There's Only 2
Tony
Cotteys

Cotts's gift for telling a story is legendary within cricket circles. He has the ability to be both funny and insightful.

Peter Moores
England Cricket Coach

An irresistibly entertaining book. Tony has the gift to make the reader feel part of his adventure. A brilliant read.

Dr David English MBE
Founder, Bunbury Cricket Club

Tony's wicked sense of humour ensured there was never a dull moment in the dressing room. His book was always going to be a lively and enjoyable read for all sports fans.

Hugh Morris
Managing Director, ECB

There's Only 2
Tony
Cotteys

Tony Cottey & **David Brayley**

Gomer

Picture credits:

All photographs are courtesy of Glamorgan C.C.C.,
apart from

First picture section:
    Cottey collection: p. 1, 2, 6 (top), 7 (bottom);
    South Wales Evening Post: 4, 5, 6 (bottom); 8 (top
    left); David Brayley: 7 (top); Press Association: 8
    (bottom right).
Second picture section:
    Cottey collection: p. 2 (bottom), 3 (bottom),12,
    14 (middle); *SWEP*: 11 (bottom), 14 (top), 16
    (bottom right); Press Association: 7 (bottom).
Third picture section:
    Cottey collection: 1 (top and bottom), 2, 3
    (bottom left), 5 (bottom), 7 (top); *SWEP*: 1
    (middle), 7 (bottom) ; Press Association: 4 (top), 5
    (bottom), 6 (top); *Brighton Argus*: 4 (bottom), 6
    (bottom); Gareth Llewellyn Williams (Origin8): 8.

Published in 2008 by
Gomer Press, Llandysul, Ceredigion SA44 4JL
www.gomer.co.uk

ISBN 978 1 84323 924 6

A CIP record for this title is available from the British Library

This book is published with the financial support of the
Welsh Books Council.

Printed and bound in Wales at
Gomer Press, Llandysul, Ceredigion

To Mam Ruth and Dad Bernard, Gail, Lowri and Seren

T.C.

To Mam Marilyn and my late Dad Derrick, Debra, Georgia and Olivia

D. B.

Acknowledgements

In 1976, outside The Cricketers pub, I ripped the cover off my Glamorgan season ticket and passed it to Dave, whilst I kept the part with all the vouchers. We were both ten years old. As he didn't have a ticket, I told him to wait for a couple of minutes and then follow me in. We both got in safely and spent the day on the big bank in front of the scoreboard. Heaven. Nearly 30 years later, we were together, back at St Helen's watching Glamorgan play Sussex in my first year of 'retirement' with Dad and his golfing buddies in one of the hospitality boxes. It was during that afternoon that we hatched the idea for this book – boosted by Craig Baron, who really enjoyed the lager-driven stories I was rattling off, many of which now appear in this book.

To get from that afternoon to now, writing this grateful acknowledgement, we have been helped by many good friends. Some read the book in its earliest draft, some have given professional advice, some have opened doors for us and dug out some great photographs and some, importantly, boosted us when we wondered if the book would ever see the light of day.

In no particular order, grateful thanks are due to all, and sincere apologies given to anybody we have unintentionally overlooked. So, to David English, Gareth Williams, Ray Mitchell, Adrian Jeremiah, Christopher Martin-Jenkins, Jim Gracey (*Belfast Sunday Life*) Steve James, Peter Moores, Alan Curtis, Hugh Morris, Stuart Button, Chris Lewis, Mike and Yvonne Llewellyn, David Evans, Chris Rees and Chris Peregrine (the last three from the *South Wales Evening Post*). Also, Steve Powell, Glamorgan's Andrew Hignell, Bruce Talbot and Simon Dack (both *Brighton Argus*), Robin Martin-Jenkins, Roddy Bloomfield (Hodder Headlines – for his wise advice), Iwan Davies (for access to the Vetch), Nick Rees, the late and much missed Kevin George, our excellent and patient editor Ceri Wyn Jones and the hard-working Lowri Walters (both from Gomer – thanks so much for the confidence you have shown in us), Stuart Davies, Bernard Lewis, Nigel Harries, Anthony Rees and finally, Greg Matthews, the very first one to tell us we might have something people would love to read.

Whilst also being grateful to all my on-field friends, I must acknowledge those off-field coaches: from the dads, through to my sporting schoolteachers such as Mrs Margaret Holledge, John Jones and Arwyn Harries, and onward to the professional ranks of John Toshack, Les Chappell, Don Shepherd, Jim Presdee, John Steele and Peter Moores. One in particular, is a man who at times had more faith in my ability than I probably did, and it is to him that I owe possibly the greatest debt – Glamorgan's Alan Jones. Thanks Al.

Thanks to you all. *Diolch yn fawr.*

Tony Cottey   Dave Brayley
Swansea, May 2008

Contents

Foreword

by Christopher Martin-Jenkins

We live in the age of Celebrities and the Big Event, especially in the world of professional sport. I have used the capital letters deliberately. Thanks almost entirely to television, familiar faces become celebrities, which means that they become more or less wealthy, and the consequence is that young people want to emulate them.

The book that you are about to read is a timely and vivid reminder that there are heroes who do not become widely known celebrities, and a level of sport that is virtuous in itself.

Tony Cottey's story is of a talented and dedicated sportsman who played professional football for a few years and professional cricket for nearly twenty, overcoming a lack of physical presence with determination of extraordinary intensity. The account of his pathway from childhood games with his father on the outfields of Glamorgan to the first-team dressing room, his passionate involvement in the winning of two County Championship titles and his struggle to progress from the smelly drying room at the Vetch Field in Swansea is authentic, colloquial and engrossing.

Its absolute veracity is what struck me after reading many ghosted cricket biographies that lack the same passion and concentrate on a world of international sport that is already familiar to most. The trouble with familiarity, as we all know, is that it can breed contempt.

I was doing some work recently on an MCC film about the 1953/54 and 1954/55 tours made by England under the captaincy of Len Hutton. Writing about the first of them, the often controversial visit to the West Indies, the late E.W. Swanton observed that international sport was becoming too important to too many people. 'National prestige', he argued, was a dangerous phrase. More than fifty years on it caused a test match to be abandoned at The Oval and the head of the Australian Rugby Union to maintain that 'hate' was what motivated his countrymen in games against England.

There is a wider and a wiser perspective here and much to be learned about the secrets of success in professional cricket, even from one who never quite made it to the international sphere to which all young professionals must aspire. Cottey had plenty of achievements for all his lack of height. At five foot four inches the smallest batsman in the county game since the Lancashire stalwart Harry Pilling, he finished with just on 20,000 runs in first-class and one-day cricket and no one who makes 1,000 runs in first-class matches in as many as eight seasons does so without exceptional ability. He was a superb little player of spin, moving his feet like a dancer or a flyweight boxer and hitting the ball as hard as anyone. I remember in particular a brilliant innings for Sussex at Northampton. When all around him were groping helplessly on a pitch where the ball was turning in feet not inches, he mixed deft sweeping with drives from well down the pitch or pulls punched to the leg-side boundary the moment that the spinners pitched it a fraction short. And to Tony a short ball was a good length to others. Throughout his career, whatever his form with the bat, his sparkling fielding and loyalty to the team cause made him an asset to both his clubs.

The unselfishness of his commitment as Glamorgan's vice-captain and later as the livewire presence on and off the field at Hove had to be learned. He talks of the three ages of the professional cricketer who makes it (as so many talented players never do). First come the early years when some of the characteristics of a rat are needed to climb above others and make it to the first-eleven dressing room. They are followed by years as an established player when complacency is the enemy: 'I'm only as good as my next innings and definitely not as good as my last' was his philosophy then. Finally come the seasons of maturity when the success of others and the cause of the team truly matter as much as personal achievement.

Dealing with failure is very much a recurring theme. He was the victim of a cull of professionals when hard times hit Swansea City. He left Glamorgan when they would not offer a long-term contract and finally said farewell to Sussex through a haze of tears. Mingled with good seasons were years when runs, luck and confidence deserted him in turn: 'I've had many, many times when I had nowhere to go,' he admits. One solution was offered by Peter Moores, now England's coach, namely to play 'without traffic in your mind'.

A host of fellow players add to the enlightenment and enjoyment of this story. Both Moores and his predecessor, Duncan Fletcher, emerge well, unlike Michael Bevan the introspective Australian whose departure as overseas player at Hove ushered in the golden era under the captaincy of Chris Adams that started with the county's first Championship title in 2003 after 163 years as also-rans. Moores brought innovative thinking that was sometimes risky, not least on the day when he confronted all eighteen members of the staff with envelopes and papers and told them to make a frank appraisal, signed and attributable, about each of their teammates.

Now Tony Cottey is in the sporting after-life, the one about which Viv

Richards, no less, cried in the dressing room when, on the point of retirement, he helped Glamorgan to win a Sunday League title. As a professional sportsman, writes Cottey through his admirably sympathetic amanuensis, Dave Brayley 'you feel immortal'. That is as true for a flourishing county cricketer as for one of the greatest of all batsmen. But for everyone the days in the sun must end.

They are to be savoured at the time, and no less so in retrospect.

Introduction

I think it was Colin Pascoe who first brought it to my attention.

'Have you seen the teams on the programme, Cotts? You're playing for them too.'

It was 1983 and I was sitting in my Swansea City kit in the away dressing room at Upton Park, waiting to take on West Ham United in a Football Combination League match. And Pasc was right. There in the programme, in black and white, was the name of the Hammers' number 10 – Tony Cottee.

So began a life of confusion between two totally unrelated sportsmen. Even though it's spelt differently, and the other TC went on to have a far more stellar career than me in a far higher-profile sport, to this day, I sometimes get asked when being introduced to people, 'You're not the footballer are you'?

Admittedly, both of us are short, and we're both sportsmen, but that's where the similarities end. The other Tony Cottee carved out a career principally for West Ham and Everton – and won seven caps for England. Since his retirement he's joined the many ex-pros in the media as an expert summariser and analyst, featuring alongside the likes of Charlie Nicholas, Phil Thompson and Matt Le Tissier on Sky TV's *Soccer Saturday*. Me? I managed to stay in the professional football ranks for just 18 months longer than our first encounter, before I was deemed 'not quite good enough' by a former Upton Park favourite – John Bond – and saw my football dreams being snatched from me, before they'd ever really begun.

But then I got lucky.

I had another string to my bow – cricket – and I was very much in the right place at the right time, and soon began a 20-year career with Glamorgan and Sussex. Even during this time, as I strived to make my name with a bat as well as a ball, the Cottey/Cottee link was never far away.

Probably the best day of my sporting life took place in September 1993, on a balmy end-of-summer day down in Canterbury. It was one of those quirks of the fixture list that saw Glamorgan travel to Kent on the last day of the Axa Equity and Law season, where the two teams scheduled to meet seven months before, now occupied first and second places in the league. It was that simplest of sporting equations: the winner of the match would win the league. As I walked nervously around the outfield that morning, only just managing to keep my breakfast down as I warmed up with the team, little did I know that in just six hours' time, I'd be hitting the runs that would win both the match and the league for Glamorgan, before running off in disbelieving delight arm in arm with Viv Richards. Yes, Sir Viv Richards! I still can't believe it. After 25 barren years, our proud Welsh county had finally picked up some silverware, and a couple of my boundaries had helped to tip the scales our way that afternoon and given our fans cause for optimism. And midway through our partnership, they gave it voice. It started over at the uncovered bank opposite the old lime tree on the edge of the playing surface that gives the St Lawrence ground its signature. I recognised the chant straight away and began to smile as it grew in volume:

'There's only two Tony Cotteys, two Tony Cotteys, there's only two Tony Cotteys. Two Tony Cotteys . . .' And on it went.

At the end-of-over break, Viv – just about the coolest guy in the whole ground – asked, 'What's that all about man?'

'Long story' I replied.

*   *   *

That long story is still going strong in September 2006 when I arrive at a sports club in Yorkshire. A mate of mine has double-booked a speaking date at a dinner and has asked me to fill in for him. I've spent 20 years of my life on the road, travelling the length and breadth of the country playing cricket. And whether it be to the big grounds like the Oval or the small ones like Scarborough, it's never been a chore: I quite like the freedom that travelling across the country gives me. Tonight, I get out of the car, walk into the function area, passing many people who politely say hello, and I ask to speak to the name of the contact I've been given. As I wait, I just begin to get the unnerving feeling that no one really knows who I am. I've never been fazed by that, after all I'm not in the Botham class. But, in cricketing circles, there's usually somebody who recognizes me. Is it going to be one of those nights, I think.

I finally meet the guy who's organised the event, the chairman of the club, who seems a tad sheepish, but there could be loads of reasons for that. He quickly points out where I'll be sitting at the top table, and where the microphone will be, then asks how long will I be on and other such housekeeping questions. He asks me if I'd like a drink. I would. I really need to take the edge off. Then, making my excuses, I pop to the gents.

I duck into one of the cubicles, pull down the top seat and sit down. I don't need the loo, just a few minutes to clear my head, get my speech sorted out and glance at my notes. I don't like to use them when I speak if at all possible; I use these five minutes to cram just before the event begins. Usually, once I've started, I'm off and the nerves vanish. Usually.

The door opens and in walk three men. From their sound, they're obviously well-acquainted with the refreshments. A couple of bawdy one-liners which make me smile are followed by a conversation which doesn't.

'Hey, did you see Frank with the speaker?' says one.

'That wasn't him,' says another. 'I've seen Tony Cottee before and that ain't him.'

'It must be him, but he's much shorter than I thought. He didn't used to have curly hair though, did he?'

'Well I don't care who he is,' says the third finally, 'he'd better be bloody good – I've paid £50 for this ticket'.

I gulp. Tony Cottee has come back to haunt me.

Once they've gone, I head off to find Frank. He's now talking to the comedian who is to kick off proceedings.

'Frank, can I have a quick word please?'

'Sure Tony, what's up'

'They think I'm Tony Cottee, don't they? Everton and England Tony Cottee.'

The sheepish response says it all.

I feel like running away.

'Look' I say, 'it's too late now. Can you just ask the comedian to do an introduction of my career and who I really am, then I'll just give it a go.'

The comedian refuses point blank. 'I don't do introductions for anyone.'

I ask Frank himself to do it only for him to protest that he wouldn't feel comfortable doing it either. I saw my life passing in front of me and started to panic.

'Look, Frank,' I said firmly, 'there's 250 drunk Yorkshiremen out there who think they're about to be entertained with stories of Frank McAvennie and Graeme Sharp. Instead they're going to get Waqar Younis and Mushtaq Ahmed. The least you can do is tell them who I really am.'

He now looks how I feel.

And I'm on. Frank stands up. He introduces me – very briefly. And I stand up to muted applause. Another gulp. Not audible, I think. Then, as I stand there, contemplating my fate, inspiration strikes:

'Thanks everyone. I understand from your chairman that you were expecting someone totally different tonight. A different Tony Cottee altogether. Well, unfortunately, he apparently had another engagement and had to pull out. I'm really sorry about that. However, in fairness, this left your chairman with a bit of a dilemma. Panicking, he just reached for the Yellow Pages and began flicking through. Bugger me if he didn't find another Tony Cottey next to the first one.'

It goes down a storm. As does the rest of the evening!

*   *   *

I'm not sure if the 'real' Tony Cottee knows who I am. Even if he does, I doubt very much if he's ever been mistaken for a journeyman Welsh cricketer who enjoyed unexpected success on the South coast at the end of his career. And I'm certain he doesn't know that he once played a couple of games of football against that journeyman nearly 25 years ago. So if he doesn't, I guess he's now going to have to accept the fact that there really are two Tony Cottees.

Or is that two Tony Cotteys?

CHAPTER ONE

A Short Story

In 1982, I made a decision that I've really regretted ever since. I had just joined Swansea City Football Club as a full-time apprentice and I had to take a medical with the club doctor. I assumed it was going to be a stringent process where every joint, muscle and tendon would be tested to see if I was going to be able to stand the rigours of a career in professional football. Nothing could be further from the truth. It lasted about five minutes. I wasn't weighed – I was merely asked by the doctor what I thought I weighed. I knew exactly. I've always been quite precise about such things, so I told him – 'Nine stone eight pounds.'.

Whilst writing this down, and without looking up, he then asked me my height.

I took a bit of a breath, and replied 'Five feet five inches,' and watched as he scribbled it down.

There. I'd done it. I'd been in professional football for about five minutes and I'd told my first lie. I was actually five feet four. Now lying about one inch is not too bad, I hear you say. But, at the time, I had a major complex about my height, or more precisely, my lack of it. Locally I had been regarded as a bit of a child prodigy because I seemed to be as skilled at football as I was at cricket. I captained the Swansea Schoolboys under elevens football team, by which time I had already made my first century in a cricket match when my primary school, Crwys (from Three Crosses on the fantastic Gower Peninsula), defeated our rivals in the next village, at Dyfnant school the previous summer.

The trouble for this particular prodigy though was that he didn't seem to be growing like the rest of the boys. It wasn't a problem at first; kids in early-years comprehensive come in all shapes and sizes, but by the time I was fifteen, I was pretty much the same height that I'd been when I was twelve, and as a result I was dropped from the Swansea Schoolboys football squad for being too short, even though I'd been good enough to be captain the previous season. I was absolutely devastated. Not only did it intensify my sensitivity about the subject, it also made me believe that physical stature was obviously an attribute of great importance to selectors of representative football teams.

1

Within a year of this heartbreak, however, my luck had changed, and I'd been selected as one of only three players in the area to be offered apprentice professional terms with the then high-flying Swansea City, under the stewardship of John Toshack. Despite this, I never wanted to experience the feeling of being deemed not good enough simply because I was short, ever again. Hence my lie to the club's doctor – however fruitless it now appears. But try as I might, my issues over my lack of height were destined to follow me into the harsh professional surroundings of Swansea City. The dressing-room environment is particularly tough when you start out – it never changes really, you just get used to it. At the time, the dressing rooms at Vetch Field were split between the first team squad in the home team's room and the reserves and apprentices in the away team's. King of our dressing room then was future multi-million-pound international striker Dean Saunders, who at the time was a bright-eyed new pro like the rest of us. Dean and I hit it off from the word go, but even I was not spared his sharp wit and humour. He was one of many who would mercilessly take the mickey out of my height. But, with Dean, there was no malice: he was just after someone who would give back as good as they got. And, in me, he found a willing opponent!

I hid my height anxiety as best I could, desperate not to show any weaknesses to anyone. The way John Toshack ran the club was almost designed to expose flaws in people's character, so I would do all I could to hide any feelings that suggested failings. That still didn't stop me being hurt by the constant jibes, but I knew I had to deal with it and get through it. Like everyone else, I just wanted to be accepted, to feel that I belonged.

I remember one particular occasion that occurred after I'd been at the club for about four or five weeks. I came into the dressing room, and sat down by my peg. Dean Saunders, who was already there with a few of the others, walked across to me, with a quizzical look on his face. He stood in front of me and studied me silently, looking me up and down like David Attenborough trying to size up some new species of ape he'd just stumbled across. After about two minutes of this, Dean spoke.

'I've been watching you closely, and there's something not quite right about you'

Inside, I started to crumple. Here we go again, I thought, I've had this all my bloody life. On the outside, though, I was poised to respond to the height-related barb that was sure to come, hoping to retain some dignity with something equally sharp in return. So I just sat there, smiling, awaiting the insult.

Dean continued looking at me closely, 'Yeah, definitely something not right, but I can't put my finger on it. What is it about you that makes you different from the rest of us? Yes! I know what it is now! I can see it clearly . . . Your eyes are too close together.' With that, he just laughed and turned on his heels and walked out.

Talk about selling me a dummy. I was speechless. To this day, I'm certain that was Dean's way of saying – don't take any of this to heart, you're gonna get the piss taken out of you, but you're one of us now, so don't worry. What is more, I don't really remember Dean mentioning my height again.

Whilst I would still struggle with the issue for a few years to come, I think that moment made me realise for the first time that part of what makes me what I am is my lack of inches. It gives me my identity – it sets me apart from the crowd. In later life, I've used the situation far more often to my advantage than others have managed to turn it against me. It wasn't always this way of course. After I'd left football behind and I'd started to chase my cricketing dreams, it was still unsettling to have to stand out on the field listening to cruel comments such as 'Dwarf', 'Shorty', 'Tattoo', 'Hod carrier for Lego', 'Bouncer for Mothercare'. And there were many insults that were much, much worse than those.

When fielding out on the boundary's edge with your back to 2,000 odd people, where you're forced to listen to their insults and their laughter (knowing that you dare not react), the world seems a very lonely place. It always puzzled me – hence my anger at the time – how a large group of people were able to get away with this kind of abuse. They were basically allowed to taunt me, to mock my physical shortcomings. And, at the time, being subject to this very public minority bullying was bloody hard to come to terms with. Central to this was the humiliation of being singled out. As a player with Glamorgan, as all our away games were in England, we'd all suffer the taunts of being 'Sheepshaggers' or hear the choruses of 'Baaaas' and we'd laugh at the crowd as it gave us a feeling of unity as a group, especially as one of us would shout out to the offending loudmouth – 'Yeah that's right mate – we shag 'em and you eat them.'

Now, I know that my lack of height was not any kind of insurmountable handicap. And I know that my anxieties about it were not disabling. But I can't pretend that I didn't have a complex about the whole thing. I was *extremely* sensitive about it, and was forced to deal with a very private preoccupation in the full glare of the public eye. For all my agonising, however, not even my mother and father or closest friends knew how I felt – and probably won't until they read this book. However, as the years have passed, and with the benefit of hindsight, I've realised that I am now almost glad that it all happened. It helped build a mental toughness that I carried with me for the rest of my sporting career and through my life in general, and it has become, in my mind anyway, a big positive.

Over time, I started to realise that the best way to deal with the insults was not to wallow in anger and embarrassment, but to humour my detractors. A common retort to the abusive fan on the boundary's edge would be to spin 'round and shout loudly, 'Sorry pal, any jokes about my height go straight over the top of my head'. 99% of the time this turned the joke on him, and people joined in the laughter, and often won me a round of applause.

Later on in my career, when I was truly comfortable in my skin, and equally importantly, in my ability as a cricketer, I'd often say to a fast bowler like Devon Malcolm (who was once warned by umpire Peter Wight for bowling six bouncers at me in one over), who may have sent down two or three short deliveries to try to soften me up, and was now standing, hands on hips, three feet away from me giving me the evil glare – 'C'mon Dev, you know me well enough now, I'd need a stepladder to get hit by one of those.' More often than not a grin would begin to crack his stern features, and I became more than happy to develop this self-deprecating 'Cheeky chappie' image – I honestly believe it helped me.

I now often get asked to appear as an after-dinner speaker, recounting stories that either happened to me, or that I witnessed, during my career – and some of these stories appear in the pages that follow. The ironic thing, however, is that I'm now more than happy to stand in front of hundreds of people, and ridicule my own lack of height without a second thought. Who'd have believed that the troubled teen in that Swansea City dressing room all those years ago would one day be sufficiently at ease with himself to tell some of the following stories in public.

The first one occurred when I was still trying to establish myself as a regular first teamer with Glamorgan. I'd played for the first team on many occasions, but was often the first player to be left out when a senior player, Alan Butcher for example, returned from injury. During this period I was never sure if a good innings would lead to a run in the side, or whether I'd be dropped down to the second team, and when you're on the fringe of the team like this, the uncertainty really gets inside your head. When you are out of the side, you try your best in the Seconds, in the desperate hope that you make it into the Firsts for either a one-day game or best of all – in those days – a three-day game. As much as I love the cut and thrust of the shorter game, the three-day championship version offered the fringe batsman that wonderful added bonus – a second chance. If you failed in the first innings, at least you knew, weather permitting, that you'd get another innings in a day or two. And, who knows, making the most of that second chance might be enough to earn promotion from the second team.

It was during this period of uncertainty that I was given the rare luxury of being told in advance that I was to play for the first XI in a couple of days' time, against Nottinghamshire at Trent Bridge. Notts were more than a decent side at the time, and included seasoned international players like Chris Broad, Derek Randall, Tim Robinson, Bruce French, Chris Cairns and Chris Lewis – I couldn't wait to test myself against such tough opponents, especially as I now had the chance to prepare myself properly. Another bonus was the venue – Trent Bridge – a test-match ground. When you start out in cricket, it's the allure of the venue as opposed to the opposition that often sets the pulse racing. For example, for many years during the late 1990s Gloucestershire won more than their fair share of games – they certainly held a monopoly on one-day trophies – yet at the same time Middlesex were very much in the doldrums, and were a shadow of the team that swept all before them in the 1980s. However, whilst Gloucester played in Bristol, Middlesex played at Lord's, so when choosing between Gloucester away and Middlesex away, there was no contest. And the same went for the other six test-match arenas. You mentally ticked them off when you played there – it was a special event. Even now as I look back at the 30-odd hundreds I made in my career, the ones I managed to score at the test-match grounds leave a certain feeling of satisfaction above some of the others. I never did manage one at Lord's though!

But back to Trent Bridge. I'd had a couple of days to get prepared and to get my head right, and also the advance notice to plan something else too. I'd been courting (I love that word!) Gail for a few years at this point and this gave me the opportunity to show off a little, by taking her to the game. Now I'm sure you're aware of those footballers' wives, and trophy wives in general, attracted by the glamorous trappings of success in professional sport – the so-called WAGs. All I can say is that Gail is about as far away from that as it's possible to be. No one is less likely to be impressed by a big-headed sportsman than Gail. When we first met, I was a struggling apprentice professional at the Vetch, and when I proudly announced to her that I was a professional footballer, the lack of response suggested she'd have been more impressed if I'd told her I was a bus conductor. Whilst she's been extremely supportive, not to mention tolerant, of my sporting existence – a cricketer hardly works regular hours – she's never really been that keen on spending day after day watching cricket, and has always preferred spending time with the family and catching the odd snippet on TV rather than attending games. A lot of that may have been a result of what happened that day at Trent Bridge!

We set off together for Nottingham, and arrived at the ground in plenty of time. I arranged for the obligatory complimentary ticket for Gail, and showed her briefly around Trent Bridge's hospitality areas, and pointed out where she'd be sitting, then off I went to work. I was feeling quite pleased with myself when I returned to the dressing room and dealt with the predictably sensitive abuse from the boys: 'Are you going to be holding hands at lunch?' and 'Would you rather be twelfth man today so you can sit together?'

Once the stick was out of the way, I prepared for the day ahead, but must admit that I was really chuffed that Gail was in the stand, and took the field with a certain feeling of pride knowing that there was someone in the ground rooting for me, and there's no better feeling knowing you've got that extra bit of support for the day's endeavours. Also, I'd be lying if I didn't admit that it's great to know that you have the chance to really impress someone who means so much to you. Imagine the buzz of leaving the field at the end of the day having scored a match-winning innings, and hearing the applause of the crowd as you acknowledge your thrilled and emotional girlfriend . . .

Never going to happen.

We won the toss and put Notts in to bat on a green pitch, hoping to take a few early wickets, and then attempt to restrict them to a manageable target for us to chase later in the day. As we shuffled around waiting for Matt Maynard to set the field, I noticed a couple of the more senior pros like Hugh Morris, Chris Cowdrey and Viv making a move away from the area of the field that lay in front of one specific part of the ground, but I didn't think much more about it. Then Matt shouted – 'Cotts, deep cover on the boundary, please.' I dutifully trotted over to the rope and looked up. I noticed there was a public bar standing out above me, and various people were milling about, underneath a sign that proudly displayed the sale of a very strong South African beer, Castle Lager. Unbeknown to me, this was Castle Corner, and I was soon to be introduced to its subtle inhabitants. Everyone on the team knew what Castle Corner meant – except me. The initial reaction from the crowd was quite muted – 'Oi, Shorty – what's the weather like down there?' and 'Has anyone got a microscope so I can see him?' and so on. I'd experienced this type of stick on many occasions in the past, so just gritted my teeth, and hoped it would soon pass – but as the morning gathered pace, so did the sales of Castle Lager. And so did the abuse.

I started to feel my plans to impress Gail beginning to unravel. In fact, this was starting to turn into a major embarrassment. I tried to adopt the customary water-off-a-duck's-back attitude, but inside, and even more so due to Gail's attendance, I started to wince every time a fresh insult was hurled. My only comfort was that Gail was sitting directly opposite Castle Corner, about 160 yards away, and I was hoping to pass off the increasing laughter emanating from the stands at my expense as me having a comical interaction with crowd. A forlorn hope unfortunately. I looked across at Matt and Hugh who were fielding on the opposite boundary – they could barely conceal their laughter. Bastards. Mind, I'd have been laughing too – if it hadn't have been happening to me!

The last ten overs of the innings were a disaster – the ball seemed to follow me everywhere, seemed to hit every divot in the pitch. What's more, a couple of catches fell short of me, but not before I'd completed a despairing dive, much to the increasing hilarity of the residents of Castle Corner. The close of innings came as a release. I ran in to join the boys walking off as quickly as I could. A couple of the lads were pissing themselves laughing, and Matt said, 'I'm sure that impressed your missus, Cotts. I bet you're glad you brought her now.'

I managed to catch up with Gail for five minutes at lunch, and kept my savoir-faire intact as she asked me what all the laughing was about. 'Nothing,' I replied, 'the fans love me up here, I was just having a laugh with them. Anyway, better get back and start preparing for my innings – see you later.' And I made rather a sharp exit.

Got away with that I thought, no more stick for me and all I need now is to get a decent score, and my plan to impress the lady who was to become my wife would be complete. No problems.

When our fourth wicket fell on 138, I jumped up, grabbed my gloves and bat, and walked out of the dressing room. At Trent Bridge you walk down an old corridor and past the famous honours' boards, which list some of the greats who have graced the famous ground, then out into the daylight, down the steps to the gate, held open by a kind attendant, and out onto the lush, manicured turf. Field of Dreams. Or is that nightmares? At the bottom of the steps I looked up and saw Viv Richards, looking supremely confident and waiting for me to join him out in the middle. This in itself gave me confidence – I loved batting with Viv; he took all the pressure off you and always boosted you publicly, especially if you played a good shot. Batting with Viv, on a test-match ground, in front of a full house, and more importantly my future wife: it doesn't get much better than this, I allowed myself to think.

As I set foot on the grass it began. Quietly at first, then with increasing volume. It started deep in the bowels of Castle Corner, then spread, slowly around the ground eventually reaching the part of the ground where Gail was sitting. By now I still had twenty yards to get to the batting crease and meet up with Viv. I couldn't pick it up at first, then I did, and when I did, I just wished that the ground would open up in front of me.

'Hi – Ho, Hi – Ho, Hi – Hooooo.' And on it went. Even as I was taking my guard, it could still be heard from the rooftops, along with the odd 'It's off to work we go.' The ever eccentric England legend Derek Randall jogged past Viv and shouted 'Which one is he Viv – Sleepy or Grumpy?' My confidence, which was as high as a kite as I walked down the steps, was now down in the depths, and even though I hung around with Viv for a few overs, I managed just 17, and then got out.

If I thought that was the end of my misery, I was mistaken. I wasn't to be alone for the long walk back either. I was doing the best to maximise my five foot four inches by lengthening my posture and sticking out my chest, hoping to create the illusion of at least five foot six. But to no avail. The Castle Corner 'Hi – Hoers' were back in full voice, and Disney's favourite theme reverberated around the ground again as I made my sorry exit. I ran up the steps as quickly as I could, back to the sanctuary of the dressing room, still hearing 'shovel and a pick and a walking stick' fading into the background.

'All right, Dopey?' said Steve Barwick.

'Piss off, Baz.' Cue hysterical laughter from the rest of the dressing room.

'At least your missus missed it, Cotts,' said Hugh, 'She was in the loo'.

'Was she?' My spirits were lifting.

'Nah – she was singing along as well'.

The trip home was a long one. It took me 'til we got to Ross-on-Wye to convince Gail that they weren't singing 'Hi Ho' because I was a short-arse, it was because of my habit of walking to the crease carrying the bat over my shoulder like a shovel.

I don't think I convinced her though and it was a long time before I asked Gail to a game again.

A few years later we were playing Middlesex at Lord's – a favourite ground. If ever you get the chance to go to a match at Lord's, make sure you take it. Quite simply it's one of the best arenas for sport in the world. From the moment you arrive at the car park, get your kit out of the boot and walk into the historic pavilion via the fabled Long Room, you realise that you are truly blessed: for the next four days, this will be your place of work. Everything about the place exudes class and history. The dressing rooms are on the first floor, and the staircases that lead to them are so ornate that they wouldn't be out of place in a stately home. In fact, from inside the building the only things that give away the fact that you are in a cricket pavilion are the paintings of legendary cricketers and famous cricketing scenes, and also the rubber matting on all the stairs, pockmarked by the studs of those who have over the years climbed the stairs in triumph or defeat. Inside the pavilion, all is polished wood. But most memorable are the honours' boards that sit on opposite walls of the dressing rooms. In the away dressing room, one board names the overseas players who have scored test-match hundreds at Lords, and the other lists the overseas bowlers who have taken five wickets in test-match innings at the ground. I was always most interested in the roll-call of batsmen. All there, in magnificent gold leaf, were true legends of the game – Don Bradman, Clyde Walcott, Gary Sobers, Viv Richards, Desmond Haynes, Allan Border, Sunil Gavaskar, and many more. It was nothing short of breathtaking, therefore, to take the same field as these players of the past, or to stand on the dressing-room balcony, surveying the scene below. Cricket is quite aesthetic really, with the ornate stands surrounding a lush green outfield with a pale, cabbage-white batting strip in the middle. But Lord's takes this to another level. I must have played there over 20 times in my career, yet every time I played there and took part in the warm-ups, I always felt guilty if I scuffed the turf as it was all so perfect

So this was the glorious setting for the game. Glamorgan had a couple of injuries at the time, so a couple of the younger players were in the team. By now I was a regular in the team, and had started to put the issues of my height behind me. If I did harbour any lingering doubts, the replacements who played that day would have made feel totally at home anyway. If it was a football match and you were looking at the pen pictures of the team in the match programme, you'd be left with just one conclusion: they might just struggle in the air!

Our team included the following towering cricketers – in no specific order:

Alistair Dalton – 5 feet 6
Stuart Phelps – 5 feet 5
Anthony Cottey – 5 feet 4
Adrian Dale – 5 feet 8
Hugh Morris – 5 feet 7

During our innings, wickets fell at regular intervals, and the order in which they fell gave the impression that each batsman was being replaced by a similar, yet slightly shorter version of himself. England's John Emburey, whose six wickets did most of the damage that day, picked up on this, and pointed out loudly in his strong London accent that, according to him, 'Every over I bowl, there's a facking dwarf on the pitch!'

This created plenty of merriment amongst the Middlesex lads, and as I got some runs that day, I was at the crease for much of the afternoon when our strapping batters were striding to the crease to hear Emburey shout out in disbelief to Desmond Haynes, 'Dessie, I can't believe it – there's another midget on his way!' I must admit it was very funny. Mike Gatting was captain of Middlesex at the time, and he had become a bit of a mentor to me during this middle stage of my career. I often sought him out at the end of a day's play over a beer for some advice on the game in general, and batting in particular. I always badgered him about the best ways to play spin bowling, and he gave me several mini master-classes around the table, which I tried to put into practice as my career progressed. He came over to me as we lost another wicket, and made a joke about how at home I must have felt in such a vertically-challenged team.

He laughed and set off to join prime joker Emburey. I laughed, told him to piss off, and reflected how differently I had learnt to deal with this banter now.

Eventually, Stuart Phelps, our back-up spinner, came in to bat, and the arrival of his five-foot-five frame, caused Emburey to announce: 'Jesus – I don't believe it, another one!' When Stuart was given out not long after, he got the usual send-off from the Middlesex fielders and trudged back across the hallowed turf toward the famous Long Room. I was just standing next to the umpire Trevor Jesty, with the Middlesex lads about ten yards in front of me, when the six-foot three-inch Steve Barwick came bounding down the steps to replace Stuart. Through the gate he came, carrying his helmet, as his long, dark hair flowed behind his round-shouldered, slightly-stooped frame.

In the face of this grand entrance, and quick as a flash, Emburey shouted out 'Who's this now lads – Snow facking White?'

Even the umpires burst out laughing. He had a way with words did Ernie.

These two stories illustrate how my attitude changed over the course of my career. At Trent Bridge I could have died. But at Lord's I was chuffed that someone as big in the game as Mike Gatting had taken time out with me to have a laugh about the situation. I now absolutely love the fact that I am apparently the shortest player ever to play for both Sussex *and* Glamorgan. I feel that it makes me unique.

I truly regret the lie I gave to that doctor at my medical for the Swans all those years ago. Not just because I feel I was actually denying myself, but also because, unknowingly, I did myself out of another claim to fame. The shortest players to have played football for Swansea City in its long and proud history are Huw Morgan and Lyndon Simmons, both five-feet four-inches tall. My height exactly! Unfortunately, due to my dishonesty with the doctor, the footballing record books have always listed me at a strapping five feet five, and will do so for eternity.

My mother always said that I should never tell lies. I should have listened.

CHAPTER TWO

Trying to Stay Onside

My first few years in sport couldn't have been better ones. I captained Dunvant and Three Crosses, my village football club, and the cricket and football teams at Crwys Primary – where Mrs Holledge always encouraged us to enjoy our sport – and later at Bishopston Comprehensive. Like my classmates, I dreamt of a career in sport – any sport. I was lucky though, and achieved a small breakthrough far earlier than I – or my classmates – could ever have expected.

St Helen's in Swansea is a sports ground steeped in history. As a kid, I spent the bulk of my summers there watching my heroes playing cricket for Glamorgan. One such day in 1976, during the tea interval, I was an enthusiastic ten-year-old playing cricket on the outfield. My dad, Bernard was bowling to me, but also throwing down some deliveries was a young West Indian, the overseas pro with Swansea, who were also based at St Helen's.

For the best part of forty years, Glamorgan County Cricket Club had been under the control of the not unsubstantial figure of Wilf Wooller. For those who don't know, Wilf was simply a Welsh legend. In 1933 he won his first Welsh cap as a schoolboy in the team that became the first Rugby Union side from Wales to beat England in a full international at Twickenham. He was to go on and win seventeen more caps. After the war he captained Glamorgan Cricket Club for fourteen seasons, including the County's first Championship triumph in 1948. He also represented Wales at Hockey and Squash, yet still found the time to play football for Cardiff City's first team, once scoring a hat-trick. Thrown in for good measure is the fact that he was a prisoner of war in the Japanese Changri camp in Singapore, and by the time 1976 came along, he had been the Secretary of Glamorgan for over 20 years. He was truly a gargantuan figure in Welsh sport and Welsh life in general.

I'd never heard of him.

Anwyay, Wilf was in the press box that day in 1976, casting a knowing eye over the St Helen's outfield, contemplating yet another mixed performance by Glamorgan. Apparently, his eyes wandered to me, batting with my tiny size-3 Duncan Fearnley, and doing my best to smack my dad's off-spinners back over his head.

Wilf subsequently said that he couldn't believe what he was seeing, this tiny boy playing all sorts of shots off his Dad's less than penetrating bowling. Apparently, he watched for about ten minutes, then, finally satisfied that he wasn't watching a recurring fluke, grabbed the microphone normally used to announce the incoming batsman, and barked out 'Will the man playing cricket on the outfield with his small blond son come straight to the press box . . . and bring the boy with you.'

Dad thought it was a joke. He was a regular in the first team at Swansea Cricket Club, and assumed it was one of his mates messing around – par for the course in those days. As a result, he just laughed, waved at the press box, and watched as his new West Indian friend bowled another ball at me. 'Stop bowling, and come up here now – I won't ask again,' came the next blaring message. Dad now recognised Wilf's regal tones, and, red with embarrassment, told me to follow him quickly.

I must admit that I was a bit confused at this point. I thought I was about to get a row for playing on the outfield, and if that was to be the case, I had my defence planned already, a tried and trusted one. It was going to be based around pointing at my dad and saying 'He made me do it.'

Dad nervously approached the press box and Wilf pulled the door open just as Dad leaned forward to grab the handle. 'Wilf Wooller,' he said thrusting his hand forward to my stumbling Dad. 'What's this lad's name?' Dad told him and Wilf replied by bombarding Dad with questions like 'Who does he play cricket for?', 'Who coaches him?', 'Why *isn't* he being coached?' and various other questions about my cricketing aspirations. I don't remember much more that was said because Eifion Jones walked into the box, and I became mesmerised by his presence. He'd been Glamorgan's wicketkeeper for the past fifteen years, and along with his brother Alan were (and still are) Glamorgan legends. To my ten-year-old mind, they were as close as a kid could get to an Andrew Flintoff or Kevin Pietersen of the 1970s.

After being grilled for about five minutes, Dad, being Dad, had by now enough of this interrogation which he, at best, interpreted as interfering, and, at worst, as Wilf being 'a right cheeky bastard'. So he asked what exactly was being proposed. Wilf responded by saying that he'd seen enough of me to realise that I had real ability, and that he wanted to arrange to send me up to the Neath Indoor Cricket School over the winter to be coached by Tom Cartwright, Glamorgan's former England test-match bowler and the man then responsible for developing Glamorgan's future players. Dad was a bit taken aback by this development and thanked Wilf for his interest, and took Tom's contact details.

We went back to our seats, but not before Dad fetched a pint to help him get over the impromptu meeting. I, of course, had no idea what this would lead to – not least the implications it would have for my mother who would spend countless hours over the next few years feeding balls into the bowling machine at Neath as I attempted to hone some sort of technique. At the time I was just pleased: I'd not had a row for playing, what's more I'd seen Eifion, one of my heroes, close up, and was now able to sit back and watch John Hopkins and Majid Khan take to the field for Glamorgan to try to avoid yet another follow-on. I always smile when I recall that life-changing afternoon, especially when I think back to the West Indian who was bowling to me with Dad that afternoon. He was only twenty years old, and was spending his first ever trip away from Jamaica. In time, he was to become one of the most successful test-match wicketkeepers of all time. Jeff Dujon was his name – a true West Indian legend.

But football was never far away in those early days. And it was football that gave me my first taste of sporting failure. I'd been a regular member of Swansea Schoolboys football teams since Under 11, and had been captain until, at fifteen years of age, I was, for the first time ever, dropped. Why? I was told it was because I was too short – and that broke my heart. If you get dropped for something that you can address – say, not being very good at tackling – then at least you can go away, practise, and hopefully come back a better tackler. But when you are fifteen and are dismissed so bluntly for something you are so powerless to change, where on earth can you go? You can't go to the gym to do more weights, or dedicate yourself to extra fitness training. Such was my despair that I was willing to give up on football totally.

So, I threw myself into cricket. And in July 1982, a month after my sixteenth birthday, I made my debut for Glamorgan Seconds at St Helen's against Somerset. To this day I can remember almost every moment, playing, as I was, with established first-teamers like Mike Llewellyn (now my boss!), Geoff Holmes, Terry Davies and John Derrick – along with another youthful hopeful you may have heard of, one Steve Watkin. I did OK, scoring 29 in the first innings and 33 in the second (out of 89), but it didn't prevent us being stuffed in two days. Tom Cartwright wiped the floor with us, and long after a victorious Somerset had headed off down the M4, we were still out on the middle of St Helen's being put forcefully through our paces. This was my first introduction to the harder edge of life as a pro, but was an absolute holiday compared to what I'd be experiencing within the next few months.

Around the time that I made this breakthrough with Glamorgan, I then received the shock of my life. After I'd pretty much abandoned my dreams of a career in football, a letter arrived offering me two-year terms as an apprentice professional with my beloved Swansea City! This created immediate turmoil at home. I'd done really well in my mock 'O' Level examinations, and with the real things on the horizon, my mother viewed this news as an unwelcome distraction. After much discussion, she pointed out the two options available to me.

Option One was to forget about the football offer and concentrate on cricket. I'd already been offered a summer contract by Glamorgan for the season ahead and if I accepted that, I could still concentrate on the exams, with a view to progressing to 'A' levels, then University. This approach would dovetail perfectly with a career in cricket, where, at the time, a university education was almost seen as obligatory, especially if a player harboured dreams of international recognition. Option Two was to accept the opportunity of becoming an apprentice with Swansea City – but not at the expense of my education. If this was to be the case, she wanted to seek assurances from John Toshack that I would be given time during the week to attend Tycoch College of Further Education for an afternoon a week to study for an 'A' Level.

To be honest, options one and two aside, I had no idea myself what I really wanted. I realised what a fantastic opportunity I was being offered by Swansea City – something I'd always yearned for – but I was still smarting from the way football had already discarded me. I was worried that history might repeat itself further down the line. Cricket on the other hand had come to my rescue when I was at my lowest, and had offered me a lifeline, and more importantly had never made my height an issue at all. My head was probably edging slightly toward cricket and I thought that maybe, if I went down that road and failed, I'd still have the option to return to soccer, with hopefully a completed education behind me. My heart though was sending different messages – football was my true love, and the more thought I gave the dilemma, the harder football was pulling me.

My mind was finally made up by Les Chappell, Swansea City's reserve team manager. I explained to him how I felt and Les listened. Then, after a few moments' silence said, 'Look Anthony, you can always go back to cricket if you fail at football, but you'll never come back here if you fail at cricket. It'll never happen. By then we'll have had two or three more intakes of apprentices who will be further down the line than you – there simply won't be an opening for you. If you were to join us and then fail though, you can walk back to cricket as the fittest player on their staff.'

Point taken, job done. I knew there and then I would become a Swan.

So, with the full backing of Mam and Dad, who had been satisfied by Tosh's assurance that I'd be allowed to continue with my 'A' Levels, I was about to embark on the toughest, hardest, most painful few weeks of my life. But gruelling though it was, I wouldn't have missed that initial training for the world. As regards my academic studies, they only lasted six weeks! Football, and the fantastic life that came with it, took over and became everything to me.

My professional sporting career began in August 1982, with one of the most surreal moments of my life. I arrived at the Vetch Field on my first day as instructed, at 9am. I was met by the club secretary and shown in. There were no formal introductions, it was pretty much sink or swim. The other new apprentices were Roger Mullen, a tough centre back from Ton Pentre in the Rhondda Valley, and David Hough, originally from Wolverhampton, but who had played with me in my junior team Dunvant and Three Crosses, so we knew each other very well. Within minutes of my arriving, the pros turned up, and I freely admit to being totally star-struck. I watched in awe as some of the biggest names in British football walked in front of me. At the time, Swansea City was one of the nation's favourite teams. They had just completed an unprecedented rise through the divisions from Four to One in just four seasons. Most football judges now agree that such a remarkable rise could never happen again in the modern game. Former Liverpool legend John Toshack, in his first job as a football manager, had masterminded the rise, and after a debut season in Division One which saw them leading with six weeks to go, (finally finishing sixth to champions Liverpool), they were pretty much everyone's second favourite team. There was a huge amount of goodwill toward the club from the football world in general as they embarked on their second season in the top flight, this time with me on board.

The players I witnessed that morning were internationals all: Alan Curtis, Robbie James, Leighton James, John Mahoney, Dai Davies from Wales, Dzemal 'Jimmy' Hadziabdic and the menacing Ante Rajkovic from Yugoslavia, Ray Kennedy and Bob Latchford from England. Bob Latchford looked over, saw me sheepishly glance at him and approached. With a beaming smile and outstretched hand he said 'Hi son – Bob Latchford, welcome to the club, good luck and enjoy it,' and he did the same to Roger and Dai. I was thrilled. Latch was a legend, and also a giant – he appeared huge to me, and I was so impressed with his friendliness and kindness, which I came to understand was second nature to him. On the other hand Leighton James, who I now know and like, looked at me as if I was something that the cat dragged in – and that wouldn't

15

change for a while either. Sorry Leighton – harsh but fair – but I was soon to learn that his respect had to be earned, and that was fine by me.

Then came the surreal moment. Harold Woollacott, the gnarled old stadium manager came in and shouted 'Cottey!' I looked up hesitantly and replied 'Yes?'

'Get out on the pitch son, the Evening Post want a photo of you'. I nearly died. I'd only been there ten minutes and I was being singled out. Uncomfortably conscious of the suspicious glances of the second-year apprentices and first-year pros, Dean Saunders amongst them, I walked down the tunnel, and out onto the pitch.

There to greet me were the Evening Post head photographer, Len Pitson, and chief sports reporter, John Burgum who was holding a cricket bat. He had his back to me and was talking to John Mahoney, Ian Walsh and our two Yugoslavs, Jimmy and Ante. I was handed the cricket bat and told to hold it out as though I was playing a shot. Nobody explained why this was happening – even though it was obvious – and nobody asked my permission, it was just assumed I'd do it. They were right. I would have stood on my head if they'd asked me. John Burgum had a quick chat with me about how it felt joining the club, and why I chose football over cricket, while Len arranged John, Walshy, Jimmy and Ante behind me in a slip cordon. A couple of snaps later, it was 'That's it son' and everyone ignored me again. During this surreal five minutes, I don't recall any of the players saying a word to me, it was as if I didn't exist. I was starting to understand my place at the club. I was the lowest of the low, and in my quest to become a first-team professional footballer, I was soon to learn that there was only one route – from the bottom up, no short cuts – and as every pro had travelled the same route, many took glee in putting new apprentices through the mill.

Coaches Les Chappell and Terry Medwin then mapped out the next two weeks for us lowly apprentices. There were about a dozen of us in total, including last year's intake, and the pre-season training arrangements, and our duties therein, were explained. It sounded like torture. And the next day the torture began!

I arrived at the Vetch at 9.00am. The only people there were the apprentices, groundsman and stadium manager Harold. We entered the pitch-black changing room, put on the lights and changed. Then it was into the drying room to get the big wicker skips filled with the first team squad's kit and boots, and load them into the two sponsored Leyland Sherpa vans – the van of choice at Swansea City at the time. Glamorous stuff!

We then drove the twenty odd minutes to the University playing fields at

Fairwood on the gateway to the Gower peninsula which, rather annoyingly for me, was located about three minutes by car from my family home. We usually arrived there at about 9.45, when we had fifteen minutes to lay out all the kit and boots in strict numbered order for Tosh, assistants Phil Boersma and Doug Livermore and all the pros, who arrived promptly at 10.00. Within ten minutes, all players (first team, second team and apprentices) would be running round the playing fields in a twenty-minute warm-up run. In the three pre-seasons I endured, the hugely talented and immensely likeable Robbie James was always rank last in this first morning run. Absolutely knackered and breathing out of his backside, Robbie always looked like he'd summered well, and I was shocked to see him struggle so much as I'd always admired him as a very forceful attacking midfield runner, not unlike Roy Keane in his pomp. However, at the end of the two-and-a-half weeks' pre-season training – where the one object that didn't figure was a football – Robbie finished the last session of the last day, where he'd be for the rest of the season, right out at the front, with everyone else in his wake. It still saddens me to think that we would later lose this Rolls Royce of a player and a man when he collapsed and tragically died in 1998, aged just 41, whilst playing for Llanelli as their player-manager.

After the warm-up run, the four or five football pitches that made up the Fairwood playing fields were set out into various 'fitness stations'. They would have been better named 'torture stations'. Station One saw benches laid out in the form of a steeplechase barrier, and laps were measured out to replicate a 300-metre circuit. This was to be run at three-quarter pace, but with the competitive element of a race. Then, after a two-minute breather it was onto Station Two – shuttles. These were referred to as 'doggies' in the trade and involved short, sharp repetitive sprints back and forth between laid out marks on the grass about ten or fifteen yards apart, and lasted several minutes. Then another brief rest before Station Three – 'Zigzag'. This was a run, again at three-quarter pace, starting from behind a goal at one end of the pitch, moving diagonally across to the left touchline, then zagging back over to the opposite touchline on the halfway mark and continuing zig zagging like this, down the pitch, then back to where you started behind the goal. Then repeat. Without stopping.

The final station was the killer, the worst and hardest training I ever endured in twenty-three years as a professional sportsman: '*The Progressor*'. Sounds like something off Gladiators. Basically, several of us would be lined up behind the goal line at the right-hand corner flag. On the clap of the trainer, usually Tosh, we had to sprint behind the goal to the opposite corner flag, 50-odd yards away. Then we'd slow down and jog around the remaining three sides of the pitch. As

17

we arrived back to the point where we'd started the first sprint, Tosh would clap again and we'd immediately sprint again behind the goal, but this time, carrying on sprinting around the corner flag and up the touchline to the halfway line, where we'd slow again and jog back around the rest of the pitch. Then from the start, another clap and sprint again, this time behind the goal then along the length of the whole touchline, before resuming jogging pace and returning to the start. I think you're getting the idea now! We would progress at each stage like this until the final lap, where the whole pitch was rounded in a total sprint. If anyone was deemed not to be sprinting by Tosh or Boersma, you were sent straight back round the pitch – it was absolutely brutal. Once these stations were completed, and repeated, punctuated by the obligatory sit-ups and press-ups, it was, after two-and-a-half-hours of torture, lunchtime!

Unfortunately, whilst all the pros looked forward to relaxing in the canteen upstairs, we, the apprentices, had to move into Phase Two of our duties. Basically, as soon as Tosh called a halt to the morning's exertions, we shot straight off to the showers. By the time we'd washed, dried and changed we were joined by the pros who, dumping their kit where they stood, entered the showers. We then scuttled around the dressing room, collecting the sweaty, manky kit and dumping it in the large wicker training skip. Then it was out to the glamorous Sherpas – oh how I miss those vans – and tossed the loaded skips into the back. We then rushed upstairs to the canteen, where we ate exactly what they ate at Liverpool apparently – soup and toast – and finished it just as the pros arrived for their food. They would spend the next hour-and-a-half leisurely eating their soup and toast with several cups of tea (energy drinks were still a figment of a nutritionist's imagination at the time) and generally relaxing, until Tosh called them back together to get changed for the afternoon session. For us apprentices though there were no such luxuries. As soon as the toast was swallowed, two of us rushed back to the Sherpas and back to the Vetch near Swansea City Centre, a forty-minute round trip. When we arrived at the Vetch, the skips were unloaded and taken to the drying room. Already hanging up there, again in number order, was everybody's kit for the afternoon – socks, shorts, tops, bibs (never tracksuit bottoms, as Tosh believed in the Liverpool way of never wearing anything in training that you wouldn't wear in a match) – and these were packed neatly into a waiting empty skip. We then opened the steaming wet skip we'd brought from Fairwood and sorted through the kit, turning socks, shorts and tops inside out so they were all correct, and again hung them on the numbered pegs. Once all this was done, the door to the drying room closed behind us, and it was back to the Sherpas, loading the skips on board, and off to Fairwood.

The horrors of the drying room deserve further explanation. The Vetch was built in the early years of the 1900s and was based around the ornate 'Centre Stand' which ran along the south touchline of the ground. Until the general offices moved into the new East Stand, which was built in 1980, all the club's rooms were based underneath the Centre Stand, and thus, like the dressing rooms, the drying room had no windows. It was a small – approximately ten foot by four foot – brick-faced room filled with hooks and pegs, all numbered so that each squad player had his own spot. The only other objects in the drying room were the red-hot water pipes at the foot of the walls, which provided the heat for the drying process. So, after every training session, every bit of wet, unwashed, kit was hung up on the allotted peg, and the door was shut. Simple as that. Prior to the next training session, usually the next day, the door was opened, and the kit was now dry. The drying room had done its job again.

Whilst the drying room was swept out occasionally, I don't ever remember the Shake and Vac being applied too often. As a result, by the Wednesday of a normal week, the stench was unbelievable. Training kit was washed at most once a week, the rest of the time it was just left hanging to dry, where the collective sweat of twenty or so of the country's leading professionals had ample time to become infused with the ghostly aromas of the players of the previous 80 years. I spent quite a bit of time in that drying room in my first two years. Do I miss it? Not exactly.

When we arrived back at Fairwood in the afternoon, it was exactly the same predictably painful process as in the morning. And thus it continued for three days. It was so hard that, after I got home at 5.30pm each night and had my tea, I would go straight to bed, be asleep by 6.30 and wouldn't stir until 8.00 the next morning, when I would wake up stiff as a board. By the Wednesday night I announced to my mother that I'd had enough.

On the Thursday morning, Mam and Dad had to force me out of the house. I remember sitting on the bus, which ironically passed Fairwood playing fields, and giving serious consideration to getting off it and ending my torture once and for all. I was happy to toss away all my football dreams there and then – it was just too tough for me, and I'm not too proud too admit that. But, of course, I stayed on the bus, got off at the station and made the short walk to the Vetch, still feeling quite sick.

Within minutes of arriving at the changing room, we were off to Fairwood for another session. It was another tortuous morning, where again, footballs were conspicuous by their absence. At lunch, I remember looking around to see if anyone else looked as shattered as I felt. I wanted to confide in someone but daren't, and I swear that if anyone at that point had said to me – 'That's it, I quit' – I'd have walked right out of the door with them. As I looked round, there appeared no takers, and, as I contemplated the horrors of the afternoon, I was on the verge of tears. Then Tosh appeared – along with my stiff upper lip thankfully – and called all the first-year apprentices together. 'No training for you this afternoon, lads – you need a rest. Just get the skips ready and get back to the Vetch, change and go home.'

I could have kissed him.

I considered later how very close I had been to chucking it all away, not realising that Tosh had already noticed that we'd gone to our limits. It wasn't to be the last time that he would appear to be a step ahead of everyone else.

By the end of our two-and-a-half weeks' pre-season training, I'd lost eight pounds in weight. Bearing in mind I was a heavyweight 9st 8lbs when I started, you can get some idea of how heavy the workload was. Anyway, I'd survived my first couple of weeks as a footballer by the skin of my teeth, and if it wasn't the dream life I'd expected, there were genuinely better times ahead. And slowly, but surely, I began to enjoy the trappings of being a Swansea City player. Indeed, the more I think about it, the more convinced I am that the three seasons I spent in this harsh and disciplined environment were the best years of my sporting life.

Football is littered with players who, thinking they've got it made, get too big for their boots and fail to make it as a professional. Tosh, and more importantly his assistant Phil Boersma, would try to clamp down on that straight away if it was spotted, and would do anything in their power to keep your feet on the ground. The lessons I learned then I keep with me today. Whilst some of these lessons were taught to us by the management, others were learnt from very practical experience. Indeed, one such event ensured that I would never take myself too seriously again; it was the annual First Team versus Reserve Team trial match, held on the Vetch Field itself.

When I heard about the match, my heart skipped a beat. I allowed myself a second to dream that this was my chance: this was when the outsider, a young pro, would force his way into Tosh's plans by providing a man-of-the-match performance. The trouble was that the club was run largely on the basis of a Premiership club today, and as a result, the playing staff numbered well over 30, and as such, I was at the bottom of a very big – and talented – pile. And seasoned pro Colin Irwin reminded me of this, bringing me down to earth with a bump: 'Don't even think about it son – you'll have to wait your turn to play in this one'. I was only sixteen, I'd only been at the club for a month, and here I was hoping I'd take the field in a match against, Leighton James (who remains one of the best players I've ever seen) Latch, Alan Curtis, Robbie James, John Mahoney and many other of our top players. I'd have given anything to be involved.

The game was a late morning kick-off and was to be my first real experience of what a match day for the players was to be like. The only thing missing would be the crowd. I'd seen all these players every day for nearly a month now, but today there was something different. There was a slight edge in the air. The mickey-taking was still in evidence, but underneath it all was a real feeling of competition and a strong sense that there was absolutely no way on earth that the Firsts would permit themselves to lose to the Reserves. There was just far too much professional pride at stake.

As the first-year apprentices were not involved in the game, we were at the beck and call of both teams, as we would be on a proper match day. I was given the home dressing room and had to make sure everyone had what they needed – kit, drinks, towels etc. The players were really up for the game, lots of bravado: 'Let's show these tossers what it's all about', 'No mercy boys', 'We'll never hear the end of this if we lose' and various other statements of intent. I remember standing there listening to Tosh giving some advice to the defenders about how he wanted them to line up as a unit, and again allowed myself to wonder what it would be like to be part of this group of players, and how would I cope. Ray Kennedy then asked me to get him a bigger pair of shorts. And as I went out to fetch them, Les Chappell was coming along the corridor towards me with a smile on his face.

'Ah, Cotts, glad I found you. Fancy being involved today?'

I nearly passed out. Did I fancy being involved? Was he joking?

'Bloody right, Les,' I blurted out. I couldn't believe it: my prayers had been answered. And as we went down the corridor, I thought 'Bollocks to Razor's shorts, he can get them himself. I'm the opposition now.'

Instead of taking me into the away dressing room where the reserves were getting ready, he walked straight past and into the referee's room. Strange I thought – perhaps he's going to give me a personal briefing on how he wants me to handle Robbie James's rampaging runs or how I could best close down Alan Curtis. Instead, Les went to the cupboard and pulled out a yellow linesman's flag and threw it to me.

'There we are – you said you wanted to be involved. Run the line'.

My face fell into my boots. Les burst out laughing. 'Bloody hell, son, you didn't think you were going to play, did you?'

21

I blushed and mumbled something like 'Of course not – don't be daft' and Les laughed again,

'Jesus, you youngsters, you want it all straight away. You've got to learn first son. Now, whatever you do, don't balls it up, Tosh and Boey will be in the stand and they want a proper game to see how everyone goes. You'll be the only linesman, so you'll cover both halves of the pitch, it won't do your fitness any harm either. Do you understand?'

I responded with a crestfallen 'Yes'.

As I walked out, Razor came out of the dressing room – 'Son, where the hell's my shorts?'

'Sorry, I'll get them now.'

Then I made my first mistake. I got the shorts, went back in, handed them to Ray, and then heard Colin Irwin's familiar Scouse tones booming out:

'Look out boys, we've got the Laughing Gnome running the line today.'

I glanced down in horror and realised I was still holding the linesman's flag Les had thrown to me.

Then came the abuse. Plenty of it. And from everyone. You can only laugh and go along with it, and hope you can escape the dressing room with a modicum of dignity. As I slipped out, Tosh and Les were smiling and I just buggered off as quick as I could.

I made my way down the tunnel and out onto the pitch. The first person I saw was my fellow apprentice Dean, who'd made it onto the subs bench for the Stiffs (Reserves). We both looked at each other, then down at the flag and he just burst out laughing. I looked around, and saw both sets of players trotting out onto the pitch, and saw the rest of the subs going to the dugout and the rest of the management staff, a couple of directors and some of the office staff all taking their seats up in the Centre Stand behind me. I wanted the ground to open up. I looked back and saw Dean, and all I could see were his shoulders moving up and down in hysterics. I took my starting position just in front of the dugout, prime target of the inevitable stick from the subs' bench.

I cleared my head a bit and then realised that I just had to get on with it, and turn it into an opportunity. Tosh was up in the stand, after all, surveying his kingdom, and this was the first time I'd ever really had the chance to stand out in front of him. Right then, I resolved that I was going to put in the best linesman's performance he'd ever seen, and earn his thanks after the game for a tricky job well done. That became my goal, and my focus. Amazing what shite goes through your mind when you're a kid!

Anyway, I kept up with play and made all the correct decisions, even if I suffered a bit of abuse from the Reserves when I awarded a 50/50 throw against them. I sarted to enjoy it, revel in it, even!

The game itself was extremely competitive: all the banter disappeared as soon as they kicked off, to be replaced by a cold, ruthless professionalism. I couldn't believe how ruthless these players were. Best mates on opposing sides thought nothing of absolutely clattering into one another with challenges that would prompt the typical footballers' scuffle – handbags at five paces.

At half-time, the score was 0-0. More importantly, and though I say it myself, I'd done OK.

Five minutes into the second half, the First Team started to launch a series of sharp attacks, which the Reserves struggled to keep out. Then, at last, came the breakthrough! Alan Curtis held the ball up long enough for Robbie James to make one of his late, lung-busting runs. Curt played the ball through for Robbie perfectly which saw him one on one with the goalkeeper. He finished clinically. 1-0.

Well, it would have been if the idiot linesman hadn't had his flag up for offside.

Me.

It was a very close decision, and I don't know if I panicked, but as soon as the ball was played through, I felt my arm shoot up. The goal was disallowed. And all eyes – and abuse – fell on me. John Mahoney delivered a particularly well-chosen tirade, matched only by Ray Kennedy. I noticed Robbie James looking at me as he jogged back, but he just smiled ruefully and shook his head.

The game restarted, and I just wanted to die. I started to lose focus. I started to believe I'd given the wrong decision, and wanted to make amends. I then started to think about Tosh. I had so wanted to impress him, but was starting to lose control.

The next thing I knew, Bob Latchford was running onto a clever through ball from Ray Kennedy, and calmly slotted it under the advancing Chris Sander. Bob never missed. 1-0.

Well, it would have been if the idiot linesman didn't have his flag up again.

Guess who?

This time the abuse was torrential. I've never realised that the words 'cheating', 'little' and 'bastard' could be used by so many people at once, at such a volume and with such speed.

As I stood there, I had no idea why I'd put the flag up. It's almost as if my arm had taken on a life of its own. Bob's run had been borderline, but it had probably been just on-side. It was as if somewhere in my deep sub-conscious I wanted to show Tosh just how honest and dependable I was and that I would not let anyone get away with anything. Even if there was nothing that they were trying to get away with! The first-team players had a much simpler view – I was a cheat.

I just wanted to walk onto the pitch and tell them all I'd made a horrendous mistake and that it was a goal after all, but I would never had lived that down. Instead, I thought about Tosh again. I thought he'd be far more impressed if I said nothing, stood my guns, and kept my flag up. Showed a bit of toughness – some character. So that's exactly what I did. I held the flag tight, and held it high, and waited for the abuse to stop.

I also resolved that whatever happened in the rest of the match, one thing I wasn't going to do again was flag again for offside.

With five minutes to go, the score was still 0-0. Suddenly, a ball was played through to the centre forward who, amid a chorus of appeals for offside, rounded the keeper to score. 1-0.

My arm – now under my control – remained firmly by my side.

My final mistake.

It was the Reserves who had scored. Ian Walsh – class finish. Except that he had been *at least* five yards offside.

So I was slaughtered again. I thought I was going to get lynched. I ran back to my mark, and I was almost shaking. I couldn't have done a worse job if I'd come down from Mars and run the line without ever having seen a football match before.

Before I knew it, the referee blew for time. The Reserves had beaten the First Team 1-0, and I had proved to be a matchwinner. But not quite in the manner I had dreamt earlier.

I got off the pitch as quick as I could, trying to ignore the abuse, and went into the Ref's room and laid the flag on the shelf in the cupboard, and walked quietly out. Then I went back toward the First Team dressing room to continue with my tasks. I took a deep breath and opened the door.

Suffice it to say that the next twenty minutes of my life were nothing if not character building . . .

CHAPTER THREE

The Apprentice

With my first pre-season out of the way in 1982, the real stuff began. Again it was quite regimented, but not as intense as pre-season training. In a normal week, the sessions, held at AWCO sports ground in Jersey Marine on the outskirts of Swansea, would start at 10am each day, and Tosh's programme would involve the following:

Monday: fitness work. Similar to pre-season at Fairwood, but no *Progressor,* thank God. Plenty of running though, but with more ball work than pre-season. Lunch at 12.15, then back in the afternoon for an hour of weights. Finish at 2.15.

Tuesday: lighter session, still plenty of running and doggies, but not as tough as Monday. Finish 12.15.

Wednesday: medium-length run to warm up then five-a-sides, one-touch football and skill drills with the ball – a great day. Finish 12.15.

Thursday: the best day – technical stuff, ball skills, free kicks and corners. Finish 1.15.

Thursday suited me perfectly. I was a central midfield player and my main strength was my ball skills. In time, over my three seasons at the club, as I eventually took all corners and free kicks for the reserves, Thursday became the day that I featured most, and had more of the ball than almost everyone else. The equivalent dead-ball expert or set-piece specialist in the First Team was Leighton James, and in training he left us in no doubt as to how good he was at it. And in case we hadn't noticed – he would tell us anyway. All the time.

In fairness, he was excellent. If he wasn't shy of talking the talk– to teammates or the opposition – he was also one of those in life who was more than capable of walking the walk, and remains one of the best players I ever saw, and I came to respect him hugely.

One thing I remember about those Thursdays was the excellence of Bob Latchford and the commitment of goalkeeper Dai Davies. In my first season at the club in 1982/83, Bob was to end up with 20 league goals from just 31 games and a further 14 in cup games, an unbelievable return for the top division, bearing in mind that we were relegated. Dai on the other hand was going through a bad trot. During the previous year, following some abuse from the fans and media in general after some indifferent displays, he was featured in a tabloid article that outlined his troubles and basically asked the fans to stand by him. Unfortunately for him, the paper decided to headline the article 'Don't call me Dai the Drop'. So, as is the way of the world, 'Dai the Drop' he became to every away fan in the country. They even made a song up about him which even a few of the home fans joined in with. That was tough on Dai, because, although he was prone to the odd error, he was as brave as a lion and a really nice guy – and fiercely proud as a Welshman.

Anyway, he always wanted to stay behind for extra work after Thursday's training finished, and Bob, being the perfect pro, was no different, and was happy to help Dai out. Between them they came up with the following drill. Four apprentices, two on each flank would alternate playing crosses into the penalty area, at about penalty-spot range, 30 times. Bob, beginning his run from outside the box, would arrive to meet the cross but insisted on them being mixed up – some high for a leaping header, some along the ground for a side foot, and some mid-height for a volley or diving header. I was always one of the four and loved being involved in this drill, watching someone as gifted as Bob from such close quarters. Dai's role was straightforward. He had to decide whether to come and claim the cross if it was high enough, or remain on his line if not, and attempt to keep Bob's best efforts out. There was only one flaw in this plan. After a month or so of this extra training drill, I think Bob had only missed about five times. Poor Dai must've been even more demoralised than he might have been at the start. It wasn't that Dai was making mistakes – far from it – it was just that Bob was so clinical. I'd never seen anything like it. He managed to adjust his body to any angle that the ball was delivered to him at. It didn't matter if it came from the left or right flanks, it was all the same to Bob – he was absolutely brilliant. He played 12 times for England scoring 5 times, and if he'd just had a touch more pace, he'd have been the Alan Shearer of his day – he was that good. I don't think he improved Dai's confidence a hell of a lot though!

As far as the training week went, that just left Friday. As this was generally the day before a game (no Sunday kick-offs in those days) Tosh and the staff were not interested in fitness, but concentrated on the tactics for the next day's opponents. Obviously this was geared toward the first team, and as such, we reserves would often take the part of the opponents, and were given instructions on how to attack in their particular style. Tosh would then issue instructions to the first team's defence, which would be Dai Davies in goal, and then any combination of Wyndham Evans, Chris Marustik, Ante Rajkovic, Max Thompson, Colin Irwin, Nigel Stevenson, Dudley Lewis, Dzemal Hadziabdic or Garry Stanley. He would pick the four defenders from that group who were playing the next day, then get six of us to attack them, and try to score. All this always took place on the Vetch and not the usual training ground, and was the time that I'd allow myself to dream that I had as much chance as anyone of making it at the highest level.

I do remember once getting a bit carried away though, and nutmegged our Yugoslav assassin, Ante Rajkovic. I knew it was a bit cheeky, but he never said anything, and I just thought it showed everyone that I had a bit about me. About ten minutes later, Tosh set up a corner for us to attack from, and the ball was headed out to the edge of the box where it fell to me. It was a little behind me, so I had to turn away from goal. As I shielded the ball and was about to play it off, I felt the back of my leg go numb, and I landed in an undignified heap on the floor. I looked up to see Ante walking slowly backwards away from me, just staring – there was no smile, no anger, just a stare. 'Not so clever now, son, are you?' said Boey. Point taken. I don't remember nutmegging anyone else in training again – certainly not Ante.

Even though training for the pros ended each day around lunchtime, the apprentices still had our chores to do after the morning's exertions. Each player was given certain areas of the Vetch to look after. Mine was the away dressing room and bath. We also had five pros to look after. My first ones were Dai Davies, Max Thompson, Jeremy Charles, Jimmy Hadziabdic and former Liverpool and England legend, Ray Kennedy. We were basically at their beck and call when they were in, and had to ensure that they wanted for nothing. Training kit – rescued from the infamous drying room – was pegged out for them, boots were cleaned (three types – trainers, rubber studs and screw-ins covering all conditions), and clean, dry towels always had to be on hand. If there was a televised match at the weekend, we also had to highlight the advertising stripes of the boots with white paint, or sometimes Tippex, to ensure the boot sponsor got maximum exposure on the day. This was more complicated than it sounded. The club at that time was sponsored by Patrick, the French company then favoured by Kevin Keegan. Their boots were black and had two small, angled, white stripes, just at the back of the boot, between the heel and the ankle. Once the boot was totally clean and dry, we had to coat the boot with thick black boot polish. This helped soften the leather, to the extent that it felt like you were wearing slippers. I seem to remember that kangaroo skin was the raw material used for Patrick boots, much more lightweight and pliable than traditional leather. When the polish was dry, we'd then have to paint over the white stripes. This became a work of art. If you went outside the line in any way, making the stripe look anything but authentic, the pro concerned would chuck the boots back at you and you'd have to start again.

This was a delicate job, but nothing compared to the dark world of the contract swappers. These were players who'd made their own deals, with say Puma, but preferred to wear another boot – say Adidas – and would then disguise it as the boot of their sponsor. With these players' boots, you needed the skill of a young Tony Hart. Firstly, you had to remove all evidence of the original boot design. Sometimes black paint would suffice to cover the white lines, or you'd have to remove the stripes altogether with a razor blade. Then we had to copy the white markings of the required sponsors' design onto the blacked-out boot. The easiest was Adidas, just applying three white stripes. The hardest were boots like Puma, which has an extravagant swoosh, almost like Nike in reverse. These were so tricky we'd have to get an original Puma boot onto the table and copy the design. When the job was done, everyone was happy – firstly the pro, as he'd conned the sponsor, but had pocketed the money – secondly, the sponsor, as he would see a pristine white advert set against an immaculate ebony boot – and lastly us, because we wouldn't have to do that painstaking job again until we were next due to be televised.

As apprentices, we always tried to do these jobs as best we could – but we did have an ulterior motive for this: the 'Christmas Box' of tips. I used to get twenty quid off each of my pros – and when you think we each had five pros to look after, and our wages were basically a pittance, such contributions certainly helped the Christmas festivities go smoother. As apprentices, we'd compare Christmas Box notes and I remember Colin Pascoe coming in looking almost shell-shocked. One of his pros was Bob Latchford and from the look on Pasc's face, Latch couldn't have given him anything. But then Pasc opened his hand and showed us his £100! Class act was Latch.

As poorly-paid apprentices, we had to be resourceful. There was a sports shop in Swansea's Quadrant shopping centre, Gilesports. One of the shop assistants was a Swans fan, and we worked out a deal with him whereby we could take a brand new pair of club-issue Patrick training boots, probably worth about £15 at the time, put them in a Gilesports bag, bring them to him, and ask him if we could exchange them for another make of boot – usually Adidas World Cup, which were about £45 and the dog's bollocks. In return, the guy would be kept in complimentary tickets for the season!

Once the personal services to the pros were completed, we had to move onto our daily chores. As I mentioned, my main task was the away dressing room. This was used every day, and therefore had to be swept out and kept tidy, but Friday was the day it had to have the real Mr Sheen five star treatment. Out came the scrubbing brush and this minging orange industrial floor cleaner. This was such hard work that we all took a real pride in it, and I've witnessed other players being thumped if they purposely walked on a recently cleaned, wet dressing-room floor. After the floor was done, benches, hallway, sinks and bath then had to be cleaned to perfection. Just as I'd finish, Terry Medwin, the club's Youth Development Officer and former Tottenham Hotspur legend of their double winning team of the 1960s would come in to inspect. He had this *unbelievable* knack for finding a pubic hair in the bath. He'd pick it out, show it to me, toss it back in and announce 'Hairs lead to boils son – do it again.' He never failed to find one, I became convinced he brought them in with him.

Ah, the romantic life of the professional footballer.

After this we were at the mercy of the stadium manager, Harold. From 1.30 to 5.00, Monday to Friday, you were Harold's and you had to get on with it. Typical jobs during the week were replacing the divots and tidying around the edge of the pitch; sweeping all the terraces and bagging all the discarded rubbish and junk from the preceding matchday; washing all the seats in the stands, and any other cleaning or maintenance duties Harold had in mind. Now I don't know how other clubs treated their apprentices, but what we all had in common, I suspect, was the carrying out of such menial duties. And, as much as I hated it, I just accepted that if Bob Latchford, Alan Curtis and Robbie James etc. had all been through it, then there was no reason why I couldn't put up with it. Indeed, our application to these tasks was probably seen as a gauge to our character and strength of mind as players. Tosh knew that a moaner off the pitch was likely to be a moaner on it, so I just shut up and got on with it.

Some time ago I watched a documentary about Alan Shearer whose duties, when he started out as an apprentice at Southampton, were similar to mine. Such low, unpleasant work is no longer part of the game for the up-and-coming pros, and he bemoaned this. He said that it had given him the discipline that had sustained him throughout his career and had made him what he was as a player. He also said it gave him the happiest two or three years of his footballing life. And I know exactly what he meant.

Human nature, however, dictates that if you put a group of youngsters together and enforce a rigid, disciplined regime on them, then at some point they will rebel. Fearing that we would be dropped, or, even worse, sacked for open revolt against Tosh and his assistants, our rebellion took the subtler form of practical jokes. These ranged from the small, off-the-cuff ones like hiding shin pads or boots, to the far more sophisticated ones such as being dared or bet to perform some ridiculous stunt. The bosses would often turn a blind eye to these, probably realising that we had to let some steam off. Then again, they didn't find out about them all. And we were happy to take the risks.

Firstly there was the blackballing. Not big, not clever, but very funny. The victim was pounced on by a few of the others. Screaming, they were dragged to the treatment room, spread-eagled and tied to the table legs. Shorts and pants dragged down, noxious black boot polish was liberally applied to the genitals of the victim. Hardly Cambridge Footlights but hysterical – if it wasn't you. I'd really love to say it never happened to me. But my turn came. I was on my own in the boot room, and was taken unawares by the rest of the apprentices. As soon as they jumped me I knew what was coming, and I fought for all my worth, but it was no good, the boys were experts. What's more, they applied the polish via a boot brush, which hurt like hell. After they were done, I looked down, and for the only time in my life, I had the credentials to play for the West Indies! OK, I didn't qualify in terms of ability, or, shall we say, dimensions, but at least the colour was right! It must've taken a month to get it all off: the polish was waterproof!

From such basic pranks, we graduated to one that needed *slightly* more thought. Most lunchtimes, highly-tuned athletes as we were, we'd feast ourselves at the Argyle Fish Bar: battered sausages, deep-fried rissoles, curry sauce and chips – straight from Rafa Benitez's Liverpool diet programme! Whenever a new lad joined the staff – sometimes associate professionals joined on six-month contracts – he would be introduced to the joys of The Argyle. However, their introduction was not as straightforward as they might have thought. We'd wait until lunchtime and then start talking about what we were going to have to eat. By now we'd have selected our stooge and instructed him to start a list, telling him that one of his first duties was to fetch the order. He had to go around everyone at the Vetch – sometimes even first-team pros who were in getting treatment – and off he would pop to The Argyle. Andrew Bennett had recently joined us, a fast, wiry striker, and all-round decent lad. He left the Vetch with a list as long as his arm, something like fourteen bags of chips, eighteen sausages, two chicken legs and the odd pastie. Just before he left he asked for money. 'Put it all on the club's account,' he was told, and off he went.

I think you can see what's coming.

Benny arrived at the chippie just as it was busying up for lunch. He put in his order and began to wait. Now the Argyle is not the biggest of establishments, and within five minutes people were queuing out of the door and onto the pavement, moaning quite loudly. Benny was beginning to feel the pressure, especially when they ran out of chips for the second time. After what seemed a lifetime, they handed him a large box, packed with freshly fried food. Stressed, he grabbed the box, and uttered the immortal words 'Put it on the club's account,' and turned to leave.

'What account?' Came the reply. Startled, Benny responded
'Swansea City's account.'

'We don't have an account with them. That'll be £29.58, please – cash.'

'I've only got £6.00 on me,' he stuttered.

'Well, you'd better give me those back and go and find another 24 quid then,' was the response as the food was snatched back from him. Benny sheepishly walked past the disapproving queue and bolted back to the Vetch. Needless to say, we were killing ourselves at his distress, and laughed all the more when his anger surfaced upon realising he was the victim of a set-up. The chips were great though – eventually!

There were, however, grander pranks – and yours truly was never far away from those. One slow day at the Vetch, as six or seven idle minds were beginning to wander aimlessly, Roger Mullen drew attention to the height of the floodlight on the new East Stand. I claimed that it wasn't as high as one of the old ones in the opposite corner of the ground, prompting a considered debate. All, bar one, agreed with me: the old vertical floodlight was definitely taller. Undaunted, Roger continued:

'Well, I don't care how high it is, none of you tossers would climb it!'

Before I could think, I heard myself reply:

'Who says?'

Big Mistake. They pounced like jackals. I was baited, taunted, called chicken, dared to do it, and finally – the money came out. A very substantial pot. There was no going back now. I took the bet. I was risking my life, but *far* more importantly my career (I'd have been sacked if I was caught), for the princely sum of £3.50.

The next thing I knew, I was standing at the base of this old floodlight pylon looking straight up to the top, about 100 feet away. Various conditions had by now been attached to the bet. One of the bastards had even wanted me to stand on the very top with my arms outstretched – but not even I would do that. Not for less than a tenner anyway!

The first thirty or forty rungs were fine, but then it started to get a bit hairy.

The ladder itself was pretty much totally vertical, so, when you start to tire you begin to lean backwards, and get the feeling that you are going to fall. Putting aside thoughts of my imminent death, on I climbed and got above halfway. It was from this point on that the wind kicked in. The Vetch Field is probably no more than 200 yards from Swansea Bay, where the prevailing wind whips across almost constantly during the winter months, and now I could feel the whole structure begin to sway. Finally, I reached the safety of the lights cage at the top of the ladder. I paused briefly to look at the view, but knew I must have taken almost half of the ten-minute time limit agreed for the bet already. I had to get on. I swung out onto the frame, where thankfully, there was a small ladder. I climbed up until my hands reached the very top, and hauled myself up so that my elbows rested on it, which meant – again as per the conditions – that my head and shoulders were above the whole thing. I stayed there for ages – a good second-and-a-half – and made my way down as quick as I could.

I'd got about halfway down when I noticed the lads scuttling away from the base. Odd, I thought. This feat deserved a round of applause at least. But then to my horror, I saw Tosh strolling across the pitch from the North Bank and heading toward the players' tunnel. I froze. If he looked up now, my fledgling football career and I would be history. As I clung to that pylon I was terrified that one of the lads would mischievously ask Tosh what was that halfway up the floodlight, but I was eternally grateful that they said nothing and kept their heads down. Just as Tosh was leaving the pitch and about to enter the players tunnel, out came Stadium Manager Harold. This was much worse – if Harold saw me, he'd have got a shotgun and blasted me off the bloody thing!

They stood there for about five or six minutes, while I remained welded to the rung, totally motionless. I was starting to feel quite cold by now as the only clothing I had on was a football shirt and shorts. After what seemed an eternity, Tosh and Harold both turned and went down the tunnel. I seized my opportunity, shot down the floodlight and jumped off the bottom rung, looking around to make sure no one saw me. The lads were great, they were almost as relieved as I was as they knew what the consequences would have been if I'd been caught. But then I was brought back down with a bump when I asked for my winnings. 'No chance – too slow' and they all walked off.

Bastards.

One of the main pranksters at the time was Darren Gale, a six-foot-plus, fourteen-stone striker, whose pace made him a real handful – a 'Gale Force' as many of the headlines predictably proclaimed. But he also proved a handful in a number of other ways – and places. In the windowless Vetch dressing rooms, for instance, where, with the door closed and lights off, you couldn't see your hand in front of your face.

The rule at the club was that the first person in at the morning would go to the dressing room and switch the lights on. Darren's party trick was to have arrived at the club about ten minutes earlier than that, and standing, poised to pounce, on the benches that ran around the walls of the room. In time, the victim would then walk into the darkness, walk round the wall to locate the lights, and just as they were about to flick the switch, Darren would jump onto their back and scream. It happened to me a couple of times, and it frightened the absolute life out of me. Darren would then switch the lights on and collapse into hysteria as he saw the fear and shock in his victim's eyes.

One day, it all came to an abrupt end though with Darren's final victim. As normal, Darren was in position, coiled like a cobra ready to strike – at least that's what he told us – when the door opened, then closed quickly. The victim rounded the wall and groped for the switch. With that Darren leapt, screamed and landed on top of yet another unfortunate soul, then switched the light on to mock his screaming victim. His delight soon turned to horror as he saw a dishevelled John Toshack trying to regain his dignity. This time it was Darren's turn to shit himself. Tosh, being Tosh, apparently just sighed, and said

'Aye Darren, what do you think you're doing there son?'

It was a rhetorical question. And we never had to worry about switching those lights on ever again.

For all the humorous hi-jinx, there were less savoury moments. And occasionally the tensions of a group of young, fit and ultra-competitive lads would boil over – as they did the day I walked in on Dai Hough (Duffer) and Phil Williams arguing. Phil revelled in being argumentative, and you often just wished he would shut up. On this occasion I said exactly that. As I did, Duffer turned around, glared at me:

'What the fuck's it got to do with you?'

I was taken aback. I hadn't been having a go at him, but now, with the attention of the dressing room turned on me, I replied just as aggressively –

'Everything when you're behaving like such a prick'!

Duffer just snapped and lashed out at me, splitting my left eyebrow clean open. And when I saw the old claret – I went nuts! I chased Duffer out of the dressing room into the kit room, where he turned round and grabbed me, thereby stifling any punches I was attempting to throw. He held onto me for dear life in this all-encompassing bear hug, until my temper subsided. When he judged that it had, he slowly let go, apologising as he did so. But he'd judged it wrong. Now, I'm not overly proud of what happened next, but my only defence is that we were being schooled in a dog-eat-dog environment where weakness of any description would be exploited.

Anyway, with this is mind – I butted him.

It was Duffer's turn to go nuts, but, luckily for me, this was the cue for the others to step in and separate us. At which point, Les walked in and, seeing the state of us, he called us into his office. I prepared myself for a bollocking – but it never came. Instead Les seemed oddly satisfied about it all. Apparently, it was good to get things like this off your chest. I think he even said 'Well done.' He then threw Duffer, who was less bloodied, the keys to the Sherpa, telling him to drive us both to casualty to see if we needed stitches. He ensured that we completed the obligatory, 'no hard feelings, lads' handshake — and off we went.

By the time they'd put a couple of stitches in my eye and cleaned up Duffer, we were back on friendly terms, and apologised to each other – this time with meaning. To this day I've got nothing but good feelings towards Duffer and I hope he feels the same about me. The whole incident was indicative of the darker, more primitive side to life at a soccer club, and I can assure you that this was just one of many altercations and bust ups I witnessed during my three years with the Swans. I wouldn't butt Duffer now, mind: not only did he carve out a career at the Vetch making over 200 appearances as a tough-tackling defender, but he's now high up in the South Wales Police Force!

As for Phil – so often the instigator – well, we had the last laugh. Phil was a very gifted player, and had the ability to have played at the highest level. Phil's problem, however, was his weight: he was just one of these people who was prone to putting on a few pounds, and to be honest, he was never the most committed of trainers. What's more, his diet wasn't typical of the professional athlete. Les was always onto him about this, and swore he'd come down on him if he caught him eating anything he shouldn't. One day, after one of our Argyle-chippie expeditions, Les caught Phil red-handed, devouring his pastie and chips! Les went nuts. He marched Phil to the minging, stinking drying room, and ordered Phil to put on all the wet gear (the stuff that makes you sweat the most, like bin bags, and believe it or not incontinence pants). He then got him to don a full tracksuit and take in an exercise bike with him. Phil would have to clock up ten kilometres before Les let him out. We were wetting ourselves when he was locked in. And when Phil came out looking like a drowned rat, surprisingly we weren't any more sympathetic.

Part and parcel of an apprentice's life were our efforts to make a few extra quid one way or another. Kit – especially boots – which had been deemed surplus to requirements, was often rescued from the bin, cleaned up and sold to friends and acquaintances. This was long before the replica-kit society of today, and a pair of shorts or boots that were available because 'Tosh didn't want them anymore' were a useful commodity. I was on only £25 per week, with another £10 for my mother for board and lodge. The club were happy for you to stay at home as, a) it was cheaper, and b) it generally kept you out of trouble. Luckily for me, Mam always let me keep this extra tenner, which was a nice little bonus, as was any kit that you managed to sell on. What always sold well was kit from the opposition; don't forget in those days the Swans' fixture list included Liverpool, Arsenal, Manchester United and Tottenham to name just four. Chelsea were still in Division Two!

On a home match day, you were assigned duties, and once in a while one of those was to look after the away dressing room. This meant making sure that the half-time teas, and the tray of Fanta orange, were also present and correct to quench the most raging thirst. It was to be another fifteen years before someone worked out that water and not fizzy orange was better at rehydrating you. Once the game had started, however, and everyone had trooped out to watch the game, the dressing room was like the Marie Celeste, and if any kit was left obviously lying about, the temptation was often too great to resist for the lowly-paid apprentice. On one occasion Luton Town were the visitors, and about twenty minutes before half-time, Colin Pascoe and I were ordered to go and start on the teas. We entered the Luton dressing room, and lo and behold, about four or five pairs of shorts were strewn across the floor. Luton had a great kit, and these royal blue satin shorts with the three Adidas stripes down the sides were some of the best around – much better than the Patrick stuff we normally had to peddle. Pasc and I looked down at the shorts, then back up at each other – not a word needed to be said. He went straight back out into the corridor to stand by the door. I swept up the shorts, jumped up on the table and pushed up one of the polystyrene ceiling tiles – the gap between the tile and the ceiling was a handy hiding place for the apprentices' stash. While I was at full stretch, pushing the shorts into the gap, the door opened. Pasc has never fully explained how he let this happen, but the next thing I heard was

'Oi, what the hell do you think you're doing!'

I looked down, to see the Luton midfielder David Preece glaring at me. He had just come off injured. 'Get them down now,' he shouted, gesturing at the shorts in my arms and the ones hanging from the ceiling. I jumped down very sheepishly and handed them over. I was in deep shit. 'You cheeky little bastard,' he said, and then, luckily for me, burst out laughing. 'I used to do the same when I was an apprentice; I didn't think it still went on – now piss off and take this as a lesson – don't do it again.' Embarrassed and relieved, I apologised and left to be greeted by an unapologetic Pascoe who thought it was hilarious.

Shame about the shorts – they were quality. I'd have got a few quid for those.

My revenge on Pasc came quickly enough though and was exacted when he was again on away dressing-room duty soon after. After the match was over and the away team left, he was expected to tidy up the dressing room before he left. Anything left unwanted – like unopened cans of Fanta – were always kept as booty by the apprentice concerned. That day, he decided he wasn't going to take them home as the rest of us would normally do, but chose to hide them above several of the roof tiles for future use. Unbeknown to him, I watched him hide them all, and after he left, I went and pinched them, and stashed them away myself.

Monday lunchtime, Pasc made a big deal that he wouldn't be buying a drink to go with his chips as he'd stashed last week's treasure away, even mocking us sad saps who had to actually spend money to wash down our lunch! I said nothing. But when the chip messenger came back, and Pasc had gone to retrieve his ill-gotten gains, I fetched a can from the stash and sat down with my chips. A couple of minutes later, red-faced, he returned and disconsolately sat down to start on his chips. One of the lads innocently asked where his drink was, at which point I popped open the can, took a long, loud slurp, looked at Pasc and said,

'Aaah Fanta – you can't beat it lads, can you?'

Everyone burst out laughing, but Pasc went crazy. Chips up in the air, he flew at me and started pummelling me until I told him where I'd stashed the rest of them. Another painful experience but well worth it for the look on his face.

The Liverpool way was never very far from life at the Vetch in the early 1980s. Tosh had never been anything less than honest in the press about his affection for the club in general and Bill Shankly in particular. Even Tosh's accent was a mixture of Cardiff, Scouse and Shankly's Scottish burr. Everyone was 'son' and a knowledgeable 'aye' was his habitual reply, especially when he was thrown a trivial question by one of us troublesome youngsters, and this often weary response, 'Aye son, aye' was regularly heard around the club. At our winter training ground at the AWCO fields at Jersey Marine, Tosh had long since installed the wall of six or seven upright boards, approximately the size of a football goal. Each was angled so that, when you entered at one end and struck a ball at pace at the board facing you, that board would then feed the ball back in your path toward the next board, towards which you again struck the ball, then back to the next one and so on until you emerged at the end. It taught you to shoot and pass with accuracy, and encouraged instant control of the ball coming back at you at pace. This wall was a carbon copy of the boards Tosh had learnt his skills on at Liverpool.

But the main thing that Tosh brought with him from Liverpool was the overall discipline, part and parcel of which was the attitude to injury. Quite simply, injuries were not tolerated. Whether you had a simple strain or a pull, or something more serious like a break or ligament snap – you were persona non grata, you were no use to anyone. Injury meant you couldn't play, and if you couldn't play, nobody wanted anything to do with you. With this in mind, you'd have assumed that we had the top medical facilities available to get us up and running again. Don't forget, this was the time of Bryan Robson, Glenn Hoddle, Ossie Ardiles, Ian Rush, Graeme Souness – legends all – and a period that many look back on as the last golden era of football. But even though Swansea City was effectively a top six club – the equivalent of say Portsmouth today – can you believe that we didn't even have a physiotherapist. Those duties fell to Boey. Happy days.

The first time I was injured and received treatment from Boey was courtesy of your regular dead leg. I remember Max Thompson (who won ITV's Goal of the Season in '81/82 for his wonder volley when we beat Arsenal) clattered me from behind in training, and caught me just on the inner thigh of my right leg. It started to stiffen up during training, and by the next day I could hardly walk. I reported to work as normal, and told Les Chapell, who had a quick look at it. He realised that I wouldn't be able to train that day – 'You'd better go and see Boey,' was his advice. Warily, I knocked on Boey's door, who looked up with the contempt only reserved for those who had no right to be any functioning part of the human race. He looked down again and asked me what I wanted.

'Les sent me – I've got a dead leg.'

'Dead leg – Jesus, son, what d'you think this is, Mothercare? You'll have to wait till I get back from training – are you coming?'

'Les says no,' I replied.

'Fuck me – what are we running here – a girls' school? If you can't train get on with your cleaning jobs till I come back.'

I limped out of the room with my tail very much between my legs, and went to find something 'useful' to do. I pottered around, enjoying the soluitude for a while, but then the spectre of Boey's return began to haunt me. I can't stress enough how daunting it was to deal with someone like Boey when you were an apprentice. You'd never strike up a conversation with him, or even say hello, let alone try to have a nobble with him. He was deemed unapproachable to our class. As I was sitting there, contemplating my fate, the players started drifting in, and a couple of them looked at me, laughed and pointed out that Boey was in a foul mood. And he was the next one through the door.

'You,' he called, 'Come on – I haven't got all day'. He took me to the treatment room and told me to get up on the table, then he disappeared. As I was nervously sitting there, John Mahoney walked past. Now 'Josh' was revered by all. He was Tosh's cousin, legendary Welsh International and, along with Wyndham Evans and Ante Raijkovic, the hardest member of the staff. He was right out of the old school and his attitude to pain was legendary. He once tried to run off a broken leg after a particularly nasty challenge at The Vetch. He looked in as he walked past, and did a double take. 'What's the matter son?'

There's kind, I thought – he doesn't really know me from Adam but he's concerned about me. I was really pleased.

'I'm injured' I replied.

'Injured? 'You taking the piss? How old are you son?'

'Sixteen'

'Sixteen? Jesus, son – I never got injured till I was 29!' and with a withering look, off he went. I was crushed.

I sat there and considered just hopping off the bench and letting nature take its course. Then Boey re-appeared. He told me to lie back and relax (relax?!) and he switched on the ultrasound heat machine. Now, for the uninitiated, these electric machines pump heat directly into a chosen area of muscle, via a long metal arm with a circular metal surface at the business end, all designed to speed along the healing process. Clear gel is first liberally spread onto the damaged area – in my case the inner thigh – to act as a barrier between the skin and the hot metal surface of the ultrasound arm. Then, the ultrasound is moved in circular motions around the injured area. Easy.

Or so you would have thought.

Except Boey had forgotten the bit about spreading liberally. Or else he was compelled by budgetary constraints to apply a blob of gel that wasn't enough to cover the end of a toothbrush. I wanted to ask whether he'd put enough on, but I valued my life too highly. You learnt early on: never, *ever* question Boey. Anyway, the treatment began, and I relaxed(!) and lay back.

After a minute or two, Doug Livermore, Tosh's other assistant, came in and started to talk about travel arrangements for a scouting mission with Boey later that day. As they discussed the respective merits of the M5 and M1, the area on my leg that Boey was working on was getting warmer. All the while, he was becoming more and more engrossed in the best way to approach Ewood Park in Blackburn, and I noticed that his hand was slipping further away from the injured area, and further along up my thigh, to a swathe of un-gelled, exposed pink flesh. It started to get hot straight away. I wanted to tell him, but he was now arguing with Doug about junctions, so I let it carry on. Another 30 seconds passed and the situation was getting desperate. I'm quite decent with pain, but my threshold was rapidly approaching, and I was starting to twitch. As Doug finally announced that as he was driving he'd decide which exit they'd take, I screamed and punched Boey across the wrist, nearly knocking the ultrasound out of his hand. He lurched around as if he was just about to hit me back, but Doug burst out laughing and said,

'I think he's done, Boey! Did he order medium or well done?'

Boey looked at me, then down at the burn on my thigh and burst out laughing too.

'Sorry son – you should've stopped me'. Yeah right I thought! Doug left laughing, Boey squirted some more gel on, and told me to relax again and lie back. This time, for once, he was quite attentive, chatty almost. But I was more concerned with getting it over with, and leaving without a trip to the burns unit.

On another occasion that season I took a knock on my ankle which swelled up quite quickly and began to bruise. Boey took a look at it and said the dreaded words 'Wax bath'. Now, I'd seen the wax bath many times, but never had to experience its horrors until now. Imagine a foot spa that you can buy in any Department store these days for about 30 quid. Sleek, colourful, ergonomically designed . . . Well, it wasn't like that at all. Imagine instead one designed in 1947, by someone who was de-mob happy and just pleased to be making electrical appliances rather than attacking beaches in Normandy. It was a big, cumbersome iron pot, with original mottled 1940s' heavy electric flex, and it was filled almost to the brim with wax. Some at the club swore it had been there since the Second World War. Terry Medwin, who had been on the groundstaff at the Vetch in the early 1950s, said he remembered it from his day – and it had been old then! Terry also swore that it contained the original wax. Apparently that wax had once been light pink, but forty years of use had seen it turn a deep, dark brown. We shuddered to think what had prompted this change in colour.

Within minutes of switching the pot on, the wax would soften and melt. Once it became fluid – and very, very hot – you had to plunge your foot in, up to the lower shin, for about ten seconds. You had to time the plunge right because if you left it too long and the wax started to bubble, you'd end up with third-degree burns to go along with the original ankle ligament strain you'd been hoping to treat.

Once the foot was coated, you'd remove it instantly and switch the thing off. You then had to sit, with foot outstretched over the bath (to catch rogue drips) for about ten minutes until the wax had hardened. The foot, ankle and shin were then peeled, with all wax being emptied back into the bath below you. As the pot was still warm, the wax within swallowed up the discarded wax from your foot and started to cool down and set, awaiting its next victim. In the three years I was at the Vetch, I was seldom without a blister, athlete's foot, crushed blackened toenails hanging off, and various other afflictions of the hoof. This meant that when peeling off the wax, anything that was loose on the foot – skin, nails, hair – went straight back into the pot. Lovely! It certainly gave a new meaning to bonding with the past legends of our great club. I'm pretty sure Premiership clubs employ podiatrists now. Norman Whiteside is one, and I wonder if he still has a place for the old wax bath on his list of scientific remedies. Somehow, I doubt it.

As I write this book, I can reflect on the fact that I've only ever taken one day's sick leave in my working life. One day in 26 years. I know I've hardly been working down the mines, but I'm proud of it nonetheless.

I'll never forget that day off, though. It was Christmas Day 1982, I'd been at the Vetch for about five months, and I thought Tosh was going to kill me. We'd been sent home early the night before so I called next door to see my oldest friend, Chris Lewis, who I'd not seen much since I'd joined the Swans, and he said lots of my old school mates would be at a party that evening at a friend's house in Pennard. I leapt at it, so we arranged to meet at 6.30 for his dad Dennis to take us over. When I got there, Chris asked if I fancied a drink before we left. I was an athlete, I was an apprentice footballer – a man of the world – of course I fancied a drink. He returned with a three-quarter pint tumbler, filled with rum and coke. Lovely.

Yeah right.

I was nearly sick drinking it – it was vile.

Within 20 minutes I was struggling. By now we were in Dennis's car travelling past Fairwood Playing Fields where I'd nearly been sick so many times during pre-season training. This time I was, all down the side of Dennis's car. I was sick twice more by the time we arrived at our drop zone at Pennard Golf Club, and proceeded to vomit, once more, in the car park. I was by now, white as a sheet, in a cold sweat and shaking. Dennis stepped in and said he couldn't allow me to go. He told Chris he'd pick him up later, and told me to get in the back seat and try to sleep. He then took me home.

The next thing I really remember is my mother waking me at about 8.00 the following morning to go to work.

It was Christmas Day.

Now I've had more hangovers than I care to remember thanks to a career in cricket, where a night out is as important as good batting pads, but without a shadow of a doubt, this was the worst I've ever felt in my life, before or since.

I told my mother I wasn't going in, but she was adamant. 'Get up, I'm taking you in,' was her reply. 'You've made yourself ill, you deal with the consequences.' On the way into the Vetch in the car, I kept telling Mam how bad I felt and asked her to turn round and go home. No way, she said – you'll have to tell Tosh yourself.

By the time I arrived at the Vetch, I was in a bad way. I was still ghost white and ice cold, but I was also shaking like a leaf, and my teeth were chattering.

'I'll wait here for five minutes – you go and tell him,' said Mam. 'If you're not out – I'll assume you've stayed.'

I got out of the car, and sloped through the players' entrance, and who was the first person I saw? Tosh.

'Bloody hell son, what's the matter with you?'

Here goes I thought – do I tell him the truth or not. I decided I'd better had.

'I'm not feeling too well, Boss – I've . . .'

Before I could finish, Tosh said 'You've got a chill son – I don't want you going in there you'll give it to everyone. How did you get in?'

'My mother – she's still outside.'

'Well get out there and go home and get to bed. Don't come in tomorrow unless you're right. OK?'

I was so grateful I could've kissed him (this was becoming a habit) and I turned round and went back to the car.

'Well?' said Mam. 'What did he say?'

I told her, and she just looked at me and dared me to drink like that again. We drove home in silence.

Later that evening Chris popped in to apologise.

'Apologise for what?' I said.

'The rum in the drink. I filled half the glass with it – there were about six measures in there. Sorry.'

I could have chinned him, but I was too knackered to care.

CHAPTER FOUR

Fields of Dreams

To the impressionable apprentice and young pro, the words and actions of the senior pros are gospel. But, with hindsight, it is impossible to understate how cut-throat and vicious some players could be. In fairness there weren't that many at our club, apart from the money-grabbing ones who would sell their grannies for an improved contract or increased win bonus. But there were some on the circuit who would break your leg as soon as look at you. These were often the pros who'd made their living in the 1970s and were now winding down their careers at Luton or Orient or such clubs. In order to prevent such intimidation, the pros at our club would always urge you to get your retaliation in first, and 'bollocks to the consequences'. I'm not proud of it, but it was advice that I followed. Like the night the youth team were playing Plymouth Argyle at the Vetch mid-way through the '82-83 season.

It was a big night because Tosh, Boey and Doug were all in the stand watching, and I was reaching the stage where I was pushing for a regular place in the Reserves. Ten minutes into the second half, we were still 1-0 down, when my midfield colleague Dean Rees was taken off. He'd been up against a big strong lad who'd run the game for them, and I was pushed on to mark him, with instructions brought on by the substitute to stop him playing. I took this quite literally, and as the game was about to re-start with me standing directly in front of him, I looked round, saw that the ref was looking the opposite way, and lashed out at him with my forearm and caught him across the jaw. Job done. Then I saw the flag being waved by local linesman Mike Birt, who'd seen my actions. Mike had refereed me loads of time as a schoolboy, and he usually missed everything – but not this bloody time. The ref ran over, spoke to Mike, and sent me off.

As I trudged off, I glanced up to the stand and saw the big three, stony-faced, looking down at me. I looked away quickly, but still caught Les's eye: he looked so angry, I thought he'd burst. The only bonus was that because the players' tunnel at the Vetch is about thirty yards to the left of the dugout, I didn't have to walk straight past him and suffer the inevitable tongue lashing. I didn't have long to wait though. I'd just finished dressing, having sat in silence for ten minutes prior to my shower doing the old head-in-the-hands routine, when Les nearly blew the door off its hinges.

'Get in here,' he shouted at me and walked into the shower area. To say he tore a strip off me is putting it lightly. I'd cost us the game, I'd blown any chance of instant promotion to the reserves, and I'd let myself down. My crime? Smacking the guy in the face? No – that was good, 'it stopped him from playing' – no, my crime was getting caught. The main point of Les's rant was that I hadn't been cute enough. That was the biggest sin. It again underlined to me the main difference between amateur and professional soccer. Basically anything went in pro football, as long as the result was victory. The only thing that I remember being really taboo was spitting – still is today. There was an unwritten code at the time, that the harder the player the more respect he had in the game. It was fine being a George Best or a Glenn Hoddle, but there weren't many of those gracing the game in the early 1980s, what really won you friends and made you a name was being capable of putting it about.

I remember reading Alan Hansen's autobiography some time ago where he dedicates the introduction of his book to his memories of Billy Whitehurst. When Hansen had the new season's fixture list, did he look to see when Liverpool were scheduled to play Arsenal, or Manchester United or maybe Everton? No. He looked to see the two dates he'd have to face Whitehurst. Was Whitehurst an international? A million-pound player? The best striker in the division? No. He was just hell on legs. Over six feet, about fifteen-and-a-half stone, he very much enjoyed putting it about. And Hansen admits to being scared of him. Back in 1983, before the third and fourth officials appeared, there was an undercurrent of violence, cheating and dirty tricks, and adopting some of these tactics yourself would see you being admitted to a special sort of club. You were a pro.

Now, Billy Whitehurst I was not! People who played with me at that time would laugh that I'm even mentioning my name in the same breath as his. But that's my point. I was never a hard man, never wanted to be, and to be frank, never had the ammunition to be one even if I'd wanted to. Nevertheless, in order to belong, I tried my best to be nasty little so-and-so. It just didn't come naturally!

I learnt once and for all, however, that I was no on-pitch enforcer in '84/85 when we were playing Chelsea Reserves at Stamford Bridge. My direct opponent in midfield was Keith Jones. He was a couple of years older than me and had already broken into Chelsea's first team. He was a bit of a prodigy, having had a couple of man of the matches which had been shown on *Match of the Day*, and he would go on to make 60 odd appearances for Chelsea before being transferred to Charlton. But this day he was in the Reserves against me – and his ass was mine!

Les had already spoken to me quietly prior to the game. 'Decent player Jones – doesn't like it being dished out though – win that battle and you'll win us the game.'

I knew what I had to do.

We'd been playing for about 25 minutes and we'd not really come into much contact with each other, apart from tracking each other's runs. He was definitely a good player, quite pacy and strong. We were awarded a goal kick, so I jogged to the halfway line near the centre spot and turned to face my goalkeeper awaiting the ball. Keith came to stand directly behind me, and got quite close in order to challenge for the ensuing header. Now I'm sure you've seen the famous picture of Vinnie Jones reaching out from behind and squeezing Gazza's crown jewels, well, here in print I can claim to have done that well before Vinnie, but, with a slight variation. Unlike Vinnie, I didn't quite so much squeeze Jones's pride and joy but instead unleashed a big punch. I waited until our keeper ran up and was about to kick the ball, then seized my opportunity and smashed my fist backward into Keith's privates. He groaned and crumpled as the contact was made and I just ran forward to meet the ball and carry on with play. I expected to be clattered pretty much straight away, but didn't really mind as that would result in a booking for him – and maybe even worse, a sending off. Advantage us.

Nothing came.

Two minutes passed – nothing. Five minutes, ten minutes – nothing. I couldn't believe it – first teamer? Chelsea? What a pussy! I thought you had to be hard to play this game, I smiled to myself. Les *will* be pleased. I turned to chase a long ball forward by us, which was swept up by Chelsea's keeper. Jones tracked my run and turned at the same time as I did, just as the keeper kicked the ball back into our half. As I looked up and saw the ball fly over my head, Keith punched me right on the point of my jaw.

Ow! It really bloody hurt.

It was one of those when you really see stars. 'Fair enough I thought – I might have been wrong about you,' and I jogged on. Then, before the ball had even bounced, he did it again! Right on the button, same spot, absolute agony – I thought he'd bust my jaw. What did I do? I lashed out like a man possessed, swung a couple of haymakers, both of which missed Keith narrowly. But, my punches were seen by the ref. The result, a booking, a bollocking (off Les) and a

44

great deal of respect for Keith Jones. He'd once more shown me the world of the pro. Wait and wait, get revenge, but on your terms – and out of the way of the ref. Another salutary lesson learned.

Such tetchiness was commonplace in the Combination League where the officials weren't of the highest standard, and when Swansea played QPR at the Vetch, I had a front-row seat as unpleasant events unfolded. I had been picked in a squad of 13 for the game, but left out of the 12 after the warm-up at the ground so didn't have to face what was a very big QPR side, none bigger than their captain for the day, Steve Wicks, a former England Under 21 Cap. He had been a regular first-teamer for years, and was using this game for fitness during his return from a recent injury. QPR's Reserves were managed by a very famous name in the world of football, former Double-winning captain of Arsenal, Frank McLintock.

About twenty minutes into the second half, and for no apparent reason, over near the corner touchline, Dean Saunders elbowed the QPR left back in the face. McLintock went nuts and was shouting at Dean, who delivered his perfect 'Who me – I didn't touch him?' look back at Frank. The score was 0-0 at the time.

From this point on, Dean, who'd spent much of the second half winding up the defenders with well-placed comments and niggles off the ball, became a marked man. The elbowed full back continued to stalk his prey in absolute fury, but instead of avoiding him, Dean continued to bait him. But when the ball bounced chest high toward Dean on the touchline, the now livid left back seized his chance. It was almost like one of those slow motion moments from *Kung Fu*. The left back just launched himself at Dean, about three feet in the air – both feet outstretched in front of him and with studs up. Like the matador he was, Dean saw him coming, moved slightly to the side, then turned and watched the player sail through the air – missing everything – and landing in a heap on the cinder track around the pitch, instantly burning the skin on the top of his backside. Lots of our team burst out laughing at this, whilst the QPR players gathered round Dean in defence of their karate-kicking teammate. Most memorable in this was the way in which Steve Wicks lifted one of our slight midfielders off his feet with one hand and just dumped him on the turf. It was all getting a little out of hand, and the referee obviously agreed because he sent Wicks off.

The game, unsurprisingly, deteriorated: the verbals and niggles became ever more nasty and less legal, but in terms of the football, QPR were still battering us. Then, with a minute to go, and totally against the run of play, Dean made a sharp run into the box and was tripped – penalty. Midfielder Huw Lake, stepped forward to take it, scored, and celebrated right in front of the QPR bench, and more significantly, right in front of Mr McLintock.

The game teetered on the brink of all-out war.

The referee managed to keep control, and within a minute it was all over, and we'd pinched a 1-0 win from nowhere.

Predictably, the game ended with a scuffle, and this continued into the players' tunnel as we all trooped off. The tunnel at the Vetch – as was common with most grounds before the new replacement stadiums that began to arrive in the 1990s – was about as wide as your normal hallway in a regular house. As narrow as four feet, and about ten yards long, it was not the place to have a fight. When it all kicked off now, there must've been about fifteen of us in the tunnel all pushing and shoving, and to his eternal credit, only one – Steve Wicks – attempted to keep the peace and keep people apart. The focus of the QPR anger was Dean and Lakey, and from behind the best peacekeeping efforts of Wicks came a big haymaker from the QPR substitute. It was one of many attempted punches thrown in this frenzy of swearing, abuse and pushing and shoving, and one of the few that connected with anything. What it did connect with was Lakey's front teeth, and instead of knocking them out, just snapped them both off, halfway down. Lakey's startled face was a picture. I didn't know whether I should fight back on my teammate's behalf, or burst out laughing. As I was deciding what to do, the staff from both teams arrived in the tunnel, and we were pushed into our respective dressing rooms.

We began to get changed for the showers, and commiserated with a totally crestfallen Lakey, who was checking out his snapped teeth and new smile in the mirror. Next thing, the door opened, and in walked Frank McLintock with the substitute who'd caught Lakey flush in the mouth. The layout of the Vetch had one problem: the only way to the physio's room for treatment was through the home dressing room. Now, to add insult to injury, the substitute needed stitches put in his hand because in the process of re-shaping Lakey's grin he'd ripped open a deep gouge across his fist. There was silence for a moment, then Dean jumped up and started screaming out 'Lakey, Lakey, he's the bastard that knocked your teeth out – hit him, hit him'. Lakey had had enough by now and I don't think he wanted to risk any more of his pearly whites, but Dean was having none of it. And in his desperation, Dean ripped off one of his boots, threw it at Lakey and shouted 'Hit him with my boot, hit him with my boot'

Again I didn't know whether to join in or just burst out laughing, but then McLintock – who no doubt had been in this situation countless times in his career – just rounded on Dean and shouted in his gruff Scottish accent, 'Hey, you son. You'd better shut your mouth and sit down right now. You started all this today, and unless you want me to end it, you better let me get this boy treated so just piss off and get changed'. I think Dean sized up the situation pretty quickly, realised that he didn't particularly want to find out if Frank was as tough as he looked and just sat down and took off his other boot, as the rest of us smiled, and put it all down to experience. Another ordinary day at the office!

When I'd settled in at the club during the '82/83 season, my goal was to become established in the Reserves, and the ritual of checking the notice board on a Friday lunchtime to see if I was picked in their squad was often a bittersweet experience. You see, I was regularly selected in the squad, but just as often left out of the final twelve. As this was in the days of just one substitute, I often went weeks without kicking a ball in anger. I remember feeling quite down about this at the time, and would enviously look at the joy on the faces of my fellow apprentices Roger and Duffer when they were selected long before me. It wasn't long before I convinced myself that I was just never going to be good enough to ever make it into the Reserves − let alone the First Team − and I wondered if my stature was again going to hold me back. The situation really started to manifest itself during training sessions. Whether I was trying too hard, I'm just not sure, but I had a couple of weeks where nothing was going right for me. After each training session, the worst player was awarded the yellow bib which had to be worn throughout the next day's session to basically signify how crap he'd been. I think I won it three days out of five during this spell. I started to let everything affect me. I looked at the players in my position during training − Huw Morgan, Phil Williams, Paul Maddy, Robbie James, Garry Stanley, Ray Kennedy to name just half a dozen − and managed to convince myself that I simply wasn't worthy of being on the same field as them.

There was a saying doing the rounds at the time that 'a good big 'un will always beat a good little 'un' − I can't remember when I first heard it, but I started to believe it was true, and the more I allowed myself to think this way, the worse I performed during training. After what seemed like months, but in reality was probably a couple of weeks, Les had noticed this dip in my form and took me aside for a chat after yet another poor performance and asked me what was troubling me.

Initially I tried to front it out and said I had no idea what he was talking about, but Les was having none of it and said that he knew something was wrong and wanted to help. I thought for a moment and decided I should tell him. I really trusted Les, so realised I'd best get it off my chest.

'I don't think I'm good enough Les' I started. 'Everyone I look at is better than me, they're all regulars in the reserves whereas I hardly ever get in the squad let alone get a game, and I just feel that I'm getting worse while they're all getting better'.

Les just smiled and said 'Is that it? That's all that's worrying you?'

I paused for a moment and said 'And I don't think I'm big enough; I just can't seem to compete with Robbie in a training game for example – he's just too strong.'

Les nearly laughed this time: 'Listen, son, half the pros in England can't compete with Robbie in a match, let alone first-year apprentices. Anthony, we all know at this club that you can play – you wouldn't be here otherwise. Just start to believe that. The reason you are an apprentice is that you are here to learn for two years – we don't expect you to walk straight into the First Team or the Reserves for that matter, in your first year. Just keep trying hard and it will come – I guarantee it. I know you're small, and maybe that will be an issue at some point, but one thing I can also guarantee you is within twelve months you will be a helluva lot stronger and a helluva lot fitter than you are now, and that's when you'll really start to impose yourself. You certainly aren't going to be a giant but there's no reason whatsoever why you can't go on and be a success in this game – whatever size you are. Do you understand – things will improve, and you'll forget you ever had these thoughts, just stick at it'

I thanked him, and he just told me to think about what he'd said, start to be more positive and just go and get changed. Then he just turned and walked off. It may only have been a short conversation, but it meant a huge amount to me that Les took the time to boost me in that way. It still does – I owe him a hell of a lot.

Within a couple of months, and as the '82/83 season developed, I began to feel I belonged and this feeling strengthened quickly once I began to appear in the thirteen for the Reserves regularly. Not only did my attitude change, but my luck improved as well! My mates Roger and Duffer were defenders, Roger an out-and-out centre half, Duffer a fullback come centre half. Unfortunately for them, there was plenty of cover in defence, and if a semi-regular first-team defender was relegated to the Stiffs, whoever had played the previous week for the Reserves at centre half – regardless of how they had done – would be dropped. Even if they were man of the match! This was the way the hierarchy at the club worked. In my position midfield, it was slightly different. If a first teamer was dropped, it was easier to accommodate a midfielder who'd excelled in the previous reserve game. This meant that during my time in the Reserves I played in all four positions in midfield: right side, left side, centre left and centre

In Nanna Olive's garden, aged two. 'Keep your head down, son!'

Little did I know this Welsh international would later become a colleague: Leighton James with me (second left) and Swansea Schoolboys teammates, Steve Thomas, Lyndon Lewis and Keith Williams

Captain of Swansea Schoolboys under 11s. Manager Stuart Davies (back row, middle) still a mate today, as is my lifelong friend Chris Lewis (front row, far right).

Like father, like son with Swansea C.C. Dad's the one with Bob Willis's Duncan Fearnley 'Run Reaper' bat. Why would anyone want one of those?!

Captain of Wales Youth at Celtic Park vs the Scots in 1983.

An early indication that a choice was on the horizon.

First morning at the Vetch, and praying for a low profile, as John Mahoney, Ian Walsh, Ante Rajkovic and Jimmy Hadziabdic crowd the batsman.

Training run in Singleton Park, with ever eccentric manager Colin Appleton (far left).

John Toshack (far left), Les Chappell (second right) and Wyndham Evans (far right), all big influences on my career.

Appleton welcomes back the smiling assassin Ante Rajkovic, surrounded (from left) by Gary Richards, Jimmy Rimmer, Dudley Lewis and Chris Marustik.

Two for Latchford, two for Cottey – Bloody Hell!

Dean Saunders – life and soul of the dressing room.

Ray Kennedy. What a player!

Phil Boersma. Very hard taskmaster.

Darren Gale signs for Tosh – before the lights went out!

With Tony Rees next to me, I'm peeking under the armpit of John Bond, who points the way forward. For me, it was towards the exit.

The best squad in Swans history – sixth in Division One, 1982. The new boy is second left in the front row. Colin Pascoe is two to my left.

Swansea City 1984-85, the slide down the leagues had begun. I'm far left of front row next to Dean. Colin Meldrum is far left, back row.

Scaling the heights and plumbing the depths! Opposite is the Vetch floodlight I climbed for a bet after training. Below is my bungee jump for a dare during the break in a one-day game against Lancashire at Hove. Age has obviously mellowed me!

Fifteen years old and picked for Welsh Schools vs England Under 19s at Pontarddulais – bounced out by Andy Pick for nought!

An early photocall in 1986 – what a barnet!

My Cap. Wales versus England at Sophia Gardens – trying to avoid the prone Ashley Giles. David Hemp and Geraint Jones look on.

right (sounds like a political party conference!). As a result, as time moved on, the Friday lunchtime ritual of checking the thirteen for the game became far more enjoyable. Once I'd made the breakthrough, I was in the thirteen – and more often than not the twelve – from then on. It's amazing looking back that my first regular partner, for about twenty games or so, was Ray Kennedy. 'Razor' was at the time the most decorated footballer in British history. He'd done the Double with Arsenal as a striker, joined Liverpool where he had a stellar career – Doubles, Trebles, European Cups, the lot – and also picked up twenty-odd England caps. When Tosh signed him in January 1982 most Swans fans couldn't believe it. Here was a true modern great, albeit now a little overweight, and entering the twilight of his career.

Razor was such a lovely quiet guy that he was a pleasure to be around. He always found time to have a word or piece of advice if we ever came across him at Hock's wine bar in Swansea, the regular hangout for the first-team squad after a game. Now us young pups knew we were playing with fire, there were, and still are, strict rules about a pro and his drinking habits – but in those days the main belief was that there was no harm in having a few beers as long as you sweated it all out in training the next morning, and never, ever drank the night before a match.

As a result we'd often hang on Razor's coat tails, and join him at Hock's as he held court. As a young, fit, professional footballer, there were always plenty of interesting people to talk to who had been attracted by Razor's presence. There was definitely an issue about something between him and Tosh, and not long after, Tosh dropped him to the Reserves. It was from here we became temporary partners in midfield, and I enjoyed every minute of it. I was required to do his running – fetching and carrying the ball for him to weave his magic. I loved running – still do – so it was a pleasure as far as I was concerned. There's an old saying that I know you've heard before about old sportsmen: 'You never lose it'. And Razor embodied this. The guy had more ability in that left foot than I had in the rest of my body. I remember a drill we had to do in training where you played to ball into a teammate who stood on the edge of the penalty area, and acted as the pivot. He'd play the ball back to you, and you'd take a shot at the goal, trying to place it either side of the keeper. Razor would go for top corners, bottom corners, as tight to the post as you'd dare. His accuracy was phenomenal; I swear he never missed.

His career at Swansea kind of fizzled out at the end of that season, and he left in the summer under a bit of a cloud, joining Hartlepool, but none of us were to know the real reasons. It wasn't until years later that I picked up a newspaper while waiting to bat for Glamorgan and read the headlines about Razor's battle with Parkinson's disease. Apparently he'd first experienced the symptoms as a nineteen-year-old starlet at Arsenal when he had problems signing his name when answering autograph requests from fans. As his career developed, so did the symptoms, and he apparently turned to booze to take his mind off the condition. I couldn't help reflecting that some of my happiest times at the club, spent playing with him in midfield, were in reality some of the most traumatic in his life. I remember finishing the article, putting it down and walking out of the dressing room alone. All my worries that day about whether I'd get runs or not went straight out the window, it made me realise, all too briefly, that life's priorities revolve around health and well being, not just bat and ball.

When that breakthrough to the reserve team came in 1983, I found myself in the most illustrious company. Up front was none other than Tosh, and also – usually returning from injury – Ian Walsh, both supplemented by the emerging talents of Dean Saunders. That first period was quite successful for me, not just in establishing myself in midfield and as a 'player', but scoring as well. I scored around ten that season, and many of them were as a result of knock-downs and lay-offs from Tosh, with me being given orders to get in and around the box as much as I could. The system we played really suited my game, and was unique at the time. Tosh is credited with bringing the sweeper system to the First Division. Previously an extra defender was viewed as a very negative approach, but Tosh turned it all on his head by the way he implemented it. Basically he'd pick three centre halves, one of whom would sweep behind the middle two. Tosh had even performed this sweeper role himself in the First Team on occasion in previous years. The players who performed it at top level were Ante Rajkovic as sweeper (and possibly the best defensive player I ever saw), with Max Thompson and Colin Irwin the twin centre backs whose job it was to win everything in the air and also be as strong in the tackle as the referee would allow. If anyone was injured or suspended, Dudley Lewis would deputise for Ante, and Nigel Stevenson or Jeremy Charles would fill in at centre back. The beauty of this system was that it allowed the full backs – Neil Robinson, Jimmy Hadziabdic, Garry Stanley or Wyndham Evans – to get forward as much as possible, with two supporting central midfielders – Robbie James and Ray Kennedy – instructed to get forward, also getting in on the act. In attack we then had the luxury of having almost three strikers – Bob Latchford the kingpin, with Alan Curtis to the right of him and Leighton James to the left. It was an attack to drool over, as we all did when Swansea announced their debut in the top flight with a 5 -1 thrashing of then mighty Leeds United.

Every Swansea team, from the Juniors through Youth to Reserves, played the same system as the First Team. This meant obviously that any player promoted up a grade would at least never have to worry about learning the system, and could just concentrate on their part in it.

The hardest part of changing managers is changing systems. New managers bring new ideas and you have to adapt, or you'll be moved on. The next managerial appointment that the Swansea Board of Directors made, apart from caretaker managers from the backroom staff, was a certain Mr Colin Appleton in 1984, and I would never have dreamt that he intended to show us his system out on the pitch, in front of a startled crowd and bemused players. But more of that later.

The worse thing about my final couple of seasons at the Vetch was the off-the-field intrigue. Financially, the bubble of the club had not so much burst, as exploded in a nuclear style. I remember being told to go and fill up one of the trusty, and now rusty, Sherpa vans with petrol, only to be told by the garage assistant that the credit account with the club had been cancelled and I'd need cash. I obviously didn't have any on me, so had to ask if he'd allow me to go back to the club to get some, and return later in the day. This I did dutifully, some petty cash was found, and the petrol paid for. From that day on all such trips meant a visit to the club secretary to get the cash up front.

The reason for this financial meltdown was the classic football boom-and-bust story. That initial, hugely successful, season in Division One in '81/82 didn't come cheap. Players were on wages as high as anyone in the league. Bob Latchford and then Ray Kennedy were believed to be the top earners, with an informed source stating that Razor was on over a grand a week, before any bonuses. Rumour had it that he was the highest-paid player in the country – I don't know if that was true or not – but if it was, it was the 1980s equivalent of having a Frank Lampard or a Steve Gerrard on the payroll. The win bonus was £220, with £80 for the draw, added to the £50 appearance money. If the First Team won two games in a week – as often happened in that first season – bonuses and appearance money would rise to over £500 a player. As the team started to underperform in the second season, crowds dropped dramatically, and as a result, so did revenue. In those days clubs were almost totally reliant on ticket sales for money as this was before the Sky-fuelled TV boom, and once the crowds started to dry up, the debt of the club increased dramatically, and extremely quickly. That was when the brutality of pro football came to the fore again. Players were just sold as a matter of course – some against their wishes – just to reduce the wage bill. I remember Bob Latchford holding out for a move – and a deal – to a club that suited him. In the end the club decided to make it as easy as possible for him to leave. How did they achieve this? Offer him an inducement to leave? Find him the best club or deal available? Write him a letter of thanks for the impeccable way he served the club during his time there?

No.

Drop him from the first team squad. Make him train with the kids. Bring him back in for afternoon training, on his own, lapping the track, being watched by apprentices. Bob eventually signed for NAC Breda (heard of them?) in Holland in January 1984. I don't know if that was the club he wanted or not. I just know he left.

Now you're probably appalled by this lack of sensitivity, by what amounts ultimately to bullying. To the pro, however, whilst it's obviously a huge pain in the arse, he's seen it happen to so many others within the industry that he just feels it is bound to happen to him at some time, so just hopes that it's all over with quickly. Some people, like Bob, deal with it with dignity and strength, others just create havoc and unsettle everyone until they get their move. I don't know how I would have dealt with it. It's all designed to break you and ensure that the club remains in charge.

In such circumstances, change at the top is inevitable. Chairmen and directors resign, managers come and go. Our management team of Tosh, Boey, Doug Livermore and Terry Medwin were early casualties. Some walked, some were sacked, some returned and were then sacked (Tosh), some were caretaker managers, and eventually all were gone. In May 1984 Colin Appleton was appointed as manager. The only member of the managerial staff remaining from our glory days was my mentor Les Chappell.

So that left us with the two Colins – Appleton and Meldrum. When we were first introduced to them, certainly from the response of the dressing room, you'd swear it was the Two Ronnies that had been appointed.

We had all been told to report to the first-team dressing room, and change for training as usual. All 30-odd of the playing staff were there, waiting to meet our new management team, and we heard a very strange clip-clopping sound coming along the corridor. The door opened and in came Colin 1, followed by Colin 2. Before Colin 1 had a chance to say anything, thirty sets of eyes looked down to the floor at the source of the clopping. There, beneath a white Swansea City shirt and black Hummel tracksuit bottoms emblazoned with the obligatory initials, 'C.A.', were bare feet, squeezed into a small pair of white, wooden-soled

Scholls. Now these weren't the closed-toe clog favoured by Queen's Brian May – he might just have got away with that – no, these were the open-toed variety favoured by your mother. Laughs were stifled.

'All right Lads? – I'm Colin Appleton, and I'd like you to call me Boss.'

Pointing at the very large, barrel-chested man next to him, with sandy hair and a florid complexion, he said, 'This is my assistant, Colin Meldrum – he'll be knocking you into shape.'

This time some of the laughs were beyond stifling, as the 30 sets of eyes moved from the lovely white Scholls, to a pair of extremely battered, but clearly very comfortable, ankle-height, tan-shade, suede Hush Puppy boots, again topped off with Swansea issue training kit, and the initials 'C.M.'

I don't think anyone that was there can remember what was then said by Colin 1. Eyes were looking skyward, lips were being bitten and fists were clenched. Colin Appleton had landed and he wasn't going to last too long!

First impressions are everything in life, and sometimes they can get in the way of the real man. Colin Appleton was very much a throwback manager. A hard defender, who had played for Leicester City in two FA Cup finals in the early 1960s, he had been the first player to captain Leicester to a Cup win when they won the 1964 League Cup. He'd joined us from Hull City where he'd turned the club around, and gained the reputation of being a trouble-shooter. Unfortunately, the fans, and in some respect the players, were expecting a big-name appointment. I don't think anyone had heard of Colin – certainly none of the players had. That in itself wasn't a problem, he'd have got away with that. The trouble was, as his choice of footwear proved, he was quite eccentric – I think he even revelled in it. Nothing wrong with that either, two of the most eccentric managers that ever lived are believed by many to be two of the best – Bill Shankly and Brian Clough – but Shanks and Cloughie had substance, and, most importantly, success to go with it. For that, the eccentric manager is forgiven everything. Appleton unfortunately didn't have much luck in the success department, and from day one, from that very first clip-clop moment, I felt he struggled to win the respect of all the players.

He wasn't really helped by Colin 2 either. If anything, he was more of a hindrance. At least on the training pitch Appleton would swap the Scholls for soccer boots. Meldrum always wore boots for training too. But they were always those ridiculous Hush Puppies. God how we came to detest the sight of them. Now for all I know he had the biggest bunions the world had ever seen and needed to protect them by wearing those boots, but to us he was just taking the piss. The initial amusement at his appearance soon dissipated to a lack of respect and general loathing. How on earth can a fifteen-stone man, on a muddy training pitch, who can hardly keep his balance as he tries to instruct you on ball retention, retain any credibility? Unfortunately, Meldrum never won anything from us, credibility nor respect. He also had this unbelievably embarrassing way of singing 'Dee dee dee dee, Dee daa dee daa' to illustrate anything that involved movement in, say, closing down an opponent or jockeying a player away from danger. You really had to be there to believe it.

Ironically, Appleton rated me quite highly. Probably more so than any other manager I played under. He was very encouraging, and really gave me my head in reserve-team games, which when you consider we were playing the likes of Spurs and Arsenal, where I competed directly against players such as Glenn Hoddle, Ossie Ardiles, David Rocastle, Paul Davis to name but four, was a big boost to my confidence. He still had us scratching our heads with his methods though. I remember he took us against Arsenal Reserves at Highbury once late in the '83/84 season, and after we'd finished the warm-up, he did one of the most embarrassing things that ever involved me as a professional sportsman, and it had to happen out on the pitch at Highbury of all places. As a lover of football history, Highbury was a venue that I'd been desperate to play at since I'd broken into the Reserves, as I'd always read about the clubs golden past and its famed marbled halls. Basically Appleton had a bee in his bonnet that the reserve team didn't understand his system, and wanted to explain how we should adopt a certain formation during the game. The Arsenal lads were just trooping off to get ready for kick-off in about fifteen minutes' time when Appleton called us to a huddle in the centre circle.

'Right lads, I want you all to know exactly what I want from you today, and I want you to play with this system – and stick to it. Mike get in goal.' Our startled goalkeeper Mike Hughes looked at him:

'You want me to go in goal boss?'

'Yes son – go on,' said Appleton, pointing to the empty net fifty yards away. Then he pointed to our fullbacks: 'Lads – left and right back – go on,' again pointing at the relevant parts of the pitch. The Arsenal lads started to look over their shoulders at us now as each one of us was sent to our respective starting positions. Our embarrassment was compounded by the sniggers from the departing Arsenal lads, and rather uncomfortably we took our positions. Luckily the combination league games didn't attract big crowds, but the 2,000 or so fans sitting in the main Highbury stand watching me take part in the first human game of Subbuteo, was about 2,000 too many for my liking. When Appleton started to run between us telling us to move to combat him, or get into space and support a run, it was almost too much for me. I'd have happily died on the spot. After five minutes of this – with no ball to be seen – Appleton called a halt. Mercifully.

'Now just keep to this system boys and you'll be fine'

Fine?! We all just wanted to run off the pitch, straight through the Highbury halls, and carry on straight back to Swansea. We felt humiliated.

Talking of running reminds me of Paul Richardson, signed from Swindon Town by Colin Appleton in my final season of '84/85, when I was finally an established member of the first team squad, and feelings of not being good enough were firmly a thing of the past, just as Les had predicted. Richardson was very much a journeyman pro, having played for Nottingham Forest, Chester, Sheffield United and Blackpool, and was at the end of his career. On his arrival he made the fatal dressing-room error of giving an interview in which he was proclaimed as 'The fittest footballer in Britain.' And it became clear to us that not only did he actually believe it, he absolutely revelled in it. By this stage my body had pretty much reached its fighting weight: I was about the fittest I was ever to be and my particular forte was running over the middle distances of two to five miles.

After about the third training session, the lads had already had enough of Mr Richardson. Colin Appleton by now had us training on the municipal soccer fields at Ashleigh Road in Swansea, about two-and-a-half miles from the Vetch, where the heavier, wetter, less tended pitches would be better preparation for the heavier pitches we would encounter at this time of the season. Anyway, at the end of training we were ordered to run back to the Vetch as a climax to the day's exertions. In common with all footballing folk, Appleton didn't trust us, so he would drive alongside us all the way back to the Vetch. I can still hear all the car horns beeping behind him as he was barking 'Race, lads, race – I want a winner here, pull your fingers out,' whilst driving at about ten miles an hour at our side.

That day, Richardson gave Appleton the race he wanted, as he bolted off from the front of the pack after about 300 metres. After a couple of moments I thought, 'I quite fancy this.' So off I shot. For a mile or so I was only making limited headway on him, I knew I was way ahead of the group as the car horns were fading into the distance, but I was worried I wasn't catching him quickly enough. Then as we passed about a mile-and-a-half, I could sense he was struggling. I was gaining quickly now, and he turned round and saw me coming, he tried to sprint again, but nothing happened; I could see he'd shot his bolt. As we got to within the final half a mile or so of the Vetch I passed him, and ran on to win, with three or four of the lads including Dean and Dudley, also finishing in front of him. Not a word was said to Richardson, but all the boys made a huge fuss of me, and even Appleton, who arrived just in front of his man-made tailback, said 'Well done.' Another big learning experience. Making glib comments, especially to the press, unless you can back them up, would always come back and bite you on the arse!

On Monday, December 3, 1984, Colin Appleton called me to one side in training and told me I'd be starting the following night for the first team in 3rd round of the Welsh Cup. We were playing a team called Spencer Works, not exactly Real Madrid I grant you, but any game for the First Team was a chance not to be sniffed at. I couldn't wait. He told me it would be a hard game as they'd be a tough team and would be out to take a few 'trophies' by kicking some of us 'pampered stars' out of the game. I knew what he meant. I'd played plenty of friendlies for the Reserves over the years against Welsh League teams. The referees were often weak, and the opposition hatchet men would have a field day. We'd have a Football League official in charge this time, so hopefully he'd limit the rough stuff.

For me, it was just one of those nights you dream of. I just played out of my skin. Everything I tried came off, and I couldn't have been happier walking off the field at the end. Apart from one small detail. We'd only managed a 1-1 draw! We were booed off the field and the South Wales Evening Post had the knives out and absolutely slaughtered everyone – apart from me. Even though I've spent my whole sporting career believing that the team is everything, this was one of the few occasions where I was happy to duck the bullets, and let others cop the flak. I felt it was an important step forward in my career.

It was about to get better.

Appleton called me into his room after I'd got changed. 'Sit down son – I've got some news for you.' I sat down and wondered what was coming. 'Well done tonight son, you had a very good game.' I said nothing, just stared back at him. 'I've decided that I'm going to give you a run in the side. If you continue to do well you'll remain in the side long term, but whatever happens in the next game, you'll stay in, so don't worry about having a mare and being dropped, play with freedom and do your best. Make the most of this opportunity, and take it with both hands. Do you understand?'

I mumbled something in the affirmative. I could hardly speak. This was all I'd ever wanted: an opportunity to show people I could play. I'd been given that chance, and I wasn't going to blow it.

'OK son, well done, see you tomorrow.'

How did my run in the first team go? What was it like to have the freedom to know you're in the side for a few games? I can't tell you. It never happened. Appleton was sacked the very next morning, and I never saw him again.

I suppose the main thing now was, as I waited to see who the new manager was, at least I was very much part of the first-team squad, and with Les Chappell back as caretaker manager, I still had a chance of my breakthrough. After all, Les had given me my initial break eight months earlier on April 7, when, again as caretaker manager, he'd picked me in the twelve for the first team for the first time ever. My league debut, a moment I'd thought would never come.

In the dressing room that day were plenty of familiar faces, who in footballing terms, I'd grown up with – Dean Saunders, Dudley Lewis, Pasc, Gary Richards and Huw Morgan. All were only a year or two older than myself. The only really seasoned pros in the team were Neil Robinson, Nigel Stevenson, Chris Marustik and the legend that was Wyndham Evans. Looking back, this was an illustration of a club in serious decline – all our 'stars' were gone, and ten of the squad of twelve were from Swansea and the surrounding area. To be honest though, I couldn't have cared less. I was seventeen years old and desperate to get started. Every pro that has ever played the game will be able to tell you of the first time they were part of the first-team squad on a match day. A very high percentage of players are introduced from the bench for their debut – we can't all be teenage prodigies like Wayne Rooney – and every pro will also tell you that they want to make their debut against the biggest side possible. With the greatest respect, you didn't want to make it against Rochdale.

My first match, however, wasn't against Rochdale. It was against the biggest club in Division Two at the time: Manchester City. Their team at the time included Paul Power, Kevin Bond and future Republic Of Ireland manager, Mick McCarthy, and when we were warming up on the Vetch, as the crowd started to roll in, I couldn't help but glance across and look at McCarthy. He was captain of the Republic of Ireland at the time and a renowned hard man, and I still found it pretty strange to realise I was on the same pitch as him. One thing had changed though. I no longer had any thoughts of inferiority. As I looked across now, I was thinking thoughts like – 'You're not as big as you look on TV', and when I saw Paul Power's ungainly lope – 'You look knackered already, mate – I can't wait to have a go at you.' I was bursting at the seams, and couldn't wait to get in on the action. There was only one problem. I was sub, would I get on?

Would I hell.

90 minutes I sat there, kicking every ball, challenging for every header, with a desperate urge to get on. During half-time, after he'd issued his instructions for

the second half, and a couple of minutes before we went out for the second half, Les came over and said 'Get warm, son.'

Fantastic – I'm going on.

No I wasn't.

About five or six times in the second half, Les sent me out to warm up, sprints and stretches along the touchline, fielding the odd ball as it went out of play and glancing up into the stand on occasion to try to see Mam and Dad. I know now he had no real intention of me going on – except in the event of an injury – and all the warming up was probably more to do with sending subliminal messages to the midfield quartet on the pitch to pull their fingers out, or the youngster would be on. Never happened. Bastards!

Still, every cloud has a silver lining. If I'd got on for that last couple of minutes, I'd now be saying that I'd made my football league debut against Manchester City. When I finally made my debut five months later, it was against a club with a far bigger history and tradition.

York City! Oh well, at least it wasn't Rochdale!

It was under Appleton that I finally made my debut at the start of the '84/85 season, now aged 18. It was only the second game of the season, and to get into the first team so early on made me think that if I did well, and we had a decent result, maybe I'd keep my place, and maybe I'd get what all players breaking into a side dream of – a run of games to try to establish yourself. They all say a good debut can often give you a career in the game. If you can get about the pitch and contribute to the game, then get subbed as you tire to a standing ovation, you become an instant crowd favourite, and from such beginnings, mighty things can happen. Players have even won contracts on the strength of their debut. Especially if it is a scoring debut.

Me? I hit the bar.

With a header!!

I thought I had a decent enough game: it was at home, and I ran myself to an absolute standstill which seemed to go down well with the crowd, but we lost 3 – 1 and there was to be no standing ovation.

I've often wondered what would have happened if my header had gone in. Believe it or not I was really decent in the air. After all, I'd practised jumping and leaping from a really young age, simply to make up for my lack of inches. What's more, I never played against a single player who didn't think I was going to be anything but useless in the air. This combination of being underestimated and busting a gut to be as good as I could be often paid dividends. Against York, I ran late into the box, gambled on a flick on from Dean and got in front of, and above, the defender and watched in agony as it clattered the bar. The fickle finger of fate. If it had gone in I might never have picked up a cricket bat again.

As it was, I was dropped for the next game, spent the next three-and-a-half months in the reserves, until being called up for that fateful Spencer Works game that finally ended Appleton's short spell with the club.

Following Appleton's sudden exit, John Bond arrived in mid-December 1984 with a fanfare. He was the big name that the fans craved, and whilst most of the players were pleased, we'd also heard on the rumour mill that Bondy could be very hard work if you got on the wrong side of him. He'd come from managing Burnley, and his departure from them was so acrimonious that he wasn't allowed to attend his first game in charge of the Swans – Burnley away!– and there were even stories of death threats against him. He was from the old school of opinion that if your face didn't fit, it was the end of you – end of story.

Bond's arrival also signalled the end of one of my last allies at the club. When it was announced that Bond was bringing his own staff, Les, still unhappy he'd been overlooked for the top job, felt totally marginalised and let down, so left the club. It was a sad day for me as I'd known him from when I was fourteen years of age, and he'd backed me in my career every single step of the way. I know you can't live life on ifs, buts and maybes, but I'm as certain as I can be that had he stayed at the club and been around during the Bond era, he'd have done all in his power to ensure I'd have had a new contract. Everyone needs an ally in pro sport – no matter who you are, and my last one had gone. That's life I guess.

To be fair, Les's leaving had nothing to do with Bond, but I can't say that I ever bonded with Bond. Part of it was my fault, I'm sure: I never liked the guy from day one. I felt he only really came alive when the press arrived and the cameras started rolling. He was straight out of the Ron Atkinson and Malcolm Allison school of champagne management, but if I'm honest, a very pale imitation.

However, I respected his right to manage me, and afforded him the same respect all my previous managers had enjoyed. A sign of things to come arrived in a five-a-side match in training. Now Bondy loved to play in these games, and made sure that he was always in the strongest side. He was into his early fifties and let's say he wasn't as fit as he'd probably been in the past. There was this one game though when Roger Mullen committed the cardinal sin of not obeying Bond's orders. Roger had possession of the ball, and Bond, who was on Roger's team, was screaming for it. Instead, Roger ignored him, turned, and played it away to Wyndham Evans. Bond halted the game straight away, turned on Roger and absolutely wrecked him for ignoring him, finishing with words to the effect of 'You'll never play for this club again.' And he never did.

I look back on what turned out to be my final season with mixed feelings. Missed opportunities, frustration, elation, and lots of fun. Underpinning, it all was sadness really, sadness at the plight of the club. Tosh was my idol. He was everything to me, and everything a top football manager should be. I learned all my best habits from him directly, or as a result of the network he'd put in place at the club. To this day, the work ethic he installed in me still drags me around the lanes of Llanedi every evening on my daily run. As the financial situation started to bite, and it all started to fall apart, you could feel the heart being ripped out of the club. Tosh went in October 1983, came back in December of that year, then, by the following March, was gone again – this time sacked. None of the managers that came in his place could replace him. Doug Livermore, Les Chappell, Colin Appleton and John Bond all held the reins for some period, and whilst all were really good blokes (with one notable exception), none came close to Tosh. Tactically, motivationally, man-management wise, Tosh was streets ahead of them all. The funny thing is, I'm not sure my fate would have been all that different even if he'd stayed. I might have got my chance, but would I have made it as a pro?

Honestly?

Probably not. I lacked pace, and at the highest level, pace is like gold. Maybe I'd have played 40 odd games and moved down the leagues – I don't know, and now, I never will.

I didn't have any say in the matter anyway. When the day finally came, I was out – end of engines. And history has proved that it was probably the best thing that ever happened to me. I was lucky, unlike so many others.

I wish someone had explained that to me at the time though.

I knew, of course, that Bond didn't rate me, but I was still very much part of the first-team squad as we came to the business end of the '84/85 season. I had two targets: avoiding relegation and securing a one-year contract extension. When we arrived for a team meeting prior to the season's hugely important penultimate game at home to Bristol Rovers, I wasn't hugely positive on either score.

With regard to the team, the table didn't lie. We were a bottom four side, who needed at least four points from our final two games to have any chance at all of staying up. With all teams around you on the desperate hunt for points, a relegation battle is pretty intense, and whilst you externally make all the right noises about being positive, winning and staying up, internally you are wracked by self doubt and a strong feeling of foreboding.

As for my new contract, I knew that Bond had plenty of cover in midfield for the First Team – Ray McHale, Chris Marustik and Colin Pascoe amongst them. The financial state of the club also meant that new signings were unlikely, and there was nobody obvious in the apprentices and first-year pros pushing for a spot, so that made it pretty much a shoot-out between Phil Williams and me. I was a year older than Phil, but he'd had more opportunities than me of late. Then again, there was always a question mark over his temperament. However, Phil was naturally left footed and, therefore a left-sided player, while I was strictly a central midfield player who needed the game in front of him. Phil's strengths were beating a player and the ability to deliver pinpoint crosses, at pace, from the left. My strengths were my work rate, my ball retention – I hated giving the ball away – and my ability to pick a pass. I knew my biggest failing was my lack of pace, but hoped my other attributes would help tip the balance in my favour. In my heart of hearts though, I realised Phil had the edge, and knew that, as there were few opportunities left to impress, the writing was on the wall.

Then came the first surprise. With only two games left in the season that would determine our fate, first-choice midfielder Chris Marustik was suspended. I knew then that I'd make the thirteen for the game. And if someone went down with injury or the dreaded lurghi or anything, I'd be straight in the twelve. I then thought to myself, 'Whoever he picks in the thirteen from Phil and me will get a contract'. My heart sank. I hadn't thought of it that way before, but I realised it made sense. Bond would surely pick the player that was going to be at the club next year, and I became resigned to the likelihood that it was going to be Phil.

Then came the next surprise, Bond didn't name a thirteen, he named a twelve . . . and I was sub! It was one of the biggest games of the season as we'd go a long way to avoiding relegation if we won, and I'd been picked ahead of Phil. I felt ten foot tall.

Come match day I was ready to go. There was a real buzz at the Vetch, and when I ran out with the team, I couldn't remember ever feeling so happy. I had a kick-in with the keeper Jimmy Rimmer to help warm him up, then the ref called the captains together, and I collected the tracksuit tops and made my way to the bench. I sat down and watched the first half unfold. Unfortunately we conceded quite soon, and weren't really in the game. I knew at this rate I'd be coming on early in the second half which again illustrates one of the odd twists of professional sport. If we scored, my introduction would be delayed. If we scored again, the best I'd probably end up with would be two minutes at the end. Given the seriousness of the situation, you don't want a disaster to occur in front of you, but at 1-0 down, I was probably going to play. And that was vital to my contract prospects. Then another aspect of pro sport kicks in.

Most of you will know that I failed as a footballer. A handful of appearances is all I can show. Only the really ardent Swansea City fan will remember me, and many of those probably only because my cricket successes were often reported as 'former Swansea City footballer, Tony Cottey.' But as I sat there on that bench that day, watching the horror of relegation unfold in front of me, the nervousness of the fans and the anger of Bond spreading amongst us – I was desperate to get on. I really thought I could win us the game. Not just affect the result, *but win it*. To everyone else in the old stadium, I was probably the last person they thought would bring us victory – but I was convinced. Strangely this was never something I would feel in cricket, even though some of my innings were match-winning ones, but that day, on that cramped bench I was praying Bond would put me on as I was convinced I'd do well.

In the haven of the half-time dressing room, Bond wasn't best pleased and shouted across at me to get changed. I was to replace Ray McHale. I was given my instructions, and before I knew it, out I ran. I remember looking around as the referee was about to start and looked at my teammates and really felt this was my moment. It was everything I'd worked toward for three years and I simply *had* to succeed, both for the club, and my own future.

I proceeded to play the best half of football in my professional life.

I got around the pitch a bit and made a real impact with some tackles, had a shot tipped over, and finally played an inch-perfect through ball for Colin Pascoe who was brought down for a penalty by keeper Ron Green, allowing Derek Parlane (former Rangers, Leeds and Scotland striker) to score the winner from the spot with just three minutes to go. I had really tired in that last ten minutes, but it was all worth it. At the end, we'd won 3 – 2, and whilst I'd never claim that I'd won the game, I'd certainly helped change it, and really felt I'd arrived as a footballer. As my Mam's scrapbooks show, I had a really good press afterwards. I had man of the match in one paper and had good reviews in all the others, most suggesting that my introduction had given us an impetus that took us forward to victory. The *Sunday Mirror* even reported 'Swansea's second-half revival began with the introduction of 18-year-old Tony Cottey. The young midfielder inspired his colleagues'. How kind! Most importantly however, I'd proved to myself that I could do it. For the first time ever, I felt I really belonged in the ranks of professional footballers.

Ten days later Bond released me.

Following the Bristol Rovers game, I was left out for the final, crucial Bristol

City game as Chris Marustik was back from suspension – fair enough – I'd never have kept him out even if I'd scored a hat-trick. The very best I could have hoped for was the bench, but that went to Steve Mardenborough, who dropped out for Chris. We drew 0-0 largely thanks to a fantastic display from Jimmy Rimmer, and the point we gained ensured we survived the dreaded drop. Bond had said absolutely nothing about contracts, but thanks to the Rovers game I was more confident about my future than I'd ever been. I played in a reserve game at Ammanford in the West Wales Cup on the following Sunday and went home more than happy.

Monday morning was contract day: a day off – and a rare lie-in. About nineish, Dad called up the stairs to say I'd got a recorded-delivery letter. Strange. I hadn't ordered anything. I ripped it open, saw the Swansea City logo on the headed notepaper and then saw a blur of words that included 'unfortunately', 'regret', and 'released'. I felt sick. It remains the single unhappiest sporting moment of my life. I instantly felt empty and numb. With hindsight, it's easy to say I overreacted, but the fact remains I was nineteen years old, as fit as I would ever be, and had just had everything I'd ever dreamt of torn away from me. Dad had seen the colour drain away from my face and knew instantly what the letter meant. 'Chin up, Ant – it's not the end of the world'. I just brushed him away and walked back upstairs, dressed and went out. I jumped in the car and just drove to the Gower feeling totally empty and wondering what the future held in store for me. I parked up and just stared out over the beach at Port Eynon, and for once, not taking in any of its sights. I was so devastated, I honestly didn't think I'd ever get over it.

Looking back now of course, I should have seen it coming. Bond just didn't rate me. I'm pretty sure he didn't like me as a bloke – again, fair enough, that's life, especially in sport. I should have realised that despite my performance against Bristol Rovers, it was probably never going to be enough to change his mind. But why did he pick me, and not Phil, in that crunch match against Bristol Rovers? Phil eventually ended up with the contract, after all. Bond didn't like me enough to let me have the game as a parting gift – some memory to cherish for the rest of my days (which I do incidentally) nor do I think he'd have picked me in such an important game just to prove, in the most public way, that I wasn't good enough. Not even he was that cruel. At least, I don't think so. So the mystery remains, and maybe I'll never find out.

Whilst I'd have happily thrown John Bond off the nearest Gower cliff at the time, I realise now that he did me the biggest favour of my life. Being released put me on the road to one of the most fulfilling sporting adventures I could ever imagine. So here, in print, I will happily say something I never thought I'd ever say publicly. Thanks, John Bond. Thanks a million.

Strangely enough, the next time my path crossed Mr Bond's was when I was on the cricket pitch at Sophia Gardens nearly ten years later. For some reason he'd been commentating on the match we were playing against Yorkshire in a Benson and Hedges cup game. Robert Croft had been fielding down at fine leg, and at the end of one over, he ran up to me – 'You'll never believe who just spoke to me down there and asked to be remembered to you – John Bond.'

I thought for a minute, and all the old memories of my sacking came flooding back.

'Tell him to piss off.'

It would have been childish to hold a grudge, after all!

CHAPTER FIVE

A New Innings

The days that followed my sacking in May 1985 are quite blurred. There was plenty of rallying round by friends and family, and as much as I appreciated all the 'Never mind you'll bounce back' and 'This could be a blessing' type of consolations, by now my cynical professional attitude had kicked in. I looked at them all and felt like screaming 'Shut up – you have no idea what you are talking about.' I was obviously a man of the world and knew a lot more than all of them. I was nineteen years old!

Within a week, however, I had a phonecall from someone at Birmingham City. They had been contacted by Les (I'll never be able to thank him enough for the efforts he made in my career) and, having been impressed by my performances against them in the Reserves, they offered me a three-month trial, beginning in August for pre-season.

I had been offered something I was desperate for – a second chance at a professional football club – yet somewhere deep inside, it just didn't feel right.

To the outsider, a three-month trial with a big club seems like the thing of dreams, and I'm sure there are thousands of men all over the country who would absolutely jump at the chance of a trial at any club, let alone one as big as Birmingham City. But again, my knowledge of the real world of the pro footballer was kicking in, and my own experience of triallists coming to Swansea was beginning to cloud my judgement.

When injuries and suspensions start to take a hold at League clubs and the bare bones of their playing staff are exposed mid-season, reserve-team players get promoted to the first-team squads and as a result, youth players, and even schoolboys start to filter into the reserve team. This is when clubs need a couple of more experienced players to come in and help them through this patch. This is where the trialist comes in. It's different from the loan system, as that's reserved for the real emergencies in the first team, and will generally involve the lending of a more experienced pro, or on some occasions, a highly-rated youngster from a top club, who is loaned out to a lower league club whose manager is trusted to look after the youngster concerned. Frank Lampard, for example, played for the Swans for about ten games as an eighteen-year-old in the 1990s.

The triallist, however, is treated in a much more mercenary fashion. There's always a pool of players flitting around the lower leagues who are either deemed surplus to requirements at their hometown club, or are more mature, in their early twenties, perhaps, and have slipped through the net of their local club as a youngster, but have now made a name for themselves on the non-league circuit. Probably the most famous to have travelled this route to success are Ian Wright and Stuart Pearce.

At Swansea, I'd seen all sorts of triallists come and go, and they were afforded no respect by anyone. One or two – like Bob Latchford – might make them feel welcome, but generally the other pros ignored them. They were no better than cannon fodder for the reserves – whatever they may have been promised. On the other hand, to the young pro, the triallist is a danger. He arrives from Basingstoke or Burnley and goes straight into the reserve squad. The young pro has fought for three years to become a reserve-team regular, and this outsider strolls straight in and starts at left back. Therefore it becomes in the interest of the young pro to make the trialist's stay at the club as uncomfortable as possible. Don't forget these are generally young, very poorly paid guys, staying in ropey digs for a couple of weeks, and hanging on by their fingernails to the dream of life as a pro. In reality the best they can hope for is a contract to the end of the season, then it all starts again for them at another club if they are subsequently released. And the professional dressing room closes ranks against such intruders, and the banter reaches new levels of viciousness. Clothes and style of dress are jumped on, tastes in music are slaughtered. God help you if you're jug-eared, hook-nosed or just plain ugly. The stick can be merciless, and shrinking violets don't survive. Indeed, it almost a release for them to be, well, released.

It was knowing all this that made me wary of Birmingham's offer. Not so much the stick and abuse. Nor did leaving home faze me. It was the lack of money and the pain of possible further rejection that weighed upon me.

The money issue wasn't about greed, it was about basic survival. I'd seen how triallists had struggled. Once they'd paid for food and lodge, there wasn't a hell of a lot left to join in the lively social scene that existed in pro soccer at the time. I was very much a social animal – at the heart of it within my peer group in Swansea – and I didn't fancy sitting in staring at four walls in Birmingham, counting the pennies. In practical terms, my income would have fallen from £100 per week including appearance money in my final Swans contract to less than £10 a day expenses.

The second issue was the possible fruitlessness of the situation in general. I couldn't bear the thought of putting my all into three months at Birmingham, but with nothing at the end of it – not because I was or wasn't good enough, but simply because no real vacancy existed in the first place. Then the obvious rejection would follow, and I'd be back to square one. Where would I go next? Crewe? Lincoln? Hartlepool? No disrespect to those clubs, but I shuddered just thinking about it. I also considered the fact that if I hadn't made it at my hometown club, why should Birmingham City be any different.

But out of the blue came a phonecall. From Alan Jones, former batting legend for Glamorgan, and now the club's coach. He said that he'd been following my trials and tribulations in recent weeks, and seeing that I was now unemployed, would I consider playing for Glamorgan Seconds?

Consider?

There was nothing to consider and it was arranged. I was to open the batting for Glamorgan seconds at my home ground of St Helen's in Swansea – my lucky ground as it would transpire – on the following Tuesday, in a three-day match against Warwickshire. Payment would be £15 per day's play. If I did OK and stayed in the team for the next game, there was a chance that I would stay in the side for a couple of weeks, and then establish myself further. If I did that, I might just swing a contract until September, and after that – who knows? I started to banish Birmingham City from my mind.

Then came the problem.

I hadn't picked a cricket bat up for the best part of two years, and in three days' time I was going to open the batting against two young fast bowlers who in the fullness of time would open the bowling for their respective countries in a test match. Tim Munton – future England bowler, and the very abrasive Brian McMillan, future South African bowler, and all-round pain in the arse!

In my first couple of seasons at the Vetch, Tosh had been great about my cricket. He understood I was quite decent and as such, was happy to let me play from football's season end until pre-season training began. But when Colin Appleton came in early 1984, he prevented me playing full stop. That meant that my last innings for Glamorgan seconds had been back in July 1983, and we were now in May 1985. Still, nothing ventured, nothing gained, and I went out to buy some kit for my re-introduction to cricket. I discovered that I didn't even own a bat!

My return went better than I'd dared hope. I scored 64 in the first innings and 81 in the second, which helped us to victory. I then kept my place for the next away match against Worcestershire, where not only did I score another 81, but much more importantly, also benefited from the three-days' meal allowance of £10 per night on top of my £15 per day. That extra tenner was hardly ever spent on food, though. I learnt from the pros in the Seconds that the trick was to fill up with food at the ground during the day – at lunch and tea breaks – so that money was then spent on more liquid sustenance in the evening. Mind you, if the club booked the team into a hotel for three nights, including an evening meal, we wouldn't get our extra £10 bonus, and, skint as I was, when this happened, I'd have to forego a night out in Darlington or somewhere equally glamorous, and would spend the night watching a film instead.

After this promising start with Glamorgan, it felt like everything was starting to drop into place, and football was slowly slipping further and further from my thoughts. In that second game at Worcester, I also had the chance to hone my fielding skills as one of their young batsmen – also a triallist at the time – scored 187, and hit the ball to all parts. He's still hitting it to all parts now. His name? Graeme Hick.

The next match saw me score another half century in a match-winning partnership with Hugh Morris in an Under-25 South-West Counties tournament. The match was played at the first Test ground I'd ever played on – Edgbaston. When I arrived there I felt as I had done that day at Highbury – before it was ruined by Mr Appleton! Hugh scored a hundred that day and Hugh would go on to have a massive influence on my career.

Incidentally, I always remember the first time I met Hugh, when as a fifteen-year-old, I was picked to represent Wales Under 19s against England Under 19s, captained by Hugh, at Pontarddulais on the outskirts of Swansea. The reason that this match is memorable to me is that it marked the last occasion that my Auntie, Perp, would watch me play cricket for the best part of twenty years. Even though she was my auntie, Perp was more like a big sister to me, and along with my grandmother Ollie, they'd both loyally followed my fledgling soccer and cricket careers since I was a kid. Perp has always wanted nothing but the best for me, and this game at Pontarddulais was the first time she'd ever seen me play for a national team.

Future England A fast bowler Andy Pick was playing for England and he was about the quickest I'd faced at the time and had taken a couple of our wickets before it was my turn to face him. I'd worked out that he was going to bowl me a bouncer first up and I'd also worked out that there was a man back deep on the boundary placed to catch a mistimed hook, so I knew I had to avoid that shot at all costs. As Pick was running in to me I was saying to myself over and over again 'I'm not gonna hook, I'm not gonna hook.' In he came, let go of a short-pitched delivery – and what did I do? I hooked!

I was caught on the boundary – out first ball.

After the match, Perp was distraught: she was convinced she'd jinxed me and vowed that she'd never come to see me play again. And she kept her word. Or at least she did for twenty years, until I was 37 years old and playing for Sussex at Taunton, where she would witness me scoring 120. She should have come more often!

So I didn't go to Birmingham City, after all. I'd had that feeling in the pit of my stomach, hadn't I? About something not being quite right? Well, guess who took over as their manager, just as my trial period would have been coming to an end.

John Bond.

As Jimmy Greaves often said, it really is a funny old game.

CHAPTER SIX

A Canny Lad

After these first few innings in Glamorgan's Seconds, I really felt I was on my way, making the most of my chance. But there was another fly was on its way into the Cottey ointment. In May and June, Glamorgan's second XI was made up of long time first teamers, now at the end of their career, young pros embarking on their career, and trialists like me. What I hadn't factored in was the 'Uni' boys.

I was the proud possessor of nine 'O' levels. I was an academic colossus. Or at least I was in a football dressing room, where generally the only graduates were ones who had studied at the University of Life. Cricket, however, is different. At any time during my career, there would be five or six university types in the dressing room, where theories on any topic you can think of were often debated at length. Never get stuck in a corner with Steve Watkin the morning after *Question Time!* In six short months, I went from the sage of the dressing room to the scourge. Nobody took my word on anything. There was always someone with a dissertation in something or other ready with the definitive response.

The Uni boys didn't appear until the end of their summer term in July, when I got my first glimpse of two of the most talented young batsmen on Glamorgan's books: Stephen James and Michael Cann. Both were on three-year summer contracts. Both were at Swansea University. Both were opening batsmen – as was I. Even I, with my non-university education, could tell that three into two wouldn't go.

Not for the first time in my career, I sized up the situation. I'd had a good start, nothing spectacular, but good. If I wasn't to be cast aside in July when the Uni boys arrived, I had to consolidate. Therefore, I set myself a target to get noticed as much as possible. Not just in my batting – that would take care of itself, because ultimately I either would or wouldn't be good enough. I wanted to shine in other areas, such as my fitness, commitment and dedication. I'd seen first hand at the Vetch that everyone loved a trier – especially the fans – and resolved that whatever else I would or wouldn't achieve in cricket, it would not be for the lack of trying. But at this point I wasn't looking long term. No way. I was focussing simply on securing more days of cricket at £15 plus overnight bonus, and above all a contract until the end of the season.

Ultimately, I was to spend thirteen seasons with Glamorgan, but at the time I worked out that, if I could secure a two-month contract, financially, I could keep my head above water until the winter. That was my only priority. Money. And with it survival.

So I set about getting noticed. I did OK with the bat, but I'd already had my top score of that 1985 season – I wasn't to pass 81 again all year. But what I did was make sure that the coach, Alan, all the other senior pros, and everyone else for that matter, could see that I was the fittest, fastest player in the club by a mile. As I didn't bowl, I desperately needed another string to my bow, so I practised my fielding constantly, and soon became known for my expertise in that department. I also made sure I became the best team man that I could be. To me that meant being one of the boys, learning the dressing-room code, and trying to win people's respect. I asked for nothing, but did as much as I could do to help others. This is where I take my hat off to Tosh and Boey. They gave me the attitude for hard work and the team ethic from day one. I'd like to think it was already in me, but in reality, it needed them to drag it out.

I needed to dig deep now to get this two month-contract, and I was determined not to let it slip from my grasp.

It worked.

By the time Steve and Canny came back, I found myself pushed down at number five in the order, and not exactly scoring heavily. Not for the first or last time, the doubts about my ability began to surface. Then, again not for the first or last time, Alan Jones came to my rescue. After one of the under-25 games at Gorseinon Cricket Club, he casually came up to me and said that the club were thinking of offering me a two-month contract for July and August if I was interested. Today, a youngster in that position would ask to see the contract, refer it to his agent, before asking for extra money, an option for an extension along with a club car. That's how it is now – I'm not judging anyone – that's just how it is. But back then, I couldn't conceal my delight, said yes instantly and signed as soon as the contract was produced. I didn't even know how much it was for. I just knew I was safe. Until the end of August at least.

By the end of August, I had about three-and-a-half months' experience behind me, and travelled to Kent for the last away game of the season. Unbeknown to me, tradition decreed that the final away game of the season would involve a team night out after the last day's play which would often be the best social event of the year. It was also one of the few times in my career that the club put on a coach for us. Alan Jones was, as usual, in charge of this motley crew, and as we arrived in Sittingbourne, he gave the driver the directions to our hotel. Soon we approached a dilapidated building with the hotel's name sign hanging by one screw and flapping in the breeze. All it lacked was John Cleese standing outside abusing potential customers. Alan told the driver that this couldn't be it and told him to drive on further into the town. After twenty-odd minutes, we realised that, unfortunately, it was indeed the place and was, without doubt, the worst hotel I was to stay at in my twenty-odd years in the game. Some of the rooms were out of commission so they'd squeezed some extra camp beds into each available room, and in some cases there were three or four to a room instead of the usual two. The layout of the hotel was really strange too. The dining area was located off a hallway, with all bedrooms opening out onto the dining area, so it would be a case of opening the bedroom door, closing it behind you, then sitting down at a table for dinner! I was in with Michael Cann and Steve Watkin. About half an hour after we'd checked in, Alan and our scorer Gordon Lewis appeared, and smiling broadly, announced that they had secured alternative accommodation further down the road in a much better hotel. We were envious, but, then again, three nights without 'the boss' might lead to a little fun.

But first we had business to attend to . . . Kent won the toss and batted – and duly proceeded to give us the biggest hiding we'd had in the whole season. Graham Cowdrey, the least famous of his clan, son of Sir Colin and brother of England captain Chris, played one of the best innings I was ever to witness. Out of a massive total of 400, he scored 255 runs in less than a day, in which he flayed our attack to all parts of the ground, and allowed Kent to declare with nine wickets down, enabling them to have half an hour or so at us at the end of the day.

Canny, despite having bowled 30 overs of off-spin during the day, opened the innings and saw us safely to the close at 30 for no wicket, having scored 18 in partnership with Steve James. We got showered and changed and then went back to the hotel for a very unmemorable evening meal, after which we all piled out to see the sights of Sittingbourne. As was often the case, the group was split up within a few hours of those who went back to bed, those who wanted to stay out and have a few more 'relaxing lagers', and also Canny and myself who decided to go to catch up with Alan and Gordon on the way back to our hotel.

When we got there, Al was having a drink in the bar with Gordon and was chatting to a few of the other guests. He bought us both a drink and did the introductions. Not long afterwards, Canny drifted off to the bar and began talking to a complete stranger, who after about twenty minutes bought a bottle of red wine which he plonked down in between himself and his new cricketing friend. Alan noticed this development with raised eyebrows, looked at me, and said 'I'll have to a have a quiet word with him if he's not careful'. I just laughed and sat back and enjoyed what was about to transpire.

Canny's new friend was a German businessman, and Canny, genius that he is, wanted to be taught some German, and the more he excelled in his pronunciation, the more he and his host bonded. After about half an hour of this, Alan thought it was time to rein in his opening bat, but Canny was now making decisions based on about six lagers and half a bottle of wine. Alan approached Canny and quietly interrupted the impromptu language class and subtly advised him that it was time to knock it on the head for the night – 'Big day tomorrow.' Canny's response was legendary. He now adopted the persona of a Bavarian burgermeister, puffing out his chest and dismissing Alan's suggestion with a lavish wave of his arm, and with his best German accent:

'No Alan, more vine, more vine. Cricket vill come tomorrow, now it is vine – more vine, more vine.'

Alan, as calmly as ever, just pointed out to Canny that he was first in in the morning, to which Herr Cann responded, sounding remarkably like a pissed Arnold Schwarzenegger,

'Zat is no prob-lem Alan, I vill score you a hundred tomorrow, now ve vill haf more vine – more vine!'

Alan came back over to Gordon and me, not the least bit fazed by this, and just looked at Gordon and said 'The best lessons are those you learn for yourself – he'll find that out tomorrow' and left it at that. Not long after, Alan went up to bed, and I managed to prize Canny away from his new pal, and exited with Canny's repeated '*Auf Wiedersehen*' ringing in my ears.

When we arrived back at the hotel, it was absolute carnage. Brown and red carnage. The owners had made the huge mistake of laying out the breakfast tables before going to bed, and had inadvertently provided the boys with all the ammunition they needed for their own gunfight at the OK Corral – bottles of tomato and brown sauce. And those sauces were now dripping from each bedroom door and doorway. It didn't take Einstein to work out that they'd been using the bedroom doors as their shields and the dining room as their battleground!

In the morning all hell broke loose, the owners understandably went nuts, and the lads – now sobered up – cleaned the bulk of it up as best they could, but there were still stains left on the walls and ceiling. We all then settled down for some breakfast along with the only non-cricketers in the place, a family of husband, wife and two kids, who all seemed a bit bemused by the situation. The only player not at the breakfast table was Canny, who was dealing with the after effects of the night before and was still in the bedroom. Unfortunately for the family, he didn't stay there for long. The door swung open, and out walked a yawning Canny. Not too bad you might think. The only problem however was that he was totally naked, and scratching his not unsubstantial genitals, blissfully unaware that he was in the dining room! The mother and father quickly put their hands over the kids' eyes, but it was too late – that picture would be burned on their minds for ever. We, as befitted the whole surreal situation, just burst out laughing.

At the ground we explained to Alan what had happened, and whilst not best pleased, he said that we should have a whip-round for the owners, so a £100 was taken back to the hotel as a peace offering. After that diversion, it was back to the match. Canny resumed at 18 not out, and not looking his best. Alan hadn't said a single word to him in the morning about his conduct of the previous night, and now Canny had to make good on his drunken promise of a hundred.

Masters opened the bowling for Kent and first ball of the morning, sent down his usual medium-quick, straight, wicket-to-wicket delivery, which Canny decided to charge with a hugely expansive lofted drive straight back over the bowler's head for six. The only problem with this majestic statement of intent was that he missed the ball. His middle stump was sent cartwheeling back and off he trudged. We all wanted to break into hysterics in the dressing room but with Alan's face like thunder, we just about managed to keep our mouths buttoned. Canny's shot set the scene for the day. Kent dismissed us twice to beat us by an innings, and the only player to score over 50 in either innings was Matt Maynard.

After the final wicket fell, Alan kept us in the dressing room for an hour and absolutely battered his. He hauled us over the coals about what we thought being a pro cricketer was all about. Did we think that we deserved a career in the game after behaving like that on and off the field over the two days? Then he turned to Canny and absolutely wrecked him. 'More Vine, more vine? I'll give you more fucking vine.' The funniest thing about this rebuke however was that Alan sounded more like he was from Dorset than Düsseldorf – but now was not the time to point that out.

Finally, Alan told us to shower and change, and after we'd had time to stew for a while in silence, he called us together again.

'Right then. You know the tradition. It's our last away night of the season, but after this behaviour, who thinks we should still have a night out? Hands up!'

No one said a word or made a move. Then Matt, who we knew had already arranged a night out with Laurie Potter, a mate of his from when he'd played at Kent, put his hand up. As he did, and Alan looked at him, a couple more put their hands up in support of Matt. I think Matt was the only one in our team with the strength of character to have done this – he was a confident lad from day one, and wasn't scared to voice his opinion. Alan surveyed the scene and said

'Right, you've all had a really good season, and apart from the last two days, there's no cricket team that deserves a night out more than you lot – but lads, you've got to learn your lessons about the last two days. The temptation will always be there to piss around off the field, but the day you let it affect your cricket is the day you'll all stop being a pro.'

We had our night out and had a great time – as did Al – but what made the biggest impression on me was how Al had handled Canny, how he had known that the young batsman would have to experience the consequences his actions brought upon himself and, more importantly, the team. Alan then laid on the line how serious this was for all of our futures. Al had an absolute gift of getting his point across. Lesson of the day? We rarely learn from warnings beforehand; sometimes we need to make the mistakes ourselves to learn what's what.

A couple of days later I experienced my first ever cricket contracts day. Unlike in football, people actually told you to your face if you were to be retained or not. Rejection was still bitterly disappointing, as I would find out twice more in my career, but at least you were treated with respect and humanity.

I was offered a one-year summer contract as a professional cricketer on September 17,1985.

It was to take effect on April 1, 1986, (the spectre of April Fool worried me for a moment too) when I was expected to report to Sophia Gardens. I was to earn the princely sum of £2,500, gross, paid over six months. I wouldn't receive a penny until April – but I didn't care – I was in, and that was the most important thing. As I walked away from Sophia Gardens, I saw Greg Thomas walking into the pavilion. Greg was an extremely quick bowler, our best player, and future England bowler. I might be playing with him next year I smiled.

I was starting to dream again.

CHAPTER SEVEN

A Winter of Discontent

After the cricket finished late in that summer of 1985, I was back to square one for a spell. I was absolutely delighted that I had my first contract under my belt with Glamorgan, but knew that I had six long months and a cold winter to wait until the next cricket season. It seemed like a lifetime.

However, I had two saviours on the horizon. The first was a familiar source – football. There's always been a healthy non-league scene in Wales, and, at the time, the highest of the Welsh non-league teams in the South was Merthyr Tydfil, who played in one of the better English non-league divisions, with most of their opponents located in the Midlands. Many of the clubs that have been in the Football League Conference Division over the past few years were in this league at the time so the competition was robust to say the least.

Lyn Jones was the Merthyr manager at the time and was on the phone almost as soon as the cricket season finished, and my signing for the coming season soon followed for £50 per game. Not huge wages, but at least it put some money in my pocket, and, with all the various cup competitions, there were often two games a week. I still wasn't earning as much as some of my friends who had taken jobs straight from school, so I decided to look for something else as well to top things up.

Option two – Port Eynon Transport to the rescue!

My Dad had started his own haulage company in 1966, naming it after his birthplace, which is also my particular favourite part of the world, namely Port Eynon, a beach-side village right on the Southern tip of the Gower Peninsula. He had built it up from nothing to a company well known and well respected in the area. He had eight lorries and operated out of a small yard on the edge of Swansea. The work was hard and the hours were long, and I had total respect for the job my dad had done throughout his life. Knowing that I needed some money to keep me going through the winter, he offered me some work. Tea boy? Office boy? Pampered duties for the son of the owner? No, Dad had far grander ideas than that. I was to be a grease monkey.

Dad believed that I needed to understand how life could be at the bottom end of the ladder. With this in mind, he didn't offer me a wage, but put me on an early version of performance-related pay. My duties were two-fold. One job was rubbing down and painting the trim on his trailers with red-oxide paint, and I'd get £10 for each trailer completed, which took about a day. The other job was his favourite, but my most hated – axle cleaning. Basically, I had to crawl underneath a lorry, and whilst lying on my back had to totally steam clean the underside of the lorry, getting right into the axles and darkest corners of the wheel hubs. He offered me £5.00 per lorry cleaned, and would only pay after he'd inspected the underneath himself. Every morning I'd strap on my oilskins, hat and mask and climb under those stinking lorries and start blasting away.

Ironically, Saturday was the busiest day as that was when most of the lorries were back at the yard at the same time. However, Saturday was also football day and I generally had to leave for Merthyr at noon – so I had about 3½ hours from 8.30 to get my Mrs Mop act going, and in that time I would try to get four lorries done. When I subsequently arrived at Merthyr, I'd often been unable to get all the grease and shite off – especially around where the goggles were – so I picked up the nickname of Bet Lynch (of *Coronation Street* fame) quite quickly, due the black rings around my eyes. Financially, my Dad was starting to flinch though, as I was generally cleaning them a bit too quick for his liking (he'd forgotten that I was a veteran Vetch Field dressing-room cleaner!), and I was starting to prove quite expensive for him. He'd have been better off putting me on a wage, but those five quids were proving a life saver for me, and as dirty and disgusting as the job was, I'd have gone in on a Sunday if he'd let me, just to earn a few more pounds.

Whilst it was in many ways a bleak winter, I secretly enjoyed it too. Working with Dad was great fun. I learned about a different side to him, and emerged with even more respect for him. I had no real idea how hard the game of the haulage contractor was. Dad had to beg, steal and borrow to make sure he always had a load for the back of his lorry. For example, if you were paid a sum to haul some steel to Bristol, for example, you still had to drive back to Swansea, but obviously with an empty trailer. Dad would do all he could to ensure he picked up a load from somewhere on the return journey to keep the money coming in. He also had to deal with regular run-ins with drivers and other hauliers, which sometimes bordered on the violent, and occasionally spilled over. Yet I never once saw him back down. I enjoyed this contact with him, and on and off spent some time during the winters with him for the next ten years or so, culminating in passing my heavy goods vehicle test in 1994 – or as some of my mates referred to it as my Tonka Truck Vehicle test – which meant almost as much to my dad as watching me score a hundred for Glamorgan.

What these winter sessions did also was instil in me an absolute determination to make the most out of whatever cricketing ability I had. Despite all the respect I had for Dad, one thing was as clear as day, I in no way wanted to emulate him and follow him into the family business – it really was too much like proper hard work. For the next two years, this prospect was always in the back of my mind, and proved a great motivator

Football at Merthyr was going well also. The standard was very good, albeit very hard and uncompromising. The travelling was a problem – it's about an hour and twenty minutes from Swansea, and what with training and games, there were times when I was travelling up there three or four days a week. The lads and manager were great, and I thoroughly enjoyed my time there. The only trouble though was my Swansea background. Historically, people from Merthyr also follow Cardiff City, and people who follow Cardiff City by and large, hate Swansea City, and it has to be said, vice versa. As I'd played for the Swans for three years prior to joining Merthyr, there was a section of the fans who simply never gave me a chance. Fair enough – I fully understood and accepted that – I just had to just deal with it. You develop quite a thick skin as a sportsman, and it's amazing how often you need the protection of that covering – not least when you're being spat at – in home games – by your own fans.

Happy days!

I actually played for Merthyr against doctor's orders one day, which was a bit more serious at the time than I realised. It was October, and I'd booked my first holiday abroad with my girlfriend Gail, to Malta for a fortnight. A couple of days before I left, I went to visit Mam and Dad, only to find that Dad had contracted shingles. He was to end up with quite a bad dose, but by then I was happily ensconced in Malta's version of Fawlty Towers in Valetta. To say the holiday was a disaster is like suggesting that Roman Abramovich has got a couple of bob put away. The flight was delayed for hours and resembled something out of Con Air. The only difference between our hotel and Basil's establishment was that there was no First World War Major in residence – although judging by the food, he could easily have been the chef! Then at the end of our first week – where we were still waiting to find out what the Sun looked like in Malta – I came out in a blaze of spots. Chicken Pox.

Tremendous.

Exposure to Dad's shingles had been enough to set the old pox into action, and I felt ill instantly. The rash was everywhere, and I mean everywhere. I don't remember if the old hotel chef had spotted dick on the menu, but I could have supplied him with a portion of it if he'd asked! After I'd been confined to bed for two days, subject to vomiting, delirium and visions of death, Gail insisted we went to hospital. It was the correct decision. They kept me in for a week. We missed our flight back, and then had to wait another seven days before any other airlines would let us fly in case I was still contagious. We'd been in Malta for nearly three weeks by now, and to compound matters, I looked like the rabid son of John Merrick. I felt like shouting out 'I am a man!' when I received withering looks from passers by, but I wasn't certain myself anymore! I'd arrived in Malta at my optimum fighting weight of 9 stone 10 pounds. When we arrived home I was 8 stone 5. I hadn't eaten a solid meal in ten days, and really wanted to just get home, roll into bed and sleep for a month.

And then, the phone rang . . .

It was Thursday afternoon; Lyn Jones from Merthyr. 'How was the holiday son? OK for Saturday?'

'No, Lyn, sorry – I've not been well.'

He spent the next twenty minutes convincing me I had to play: 'Big game', 'we've missed you', 'the lads want you too play', the usual mind games. He said he'd ring tomorrow, and that I'd feel better by then. He did and I didn't! And whilst I was still resisting, two things preyed on my mind: that unscheduled third week in our Maltese paradise had left me skint; and Lyn assured me that he only expected me to play the first half.

I could last 45 minutes. Surely.

The first half was typically hard fought and bruising, and despite feeling only 50 or 60% and struggling, I'd done my job as best I could. At half-time, it was 0-0, but in the dressing room, Lyn avoided my pleading eyes like the plague. He knew I'd never ask to come off in front of the rest of the lads. In no time at all, the linesman called us out for the second half, and out we went. Me included. This wasn't part of the script.

After twenty minutes I was really struggling. Mile Oak Rovers (heard of them?) were as good as their name, a huge side, and none too subtle. I was running myself to a standstill, and was feeling very ill and light-headed. Eventually we scored and hung on for the win. As I walked wearily off down the tunnel, I was just glad it was all over.

Lyn was great. I was just slumped on the dressing-room bench, too tired even to undo my bootlaces. He made a point of putting a halt to the lads' rowdy celebrations, and singled me out for praise. I've never been one for accepting plaudits, but I must admit I appreciated his kind words and the round of applause from the lads. It took me a good week to get over the day's exertions though!

Following my winter of discontent among the axle grease and red oxide paint, I was raring to go come April 1986. It was to be my first pre-season with Glamorgan as a fully-fledged cricketer, and I was very much looking forward to the challenge. I was still reasonably fit as I'd carried on playing football throughout the season, although not with Merthyr. Around January, when fixtures started to back up, I'd grown really tired of the travelling. I'd agreed with Merthyr that I'd train in Swansea, with Wyndham Evans, one of my mentors at Swansea City, who was now manager of the Welsh League side Pembroke Borough.

I used to really enjoy those sessions. I knew all the lads: many had played for the Swans in some capacity at some time or other, and even my collaborator on this book, Dave, trained there, so I knew there was at least one person I'd beat in the sprints! Anyway, it was a natural progression that I'd end up signing for Wyndham, and the deal was done over Christmas, with me making my debut in the January. Lyn Jones was great about it. I think he knew I was never going to be a crowd favourite at Merthyr, so he thanked me for my efforts, and signed my release forms.

My time at Pembroke was short but sweet, punctuated by winning one of Welsh football's most prestigious trophies, and almost killing myself and four friends in a car crash. Life was never dull in the 1980s.

The Pembroke side was full of good players, such as former Swansea colleagues Anthony Rees and Steve Price. We got on a roll in the Brains Cup, the second most prestigious of trophies in Wales behind the Welsh Cup, which at the time was competed for by Swansea, Wrexham, Cardiff and Newport, and for those teams was a passport into Europe to play in the European Cup Winners' Cup. But whilst none of these pro teams could play in the Brains Cup, every other semi-pro team could, so the trophy was much sought after. Pembroke had never won it in their long history.

We eventually made it to the final, where we would play Cwmbran Town. They were clear favourites, not least because they were known as a money club, and seemed to have the pick of players released from Cardiff City and Newport County. And they were an uncompromising team, to say the least.

One thing that never ceases to amaze me about sport is the fans. When we arrived at the ground that Tuesday night, it appeared that half of Pembroke was there. There was coach after coach lined up in the car park, and even though less than a year earlier I'd run out in front of nearly 10,000 people at the Vetch, it was quite humbling to run out in front of these fans who'd travelled well over 100 miles into the heart of the Welsh valleys to cheer us on.

Oh, the venue? I forgot. Penydarren Park, Merthyr. The prodigal son had returned!

We took the lead after about seven minutes from one of my corners, but as the game progressed, so Cwmbran got stronger and stronger. We held out until the last ten minutes, which resembled something from the Alamo. Eventually the referee saw sense and blew the final whistle! We'd won 1-0. I remember seeing our chairman, Des Shanklin, who'd always been great to the boys, going round each one and thanking us all. He was close to tears – that's how much all this means to people.

If only he'd known that three of his players were lucky to be there at all.

About a month earlier, I'd travelled down to the game in west Wales as usual, but this time with Dave and our great mate from school, the man behind my run-in with the rum, Chris Lewis, who was back from Liverpool University. The game was against Pembroke's local rivals, Milford Haven. After the game, we all went into the bar, and had a couple of pints. Both Pembroke and Milford had their fair share of Swansea boys, and pretty soon the Milford clubhouse became a scene of all our yesterdays. We all agreed on the spot to get back to Swansea as soon as we could, meet in The Builders Arms in Oxford Street, and carry on our reminiscences into the wee small hours. Anyone who had a car offered the others lifts, and off we went. Quickly.

I had a Mark III Ford Escort at the time, 1.6 engine, and if truth be known, I was a bit of a boy racer. Swansea was an hour-and-a-half away. I thought it might be fun to get there in an hour.

We didn't get very far.

In my car were Chris in the front, Reeso and Pricey either side on the back seat, and Dave between them. As we hurtled away from Milford, Chris started rummaging around for a cassette to play which suited the mood. He didn't like any of my Elton John back catalogue, but found Marc Bolan's greatest hits. If that wasn't a portent of doom, I don't know what was.

I remember the hilarity in the car as we all screeched along to '20th Century Boy', and on a couple of occasions the corners of the country lanes nearly proved too much for me. The next thing I knew – one of them did. I was just carrying too much speed and when I saw the black and white chevron sign coming out of the darkness to warn me of the sharp left – it was just too late.

I yanked the wheel left, but nothing happened, and the car just flew straight across the road. As it was about to smash into the road sign, it hit something in front of it (which turned out to be a high-raised concrete culvert), which threw the car back across to the opposite side, where it hit another curb, before we were deposited back in the middle of the road. It all happened in about three or four seconds, but as most people tend to say, it appeared to occur in slow motion. The thing I remember most, apart from Dave, in my rear view mirror, sitting bolt upright at point of impact like a rabbit trapped in the headlights while the others were braced for impact, was the noise. It was a real loud crack and bang – hard to describe, quite high-pitched – then screeching rubber and grinding metal, followed by complete silence. Even Marc Bolan had shut up – really weird. We all got out of the car, and saw that the two wheels on the driver's side were folded slightly under the chassis, where it had smashed against the culvert. We all started to shove the car off the road, then looked around at the scene. The first thing I saw was a pub, about a hundred yards up ahead, with its lights radiating out its highly appropriate name.

'The Sporting Chance'. We certainly felt we'd been given one!

I'll never forget it until the day I die. We were really lucky. How the car didn't flip over when it hit the culvert, I'll never know. If it had, we'd have all died, as we would have landed in a water-filled ditch. I think it was only the extra height of the culvert that managed to throw us back across the road.

We walked up to The Sporting Chance and went in. It was a bit like The Slaughtered Lamb in *American Werewolf in London*, and the half a dozen or so locals went quiet as I asked for a phone to ring Dad – who proceeded to give me the bollocking of my life, despite my protestations of innocence. He knew I drove fast, and knew that I'd have been caning it to get home. I'd only had the car about a month, and he'd bought it. It was a long hour-and-a-half waiting for him to turn up. The rest of the lads were as sympathetic as ever: they put the Cars song 'Drive' on the jukebox and dedicated it to me. They then proceeded to get blasted, inspired by their near-death experience, and laughed at me as I sat there sober, wondering if I'd survive my second near-death experience of the night – when my Dad got hold of me!

By April 1986, and with all things football – and mechanical – behind me, I arrived at Sophia Gardens in Cardiff for my first ever cricket pre-season. From a physical point of view, I didn't know what to expect, but I was prepared for anything following the horrors of my three pre-seasons with the Swans, but a small part of my masochistic soul was hoping it was going to be really tough!

How wrong could I be.

Today your average county has about 18 players on its staff. Back then it was nearer 30, and as such, when we all arrived and got changed, it was not too dissimilar to the football. Until the first run started.

That run was to be the backbone of our session, and I looked forward to laying down a marker with my fitness levels for all to see. After the briefest of warm-ups, off we went. After the first twenty-odd yards, I heard a strange clip-clopping sound behind me on the road out of Sophia – and for a horrible moment thought that Colin Appleton had joined us. When I looked round, I wasn't really prepared for what I saw. One of our senior pros was the excellent Pakistani test player, Younis Ahmed. He was one of the most gifted batsmen I ever played with, all left-handed grace and timing. He was coming to the end of his career now – hence his appearance at Glamorgan – and was starting to show a little expansion around the waist. Younis looked like your archetypal Pakistani prince: dark good looks, flowing jet-black hair and a million-dollar smile. But here he was, breathing out of his arse in his tight white rugby shorts, cricket top, and most bizarrely, Adidas football boots with plastic moulded studs. For a road run? Hence the clip-clopping.

But after about half a mile it all clicked into place. By now Younis and John Hopkins ('Ponty') were right at the back of the group tailing off. Ponty was a truly great bloke, hugely popular, and always ready with a funny line for any occasion. He won't mind me saying that he too was also one of the squad that Dr Atkins might have had his eye on. Anyway, as we headed further away from Sophia Gardens, the clip-clopping stopped, I didn't think too much about it at the time as I was up at the front with Matt and Jamer, and assumed Younis and Ponty had just dropped further back. We carried on until we came to the furthest point of the run, then turned, re-crossed the river and headed back, on a different road, to Sophia Gardens. As we got to about half a mile from the end, I noticed a hedge. It ran directly across from where we were now running for about 200 yards to where we initially set out from on the other side of the river. The closer I got to the hedge, the more obvious became the two figures crouching there. One looked like an ageing Magnum PI, the other a rotund Pakistani prince!

Yes, Ponty and Younis had basically run as far as this hedge – 200 yards – then turned left and run along the whole 300-yard length of it on the boggy grass, hence Younis's football boots! They then waited, and joined the group as we ran past. And so it was each time. We always had 21 minutes to complete the run, which was about three miles, and Ponty and Younis always managed to get back within the time limit. Strange that.

A player I got to know much better around this time was Mike Cann, he of the 'More vine' incident in Kent. He was a talented opening batsman from Cardiff, educated at Swansea University and had achieved heavy-duty qualifications in biochemistry, and he basically bordered on being a genius.

Our paths had first crossed after I'd joined Glamorgan the previous season, but unfortunately, we both identified each other as rivals for a batting spot at the top of the order, both sensing that only one of us would eventually end up with any sort of long-term future at Glamorgan. Unfortunately for Mike, that's exactly how it turned out, and I was to be the one who would inch ahead as time went on – at that time probably on the strength of my fielding – but I'm certain that had fate delivered a different hand to us both, there's absolutely no doubt that Canny would have succeeded as a first-class batsman.

When we first met, I had just been released by the Swans, and as I mention elsewhere in this book, despite the brave face I put on as a brash and confident nineteen-year-old, not far below the surface was an open wound of disappointment, resentment and rejection, but above all a towering fear of failing again. And this was hugely motivating. It also explains why I'd identified Canny as the one I needed to eclipse if I was to achieve my sporting dreams.

It's important here to dispel one myth about young, aspiring sportsmen: they do not always revel in the successes of their rivals! If your rival, albeit a teammate, has a better game than you, and, perish the thought, scores a goal or hits a century, and you yourself have a bad game, there's only one thing you feel – desolation, utter desolation. This is one of the secrets of pro sport. Nobody talks about it and nobody admits to it. You'll even say well done to your rival, shake their hand and congratulate them, but you walk away feeling totally empty. You almost take it as a personal slight. It's akin to seeing your girlfriend kissing the captain of the rugby team at the school disco!

It was because I was so worried about failing again, that I was desperate to upstage Canny at every opportunity. I'd never resort to anything underhand, never did at any stage of my career – but if I could be fitter than him, I would be. In training sessions, I'd try to run faster and further than him; in net sessions I'd attempt to put more effort in than him, and in matches I'd try and outscore him and outfield him. I definitely targeted him. In a perfect world, of course, we'd have both had a contract – but, as I'd found out all too recently at the Swans, sport and the perfect world are poles apart.

But why did I have to target him at all? It wasn't that I was a bitter and twisted person; it was that Glamorgan had five opening batsmen at the club at the time, all competing for only two first-eleven batting spots:

1. Alan Butcher – former England opening batsman, senior pro and captain. Unless he was injured, he would never miss a game;
2. Hugh Morris – future England opening batsman and future Glamorgan captain, a batting prodigy with a glittering future. Again, he was always going to play;
3. Steve James – future England opening batsman and future Glamorgan captain. Most people on the outside, including friends and family, saw Jamer as my obvious rival, but I knew from an early age he'd always be a little bit ahead of me.
4. Canny.
5. Me.

With regards Canny and me, I believed in my heart that I was ahead of him at the time, but it would only take a big score from him and a failure from me to bring the doubts and worries about my ability and long-term future with Glamorgan straight back to the front of my mind.

Sportsmen's ability to deal with pressure is forever a point of popular debate. I can tell you from bitter personal experience, that any sportsman or woman you ever see, unless they're a prodigy like Wayne Rooney or Graeme Hick, will have endured a couple of years of the most severe pressure, long, long before anyone in the public will have ever heard of them. There is no greater pressure than knowing time is running out on securing that elusive first contract which enables you (for a season or two at least) to relax and concentrate on you game. The fear of not getting a contract and being lost to the game at a young age forever consumes you totally. One of my sporting heroes, Wyndham Evans, who had the impressive achievement of representing Swansea City in all four divisions of the football league in over 400 games, told me years after he finished playing, that he had earned twelve one-year contracts at the Vetch, which meant that every season from Christmas onwards, the spectre of being released hung over him, so he had no option but to perform.

It was with this 'competition' as a background that Canny and I set out on a three-year tour of cricket's backwaters on the second XI circuit, in search of a long-term future in the game. Whilst you don't really care at the time, the glamorous venues are slightly out of reach for a second-team player. For Lords read Uxbridge, for Old Trafford read Aigburth, for Headingley read Scarborough, and so on. It just adds to your education, and on the odd occasion you get called up as twelfth man at somewhere like Trent Bridge, it just whets your appetite even further for a career in the game, before you are released back to play for the Seconds down in Llandarcy or somewhere equally austere.

On one of these trips we played Leicestershire Seconds at Hinckley, again under the guidance of Alan Jones. The game was heading for a draw, and at close of play on the second day, plans were made for a quiet night out. It was the mid-1980s after all, and sports science was still about ten years away, so lager, and not energy juice, was the drink of choice for a group of young, fit cricketers with expenses to burn. Thus, heading into the centre of Leicester seldom resulted in a quiet night!

I remember leaving the pub with Canny, Ian Smith ('Smudger'), Jamer and Martin Roberts our wicket-keeper, who hadn't himself indulged, and therefore drove the club car back to the hotel. It had been a typical Glamorgan night: plenty of drink, plenty of fun and plenty of banter. The trouble with banter, especially when it's drink-fuelled, is that it can (often) result in someone getting the wrong end of the stick. Now some banter merchants enjoy a reaction. I, for instance, am a pain-in-the-arse banterer. I'm the little swine who generally starts it – always in the name of humour, mind, viewing it as a test of mental sharpness. I picked this up in the dressing room at Swansea City where it could be really vicious, but it was also a great forger of team spirit. When the honourable bantererer is outbantered, he holds up his hand, says 'Well done' and takes it all on the chin. And 90% of the time that's exactly how it all ends up, and bonds are formed in this environment which last a lifetime. But on occasions, despite best intentions, it can backfire.

In the car going back to the hotel, Canny kept saying 'Calm down now, Babes' in reference to something I'd reacted to earlier. It had annoyed me all evening. And Canny kept on. And on, and on. In the banterers' school, Canny was definitely a seek-a-reaction type, never in a nasty way, but pleased when someone bit and blew their stack. In the car that night, my stack (full of Bud) was definitely close to blowing, and like Fred Dibnah, Canny just kept chipping away at it. In the end I snapped:

'Say it again, Canny, and that's it – I'll have you.'

As the car pulled into the car park, just in front of the main entrance to the hotel, Canny's response was 'Ooooh'. And then he said, for the last time,

'Calm down now Babes'.

The stack well and truly went. I swung a punch at him and we soon fell out of the car brawling. A couple of the lads ran into the hotel to get help, while the others just watched. Real schoolyard stuff.

Apparently the rest of the squad had watched this particular drama unfold from inside the hotel. At first, they hadn't paid much attention to the young pups arriving back from a night out, not until Simon Dennis, our Yorkie seamer, shouted out: 'Bloody hell, Cotts has just punched Canny in the car park!'

Coach Alan Jones looked out in horror at a perfectly-floodlit view of me on top of Canny in a total rage, trying to knock his head off, with Canny responding with as many counterpunches as he could. The next thing I remember is Alan screaming at me to stop. I ignored him until I felt his strong grip, one which had held a bat in scoring nearly 40,000 runs for the club, tighten around my curly mop and drag me off Canny by the hair. I was frogmarched upstairs to my room, where I continued to lose it, to such a point that Alan was shouting at me to stop or I'd be throwing my whole career away right there and then. He bundled me in my room and shouted at me to stay there until the morning.

I started to calm down straight away and realised what I'd done. It was the classic cliché situation. I'd let myself down, my teammates down, my club down, but most of all, I'd let Alan down. It didn't take long for the remorse to hit me hard. I wanted to go straight back down and sort it out, but thankfully I didn't and waited 'till morning. I didn't sleep well at all, and really did worry that I'd done some irreparable damage to my career prospects. I almost didn't want morning to come at all.

But it came. Alan totally read the riot act. I was warned that I'd come as close as it was possible to being dropped for one game but Al had decided it against it and decided to keep it in-house. He was basically putting himself on the line to save me. He told me years later, he really believed I'd have been sacked if the club officials had found out about it, but his view at the time was that it would have been better to have left the club for cricketing reasons, rather than for disciplinary ones. This speaks volumes of Alan. I've never discussed it with him, but I think he must've seen something in me that others didn't. Without his judgement I may never have had the life that I've since had. I will never be able to thank him enough.

As for Canny and I, we met at breakfast, shook hands and got over it straight away. There were no grudges to bear and we were to spend plenty more nights out where the stick flew rapidly between us, but it never ended up in a car-park scuffle again.

Looking back now, I guess this incident illustrates a subtle difference between football and cricket. When a similar thing happened to me at Swansea City, it was almost welcomed by the management because I'd proved that I was more than capable of handling myself. In cricket, this was not the done thing at all. It was way out of line, so much so that my very career was at risk, especially if I repeated my behaviour. Thankfully, I never did.

CHAPTER EIGHT

Driving Miss Daisy

How many times have you watched a Premiership game on Sky Sports when they show the Liverpool team turning up at Anfield in preparation for the big match? The superstar players troop off a futuristic-looking coach, often to be greeted by hordes of cheering fans . . .

In nineteen seasons of cricket, I travelled in a coach on no more than six or seven occasions!

Cricketers are the car-sharers of the sporting world. In my early days three or four of us would cram into a car, and set out from Cardiff to somewhere exotic like Hartlepool for a three-day game. It wasn't until the mid-1990s that each player has a sposnored car. In the early days, the captain, coach, overseas player and one or two of the senior pros were allowed such a luxury, and as a result we'd pile in to their cars with kit stuffed in any available nook or cranny.

Looking back, this was great fun and I wouldn't have missed it for the world. After all, when you've got a six-hour drive to Durham ahead of you, there is no option but to get on with each other, and it's no exaggeration to say that we all made friendships for life on these trips.

I forged an unlikely friendship with John Steele as a result of these car journeys. John was the younger brother of the famous England batsman David Steele, who in 1975 won the Sports Personality of the Year award for the way he stood up against the Australians – Denis Lillee et al – and secured a place in the nation's hearts as a result of his stubborn, unflinching resistance. John, whilst never grabbing the headlines, was a well-respected opening batsman and left-arm spin bowler. By the time I met him, he'd already spent thirteen years at Leicestershire, and was spending his final couple of seasons with Glamorgan as second-team coach. To say we were from different eras was an understatement. John was 38, and to a nineteen-year-old, someone of that age was almost pensionable. but when I eventually ended up in the same team as John, we hit it off straight away. He was, and remains, a really lovely, knowledgeable guy. He could've been forgiven for thinking that I wasn't as professional as I should be, but John saw past my immaturity and realised that I did want to learn and I did want to be the best that I could be. John had a big impact on my thinking, and he passed on a lot of his thoughts while we shared the long journeys around the country. As we both lived in the Swansea area we often ended up travelling together, and I must admit I thoroughly enjoyed his company, even if – on the surface – we were poles apart.

John had one major failing though. Lionel Richie and the Commodores. If I heard 'Dancing on the Ceiling' once, I must've heard it a thousand times. But it was his car, so it followed it was his choice of music. It also followed that in the pecking order, I was the youngest, so I was handed the driving duties. Depending how far from home we were, we'd chat for the first hour or so about the events of the previous couple of days, John pointing some of the more subtle moments that had occurred, and advising me on how to deal with them in future. By the time we were nearing Wales though, the old devil would generally start to flag. The conversation would start to tail off as the toil of looking after us exuberant youngsters over the previous three days would start to take its toll on his ancient bones, and he'd recline back, close his eyes and crank up Lionel and the lads.

Being a thoughtful boy, I took this as a hint to stop asking questions, and let him doze off. What it then enabled me to do was give the car's accelerator a gradual tweak, to get us home that little bit quicker. But every time the needle exceeded 80mph, and without opening his eyes, John would quietly command 'Slow down, youth,' and back down the needle would go. It almost became a game as this pattern would be repeated all the way back to Swansea, with this particular 'youth' obeying the friendly rebuke each time.

Only once do I remember John failing to spot that I was speeding up. I'd got up to around 90mph on a stretch of road approaching Monmouth, and was giggling to myself that, this time, John had actually dropped off. Lionel was banging out as usual, mind, and all was well with the world.

And then I saw the flashing lights.

After I'd answered all the constable's questions, given him my details and accepted I was doing 91 in a 70 zone, I got back in the car, proud possessor of three points and a fine. Gutted. I looked at John who was still sitting there listening to Lionel. He just glanced across knowingly and said, 'Told you, youth, you should slow down.'

Point taken.

Not everyone at the club could drive, mind. When former England batsman Alan Butcher joined the club as captain around the same time in 1987, one thing was overlooked on his CV. Having spent his life in and around London playing for Surrey, he'd never had to drive, therefore, he'd never bothered taking his driving test. When he realised that Glamorgan split its matches between Cardiff and Swansea, and our nearest away match was a good hour-and-a-half from base, Butch decided to take the plunge. He booked some lessons, took his test and passed. The trouble was that, having been chauffeured to most of the grounds around the country in the past, now he'd have to drive and, therefore, he needed to learn the roads. To help in this task, someone would have to go with him to help him find the best routes. Guess who was picked.

Now I always got on well with Butch; he was as solid a bloke as you could find, so I enjoyed our trips. He was, however, a bloody awful driver! He wasn't too bad on dual carriageways, but he could be a bit ropey on motorways when the traffic flow got a bit heavier. On one occasion we had a match against Hampshire at Southampton, and as we left the M4 and headed toward the A34, the conversation got to Butch's driving. He was feeling a lot more confident now, was enjoying it more, but apparently, he still had one problem.

Cones.

'Cones?' I asked. 'What do you mean, "cones"?'

'You know,' he said, 'traffic cones. The ones they use for roadworks or when they narrow the lanes.'

Oh, OK,' I said, trying to suppress my concern. 'I know what you mean. Hopefully, we should be all right today though'.

I was mid-sentence when we left the roundabout at the A34 and joined the M3 to Southampton. As we merged with this busy stretch, we looked ahead, and both took a sharp breath. It appeared that the whole British supply of motorway cones was laid out in front of us for as far as the eye could see. There were lane merges, contra flows, diversions – you name it, they had a cone for it. I glanced at Butch, but he was displaying the concentration he normally reserved for facing a brutal new-ball opening spell from Malcolm Marshall.

He was fine as we approached them, but after about half a mile, it felt as if we were in a tunnel of cones as the red and white colours flashed by. Then he started clipping them on the driver's side. At 70mph. After he'd nailed about a dozen, I thought it was time to speak up.

'You're a bit close to them, Butch,' I said.

'I know,' came the terse reply.

He immediately adjusted and stopped hitting them on the driver's side. Instead, he started clipping them on my side.

'Jesus, Butch! Can't you see them?'

'Of course I can fucking see them, I just can't keep inside them.'

'Bloody hell,' I said. 'Just keep your left wheel inside the left ones, and your right wheel inside the right ones.'

'That's what I'm trying to do. I told you. I'm not good with cones'

Mercifully, the roadworks soon ended and with cones sprayed out behind us, we made the rest of the journey to Southampton without incident. As we pulled up at the hotel, Butch spotted a parking space.

'Do you want me to get out and watch you back Butch'?

'No,' came the curt reply, 'I'm fine.'

As he manoeuvred into the space, I was looking back, and could see we were a bit close on my side.

'Bit close here, Butch.'

'I can see, I can see,' said the irritated skipper. 'It's fine'. Then he smashed into the wall.

Silence.

I got out of the car to look at the damage. I also glanced up at the name of the hotel.

'The Park'. Enough said.

As much as those days in the car were fun, there was a very real risk involved. In those days the fixture list wasn't always that kind. You could end a game late on a Tuesday, and have to be at the other side of the country for an 11am start the following day. These very circumstances had disastrous results for Rodney Ontong and Steve Barwick in 1988.

We had just completed one of the best first-class matches I ever played in. It was against an excellent Essex side at Colchester. We were generally nip and tuck for the three days. They outscored us in the first innings, and we outscored them in the second, and as we approached the final session on that last day, all four results were still a possibility. The match ended in a tie – the only one I'd ever played in – but owing to a fluke in the rules, they were awarded the tie, and we had to settle for a draw, gaining fewer points than Essex, even though we technically bowled them out. Confused? This outcome occurred because Essex's England spinner Geoff Miller had been absent hurt for the bulk of the game. When we took their ninth and final wicket to effectively tie off the last ball of the game – Matt running out Derek Pringle as he went for the winning run – we were ready to leave the field in high spirits. But because Miller had been hospitalised and couldn't bat, a rule was invoked which, even though he hadn't even been at the ground for two days, meant that technically he could still have batted and as we'd taken only nine, not ten wickets, the umpires had no option but to give us a draw. If we'd taken that ninth wicket just one ball earlier, as Miller wouldn't have been there to take the field, we'd have been awarded a tie. It was a very annoyed dressing room when we all found out. Personally I was happy though, I'd got 40-odd in my second innings, opening with Butch, and the fact that England Captain Gooch was fielding at first slip and standing next to Aussie captain Allan Border throughout my knock, was all the more pleasing.

As we showered and changed, the talk centred on the next day: another Championship game, this time away at Northampton. We all piled in the cars and set off. It was well after 8 o'clock in the evening when we left, and after we arrived at our hotel in Northampton, an hour or so passed before someone mentioned there was no sign of Rodney and Baz. This was pre-mobile phone days, and as such, we didn't get a phonecall for another two-and-a-half hours, and when it came, it confirmed our worst fears. Apparently, they were driving along a dual carriageway, when a lorry pulled out in front of them and forced them across the road and down a bank into a field. Baz was bashed about and generally shaken up, but the news on Rodney was far worse.

He had taken a bad hit on his legs, and had smashed one of his knees. It effectively ended his career. He'd played for Glamorgan since the late 1970s, and even though he was South African, he had become a British citizen, so was now qualified for England. As often happens in cricket, his best form had been reached later in his career, and as his bowling and batting had matured, he developed into a quality all-rounder, and was being spoken of in terms of England selection. The crash ended all that. He was out for the rest of the season, and only managed five more games the following season before he had to bow to the inevitable and announce his retirement through injury. A great loss.

At the time, when the seriousness of the situation sank in, we all thought 'There but for the grace of God . . .' The amount of miles covered by a cricketer was massive in those days – it hasn't changed too much now – and we all realised that for the whole length of time we were driving, we really were at the mercy of so many things – the weather, the state of the roads, other drivers, and of course, traffic cones.

Rodney's passenger that fateful night was, however, spared any lasting injury, and would remain one of the happy constants of my career at Glamorgan.

When Stephen Royston Barwick was released in 1996, with some bad feeling unfortunately, I was genuinely sorry. He was an absolute one-off. About as far away as you could get from the text-book image of a 'true professional', but as close as you could get to the real-life version of a 'true professional', he had become loved and revered in equal measure by the time his career ended.

His constitution was truly amazing. In ten or more years of sharing a dressing room with him, I honestly can't ever remember seeing him eat. Off the field he was never without a cigarette, and at the end of a day's play, his other hand was never without a beer. I don't ever recall seeing him 'legless', he was like a sump – he just went on and on, without any apparent effect. The times the rest of us joined Baz for a session, and turned up at the ground the following morning like death warmed up were far too numerous to record. All the more galling for us was that he'd burst into the dressing room like bloody Tinkerbell, full of the joys of spring. Then he'd just go through the motions in the warm-ups, but proceed to bowl 30 or 40 overs in 70-degree heat, whilst the rest of us walked around in purgatory. He was legendary.

His reputation was built on bowling medium-paced off-cutters, often with spectacular success – especially in one-day cricket. He had the ability to extract bounce and movement from a pitch, at a pace far quicker than an off-spin bowler, and on his day he was unplayable. At the peak of his career – the year we won the Sunday League in 1993, probably – teams were making it public that they would have meetings the night before playing Glamorgan, in order to prepare a plan on how best to deal with him. It meant nothing to Baz though. He was as uncomplicated a cricketer as you could get. He was a master of his art, and took it all in his stride. His view was simply, 'I'm in the side to bowl 10 overs, take some wickets, and not go for many.' That's about as technical as I ever heard Baz get. It was certainly a winning formula though. The number of times he came onto bowl for a second spell when the opposition were looking to push the score along and return figures like 4 overs, 2 maidens, 3 wickets for 7 runs were many. He could be totally relied upon, and in a team of match-winners, for many years he was maybe our key one.

I remember one night in Colwyn Bay Cricket Club bar when England's John Crawley joined us for a drink. After a while he turned to Baz and said

'Come on Baz – give me a clue – how can I play you?'

Without missing a beat he said in his deep South Walian accent, 'You can't play me mun'.

'Oh come on, Baz gimee a break – just give me a tip.'

Baz jumped up and stood over John like a wizened old sorcerer instructing his apprentice.

'Right then – listen here'. Baz stood in the middle of this bar and brought his right arm straight up alongside his head, gripping an imaginary cricket ball, his face as serious as an undertaker's.

'If you start to come down the wicket when I got the ball 'ere – I got you.'

93

He moved his arm, slightly further around. 'If you start to move when I got the ball 'ere – I still got you. You'd be helpless. Nothing you can do. I got you.' He then moved his arm to the point of delivery of the imaginary ball, and said 'But if you move when I got the ball 'ere – you got me. Right? The only time – you get me. But it'll never 'appen. Never 'appen – right?' After which, he promptly sat back down.

Crawley looked as stunned as we did. Baz just picked up his pint and swigged it as though nothing had happened.

Baz took five Lancashire wickets the next day – including Crawley's!

Later in the year we played Kent at St Helen's in Swansea. The ground was starting to bare its teeth a bit now after many years of neglect which would eventually see regular cricket moved to the new HQ of the Swalec Stadium. A very strong Kent side included one of the best batsmen in the world at the time, West Indian captain Carl Hooper. If Hooper didn't score a fifty or a hundred during a game of county cricket, there was an inquest. He was simply brilliant. He was their key man, and to stand any chance of putting pressure on Kent with a view to winning the game, we'd need to get him early.

On four runs, he tried to hook a short ball from Darren Foster which had got a touch big on him, and he only succeeded in catching the ball high on the splice of the bat and spooned a dolly of a catch to our fielder at mid-on. Baz.

He dropped it.

We were stunned. As was Hooper. As was Baz. The air was blue, and Baz was looking everywhere in desperation for an excuse, blaming everything he could think of: the sun, the turf, his boots, but preceding them with the word 'Fuck' every time. As serious as the moment was, it was hysterically funny. Hooper however, took advantage of the let-off, and just over an hour later he celebrated his hundred, and was going like a train. Now, when you fielded at St Helen's in high summer, there was one place you didn't want to be. It was at deep long-off, right down underneath the old rugby stand. It's the area of the outfield where the rugby pitch encroaches onto the cricket field, and as it's hidden from the sun for long periods, it takes months to repair. The groundsman had resorted to scattering loads of sand on this area, and when mixed with the dry earth of the summer, the area became pockmarked with parched areas of sand and dust, which exploded like a grenade when the ball pitched on it. The players affectionately referred to it as 'Beirut on a Saturday Night'. Baz was stood right in the middle of it.

Steve Watkin was bowling and bowled the first ball to Hooper just after he'd finished celebrating his rapid century – and served up a low full toss. Hooper just leant back and with awesome power smashed the ball straight back at Watty, just a few feet to the right of him and rising towards deep mid-off. Towards Baz. The ball went like a gunshot. It didn't get higher than ten feet off the ground, and arrived at Baz at about 80mph, arcing towards the ground at no more than shin height and just to his right. Baz crouched down, flung out his right hand, and the ball flew in and stuck like glue. Now what Baz didn't see, and that quite a few of the rest of us had seen, was that the ball had pitched about a foot in front of him, and reached his hand, Dambusters-like, on the half volley. The reason I know that Baz didn't see it was because he had his eyes shut. So there's Baz, hardly visible due to the dust and sand thrown up by the pitching of the ball in 'Beirut', claiming the catch. Vanburn Holder the umpire asked the fielder if he'd caught it cleanly. Baz replied, with all sincerity, 'Course I bloody caught it, mun!' And that was enough for the umpire. Hooper had to go.

We were all stood there, either in disbelief or on the brink of laughter, especially as we watched Baz loping in with the ball in his hand, smile on his face, and covered from the ankle up in dry mud as a result of his 'catch', which had turned his whites the colour of a horse rustler's jeans. Carl Hooper took it all in his stride as usual, he just smiled, casually about-turned and strolled off the field. His nickname in the Glamorgan dressing room was always 'Cool Carl' – it fitted him perfectly.

CHAPTER NINE

Learning to Win

In September 1992, I finally achieved one of the many goals I had set out for myself when I first signed that two-month summer contract with Alan Jones back in 1986. I was capped for Glamorgan. Achieving your cap in cricket is a curious thing. It means basically that you've now been accepted as a senior player, a player recognised with stature and substance within the club. There are several ways you can become a capped player. One way is the way it happened to me and countless pros before. You get recognised for your steady improvement as a player, up to the point that you become pretty much an automatic selection for the team in both first-class and one-day cricket. It's a reward for consistency and durability more than anything, and I was 26 years old when it happened to me.

Other players get capped because of their stature when they arrive at the club. For example, Viv Richards was awarded his cap before he even set foot on the pitch – he was such a big star and didn't have to prove anything to anyone. I was extremely flattered that when I joined Sussex they did exactly the same thing to me – although for several seasons afterwards I still felt I had plenty to prove up there, not least to the fans. But more of that later.

Another route to a cap is rewarding a young player who may have secured an England A-tour place, for example, or even an unexpected call-up to the full England team. There's method in the club's madness here though, because these days, the extra salary money a county cap brings with it acts as a carrot to keep the talented youngster at your county, especially if the sharks at the larger counties come circling to snatch up your young prized asset.

There are other fringe benefits to receiving your county cap. At Glamorgan a very subtle one is in relation to the emblem you are permitted to wear on your sweater and cap. When you are an uncapped player, the famous daffodil of Glamorgan appears on your cap and sweater as a small unopened bud, drooping ever so slightly – to represent the early, young, unfulfilled cricketer, awaiting his blossoming career. On award of your county cap, that emblem is replaced by the bright, proud, fully opened flower, to signify your arrival on the big stage. Achieving this honour is about as proud as you get as a County Player, as it's a recognition of your ability, commitment, and more importantly to me, staying power. Little did I know then how the circumstances of my capping would lead to such bad feeling and bitterness six seasons later, resulting ultimately in my leaving the club.

At Sussex, before my time there, the award of a cap also had another strange benefit. You were able to move changing rooms! Sussex had more than just home and away dressing rooms: they had the home 'capped' dressing room, another, much smaller, 'uncapped' dressing room and also a 'potting shed' in the dungeons of the stand for the uncapped youngsters. This had been the way for over a hundred years I'm led to believe, and after a long day in the field at Hove, Sussex would all troop off together, maybe being led off by an uncapped bowler who'd taken a few wickets in a particularly good late afternoon spell, into the clubhouse and up the stairs. At this point the uncapped players made their choice and would continue either to their primitive potting shed changing room in the bottom of the stand, or to the other 'uncapped' dressing room. The capped players, of course, would carry on to the far more spacious surroundings of the capped players' dressing room upstairs. Worse than that though, if an uncapped player who'd just spent seven hours on the outfield wanted to return something – say a pair of boots he'd borrowed – he'd have to knock on the capped dressing-room door, wait, and then ask the captain's permission before being invited in. Local customs can be very strange.

But back to 1992. I was capped towards the end of the season and after a winter away, returned in 1993 with renewed vigour and the confidence of a player who had 'arrived'. My good fortune of being capped came at the same time as Glamorgan's good fortune to run into an extremely successful businessman by the name of Paul Russell. Paul came on the scene late in 1992, and the first time I ever clapped eyes on him, or more accurately, heard him, was at the bar at an away game at Hartlepool. 'Who would like to be bought a drink by a man who has just completed a two million dollar deal?' was the question I heard emanating from this small, trim bespectacled 'suit' with a moustache, standing at the bar. A couple of the players looked at each other and the look on our faces all read the same 'Who the hell is this beauty?' Little were we to know that this man would not just alter the standing of Glamorgan County Cricket Club on the domestic scene and also secure a test match for Wales, but, indirectly, he would alter the courses of all our careers – and largely for the better.

Paul saw himself very much as a visionary. He was employed by the global company Anderson Consulting, and was based in London, and held a very senior position with the company. He enjoyed the sporting environment, along with his brother Marcus who managed a successful up-and-coming band in the music business that you may of heard of, Oasis. Paul recognised the hard work done by Tony Lewis and captains Alan Butcher and Hugh Morris in moving Glamorgan away from the laughing stock of county cricket to a more positive position in the mid-table area of the league. Paul's vision however was to take this further: he didn't want Glamorgan just eating at the top table, he wanted us at the head of it, and for a time in the mid-1990s, that's exactly what he achieved. He basically adopted a two-pronged approach. He believed that if the players were treated well, with the best facilities, best equipment, best travel arrangements, best cars – not to mention improved salaries, he would be halfway there. Who were we to disagree? We thought all our Christmases had come at once. His other plan of attack was aimed at the supporters. He recognised instantly that Glamorgan had a very loyal fan base of around 3,000 members, paying around £45 a year for a season ticket – one of the highest prices in county cricket at the time, for a team that hadn't won a trophy for the best part of 25 years. His idea was to slash membership to just £15, working on the premise that slashing prices would hugely increase members, and in so doing, all other revenue streams within the ground – food, drink, souvenirs, programmes etc – would increase hugely too, which would go a long way to putting the club in a very rosy financial position. He succeeded spectacularly, and during 1993, Glamorgan's membership soared past 10,000 and almost overnight we became the best supported club in the land.

To get the all-Wales interest however, Paul also knew that it would need more than just price-slashing. There would have to be the pain before the gain.

In the spring of 1993, all the pros that were not still engaged abroad on tours or club commitments were summoned to Sophia Gardens. Paul had the idea that we needed to take Glamorgan on the road to spread the gospel of the mighty daffodil. As 1993 was also the year that coloured clothing was introduced in cricket, his idea was to dress up in our new blue-and-yellow one-day pyjamas and travel the length and breadth of Wales, meeting kids, attending question-and-answer sports forums and generally acting as ambassadors for the club, with a view to enticing the people of Wales to get behind us. It sounded great to us – Crofty, Jamer, Baz, Colin Metson, Adrian Shaw and me to name but a few – all fancied the idea of this national tour aboard a luxury bus, being feted like sporting Gods wherever we went. Bring it on!

We were told that we would be travelling in two vans.

The room went a bit quiet. This didn't go down too well with a couple of the players, but it was explained that we'd lose the intimacy if we were aboard an executive coach. The club didn't want to convey a them-and-us situation, and wanted to remove the barriers, to make sure we included people and made them feel part of the club, even part of the team. That's why we were going in vans.

We were to be split up equally, and share the driving, and were given a detailed itinerary for each day, but basically we'd be driving to North Wales to Caernarfon, then down through mid and South Wales over the week, and ending up in Newport Town Centre.

It all sounded fine to us, and we were already planning which were the best towns to stay overnight in with regard to their hostelries.

Then someone from the club said 'The only other thing you'll have to do is work out a rota for using the loudspeakers'

'Loudspeakers?' questioned Crofty.

'The ones on top of the vans. You know, like on polling day. We've got to get our message across to people, they've got to be aware of the product we are trying to sell.' I think they noticed the mortified look on our faces. 'C'mon fellas – it's going to be great. As soon as you get used to it, you won't want to give the microphone up'.

There was no reply.

A week or so later we climbed aboard our respective Skylarks, and drove to Caernarfon. We were to meet in the car park of the castle and spend the morning walking around the town centre, before embarking on our first loudspeaker engagement in the afternoon. I was driving our van, and pulled into the massive car park at 10am. You know what it's like when you drive into an empty car park, you can never find the right space – it's always easier when there's only a few spaces to choose from. So there I am getting stick off the boys for faffing around: 'Just pick a space, Cotts, there's a thousand options'. I finally picked a space and drew to a halt. As I did so, Colin Metson, who was driving the other van, pulled into the car park and surveyed the remaining 999 spaces at his disposal, and picked one. The same one I'd chosen.

He smashed into the back of us.

'Fucking hell, Meto, there's only one other vehicle within half a mile – and you hit it!'

It set the tone for the week.

We walked into Caernarfon centre and began handing out the leaflets to an unsuspecting population. At first we were nervous and tentative, but then we settled into our roles as season-ticket salesmen and started to enjoy ourselves. The people were great and we had a good laugh. This was the pattern for the week. Admittedly a bit of boredom set in when travelling in between towns – especially in mid Wales – but that's when the loudspeakers really came into their own.

Until you've been travelling, in a van with several bored professional cricketers, through the beautiful, yet lonely mid-Wales countryside, where someone spots a huge flock of sheep at the side of the road, and decides to bark like a dog through the strategically-placed loudspeakers to witness the scattering of the said flock – you've not really lived. Childish it may well be, but spectacular doesn't do it justice.

Crofty's favourite was to wait until we were driving through a small, built-up area with just a pub and a couple of shops, spot a couple of girls walking along, and then, with the volume turned up to ten, would shout 'Corrrrr, look at herrrr' like a deranged Leslie Phillips. I know what you're thinking – but we were getting stir crazy.

Finally we made it back to Cardiff. Officials met us in the city centre and said that whilst the campaign was going well, we really needed a bit of a boost in the Capital City.

That's when the sandwich boards appeared.

We looked at them with horror.

'You're not asking us to wear those are you? All they need is 'The End Is Nigh' on them! No way,' declared Crofty.

'C'mon boys,' they said. 'It's only for a couple of hours, it'll send the right message, all the details of the new membership price are on it and everything. There's only two, and the rest of you will just be handing out leaflets, so you can take it in turns. You're not going to see anyone you really know, are you?'

Fair point, we thought. We weren't happy really – most sports people have decent ego and vanity levels at the best of times, and we were no different. But it was for a good cause, so we decided to put our pride to one side and get on with it. Like he said, nobody we knew was likely to see us.

They hadn't told us about the cameras.

There we were, in the centre of Cardiff, wandering round like a bunch of gaily-dressed Mormons with the sandwich boards and the leaflets, and who's there to greet us but BBC and ITV Wales news crews! We were gutted. Or at least the ones in the sandwich boards were, Crofty in particular was mortified; the rest of us were wetting ourselves laughing.

Our final day was in Newport. This was to be a marketing man's crowning glory. A large cardboard box was produced which immediately aroused our suspicions. Out was pulled a bright green pair of polyester trousers, quickly followed by similar coloured top, with arms that looked like leaves or stalks.

100

No – it can't be.

Then out came a great big sunburst yellow daffodil head.

Oh yes it is.

'Right boys – who's going to be first in the daffodil suit?'

That was it. We refused point blank. We thought it was a joke at first, but no, it was serious. We ended up having an almighty row in which we all refused to back down. The sandwich board was definitely the furthest we were willing to go. And a good, old-fashioned stand off ensued.

To his eternal credit, our marketing man Tony Dilloway stepped in and volunteered – or was he pushed, I can't remember. But that afternoon, after walking around the city centre of Newport with a grown man dressed as a daffodil, we finally said goodbye to our off-field efforts. We'd done our bit for the sales department and were quite relieved it was all over. It had been a very surreal week, but the best six months of our professional lives lay ahead.

Just prior to the start of that 1993 season, Paul held good on his promise to ensure that the players were to begin receiving the best treatment in terms of facilities and spin-offs for our endeavours on the field. I was nearly 27 years old and I was about to receive my first sponsored car. If a player these days had to wait until that age now, he'd probably instruct his agent to take his case to the European Court of Human Rights.

Paul invited myself, Watty and Matt up to the Anderson Consulting building in London. When we arrived there he met us and strangely showed us down into the basement. From there we were taken to a brightly-lit car park. Lined up were about a dozen gleaming new cars owned by Anderson Consulting who were going to be sponsoring us for the foreseeable future.

'Take your pick, lads'

We were like kids in a sweet shop. Watty and Matt chose a BMW each, but I fancied something more compact, more akin to my size. I choose a beautiful cherry red VW Corrado. I'd always been a bit of a boy racer, and this fitted the bill perfectly. At the time, I was knocking round in Gail's Vauxhall Nova, so this car sponsorship lark was a very welcome development.

As we left our newly acquired toys so that name, county and sponsor could be emblazoned on the doors, I couldn't help but think back to my old teammate John Derrick's foray into car sponsorship. JD is a big lad. He's six foot plus, and shall we say, well covered. In the mid-1980s he was a regular first teamer with Glamorgan and held down the club's all-rounder spot as a useful medium-pace bowler, and hard-hitting middle-order batter. He was of good Welsh valleys' stock, born in Aberdare, and as such, had negotiated his own personal sponsorship deal with a local Ford Dealership in the town.

The first time I had the pleasure of being chauffeured by John in his luxury car was when we both played at Folkestone in the Seconds and after the match, we were both called up to Chesterfield to cover for injuries and play for the first team. John was returning from injury in this match, and had the dubious honour of running me out in the second innings for 80 after I'd scored a 100 in the first. I never managed to score a century in each innings in my whole career. Still, no grudge against JD. Until I saw his car for the trip to Chesterfield that was.

This fifteen-stone-plus cricketer now showed me to his sponsored 'John Derrick – Glamorgan Cricket Club', red Ford Fiesta 850. I'd seen sewing machines with bigger engines. We squeezed our kit into the back seat and got started. It took a few moments to generate the friction to move from the parking space.

'Put the radio on, JD.'

'Sorry mate, this car doesn't come with one,' came his sheepish reply.

So we embarked – in the slow lane – on our five-hour-plus journey up north, which normally only took three. I seem to remember that on our interminable journey we resorted to playing 'spot the car badge' just to pass the time.

How times have changed I smiled to myself as I cast one last longing look back at my shiny new wheels, here in a basement in the City of London. Paul then took us up to the company penthouse suite where we met some of the senior people and were treated to an exclusive buffet washed down with Verve Cliquot Champagne. It was superb. I could get used to this I thought, as I watched Watty ask the waiter if he could have a bigger glass. (Only joking, Steve).

As I've mentioned though, Paul was true to his word about introducing quality to our environment. For the season ahead we were all fitted out with several new club 'uniforms' – Chinos and club blazers for four-day games, different-coloured Reebok polo shirts for the different one-day competitions, and all players had to wear the correctly corresponding outfit or they were fined. I remember turning up at away grounds, stepping out of our luxury cars like a million dollars, and seeing the envious looks from opposition pros, stepping out of their Vauxhall Astras or Rovers, wondering where in the hell have Glamorgan got their money from all of a sudden. We certainly felt we had the edge, even before we set foot in the ground. I think Paul realised that if you feel good about yourself, then a positive outcome is generally the result, and that season – and for the next four or five years in fairness – that was generally the case.

The final idea that year was to take the cricket out to the masses. As a result we ended up playing in seven or eight 'outgrounds' for our Sunday league games, away from the traditional St Helen's and Sophia Gardens. Places like Pontypridd, Abergavenny, Colwyn Bay and Ebbw Vale all saw us perform, and this proved to be a masterstroke. We'd turn up at these grounds a couple of hours before play began, and they were already nearly half full. By the time we took the field to start the match, the ground would be packed out and the crowd simmering nicely, thanks to the various beer tents dotted around. Opposing teams came to hate playing at these grounds because of the edge it gave us, and the unnerving atmosphere that they had to combat. The crowds in these very important games certainly played their part in our success that summer; we always felt they were worth a twenty-run start.

Never was this more true than when we played one-day games at Ebbw Vale. The supporters there were as about as partisan as I ever played in front of. And as the day wore on, the stick they gave the opposition in the field became merciless. God forbid if you made an error in the field, like a slip for example. Up would go a really loud 'Way – haaaay' followed by 'Come on, Bambi – up you get butt,' and the player concerned would get the bird for the rest of the match. After my treatment at Trent Bridge in front of Castle Corner, I must admit I'd sit back and watch this unfold with a self-satisfied smile.

I remember one incident where it bubbled over a touch, though. We were playing Notts in a game umpired by a certain Dickie Bird, and Notts gave us a bit of a pasting as we struggled to chase down 200 or so, falling 40-odd short. As the crowd started to work on the Notts players in the field as our wickets steadily fell, the ever-eccentric Derek Randall began to revel in the atmosphere and was giving as good as he was getting. Trouble was, one or two in the crowd had developed a sense of humour bypass due to the liquid excesses of the day, and as Derek was getting in his car to leave after Notts had sealed the victory, someone chucked a punch at him through his car window. Derek sized up the situation pretty well, and sped off into the distance. I didn't blame him. It's the only time I remember things turning quite so ugly, mind.

Incidentally, Glamorgan suffered once or twice ourselves on tight outgrounds, most notably in 1993 in Middlesbrough against Yorkshire. Our great Dutchman Roland Lefebvre (pronounced Luh – fev) had just finished yet another tight spell of bowling and retreated to the deep mid-on boundary for a well-deserved rest, when a well-oiled Yorkshireman in the crowd shouted out at the top of his voice just as there was a lull in play, for us all to hear:

'Oi, Lerferverer, I shagged your wife the other week in Amsterdam, and she only cost me ten guilders'.

Roly's face was a picture, and, as good strong teammates, we all looked at Roly's exasperated features and just burst out laughing – along with the crowd. Sorry Roly – it was funny though!

Paul Russell is still at the club, and now holds the position of Chairman, and in recent years has come in for a bit of flak over his plans to turn Sophia Gardens into a regular test-match venue at the expense of the Glamorgan team. In my weekly column for the South Wales Evening Post, I too pointed out that I felt this approach was the wrong one, and Paul decided to have a real go back at me with a full-page letter to the editor. Whilst I've always understood the vision for the stadium, and having now seen it, would have absolutely loved to have played in it during my career, it was so at odds with Paul's fantastic treatment of our playing squad back in my day. Back then, Paul's view was that the playing squad was everything, and key to the long-term success of the club. Success on the field in terms of silverware – and there was plenty of it – led to success off it. It was this apparent change in direction that I found most confusing.

This led to the situation in 2007 of a group of players taking the field for large parts of the season who were simply too young and inexperienced to provide Glamorgan with a consistent and competitive team. The facts were undeniable. Since 2005, Glamorgan had waved goodbye for various reasons to Matt Maynard, Steve James, Adrian Dale and Darren Thomas. The going rate for top county players like them was an absolute minimum of £45K to £60K per year. Add to that the cost of an above-average overseas player – £80k minimum – and you'll see a playing investment of at least £320k left the club. The only player taken on from outside the club since those players left was Nicky Peng, who according to my information, earned less than the £45k to £60k range. At the start of the 2007 season, the club announced that there would be no investment in overseas players. Then a benefactor stepped forward, and to common belief announced that one would be funded – but only if that one was Jimmy Maher. Matthew Elliot played for free for the first month until Maher belatedly arrived – at no cost to the club. So, if we did our sums, £320k of investment into the playing staff in 2005, was, apart from Nicky Peng's salary of say £35k maximum, missing from the 2006 and 2007 squads. It appears reasonable to assume therefore that the balance, saving – call it what you will – of £285k per year was being redirected to the stadium costs, which by definition would have had a massive detrimental effect on the strength of team Glamorgan could have put out. To put it in perspective, £270k buys you a Darren Maddy, an Owais Shah and a Stuart Clark for the season.

The people I felt sorry for most in this – in no particular order – were the players, the coaches and the fans. My very real fear was that it would take years to bring success back to the fans of Glamorgan as even in the three seasons since I have finished playing, the game has become even more professional and has moved forward more quickly than at any time in its history. Especially with two-division cricket here to stay and the intense competition that format now brings. Glamorgan on the other hand, at the end of the 2007 season, were in the worst position they'd been in since the revised format began, and were further behind the rest than at any time in the past.

However, I have to also look at the other side of the argument too. Paul Russell and the committee have without doubt succeeded in producing a stadium that apart from Lord's and the Oval, is probably going to become the best cricket arena in Britain. An Ashes test match has been secured, and surely more will follow. This means that in five or maybe ten years time, the club will hopefully be on a secure financial footing as never before. The only problem however is that there are only a maximum of seven test matches per year, sometimes only six. We know that Lords always gets one (sometimes two) and the Oval one, then the other four matches will need to be shared by Headingley, Edgbaston, Trent Bridge, Old Trafford, The Rose Bowl, Durham's Riverside and now the Swalec Stadium. My question always was whether the guarantee of maybe one test match every two to three seasons worth setting against the investment – or reduced investment – of the playing side? In fairness, changes were made for 2008. Investment, in the form of Matthew Wood, Jamie Dalrymple, Jason Gillespie and Herschelle Gibbs, was made to the playing staff, which is all I, and all Glamorgan fans, ever wanted. Despite this, I will never be convinced that the ultimate aim of the redevelopment of Sophia Gardens couldn't have been achieved without basically sacrificing the 2006 and 2007 seasons and the players who had to suffer it. But, sport and life move on. I respect the fact that Paul Russell had a vision, and respect even more his determination to see it through. I genuinely wish him and Glamorgan well and hope that one day he can sit me down with a glass of wine, watching a trophy-winning Glamorgan team, and say 'I told you so.'

CHAPTER TEN

A Canterbury Tale

The funny thing about sport – and I guess it applies to life in general really – is that when you're having your best day, when you're hitting a peak, you never know at the time that this is the best it will ever get. You always assume it's the stepping stone to something greater, some other great day that will come along to replace the one you're now experiencing. Sadly, that day will often never come. I remember reading something about John McEnroe and he said that when he became world number one he was about 26 years old and the match he played to get there was one of the best he ever played, and felt that after that match he never reached those heights again. Even though he played on for years after, he felt the rest of his career was a bit of an anti-climax. I understood exactly what he meant.

The best run of form in my career was in my penultimate season in 2003, but I reached my career peak ten years earlier in the space of a single afternoon. For about the only time in my professional life, I was centre stage at the most important moment of the season, the moment when a trophy was won. It was Canterbury 1993, the first time Glamorgan had won a trophy since 1969 – and I was fated to play a major part.

Five months earlier we had been whisked off to Cape Town, South Africa for a pre-season tour. During the tour, captain Hugh Morris held a few team meetings to discuss the coming season. I think he recognised that he had the potential for a special team, and that the coming season could be our breakthrough year. Hugh was one of the best batsmen in Glamorgan's history, coming to the very peak of his powers, and he seemed to score runs every time he took to the wicket. Behind him he could call on ten other players all beginning to peak at the same time. The bulk of the team were pretty much the same age. I was 27 and a school year either side were Matt, Jamer, Daley and Watty. The experience age-wise was provided by the incomparable Steve Barwick, Roland Lefebvre, the flying Dutchman whose unbelievable catching ability in the deep suggested that he could probably catch flies – and the complex Colin Metson, who was simply world-class behind the stumps. The youngster in the team was Crofty, who would go on to greater things after this, his springboard season, all backed up by the Daddy of them all, King Viv. Viv Richards – I can still hardly believe that I can call this true legend a friend and teammate, but that's what he'd become by his third and final year with us in 1993. We didn't know it at the time but he was also to become our talisman.

During these team meetings in Cape Town, Hugh had reinforced in our minds that we were a whisker away from being a top team, and if we individually and collectively added five or ten per cent to our game, he was convinced this would be our year. He wasn't only focussing on what we were in the team to do – say, to bat, bowl or keep wicket – he was more interested in the small areas that supplement those skills. These were sharper running between the wickets, more athletic fielding, being more aggressive generally in the field and not allowing our heads to drop. These messages really got through to us all, and as a result we became excellent as a fielding unit. It became a matter of pride: no one wanted to be the one who let a catch slip through their fingers or be responsible for the opposition pinching a run due to a misfiled. We began to exert pressure on opposition teams who'd probably never come across such a combined intensity of commitment. This pattern was picked up and even improved by the Gloucestershire side of the late 1990s, who ended up winning one-day trophies for fun, but I like to think that Glamorgan set the blueprint back in April 1993 in South Africa.

As predicted by Hugh, 1993 really was to be our breakthrough year. With a month to go in the season, we were in second place in the County Championship, in the semi-finals of the Nat West Trophy, and were top of the Axa Equity and Law Sunday League. At the start of the season, I'd told Dave how confident I felt that this was to be the year when we would win something, and as such he went away and got the odds from William Hill. We were 66-to-1 to win the County Championship, 50-to-1 to win the Nat West and 33-to-1 to win the Sunday League. He asked me if I was happy to put my money where my mouth was – I agreed – and we both invested £15 each on a bet called a patent. The bookies reduced the odds because when you bet on one team to win certain events, they have to lower the odds offered – for some strange reason – but if all three were won, we'd be sharing winnings that were the best part of £300,000. If we won two trophies, it dropped to about £70,000, and if we won one, it would be about £350. With a month to go, I must admit to feeling not only the pressure of picking up Glamorgan's first silverware for 25 years, but also pondering the most spectacular cricket win bonus of all time! It became a bit of a talking point in the dressing room – especially as it appeared we were in with a definite chance in all three competitions. In the end we both had to settle for the £350 our Sunday League win gave us, and because I picked up a decent few quid in bonuses that season due to our success, I told Dave he could keep it all. He didn't protest too much as I recall!

The season didn't start too well, though. We lost our first two Sunday League games, and had a no-result in the third, which left us bottom of the league. A spectacular run of form followed, however, that saw us win the next thirteen games on the trot and helped hoist us to the top of the league. With a few weeks to go to the end of the season, it became obvious that it was going to come down to us and Kent, and as the quirky fixture list would have it, not only would we play Kent in the final Sunday League match of the season, we would also have to play them in the final four-day game too.

On the same weekend. Both away from home, at Canterbury.

Whatever happened, we were going to have to earn our victory the hard way. As each week passed and another game was won, Matt would start to pack away his kit after each victory, and shout loudly to the dressing room in a strange Scouse accent 'Well, it's looks like we're gonna be heading to Canterbury for the final sceeeenaaaario!' It got us all laughing, and by the end of the season we were all saying it. We couldn't wait.

All the time I played for Glamorgan, all everyone wanted, fans, committee, even many of the players, was a Lord's final. Yes it would be great to win a league, but a Lord's final was something special, and to a small county like Glamorgan, it seemed a more reasonable expectation after years of non-achievement, than the all-round consistent level of performance needed to win one of the leagues. The best atmosphere I'd played in prior to our day of destiny at Canterbury was in the Nat West semi-final a month before, down at Sussex of all places. Anyone that was there will tell you that Allan Wells was run-out before he got off the mark – all the TV replays confirmed it – but unfortunately the third-umpire replays would only be used in the final. Mr Wells went on to score a hundred and won them the game, and that was it. We were always in the game, and only lost by three wickets, but because we were always in it, the atmosphere was electric. The Welsh fans were superb; they never need an excuse for a good day out at the best of times, and they'd turned up in force on the south coast that day. For three-quarters of the day it was like a cup final, but as the game began to slip away, so, understandably, did the vocal levels from our great crowd. I remember catching the big-hitting Franklyn Stephenson on the boundary right in front of the Sussex members stand, and hearing the ground going quiet behind me, but as I jubilantly ran into the middle to join the boys, the roar from the opposite side of the ground containing the bulk of the Welsh support greeted me like a wave. I can't begin to tell you how good I felt. But that was to be the end of the jubilation for us, and me in particular. As we trooped off, defeated, listening to the Sussex players whooping and hollering above us, I remembered the comments of veteran sportsmen who always said that the worst match to ever lose is a semi-final. This is because if you lose in a final you've still had a massive day out which fills the memory banks, but the semi-final defeat is like a big empty void.

I joined the rest of the lads in the dressing room, Crofty was bemoaning the fact that Wells was clearly out. But that was life, and we'd have taken it if the roles had been reversed. The odd word of commiseration was passed round by Hugh and Alan, but I was totally gutted and just sat there motionless, still in my kit, just consumed by feelings ranging from gross disappointment to downright self pity. After a few minutes, Steve Barwick traipsed out of the showers, wrapped in a towel, but with plenty of soapsuds still covering him.

'All the bloody hot water's gone, mun!'

I nearly laughed. It couldn't get much worse. After a few minutes the Sussex and England spinner Eddie Hemmings – a great bloke – came in to our dressing room.

'Sorry about the hot water lads, most of our boys have finished, we've still got hot water in our room, and the bath is full.'

A few of us who hadn't begun to change glanced at each other and couldn't face the thought of a cold shower, so off we went with Eddie. Lots of the Sussex lads had gone by now to celebrate in the bar, and the ones that were left were as good as gold – they were genuinely sorry for us and didn't take the piss. At that time Sussex had a big communal bath similar to the older soccer dressing-room baths, so I decided to take a long soak in there, and Eddie was climbing in too (not a pretty sight), so I knew I'd have some good company to talk to. I sat on the side of the bath, swivelled around on the tiles, and lowered myself in. It was a bit deeper than I thought, and I went in a bit quicker than I should have. My arse hit the bottom with a slap, and the water went straight over the top of my head. I surfaced and spluttered, dignity in tatters, to see Eddie pissing himself laughing. 'Jesus, Cotts,' he said, 'I never knew we had a deep end! Hang on a moment.'

He jumped out and came back with an old wooden contraption, which he opened and plonked in the bath. And there I was, sitting on a blue-and-white striped deckchair, water up to the belly button – the final indignity!

Sussex were sponsored by Merrydown cider that year, and before Eddie got back in, he brought a slab of them and placed them on the side of the bath.

'Help yourself Cotts – things can't get much worse.'

I spent the next hour sitting there talking to Eddie, getting more drunk as the time wore on. As I finally changed, there was a message in the dressing room stating that my Mam, Dad, Gail, Dave, Paul Gallagher and wives would be waiting for me in the Cricketer's Pub, just outside the ground. I stared at the note, but I was so down, I just knew that I couldn't face them. So I just packed my kit away – walked out of the ground alone, and headed for Hove. A selfish thing to do I know, but I just genuinely couldn't face all the kind words and commiserations – no matter how well intentioned – and so off I sloped. The place I eventually found was the less-than-exotic basement bar, The Green Parrot, which I would visit frequently years later when in the midst of a bad run for Sussex.

Those awful thoughts of failure weren't far from my mind when we travelled down to Canterbury, and I was determined that I was not going to experience that crushing feeling of disappointment again. We were told that we were to expect in excess of 10,000 Welsh fans, for what in essence was going to be a cup final. If we won – we would win the league; if Kent won – they would. Simple as that. But before the fun of Sunday, we had the first three days of the four-day match to get out of the way. We wanted to really smash them in this curtain raiser and really set the tone for the Sunday, and put them firmly on the psychological back foot. We lost the toss and they chose to bat. We didn't care; we were so confident and positive and all felt that we'd bowl them out by lunchtime for about a 150.

They batted for two days and declared on 524 for 6.

They battered us. More importantly, we began to doubt ourselves.

But then the sporting fates took a hand, or more accurately a sporting god. Viv Richards.

As we trooped off late on Saturday afternoon, dismissed for 144, a whopping 380 runs behind, we prepared to lick our wounds, and go back out for the second innings and the inevitable follow-on. For non-cricketers reading this, a follow-on is when the team batting second fail to get within 150 runs of the first innings total of the team who batted first. The team who have batted first are then asked by the umpires if they'd like to bat again, or invite the other team to bat again straight away – thus 'following on'. In 95 per cent of these situations, the decision will always be to ask the team to bat again, with a view to bowling them out for less than the amount of runs they are behind – in our case 380 –

therefore winning the match having only had to bat once. It is the ultimate crushing victory in terms of first-class cricket.

There are occasions, few and far between it must be said, when the other team, Kent in this instance, will choose to bat again, but generally that will only happen if there's plenty of time left in the game, or if the pitch might be awkward to bat on during the last day. This wasn't the case with our match as there was only a day and a session left, and that gave us little or no time to get up to their massive first innings score let alone pass it, even if we were able to. Therefore, we prepared for the follow- on. Hugh and Jamer were already padded up. Umpire David Constant popped his head in, and announced that Kent weren't going to ask us to follow on, they were going to bat again instead. It raised a few eyebrows in our dressing room: there was no real reason for it, they were so far ahead already. We quickly realised why when we saw their batting line-up. Basically they put in batters who either hadn't scored any runs in the first innings, or would be batting tomorrow – Matthew Fleming being one of them – and basically turned the rest of the Saturday of that four-day game into a batting practice session for the following day's one-day 'final'. There was nothing against this in the rules, but what it was certainly doing was manipulating one match to help them prepare for the big match tomorrow. The other thing, and much more importantly to us, was that they were obviously taking the piss. Viv was beside himself with rage. He had displayed his anger on more than one occasion in his three years with us, but this time he was absolutely boiling. I'd never seen him so wound up.

When the umpires mercifully called a halt to the day's play and put us out of our misery, we trudged off, most of us fed up, but with an eye on tomorrow. Kent on the other hand couldn't have looked happier. They all stood on the balcony smiling, laughing and clapping in their batters – especially Fleming who'd scored 80-odd in no time. That just about sent Viv over the edge.

He burst into our dressing room with eyes as wild as fire and began banging the wall to the Kent dressing room and shouting and swearing with such proliferation that I couldn't do him justice by recording it here. To paraphrase, his basic message was – delivered at the highest possible decibel level – 'You mess with the game, man, and it'll mess with you. You won't win tomorrow man, the game will bite you.'

And on he went. And on, and on. It was spectacular.

We were silent and just watched him. Out he went onto the shared balcony, which was obviously full of Kent players and continued his tirade. We could see supporters from the stand below craning their necks to see what was going on, to witness this legend of the game in full apoplectic glory.

The general lack of response from the Kent dressing room was telling. No one said a word. Viv marched straight into the showers and left us all looking around – stunned. But then it all started to dawn on us. Viv had shifted the mood. He'd shifted the balance – certainly in our minds anyway – which was the most important thing after all. When he came out of the shower, he was still angry and kept shouting, 'Have those pussies said anything yet? No? Big surprise – they won't win tomorrow, man – no way, the game won't let them.'

We started to believe he was right. He was like a man in a trance – in total belief that Kent had in some way transgressed against the cricketing gods and they would get their comeuppance tomorrow. I started to believe him and I'm sure some of the other lads did too – it was the sheer power of this man's spirit and personality that had lifted us up and turned our moods around totally.

He was to be proved absolutely right of course.

Sunday, September 19, 1993 started normally enough in the hotel. The usual suspects were there helping themselves to breakfast – some more than others! But this morning had an edge to it. I allowed myself to think back to FA Cup final days when I was a kid, when they'd have the cameras at the team hotel filming them live for BBC. We were filmed that day too – not live – but for a documentary by S4C who had been following us for some weeks when it became clear that there was a chance of winning some silverware. Also among the media ranks was Bob Humphrys from BBC Sport who helped provide some comic relief when things started to get a bit tense. The main thing I remember about that breakfast though was the feeling of an almost unspoken understanding of what the day had in store for us, and how vitally important it was to us, the Club and the supporters. You could sense it almost by a glance of the eye to different members of the team when you went to get some more orange juice or coffee or something.

After breakfast was done, Crofty and I jumped into his lavishly-sponsored VW Vento and left for the short trip to the St Lawrence Ground, Canterbury. As we got nearer the ground, the scenes reinforced that this was going to be no ordinary day. The nearer we got, the thicker the crowds became. We then became aware of the proliferation of blue-and-yellow Sunday-league tops – Glamorgan's, of course – and also an equal amount of red rugby tops – Wales. We both looked at each other and took a bit of a breath. This was our Cup Final. Our Grand Slam decider! I felt both excited and nervous. It was a feeling I'd have to get used to as the day progressed.

A mile or so from the ground, we hit a queue of traffic. We were stationary for two or three minutes, then five, then ten. We started to panic. We weren't late yet, but within half an hour we would be. Another five minutes passed but still no movement. It was becoming more like that FA Cup final day on the TV when I was a kid that I'd remembered at breakfast, with masses of people going to the ground, waiting for the team bus to appear and then parting – like the Red Sea – to let the bus through.

Except this wasn't Wembley, we weren't in a bus – and Moses wasn't around!

Crofty looked out of the window then jumped out and shouted at someone. I had no idea what he was doing but got out to have a look. Luckily it was one of his mates from his native Hendy, and he explained our predicament and handed over the keys of the car to him. He happily obliged to Crofty's request to drive the car to the ground for him, and off we jogged. I had a brief panic attack halfway to the ground about our kit, but remembered that as we were in the middle of a four-day game, we'd left it all at the ground the night before.

When we arrived at the ground it really did resemble match day at a rugby international in Cardiff. There were loads of daffodil-clad fans milling around and shouting across their best wishes. The knot in my stomach tightened.

We made it past a rather vigorous security guard, and reached the dressing room. Most of the lads were there, and they too seemed genuinely moved at the number of Welshmen that had made the effort to get to Canterbury. After all, the bulk of Glamorgan's support is based in and around Swansea and Cardiff, and the Welsh valleys around Merthyr and Ebbw Vale. Added to that is the stronghold of support that exists in west Wales right into Pembrokeshire, and in mid and North Wales for that matter. From any of these destinations to deepest Kent was a very decent five or six hours on the motorway and, as our game was scheduled to begin at 12 noon, as it was a 50-over match, it would have meant that a pretty loud dawn chorus of alarm clocks had rung through the Principality at around 5am.

David Hemp, who was twelfth man, said 'Cotts, go and have a look from the balcony'. Out I went and what I saw took my breath away. All four corners of the ground were now Welsh encampments; everywhere you looked people were streaming in and taking up every available space. The buzz of excitement and expectation could almost be touched. I remember standing there, hoping desperately that we would repay them. Maybe *I* would repay them. The knot in my stomach tightened still further.

We all changed into our tracksuits for the warm-ups. I don't remember much contact with the Kent side – perhaps they were still in shock from Viv's antics from the night before. They certainly didn't look hugely confident as I glanced over at them. Maybe it *was* Viv, maybe it was the crowd – it felt like our home game not theirs. Or maybe it was just the winner-takes-all occasion. I just hoped some of them felt as bad as I did.

As a pro, the image you project is important. You have to appear super confident, taking everything in your stride, rising aloofly above the occasion. You feel yourself putting on a 'what's all the fuss about?' façade, totally in control. A well-oiled machine, no less. The truth is that day that I felt my machine was about to go on the blink! I couldn't share this with any of my teammates, that would be showing weakness, or so you think at the time. Instead you just have to carry on, and just grin and bear it.

I looked at Viv. He was laughing and joking and looking relaxed. Maybe to him this was just another game. He'd played on the highest stage for twenty years. I'd love to know how he felt, know what was going through his mind: was he really as supremely confident as he looked? As it happens, the way the day unfolded, it was to mean a hell of a lot more to him than any of us would ever have guessed from his relaxed demeanour.

Kent won the toss and decided to bat. We gathered together in the dressing room, listened to some final words of advice from Hugh and Viv, which basically involved telling us that every single run today would be at a premium. Their batters must be put under pressure from the very first ball, Viv was insistent about this. We then all took a collective deep breath and walked out into the bright sunlight. The cheers and shouts that greeted us were sensational. 'Oh Glammy, Glammy' rang around the ground accompanied by the odd Welsh hymn. We could've been playing in Swansea or Cardiff. It really took our breath away.

Then it was game on. Kent made a decent start: Mathew Fleming got 40-odd, and after about twenty overs, they were 103 for three, with the extremely dangerous Carl Hooper going along very nicely on 50 not out and he had the ability to take the match out of our reach. The day before, Kent had declared against us with him undefeated on 263. He must've been seeing the ball like a melon – we needed to get him out.

Step forward the legend. Steve Barwick. In the middle of his ten-over mid-innings spell he snared Hooper, caught at short midwicket by the ever-reliable Adrian Dale. We were absolutely over the moon. All you could hear was Viv screaming out something guttural from his massive chest. He was perfectly aware how dangerous Hooper could be, and even though he topped scored with 60, we all felt that he'd missed out. As he sloped off the pitch, disconsolate almost in slow motion, I couldn't help thinking that we now had one hand on the trophy – even though we hadn't yet batted. As I then watched Mark Ealham walking to the middle, I went back to my fielding position at deep cover, and realising that there was still plenty to do, switched back on.

The next 25-odd overs were a dream for us. Our bowlers, as they'd done all season, began to exert a real strangle hold on the opposition batsmen. They shared the wickets between them, taking them at regular intervals, which helped keep the Kent run-rate down for the duration of their innings. Roland and Baz ended with a wicket each, Crofty and Daley put the brakes on mid-innings – each ending up with two scalps, and the excellent Steve Watkin finished with the impressive figures of 3 for 33. When Alan Igglesden managed to squirt the final ball of their innings away for a single, we walked off knowing that 201 would win us our long dreamt of trophy. At almost exactly four an over, this was far from an insurmountable task.

We were now favourites. The bowlers had done their job superbly; it was now down to the batsmen. That meant me. The knot in my stomach returned with a vengeance.

I returned to the safety of the dressing room feeling very ill indeed. I don't remember much about the innings break; I don't think I ate anything, I just had some water. Before going out to field, I had, of course, been nervous – but not worried. I remember looking at Watty, Baz and Crofty though, and seeing the strain on their faces. They had it all to do, and to their everlasting credit they'd done it. As I looked at them now, laughing, smiling – totally relaxed – my paranoia and fear led me to believe that they were glancing over and thinking 'God, Cotts looks worried – if he gets his chance, I hope he's not gonna balls it up for us now after all our hard work.'

The next two hours was as tortured a time as any I can recall. Every shred of self doubt returned. All my old concerns about my inadequacies from my early days at the Swans came flooding back. Was I good enough? Did I deserve to be here? How on earth have I ended up in the same dressing room as Viv Richards? Would I balls it up for everyone?

Crofty broke my trance: 'I just saw your old man and Brayers down there looking out for you. Do you want to go and see them?'

'Yeah, I'll go in a minute,' I said. What I actually meant to say was – 'Shit – no way!' Thinking of my Dad, who was there with Mam and Gail, and Dave, who was there with his wife Deb and his Dad, Derrick – not to mention all the other familiar faces I'd already seen – just added to the weight that was now noticeably heavier on my shoulders. I couldn't let all these people down, I daren't – but still the nerves grew worse, and so did the nausea. There was only one thing for it.

I went to sleep.

Well I tried to anyway. I put my pads on, found a quite corner in the room, lay down and shut my eyes. I tried to retreat into my own little world, and ignore everything that was going on around me. Before I knew it, our hugely reliable openers, Hugh and Jamer, left the dressing room and strode to the wicket. Opening the innings is challenging at the best of times: the ball is hard and new, the pitch has been rolled and is flat and hard, and the bowlers will be really psyched up. A wicket will often fall quite early, and on this occasion, Jamer was the unlucky one: back in the dressing room for 3. He was disconsolate, and I felt genuinely sorry for him. Daley joined Hugh, and they stuck together for about twenty overs or so, and took the score to 84, before Daley was out for a very steady 33.

This brought Matt to the crease. He'd barely been passed fit in the morning, but such was his talent and reputation that all concerned decided, quite rightly, that we had to risk him. We tried to keep the news of his neck injury quiet, but as usual, it leaked out. Unfortunately for Matt, the gamble didn't work and he looked very uncomfortable at the crease and finally succumbed to Duncan Spencer for just 2

Enter King Viv.

As I was due in when the next wicket fell, I started to pull myself together and attempted to banish all my nerves and concentrate on the job in hand. As I watched Viv swagger to the wicket like he was some sort of gladiator about to slaughter the lions, I truly wished I'd been blessed with just an ounce his confidence. Instead, I began to worry again. I could be called upon within a couple of deliveries. I nearly was.

Viv had only been in for a couple of overs and, if I'm totally honest, had scratched around for his seven runs when he attempted a pull shot, mistimed it, and lobbed a catch to a fielder at short midwicket. Shit – I was in. My stomach nearly hit the floor.

The umpire's arm was, however, stretched out horizontally at his side. No ball. A reprieve for Viv. This was going to our day – surely. Hugh and Viv took the score on to 141, until Hugh, who played superbly, was caught in the deep trying to push the score on, and was out for 67, the highest innings in the match.

As I walked down the steps again, and onto the field, I passed Hugh who said something to me. I nodded. I hadn't actually heard a word he said because I was concentrating on walking to the wicket as confidently as my nerves could manage. I felt as if I was treading water, but I managed to take my guard, heard

Viv shout something positive (and loud!) down the wicket and waited for the bowler to come in.

I could hardly grip the bat.

When I entered the fray, we were 141 for 4 off 38 overs chasing 201, which was the biggest total we'd had to chase all year, such had the strength of our bowling and fielding been. That meant we needed 60 to win off twelve overs. The run rate to win at the start of the innings had been four an over, by the time I made it to the crease, Kent had put the brakes on us a bit and our rate had dropped to three-and-a-half. That meant, to win, we'd have to score at five runs an over – not a monumental task by anyone's standards, but throw in the pressure of the situation, the lack of overs to go, and the fact that my central nervous system appeared to be on the verge of shutting down, you can understand the concerns I had at that moment.

I faced my first ball. I managed to jab a bat down on it and it squirted out towards point – no run. Pressure building. Next ball – no run. More pressure. I finally got off the mark from my third ball from Carl Hooper bowling his gentle off-breaks. I built a bit of a reputation by the end of my career as having a decent record against spin bowlers so I started to settle down, and began to nudge the odd single here and there. At the time, I was still hoping that Viv would explode into life, get a quick 40 off twelve balls, and I could retire to the dressing room 5 not out and all the anxieties would be over. Unfortunately it wasn't to be that easy.

The next ball nearly sent me over the edge. Hooper loped in and Viv played a little paddle sweep off his legs, but as he made contact, the ball just bounced slightly higher than he anticipated, and it lobbed straight up in the air off his bat, towards Nigel Llong at a sort of short fine-leg position. It was as if time stood still for me. I stood there, rooted to the spot, watching this ball – containing all Glamorgan's hopes – slowly dropping into the hands of Llong as he moved in to send Viv back to the pavilion. In the split second that the ball looped towards Llong I can't explain the shudder that went through my whole body. I could see that all the hopes were about to be transferred from Viv's broad shoulders to mine, and at that exact moment of my life, I didn't feel that I'd be able to deliver. Then, a truly wonderful thing happened: the ball lost all of its pace, and it dropped out of the sky and hit the ground just short of the despairing Llong. Viv had survived, and no one in the ground was more relieved than me.

After I'd nudged and nurdled my way to six runs came the turning point. Hooper came into bowl, slightly down the leg side, I went down on one knee, and played a powerful slog sweep, which sent the ball flying like a pea to the deep square-leg boundary.

Straight into the hands of Matthew Fleming.

And straight back out and fell to the ground. He'd spilled it. I was still in.

He hurriedly picked up the ball from the grass and flung it in to Steve Marsh the wicketkeeper and captain. I jogged through for the single, and looked back down the wicket at Viv. He didn't say anything – he just looked knowingly at me with his piercing eyes – and coolly nodded at me, before a little grin broke out from his stern exterior.

At that precise moment, everything changed. Every single worry, every feeling of inadequacy, every ounce of stress just slipped from my shoulders. I can't explain to you how often this type of thing happens. In sport, of course, you get your ice men like Bjorn Borg and to a lesser extent Mike Atherton, but largely the rest of us are just like you, affected by the worry of things going wrong and not turning out as we'd hope. But often, something just happens, something to snap you out of your nervous malaise, and then it all just clicks back into place. You get on with what you're paid to do. And that's exactly what happened to me. I started to bat with more freedom. Instead of the bat feeling like a heavy railway sleeper in my hands moments before, now it felt like a natural extension of my body. Everything began to work, my shots gained more timing and power and started to evade fielders, and that most important commodity that all sportsmen need to function, began to surge through me. Confidence. Confidence by the bucket load.

Viv was fantastic. He didn't play the best innings of his career, but the sheer force of his personality came to the fore. Lots of people ask me what batsman talk about in between overs when they meet halfway down the pitch for a chat. To be honest, everyone is different. Some like to make jokes and not discuss the situation at all. Some are neurotic – 'How do I look?' 'How am I playing?' 'Am I timing it well?' Others are more methodical: 'We need at least three fours off the first four balls here,' and so on. Viv, as usual, was different. All he did – extremely loudly – was to tell me how well *I* was doing. We'd approach each other and loudly, for all the Kent players to hear, he would boom in his magnificent Antiguan accent:

'Well played Tony Cotteeeey. Keep this going now huh? All good, all good.' Then he'd punch me on the shoulder, turn and walk back to the crease. It was like being the best mate of the hardest lad in the school. This very public display of his faith in me made me feel ten feet tall.

One over later came the moment that changed the match. We knew that one big over would in all probability deliver us the game. Hooper again came in to Viv, who played a beautiful leg glance down towards the long-leg boundary. With the fielder in hot pursuit, I ran the first two runs as quickly as I could, before gambling on a third. I just went for it, hell for leather, and was a quarter of the way down the track whilst Viv was still turning at the other end. He heard my call, looked up and saw me, sprinting to pinch the extra run. He could see I was putting myself up for sacrifice, and jogged through and let me go.

Halfway down I knew I was in trouble. Two more strides and the ball was arrowing toward the stumps: flat, fast and on target. Shit, big trouble. I just put my head down, grounded my bat and slid it toward the crease at absolute full pelt, just as the ball landed in Marsh's gloves and he whipped off the bails. At that exact moment my bat broke the line. I was in. I was certain. You always know – no matter how tight it is – you always know. But what about the umpire?

I heard a huge appeal go up from the whole of Kent, but the groans and silence that followed indicated that the umpire agreed with me. My sprint had taken me about twenty yards past the wicket keeper before I stopped, turned and began the stroll back to the crease. I then heard this huge whoop coming from 40 yards away, and looked up to see Viv punching the air with delight. Again, he was publicly recognising what I'd done, and again, succeeded in making me feel ten feet tall. I was so pleased and proud I wanted to burst out laughing. Next ball I played a fine late cut that sped to the boundary for four. Viv marched down the pitch to me, and, loud as ever, punched me on the arm and shouted 'Biiiiiig shot' at the top of his voice. Next ball was a single, and then a wide to Viv that also went for four. A couple more wides were followed by a couple of singles that totally changed the complexion of the match. At the start of the over we needed 33 runs to win off 36 balls. By the end of it we only needed 17 from 30. It was certainly ours to lose now.

The next over saw me get another boundary, despite Alan Igglesden's best efforts on the boundary, which again saw Viv punching the air and screaming 'Big shot again, little man' at the top of his voice. I don't think I've ever been so pumped up in my life. If only I could have bottled that feeling and taken a swig of it every so often for the rest of my days!

We then continued to reduce the target until we entered the 47th over needing just five to win. By now the ground was reverberating to the sound of Welsh voices singing, 'Hymns and Arias' and 'Calon Lân', not to mention 'There's only two Tony Cotteys' – I don't think I've ever felt so proud. I remember looking up into the stand where my Mam and Dad were sat, trying to find them. Dave, who was sitting next to them, confirmed later that when they saw me looking up, Dad had tears rolling down his face. When I teased him about this later on he said not to take the piss – he was just 'full of emulsion'.

Viv walked down the pitch and spoke. I can't report a pearl of wisdom here, or a moment of clarity or a personal message to me from this legend that I'll be able to take to my grave. No, he just said rather gruffly and sternly, 'This is it now, this is our time, this is it.' Then he banged me hard right on the top of my helmet with his fist, pushing it down so much that I looked like Freddie 'Parrot Face' Davis. It was all starting to get a bit surreal.

Viv played the first ball away for a single. I took guard and waited for Duncan Spencer to begin his sprint to the wicket. Interesting character, Spencer. He was Australian, extremely talkative out in the middle, seldom in a complimentary fashion though – and by far the quickest of the Kent bowlers. His first ball was very quick and I let it pass through to the wicket keeper. As he walked back to his mark for the next ball, I had a gut feeling he was going to try to stick one right up my nose. As he released the ball, I took a small step back. In that split second I resolved to hook him, whatever happened – hopefully for four or six – however fast or high the ball came. The ball did in fact pitch short, and in truth was a bit quicker than I thought. 'Shit – I'm in trouble here,' I thought, but stayed committed to the shot. I got a big top edge to it, and the ball flew about sixty feet in the air – straight over the wicket-keeper's head – and I watched it bounce just inside the boundary rope and smash into the sight screens for four.

We'd won!

And I'd scored the winning runs. Me! Batting with Viv Richards! Told you it was all a bit surreal.

The rest is a bit of a blur. Viv dashed across and we embraced, then sprinted off to beat the crowds who were streaming on. All hell broke loose in the dressing room. There was the loudest cheering I remember, slaps on the back and the general hi jinx that go with such a victory.

Then Viv arrived.

He was crying like a baby in an outpouring of emotion that shocked even the most hardened soul in our dressing room. He hugged Hugh, wouldn't let him go as I recall, and was saying 'I love you, I love you' over and over. I don't think Hugh knew what to do so he just kept hold of him and laughed.

In hindsight – as I was to appreciate in altogether different circumstances eleven years later – Viv was not only celebrating a real underdog victory, but was also saying goodbye to the most active part of his life. Apart from the final day of the now pointless four-day game that had to be finished tomorrow, Viv's legendary career was over, and he'd done something that very few sportsmen –

even the very best – get to do: leave on the highest note possible – with a championship win.

The rest of the evening was memorable to say the least. First we had the presentation of the trophy on the balcony, the obligatory champagne party, with more being wasted than drunk. I remember seeing a good mate from Swansea, Paul Gallagher – known to all as the leotard-wearing bank manager Larg – under the balcony and lots of other familiar, extremely happy Welsh men and women singing their hearts out and sharing in our moment of joy. Without them it would have meant nothing at all, it was just a joy and privilege to have played a small part in making them so pleased. It was a very long night of celebration, and was one of the happiest nights of my life.

Three days later, on the Wednesday back at home in Swansea, I went to collect the morning mail, and in amongst the bills was a pristine white envelope, with Mr P.A. Cottey typed out on the front. I opened it eagerly.

It was from my kit sponsor Gunn and Moore, one of the most famous cricket suppliers in the world. I saw the letterhead and my heart leaped – bonuses, surely! Bonuses for good performance were not uncommon from your sponsor, but in those days, they were usually reserved only for the top test-match players, but in certain cases payments were made to lesser players like me. I'd just won the Sunday League, after all! I read on eagerly.

They were ending my contract and were threatening legal action.

I nearly died.

Leading up to the final weeks of the season I'd borrowed a bat from Crofty. It was perfect for me, and just felt better than any of the four Gunn and Moore bats that I had. This was no slight on Gunn and Moore or their equipment in any way, it was just that when I'd used the bat the first time, at Leicester in early August, I scored 105. The scores that followed whilst using Crofty's bat were 63, 44 not out and the 79 I scored the day before the Canterbury finale. The only time I failed to get runs in this period was against Hampshire in the four-day game that began on August 19, when I scored 6 and 0 – and that was when I'd reverted back to the Gunn and Moore bat. It persuaded me to use Crofty's bat again in the Sunday League game that weekend against Hampshire, and I scored 75 not out! It was at that point that I decided to stick with Crofty's bat for the rest of the season. To be honest, this decision was based purely on superstition more than anything else (I still salute magpies to this day!), not that I would have admitted it to anyone then. Like most neurotic sportsmen, I was desperate to get any advantage I could!

What I didn't consider of course was how Gunn and Moore would react. Their letter went on to outline how disappointed they were with my behaviour, how I had breached my contract with them, amid the full glare of publicity – the match was televised live across the UK – and that, and any commercial value they might have made out of me batting at the most crucial time, hitting the winning runs, and running off with Viv, had been lost totally.

The letter ended stating they were considering their position in relation to pursuing legal action against me, and would in all probability be terminating my contract with them due to this breach.

I was stunned.

Of course, I was guilty on all charges. Mind you, what I had done was not uncommon practice among pros at the time. Seeking to find that extra little advantage, players would often swap bats in their search for that 'lucky' one. There's not a pro cricketer born who hasn't taken a shine to a colleague's bat, tried it out in the nets, and then tried it out further during a proper innings. I know of players who played for England for years who had lucrative sponsorship deals with certain companies, but who often reverted to a 'special' bat, not related to that company, but simply peeled the original stickers off, and replaced them with those of the sponsor. It was an extremely common occurrence, and I'd never heard of anyone being caught for it.

Until me that is.

It was my own fault I guess because on the Saturday of the game, Matt asked me what bat I was going to use and when I told him, he mentioned that it was bald (had no stickers on it) and asked what was I going to do. I told him that I might stick the Gunn and Moore ones on, but it wasn't a big deal to either of us. Even though I knew it was going to be televised, I never in my wildest dreams thought I'd take centre stage in the match, and had I not batted – which can often be the case when you bat at number six in a one-day game – Gunn and Moore would have been none the wiser.

I fretted over it for a couple of days, then bit the bullet and rang the guy I had always dealt with at Gunn and Moore. He was quite cold with me straight away and continued the line about legal action, how I'd lost them a huge amount in exposure, and how that occasion was probably the only one time that they'd ever get an opportunity to make money out of 'a player like you', and I'd lost it all. He then asked me why I hadn't used it.

I stuttered for a moment. I didn't want to tell the truth I felt enough of a prat already without admitting that it had been down too superstition , so I told him that I'd only taken one Gunn and Moore bat with me to Kent. That much was true. But it had broken in my first innings knock of 79. Not true.

I can still hear his response now.

'Broken? What do you mean broken? Our bats don't usually break. Where did it break?'

I started to panic, so I fumbled a bit and said it had cracked on the splice and the edge.

'The splice *and* the edge? I've never heard of that happening before. You'd better send it up for us to examine.'

I had little option but to agree.

About half an hour later, Dave came round to the house, and saw me trying to break one of my bats against the garden wall. I usually gave him a bat at the end of a season, and even after I'd explained what had happened and why I was doing it, he was still more horrified that his next freebie bat was about to be smashed to bits in front of his eyes, rather than the possibility of me being taken to the High Court!

As it turns out, I needn't have resorted to vandalism. After another couple of phonecalls, the matter was laid to rest. Having frightened the life out of me. Gunn and Moore didn't carry out their threat to end my contract, and confirmed they'd be taking no further action. I was so relieved. I'd learnt my lesson, and was just glad it was all over. I'm more than happy here to apologise publicly again to them all at Gunn and Moore, I shouldn't have done what I did, and I'll happily go on record now and say what excellent bats they made for me, and how well they always looked after me.

There was an ironic end to the story though. Firstly, the bat I tried to break proved to be unbreakable (another testament to its quality!), and was quickly snaffled by Dave for use in Swansea's Guildhall League the following season. It was such a good bat, even he got runs with it. Then, years later, when playing for Sussex away at Northampton, the Newbury bat I was using at the time broke when I was on about 9 or 10, and as I only had that one with me I had to borrow a bat to continue, Murray Goodwin coming to the rescue with one of his. I went on and scored 112.

The bat I borrowed?

Gunn and Moore, of course.

CHAPTER ELEVEN

A Land Down Under

A massive part of becoming an effective batsman is learning to deal with all the stuff that goes on around you in between deliveries. Whether you are a batsman or a bowler, the moment the ball is in play you are doing what your talent and ability has put you there to do. On average, this actual moment lasts about five seconds, from the bowler starting to run in, the batsman hitting the ball, the ball being fielded, returned to the keeper and thus going dead again. When you consider an average day's play may contain 90 overs, and last, say, six-and-a-half hours, that means 540 balls are bowled in a day. This means that the ball is 'live' for only 45 minutes during that day. That leaves an awful lot of time for the mind to wander and worry about other stuff.

Some deal with it better than others, of course. Mike Atherton mastered the knack of switching on and off. He'd begin concentrating the moment the bowler began to move, then switch off the instant the ball became dead again. As such, he was never flustered by sledging or affected by the pressure of the occasion in general. Lots of people believe that the reason that Colin Montgomerie is yet to win a Major is that he has 'rabbit ears', and has reacted and lost focus because of things he may have overheard yards away. I've no idea if that's true, but if it is, all I can say is that I doubt whether Colin would have played Test cricket , because the higher up the professional ladder you go, the greater the abuse. The Aussies began this approach years ago and perfected the art under Steve Waugh and called it 'Mental Disintegration'. They were the first to recognise that cricket has a massive amount of 'dead' time during the day, and they would use this time to attempt to get into a batsman's head. Nothing was taboo – apart from racism – and everyone was fair game. In my case my lack of height was the obvious target. But wives and loved ones were not left out of it either –

'Hey Shorty! Tell that pretty wife of yours that if she wants to try a full-size man, I'm staying in room 216.' Cue the laughter from his mates, followed quickly by 'Oh, I forgot – she knows the number, she was with me last night.'

You'd be amazed by the number of people affected by this sort of stuff. And the minute a batsman showed that it had got to him, that's when the opposition would really crank it up. They would then deliver the most crude sexual insults to the batsman, who could only stand there with steam coming out of his ears, desperate to turn around and just smash his bat across someone's head. Then, before he knew it, the ball would be 'live' again, and he would have to switch on for his five seconds of fun. I've witnessed plenty of players – some with much more ability than me – who have been lost to the game because of their failure to handle the 'dead' time.

When I broke into the Glamorgan team, I was really lucky. I'd come from the footballing background of Swansea City where not only were you abused by fellow players verbally as a matter of course either in training or a match situation, but opposition players took no prisoners either, mentally as well as physically. Added to that was the treatment I'd endured from Phil Boersma, who from day one basically set out to break you. His point being: if you could put up with him and rise above it, at least mentally you'd have the equipment to succeed as a professional footballer. As much as I absolutely hated Boersma at the time, I have to admit that without him, I very much doubt if I'd have mentally hacked it as a cricketer. When you've been slagged off by Boey for the 'Way you looked at me' or 'The way you collected those bibs in', some fella making lewd jokes about your wife become pathetically tame in comparison. I never thought I'd ever admit it, but I owe Boey a hell of a lot. I'm guessing that all that is the sporting equivalent of the army's square-bashing at the hands of some obnoxious sergeant major

However, in addition to those early mental lessons, there was still another grounding I would need in my quest for a successful cricketing career, one that was often described as going into the Lions Den. The lions den in question was grade cricket in Australia.

I could write you a list as long as both arms of England test players who spent a couple of seasons of their formative years playing out the winters in the Lions Den. The most famous is probably Alec Stewart, who has often acknowledged how his seasons playing grade cricket in Australia gave him the mental tools necessary to play internationally. He believes that without that grounding, he'd never had the career he had of over a hundred tests for England. I found Stewie a really great guy, but on the pitch he played his cricket as hard as anyone. I don't mean the base insults or anything like that; rather that he played to win every second of every match, yet was the first to acknowledge an opponent's achievements during the match. He was the total pro, and I must admit I tried to follow his lead in my own career.

I first went to Australia in the winter of 1986. I was extremely lucky as Glamorgan's wonderful voluntary benefactors, the St Helen's Balconeers, based in Swansea, picked me as a recipient of their annual young players' grant, and covered my airfare to Australia. I'd known for some time I'd be going, and, as such, had made a final decision with regard to my football career. I was still playing in the Welsh League at the time, and was picking up £50 or £60 per game, which was very useful. But the season I departed for my winter in Australia meant I didn't kick a ball that winter, and would hardly ever play again. Given the part that football had played in my life, this was difficult to imagine. Nonetheless, I knew that my future was cricket, and therefore I saved as much as I could throughout the season, and left with £2,000 in my pocket for the winter. I went with Phil North, our left-arm spinner, and we headed off to Penrith in Sydney. I'd read a bit about Sydney, and loved the look of the place. The harbour is simply majestic, and I couldn't believe I was going to be living there for six months.

I wasn't.

Penrith is an hour in-land from Sydney. The further in-land you get, the hotter and drier it becomes, and when we arrived in Penrith, I thought Northy and I were going to pass out. It is a town of about 170,000 people and grew up as a travelling post in the nineteenth century as a result of the railway arriving there in the 1860s. I'd never describe it as a one-horse town, but Sydney harbour it was not! I remember the first walk Northy and I took along Penrith's main street. We were swaggering along like a pair of superstar jetsetters when I noticed something odd about the back of his white t-shirt. I thought I saw it move. Then I squinted in the sun and saw that it was covered in flies. I counted at least 25 before I pointed it out to Northy, who proceeded to scream and swish them away like Norman Wisdom – so much for our jet-set image! I'll never forget those bloody flies – they were absolutely huge. They followed you everywhere but were so big that they were quite slow, and one of our beer pastimes was catching the fat ones. Such is the glamour of overseas travel.

One of the first locals I was to meet was Michael Wholohan. He remains one of the biggest characters I've met on my travels and some of his antics are legendary. He's earned a living out of sport – I'm not sure how the hell he does it – but he's always had the knack of making friends with people who go on to achieve fame in the game. Angus Fraser is a mate, as is Glenn McGrath, not to mention plenty of top-class Rugby League players. As recently as 2005, I had a call from him saying that he was in Wales staying with a mate, and would I like to go out for a drink with him up in Porthcawl where this mate lived. Never one to turn down a night-out, off I trotted and ended up spending a lovely evening with

Whoolie, and discovered that his mate was none other than Scott Johnson, the Welsh Rugby coach who was about to become embroiled in one of the great sagas in Welsh Rugby history. I wouldn't be at all surprised if Whoolie had a hand in it!

We quickly became big mates in Australia, and I never ceased to be amazed by the number of people Whoolie knew, nor the scrapes he would find himself in. Like the one at the Penrith Panthers Rugby League Club. Now I don't know how many British Rugby clubs you've been to, but generally – you've been to one and you've been to them all. By and large they are neat, small buildings that sit at the side of the pitch with a bar and a lounge and various items of memorabilia displayed on the walls, along with gold-leafed lists of past captains and presidents. Penrith was just slightly different. It basically formed part of a massive entertainment complex of three nightclubs, several restaurants and pubs, some shops and an enormous marble-floored foyer.

One of the pre-match rituals on a Saturday match day – organised by Whoolie, of course – was to go to the nightclub at 8.30 in the morning, to buy our tickets for entry after the game that night. It would get so busy that if we waited until after play, we simply wouldn't get in. I was all for just going home and having an early night, but just went along to be sociable. (Yeah right.) On this particular occasion Whoolie came up with a master plan, based on a feat of such endurance that he was certain that it had never been done before, and would surely make us all legends for ever.

Now I should point out, that for all its sporting excellence and professionalism, Australia remains the nation that gave us both Merv Hughes and lager-drinking world-record holder David Boon. Boon is still revered as the man who broke Rodney Marsh's long standing record of drinking 44 cans of lager on the non-stop flight from Australia to England for an Ashes series, and his record of 54 cans still stands. I think the phrase 'Work hard, Play Hard' appears somewhere in the Aussie Constitution. Whoolie certainly bought into this concept big time. We were to play a two-day weekend match for Penrith Under 21s against Manly of Sydney, and his plan centred on not going to sleep from waking on Saturday morning until going to bed on Sunday night/Monday morning. This would be punctuated by spending Saturday Night in the nightclub and then returning there on Sunday night, celebrating hopefully both a win in the match and also this unforgettable feat of staying power. Just for the purposes of team bonding you understand, we all agreed to go along with his plan. We had a decent day in the field on the Saturday, and, armed with our nightclub tickets, we set about getting some post-match refreshments! After an hour or two, Whoolie went missing. A short while later, as we wondered where he was, the doors to the pub swung open, in he burst and shouted 'C'mon you lot – time for the club!'

Do you remember Wal in *Crocodile Dundee* with the wide-brimmed hat, khaki waistcoat, khaki shorts, socks pulled up to his knees, and finished off with a pristine pair of suede desert boots? Well that's what was now beckoning us to join him in Penrith's plushest nightclub. I just shook my head and thought 'This is going to be a hell of a long night!' We proceeded to the usual drinking games and songs, and had made it to about 4am, when we all started to flag. A couple of the boys just bolted and left, and one of those who remained asked if anyone had seen Whoolie? None of us had and we realised that no one else had seen him for a couple of hours. The bastard! He'd taken us as complete mugs and had probably been home, tucked up in bed for ages. We finished our drinks – waste not want not – and called a halt to our mammoth endurance challenge. The prospect of having to play cricket in 90-degree heat in about six hours' time started to sink in with me.

We came out into the large foyer of the complex and blinked as our beer-filled eyes got used to the brighter lighting. As usual there was a large display right in the centre of the foyer, cordoned off by thick, regal, red-velvet rope, linked to golden poles. In my time in Penrith everything appeared in this display area, from cars to kitchens to speedboats. This time, on a three-foot pedestal platform, under soft lighting was a magnificent, solid-oak, king-sized, four-poster bed.

In it, fast asleep, tucked up and cuddling a pillow, still with his bush-tucker trial hat on, was Whoolie. How he'd snuck in past the security, I don't know. He'd even taken his boots off and placed them neatly at the side of the bed! We just left him there sleeping like a baby. He would have to deal with the consequences in the morning – as indeed we would have to, chasing a cricket ball around under a baking sun. Not a good day.

The structure of the Australian game is far removed from the one in this country, and if it taught me one thing it was that, as a batsman, I had to value my wicket. This was less and less true of the young players I saw coming through toward the end of my career. As a batsman in a typical two-week period of first-class cricket in this country, you pretty much know that you are going to bat, usually twice, over the period of a four-day game. Then you'll probably have a one-day game for another innings then back to a four-day game – that's another two – then a Sunday League game again, with a few days off in between. That means in about two weeks, weather permitting, you know that you'll probably have six attempts to get a couple of big scores.

In the same time frame in Australia, you'd get one chance.

Their whole structure is based around grade cricket, which sits just beneath their equivalent of first-class cricket, state cricket. As they've got so few states compared to our counties, many of their top players drop down to play for their clubs in Grade One. The way grade cricket works is that a match starts on Saturday morning at 11.00 and the day will last 100 overs from that point. That day, Team A will attempt to bat the whole day to get the biggest possible score. For Team B, and batters like me, that means a whole day in the field in the scorching sun with little or no chance of having a knock. Play ends for the day with Team A declaring at whatever total they achieved after 100 overs, and the game resumes, wait for it . . . a week later!

So there I am. I've waited all week for my game, I've fielded all day in the most oppressive heat you can imagine, then have to wait another week to have my reward. Next Saturday I stride to the crease, play an extravagant shot to get off the mark, get caught at slip and slope off *via* a barrage of abuse in which 'short pommie bastard' features prominently. Worse than that though, I have to wait at least a week, maybe two, if we lose the toss in the next game, to get back to the crease. After you've done that once or twice, you certainly keep the extravagant shots hidden away until you're well into your innings. That's what I mean about valuing your wicket.

And in Australia, even the humble tail-ender valued his. During my career I played with lots of bowlers who revelled in their lack of prowess with the bat. It was often good fun watching them try to heave at a ball, adopting a 'six-and-out' approach that more often ended in 'out' more than 'six'! In Australia it was totally different: stands of 80 to 100 were more than common occurrences for the final two or three wickets, as everyone knew there were so few opportunities to actually have a bat. I'm not suggesting this approach could ever work here, but valuing my wicket became an important development in the maintenance of my discipline as a batsman back home.

When I first arrived in Oz, I was placed in grade three out of six. As I'd already played first-class cricket, I must admit I was more than a little put out at this. 'Don't they know who I am?' – well frankly, no, of course they bloody didn't. And they wouldn't have cared anyway if they did. There were absolutely no favours in Australia, it really was sink or swim. If I failed for a game or two in grade three, I'd be dropped to four – simple as that, reputation or no.

In my first game I scored 13. I didn't bat again for three Saturdays. When I walked out that next time, I was really under pressure because not only did I know I'd need a high score to start climbing the grades, but another low score could see me slip down to grade four. Luckily I managed 90-odd, and was subsequently pushed up a grade. But I must admit, after that first match against Hawkesbury in my third-grade debut, I did wonder what I'd let myself in for. When I walked to the crease and took my guard, I looked round to see where the wicketkeeper was standing, as I always did throughout my career, to be greeted by a human panda. Underneath a white sunhat was this stocky guy, with his nose smashed all over his face and two of the biggest black eyes I'd ever seen. At the end of the over I walked to meet my partner in the middle and commented that the keeper must've been in a car crash.

'Nah, mate,' came the reply. 'He got smashed in the face by a batsman last week for too much sledging – hit a bit of a raw nerve, apparently. The batsman's had a life ban I think.'

Oh great, I thought. It wasn't so much the state of the wicket-keeper that bothered me; it was more the matter of fact way that my batting partner described it. I hoped it wasn't the sign of things to come. Thankfully it wasn't.

At that stage in my career, if I'm honest, grade two was probably where I was at, but I was still striving for grade one. My promotion to the top flight was not achieved by results alone; I benefited from grade-one players being called up by the state side – and there was also the chance to stay in the side, if I had done well, when the state boys came back. This is why I like the Aussie system: it may have been tough if you had a bad run of form or a couple of bad umpiring decisions, but they really rewarded success and as a young up-and-coming player. Even if you started in grade six, the path to the top was clearly marked out for you incrementally. This performance-driven approach to cricket made a huge impression on me.

The other bonus from this first trip away from the apron strings was the independence wake-up call. You basically had to do everything: washing, cleaning, cooking, ironing and everything associated with domestic life yourself. Now before I upset the politically-correct reader – of course, men should do these things anyway – it's fair to say that back in 1986, if you took a poll of young, up-and-coming British sportsman, asking how many carried out these duties regularly, I'm not certain they would've reached the top three answers on *Family Fortunes*. What it did for me was add to the disciplines I was now steadily picking up. I'd already had my grounding at Swansea City with Tosh and Boey; I'd had the grease-monkey lessons from my dad; I'd learnt to value my wicket more than ever, and now I realised that there were other duties to be done that enabled me to stand on my own two feet. Australia taught me a hell of a lot.

But I never actually got paid for playing, so in between cricket, I also had a few jobs. These were usually pretty unspectacular, but two are worth recording: indoor-cricket umpire and my spell engaged with 'Aussie Fluff'.

In Penrith there was a large indoor-cricket centre where there were several 'courts' encased in springy netting where six-a-side matches were played. The netting created almost a cage effect as it went upwards and formed a roof above the court. Behind the bowler's arm at one end, and outside the netting, was what can best be described as a tennis umpire's chair, just a bit higher. Whoolie and I got jobs as umpires, and basically we had to don an identification top, climb to the top of our perch and basically manage the game. Not only did we act as the sole arbiter of the rules –LBW's, run outs etc. – but we had to score, and also work the large electronic scoreboard. And such was the pace these games were played at, I sometimes lost the plot completely. Despite these troubles, Whoolie and I started to get the hang of it, and managed to work it so that we always umpired on adjacent courts so we could have a quick chat or a laugh. True to form, Whoolie soon came up with another grand plan.

Each match would last sixteen, eight-ball overs, and after the seventh ball of the over, it was our job to call out 'Final ball, gentlemen' so that the players knew exactly where they were. The abuse we used to take from irate players was almost too much to take at times, so we'd always try to nick a ball from the over, and call last ball after six not seven, thereby shortening the game. And most times we'd get away with it. Whoolie's grand plan however was to see which one out of the two of us could call the shortest over. We'd got down to six several times, and I think Whoolie had called a five once, but getting lower than that would be quite perilous. These were intensely-contested games, after all. Brave as we were, we decided we'd try to do it on ladies night, when there was less chance of abuse if we got rumbled. We both took our respective positions and began, and soon I realised how tricky this was going to be because the ladies were quite intense themselves. Whoolie had already been corrected after trying a six-ball over, so this was going to be quite a tough challenge to win. Just then there was a bit of controversy in my court: one of the ladies was claiming a catch that had obviously bounced before she caught it and a couple of the girls were going at it hammer and tongs, even after I'd given it not out. I thought it was going to come to blows at one point when the phrase 'Cheating little bitch' was thrown out there for good measure. I sensed my opportunity – 'Ladies, c'mon let's get back to the game, she's not out, so let's carry on. Last ball, ladies.'

I caught Whoolie's face from the corner of my eye, I'd called this after three balls and no one batted an eyelid. He was gutted – a four-ball over; he'd never beat that.

Never underestimate Mike Wholohan, however.

About five minutes later on his court, as mine was taking a break after someone got hurt, and I was basking in the glory of certain victory in our bet, a lady ran in to bowl the *first* ball of the new over. She delivered a full-length delivery – some of these girls were very decent cricketers – and the batter carved it straight to a fielder. Her batting partner, missing this important fact, charged down the track for a run, the batter – horrified – screamed at her to go back, which her partner tried to do, but only succeeded in slipping on her backside as she turned. In the panic, the fielder threw the ball to the wrong end which gave the stranded lady the slightest of chances to get back in. As the ball was hurled now by the wicketkeeper to the bowler who fumbled it, the lady batter threw herself at the crease and succeeded in taking out the stumps, the bowler and a covering fielder, just as the bowler appeared to break the stumps. A huge appeal of 'Ooooowzaaaat' went up to Whoolie. He paused. And then, in the regal accent of some eighteenth-century English landowner, politely but firmly said – 'Not Out.' I thought the roof was going to cave in as all the fielding team started to abuse the shite out of Whoolie. Yet there he sat, defiantly, saying 'Not out ladies, not out.'

As the abuse subsided after a couple of minutes and they all returned to their positions, Whoolie then called 'Last ball, ladies.'

I couldn't believe my ears! Surely they would lynch him. Only one fielder turned round and looked a bit quizzically at Whoolie, who just motioned to her to play on as if he was swatting away a fly. The bowler took a wicket with the next delivery, all was forgotten and Whoolie had got away with a two-ball over, which in my opinion should be a Guinness World Record. I don't like losing bets generally, but sometimes you've got to accept when you're in the presence of greatness.

My time as a cricket umpire ended unpleasantly though. The graveyard shift was Thursday night at 10.30 when the 'eighth graders' played. They were generally pissed by the time they got on court, couldn't play anyway at the best of times, and used the session as a 'Let's abuse a pommie' training course. Not long into the game, after plenty of stick already, I turned down an LBW appeal and the bowler just swung around and told me to 'Fuck off'. I just responded by sending him off, which in the scheme of things didn't go down too well. The team refused to carry on until I reinstated him, which I obviously refused to do. The stand-off lasted five or so minutes, during which one older guy just kept abusing the hell out of me.

I sat there for a moment or two, then thought to myself – 'What would my Dad do now?' At which point this guy shouted

'Why don't you come down from your chair, you pommie dwarf,' so I did what my dad would have done, got down from my chair, and walked through the breach in the net – closely followed by Whoolie, I'm thankful to add, and proceeded to take part in what can best be described as a 'vigorous scuffle'. Everyone soon pulled us apart, and I just took off my umpire's top, threw it at the guy and walked out – and am pleased to say, never went back. It really wasn't worth the hassle.

However self-satisfied I felt about my actions, it did leave me with one major problem – I no longer had an income. I wasn't overly concerned though, as by now, Gail had joined me on a six-month holiday visa and was working at a bank in Sydney. We hadn't seen a huge amount of each other either because she left at 6.30am and got back by 5, then I'd leave at 5.30pm for the umpiring, and would get back at midnight. So part of me thought I'd take this opportunity to act as a man of leisure for a while and sponge off Gail.

I think my plan lasted two days before Gail handed me a local newspaper where she'd circled plenty of vacancies, including one with a company called 'Aussie Fluff'. Gail pointed out we needed all the money we could get, and, suitably chastised, I rang the owner of the company one Mr Steve Morea.

I went to meet him, we had a chat and he offered me the job. Basically he'd invented loft insulation designed to keep the heat out – not in. It was based on pumping recycled newspaper into the loft space under the tin bungalow roofs, which then provided a barrier to the sun's heat during the day. The first part of the job saw my partner Mick and I call up to the local dump to collect the bundles of newspapers from the back of the recycling area. Remember I mentioned the size of the flies? Well, they were nothing compared to the size of the rats! When we moved these bundles, these massive bastards would squeal and scurry off everywhere. It still makes my skin creep thinking about it.

Once we'd filled up the van with newspaper, Mick and I would go off and meet Steve. The process involved driving another van to the bungalow concerned, parking up outside, and unravelling the massive hose which would pump in the insulation: the reclaimed newspaper now shredded and mixed with some sort of dry chemical. Now if you think of a fireman's hose as being the circumference of a cricket ball, this hose was more like a football, and had to be secured tightly under one armpit. It was about 30 feet long, and after removing some tiles and cutting through the felt in the roof, both the operator and the hose would enter the loft space from the outside. The plan was then to manoeuvre as far as possible toward the opposite corner of the loft, give the shout for the hose to be switched on, then pump this gunk, best described as chemically-treated confetti, throughout the loft, until there was a covering about three feet deep, levelling it out with a big stick as you retreated. For some reason, you had to pull up the manhole loft cover from inside the house to allow air to come in from the hallway below. Then when all was done, you'd close the loft cover, leave a bag of the confetti filled to the brim as spare in case we'd missed any areas, and then back out along with the hose through the hole in the roof. Once outside we'd reaffix the felt, replace the tiles or tin sheet and job done. Simple as that. For this I was paid 600 dollars for four shifts a week which was great money. It was bloody hard work, and we could only work between 6am and 11am due to the dangers of heat exhaustion. The other main difficulty was the lack of headroom that forced you to squat your way through the whole process. Yes, even me!

Steve made sure he accompanied us on our first half dozen jobs to make sure we were doing it right, and also because it was so bloody dangerous too – the hose took some real hanging on to when the confetti was being pumped out, and if you did let it go it would spin around like a demented snake. On one of my early jobs with Steve though, it wasn't the house that worried me, it was something of the canine variety. Steve and I were up on the roof, and had removed some of the lower tiles, and cut through the felt for access to the loft. As I walked along the roof to help Steve, I slipped on the early morning dew on the roof, lost my balance totally, and started to arrow down toward the ground. It wasn't that high – about 12 feet I guess – but it would've hurt, I know. However, my foot snagged in one of the holes, and I was there dangling down, almost waiting to fall. Then I saw them. Two Dobermans who'd been locked in the back yard by the owner in case, as he so beautifully put it, 'They bloody well kill you.'

They went absolutely ballistic. They were jumping up as high as they could, twisting in the air as they did, teeth bared, saliva spraying everywhere, but thankfully for me, I was just out of their reach. Believe me, I really started to panic, here I was looking head first at something out of *Cujo*. I started to scream, and that's when I felt the firm grip of Steve's hands on my ankle and he hauled me back up onto the roof. We laughed about it and I thought later, well if that's the worse thing that's going to happen to me on this job – then that's fine.

Unfortunately, that wasn't to be the case.

A few weeks further on I had a job at a posh bungalow on the outskirts of Penrith. Mick and I arrived together, and Steve said he'd be joining us later on. I did what I had to do to prepare everything, stepped into the loft, got in position, crouched down right in the corner of the loft and shouted to Mick to start feeding the paper into the compressor on the van, and waited the ten seconds for the first lot to start getting pumped through. Once the hose went 'live', you started to earn your money and I held onto it tightly and started to level out the insulation with my stick and scuttle backwards. Halfway across I remembered I hadn't opened the internal hatch yet, and that must have been why I was having trouble damping it down. I put down my stick, reached down and flipped open the hatch, I then leant forward to pick up my stick. As I stretched for it, so I lost my balance and in an attempt to stay upright I kind of hopped to my left side onto a beam, but in so doing lost my grip on the hose, and, subsequently, my footing. I went straight through the open manhole. Somehow I'd managed to grab hold of the beam and was hanging half in, half out of the ceiling of the hallway. With that, as I desperately clung on, screaming for Mick to switch off the hose as it was snaking above me, the hose just dipped and shot through the hole beside me and started spewing chemically-treated confetti into the hall of this guy's immaculate bungalow. I kept screaming and had managed to grab the hose whilst hanging there, but was powerless to do anything else than watch it belching out gallons of this shredded paper that was neatly filling up one part of the hallway which was now up to the ceiling with insulation. By now the owner had seen what was happening and he was outside screaming at Mick to switch it off and at Steve who had also now turned up. Thankfully, the hose went limp, and I was able to drop to the floor, my shoulder in agony, to survey my damage.

It was as if someone had just held a Mardi Gras in the guy's hall the day before, and had now swept up all the confetti left behind, right up to the ceiling at one end. There was no wall to be seen. The owner was absolutely going nuts, but my boss was brilliant, he just kept saying 'Calm down, mate, calm down, it's only paper we'll clean it up in no time.'

'Calm down? Calm fucking down?' screamed the man.

He came inside, brushed past me, swung open a door to the bedroom, and in there was a man painting the ceiling, totally unfazed by the chaos around him. The owner turned to my boss 'This is the nursery for my daughter who was born yesterday, and this bastard fell through that ceiling the day before yesterday when he went up to fix my ventilation pipe, so don't tell me to calm down, my wife's coming out from hospital tomorrow and now this happens – I can't take it any more.'

At that point I quietly made my exit and went back to the van to join Mick, who was absolutely pissing himself: 'Welcome to the club Tony – it's happened to me twice.'

I've often wondered if Aussie Fluff is still a going concern, out there filling lofts as we speak. There was one more serious problem about my time with the

Fluff, however. My left knee started hurting. It got so bad that I started to have problems with the feeling in my lower leg and foot. I left it for a while, but after a few weeks I was really struggling. I woke up one morning and couldn't move my foot at all. I got out of bed and stood up but when I moved forward, my leg would move OK, but my foot would just hang there at a sort of limp 45-degree angle. I had to lift my leg really high to avoid tripping myself up as I walked. I knew straight away I had a problem.

The club arranged for me to see a specialist the next day. He put it down to all the squatting I'd been doing in the lofts and that in effect the nerves in my knee which aided movement of the foot had been crushed. He gave me a leg brace which he said would keep the foot level, but immobile, and would stop it dropping. This would mean that I could walk and even run, but was still very painful on the knee, and quite cumbersome to get used to. At the end of the consultation, he stated that I was suffering from Anterior Compartment Syndrome, and announced brightly that the effect of the crushing of the nerves meant that for all intents and purposes the calf muscle had sheered off from the foot, leading to the described instability, and in his opinion was likely to be a lifelong condition.

A lifelong condition? All of a sudden I felt a long way from home.

I asked him to clarify. He basically repeated what he'd already said, casually adding for good measure that my cricket career would probably be over. I didn't know what to do. I had a game the next day, and also an under-21 limited over match on the Sunday. I instantly went into denial, didn't tell Gail the full outcome of the consultancy, strapped up my foot within the calliper and played both games. Not only did I look run Forest Gump, I played like him too. I was really worried. I finally plucked up the courage to tell Gail, and she quite rightly said I had to ring Glamorgan straight away. I rang them, told them everything, and they ordered me onto the next plane home and would arrange for me to go and see the club's specialist the minute I arrived back. Gail and I had saved up so that when we flew back we'd holiday in Bali and Singapore, but that was out of the question now. Within 72 hours I was back in a cold, damp Cardiff in with the specialist who gave a different diagnosis. He believed that I had trapped the perennial nerve in my knee, and it was just a matter of time before the body released it. There may be cause for an operation if it didn't recover itself, but in his opinion it almost certainly would, he just didn't know when. He was of the opinion 'most certainly' that this was not a lifelong, nor career-threatening injury. I can't explain just how relieved I was.

I had to stick with the calliper for a while. It was early March by then meaning there were still six weeks before the season proper began, so I just set about getting as fit as I could. About two weeks later I was in the gym doing some bench pressing and as I relaxed between lifts I just felt something sort of tingle in my knee, then settle. I sat up and moved my foot and it was as good as new. I stood up, walked around, took the calliper off and walked again, and it was fine. I never had a moment's trouble with it in my career again. The thing that frightened me most about the whole episode is the first opinion by the Aussie consultant. I've learned since, for anything that appears serious, to get a few opinions if necessary and never, ever worry about going down that route.

When I look back at my two years in Australia, I truly realise how lucky I was. Socially, it was about the best time I'd had in my life up to that point – thanks to Whoolie. But at the end of the day, the reason I went was for cricket, and all the fun and happy stories were a bi-product of that. In hindsight I'm most proud that I did enough in my first season that Penrith paid for me to return the following year. By the New Year I'd made it into the first-grade team, and cemented my place with a hundred on debut against St George, who included then current Aussie test spinner Murray Bennett in their line-up. I stayed in the team until the end of the season averaging over 50, which resulted in the offer to return the following year. To say I bit their hand off is putting it lightly.

When I recently revisited my parent's scrapbooks to refresh the memory banks about my matches over there, I was astonished to be reminded of some of the players I played against in those two years. I had no idea as a twenty-year-old back then what the future had in store for a few batsmen I competed against: Mark Waugh, Mark Taylor and Michael Slater, not to mention the Aussie test players of the day – Geoff Lawson, Mike Whitney, Dave Gilbert, Trevor Chappell and Peter Taylor. It was truly a fantastic experience for a budding cricketer. I can't really remember now the circumstances of my not returning to Australia for a third spell, but I would be heading south on my cricketing travels again. And in 1989, I went to South Africa.

CHAPTER TWELVE

Beneath African Skies

In 1990 I scored 1,000 first class runs in a season for the first time in my career. I'd spent the summer batting at number six in the order, one place behind the living legend that was Viv Richards. The amount of confidence he gave me cannot really be quantified. As I describe elsewhere in this book, he never gave me any technical advice as such or any quietly chosen words of inspiration that lifted me, but what he did do was shout out loudly for the opposition to hear how well I played a certain shot or stood up to a barrage of quick bowling, for example. The very fact that he so publicly flattered me in this way made me feel on top of the world and all my previous fears and insecurities seemed to fade as the summer went on.

He also took the pressure off the rest of us by the way he dominated opposition bowlers from the word 'go'. He was so totally dismissive of them that you couldn't help laughing at the absolute disdain with which he treated them. One such bowler who suffered at his hands was Warwickshire's Adrian Pierson.

We were playing at Swansea in a three-day championship match, the first two-and-a-half days of which were spent watching Warwickshire dominate. They compiled 443 for 3 declared in the first innings, which included an exceptional first wicket stand of 220 between the two Andys – Moles and Lloyd – and which saw Mr Moles score a superb 224.

Our reply of 373 for 7 declared gave Warwickshire a chance to bat again, during which time they set us a far from probable run chase of 282 to win off just 56 overs. There was only one way this match was heading – a draw. The main reason for this was that the wicket at St Helen's was pretty much turning square, and we lost a few wickets to the spin of their confident young spinner, Adrian Pierson. I remember getting out and we were five wickets down when Crofty trotted out with instructions from the captain Butch to let Viv know that we were happy with the draw, and so we could basically begin to shut up shop and take no more risks. It was the usual plan for a situation such as this in a match. Pierson was gaining a bit of a reputation on the circuit of upsetting the odd batsman with his antics, one of which in particular really pissed a few people off. He had developed this habit of moving in to bowl, getting right into his delivery stride, but at the point of release, rolling his arm over and not letting the ball go. This would give him an insight into the batsman's intention to move down the pitch to charge him and play him aggressively or not.

Now if this wasn't enough to wind up even the most patient of batsmen, what he then did sent the odd one over the edge. He would just hurl the ball from where he was now standing, on the bowling crease in front of the umpire, straight toward his wicketkeeper, closely passing a bewildered batsman on the way. This he proceeded to do at the precise time that Crofty came to the crease. But unfortunately for Pierson, he did it to Viv, not Crofty. All hell was about to break loose. Up to this point, Viv had been quite circumspect and watchful in his play, which was exactly what the situation had demanded. But the way Viv spun around and glared at Pierson, we could all tell, even from the balcony, that he'd just lit the Antiguan's fire. Or as Crofty later put it: 'Viv's eyes lit up like searchlights.' At that moment, he motioned to Crofty, met in the middle of the pitch and told him in a chilling, cold and angry voice, 'Hey Crofty man, tell that boy I'm gonna lose his ball.' Crofty said that even he was frightened and in case Viv lost it with him too, he just turned round to Pierson and said

'Viv said he's going to lose your ball, mind.' That raised a laugh when he told us that.

Credit to Pierson, the next ball he bowled to Viv beat the great man in the flight, but it didn't really matter, because Viv played what remains one of the most magnificent cricket shots I've ever seen. Off balance, he let go of the bat with his bottom hand, but continued to throw the bat, with immense power, right through the ball, which resulted in him smashing it straight back at Pierson, just above head height, where the ball continued at the same trajectory, and ploughed into the sightscreen at the Swansea Bay end of the ground, hitting it about halfway up, for six.

As Pierson stood there looking slightly bewildered, Crofty said that Viv just looked back down the pitch and shouted to him in his fantastic broad West Indian accent

'Crofty – you tell that boy that the next ball will come back with seaweed on the thing.'

Over the next few overs, on a turning wicket, Viv took Pierson and the other spinners apart, and we won the game with overs to spare. It was an awesome sight, and it made me realise that sometimes, genius needs a spark to set it all in motion, and that's certainly what happened that day with Viv: he was absolutely awesome.

Apart from Viv's massive influence, the other factor that I feel definitely contributed to my maiden thousand-run season in what I realise now was my all-important breakthrough year, was the fact that I spent the winter months prior to this season playing in South Africa.

Whilst I was a veteran of two reasonably successful and character-building Australian trips, success in the Glamorgan first team had still not been forthcoming. But in the winter of 1989, as a late replacement for Steve Barwick, I joined a club deep in the Transvaal called Benoni. Glamorgan had built up a link with the club for many years through my former coach and Glamorgan legend Jim Presdee. I didn't really know what was expected of me when I stepped aboard a LuxAir jet along with Leicestershire's Russell Cobb, who was also flying out to spend the winter in the high veldt. At our stopover in Luxembourg, we both became young men behaving badly, and like kids in the proverbial sweetshop of the departure-lounge bar during our stop over, both got absolutely blasted. When I finally arrived in Benoni, hours later, I was a mixture of still inebriated youngster, complete with an increasingly giant hangover. I've no idea what impression I made on club chairman Don Campbell, when, along with several other members of the club, he offered to take me out for a welcoming drink and meal, only to be greeted by my stark refusal, and request to go straight to my room so I could sleep – which I did!

Eighteen years later, Don remains one of my closest friends and a mentor, someone I've turned to for advice throughout my career, so I guess things must've got better from that inauspicious start. Once my hangover had abated late during the following day, I was shown around the club, and introduced to various players and club members. Benoni is a largely industrial town, with a population of nearly 300,000, in north east South Africa, in what is now the Gauteng province. Back then it was known as Eastern Transvaal, and the population was largely employed in gold mining and other associated industry, and was largely white – a fact that assumed its own importance on more than one occasion.

I was soon introduced to a chap called Terrence Marsh, who was to become my soulmate during my African adventures, and the friendship was cemented further when I was able to return the favour and set him in contact with former England and Glamorgan bowler Jeff Jones, father of Simon, to allow Marshy to come over and play for Dafen in south west Wales in several following summers.

Anyway, as I stood there at the end of the 1990 domestic season armed with my season's figures of 20 matches played and 1001 runs scored, I reflected on the fact that my successful pre-season South African winter (allied to Viv's influence) had resulted in my scoring 157 runs more in that single season than I had in my first four seasons as a professional all together. I had made it. I was a pro, a successful career would now become a matter of course.

How wrong could I be.

The next season, 1991, was the worst I was to experience in the whole of the remaining years of my career – even worse than my ill-fated Championship season of 1997. I scored just 299 runs in 14 matches at an average of less than 23. Just six months on from my feelings of self-satisfaction of the sporting life that awaited me, I now thought that any chances of a career in cricket were fading fast, but worse still, I'd received a couple of wake-up calls during the season that made me honestly begin to believe that I simply was not good enough to make a career as a top-class batsman. It was the worst I'd felt about myself since my days of self-doubt and low esteem when I first joined Swansea City, and this time – as then – I was exposed by top-class players.

The first one took place at my beloved St Helen's in Swansea, in mid-July 1991. Glamorgan were hosts to the West Indies in a three-day game, and these were in the days when both county side and tourist side would – barring injuries – pick their strongest available teams, and pretty much, both would try their best to win the game. The county side wanted to win for the credibility and bragging rights over both the opposition and other county teams who had maybe already been stuffed, and also the touring side had the pride of not being beaten by what they saw as inferior opposition. There was also something else riding on the game. Even though I'd never admit it to any of the lads, I knew that if I had a big innings or played particularly well – or best of all both – I'd be putting myself in the shop window for England A recognition and ultimately the Test team. I fully appreciate that people who have followed my career may well be thinking that I must have been getting ahead of myself a little, but when you are young and playing the game to a decent standard, in your heart, you pray that a big innings, against the right opposition, at the right time, may catapult you to a level that you had previously only allowed yourself to dream about. It's happened to many people in my time in the game.

That day in July however, wasn't to be the time or the place.

When I look back at the team sheet for that match, I can hardly believe that I took part in a cricket match against such talented and legendary opposition. The Windies included Test players such as Clayton Lambert (who scored 99), Des Haynes (45), Richie Richardson (109), Carl Hooper (80), not to mention a couple who didn't score many that day – Gus Logie and a certain Brian Lara, batting at number six. But as good as those players were, my attention was taken by the bowlers. This was going to be my chance to see how good I really was (or wasn't as it turned out). The bowling was opened by Curtly Ambrose and Patrick Patterson, first change was someone you might have heard of – Malcolm Marshall – and the attack was finished off by a young paceman starting out on his career, Hamesh Anthony.

When it was my turn to bat, Glamorgan were 38 for 3 and Marshall was bowling in tandem with Ambrose. I'd love to know if there's a photo anywhere of me standing by the 6ft 10in Ambrose at the end of an over – it could be a prize winner! Anyway, both he, full of brooding arrogance, and Marshall gave me a right going over. Talk about being exposed.

My innings – or torture – lasted about half an hour, in which time I began to feel like an impostor on the cricket field. I was hit a couple of times (once on the head by the apprentice, Anthony); beaten for pace plenty of times; beaten by brilliance (Malcolm Marshall – if he'd put a bell in the ball I still wouldn't have known where it was going), and in the end, I was beating myself. I didn't show Daley, who I was batting with at the time and who went on to score 60-odd, but I was really struggling. Marshall dominated me so much that he was even showed me the shiny side of the ball in his hand as he ran in so that I had an idea about which way it was going to swing – and still I couldn't lay a bat on him. In the end, when I was beaten by a leg cutter from the magician Marshall, and was caught by Richie Richardson at slip for just 8, it came as a release. But psychologically I was done in.

Any aspirations I had of being a future England batter died that day, a small part of me told me what maybe other people already knew – I wasn't good enough. Sport's a funny thing, because the first thing you do when you return to the dressing room is put on a brave face. You end up saying things like 'I wish I'd just been able to hang around a bit longer to see him off,' and other such positive statements, when what I really wanted to say was 'Can anyone help me? I'm not good enough to play this game.'

The next day, when I was sitting there waiting to go in for the second innings as the game was petering out for a draw, I remember watching Matt and Daley batting almost praying that they wouldn't get out. My confidence was in pieces. It had been such a public humiliation, and I couldn't bear the thought of having to deal with it for a second time. Luckily for me, the lads held out, the match was drawn, and I was spared further heartache. Until we played Surrey at the Oval ten days later that was.

A player who was to become a teammate in the future absolutely murdered me. The bowler? Waqar Younis. My innings lasted twenty minutes and was again, absolutely painful to behold. He beat me time and time again with reverse swing at over 90mph, and my extremely fragile confidence was shattered once again. Eventually, I was caught in front of my stumps like a rabbit in the headlights, LBW. I can still see and hear Waqar's and Alec Stewart's hugely vociferous appeal, followed by laughter even now. My contribution? One poxy run. Again I felt desolate, and embarrassed, another public confirmation that I simply wasn't good enough – it was about as low as I'd felt in my career.

These two moments contributed to my season going downhill fast. My confidence was gone – shot to bits – but worse still, I had no belief and no one to turn to. When you lose your belief in sport, there's often no way back.

At the end of the season I took time to think things over. The facts I came up with were as follows:

1. I had a year left on my contract.
2. I would not start the next season in Glamorgan's First Team.
3. I couldn't see how I was able to improve anyway, especially after the way I'd been exposed on those two occasions by Marshall, Ambrose and Waqar.
4. I doubted whether I had the ability to sustain any sort of career in the game.

With these four points in my mind, and with winter approaching, I reviewed my close-season options:

1. Winter on the Lorries with Dad – please no!
2. Sporadic coaching at local clubs and schools.
3. Unemployment.

I really felt rock bottom.

I then made one of the most selfish decisions of my life. Professional sportsmen are often perceived generally as some of the most selfish people on the planet. You won't get much argument from me on that. Some of us, yes, me included, try to hide it as best we can. Some don't bother. But when push comes to shove and someone is about to take something away from you, in my case a career, something inside you rises up and basically says 'Bollocks to everyone else – I'm going to do what I want to do and what's best for me.'

With this in mind I picked the morning of Tuesday, October 12, 1991 to announce to Gail, as she left the house for work, that I'd be going to play in South Africa for a second time, for the winter. She thought I was joking and said that we'd talk about it when she got home.

When she walked back in at 5.30, I presented her my ticket from Trail Finders showing me booked on a flight to Johannesburg on October 14 at 8.10am. I'll never forget the look of hurt – and anger – on her face. Now, as I look back, I can publicly apologise unreservedly for the way I behaved – I'm so lucky that she still stuck by me over all these years. But the decision I made that day was to give me back a cricket career that would run for another fourteen seasons.

During my day of deceit while Gail was in work to support her income-less partner, I'd rung my best mate in South Africa, Marshy, and outlined the situation. At this point I have another admission to make. I guess I've implied that I made my decision purely on the basis that five months cricket in the South African sunshine would redeem my stumbling career. But there's one big hole in that view. I'd lost my confidence and belief totally. I really did think there was no way back once the following year of my contract had been completed – in all probability in the second team – and that my time as a professional sportsman would no doubt be over. What kept going through my mind, as Marshy and I hatched a plan, was that this would actually be my last hurrah. My final stand. My last freebie trip as a player representing Glamorgan Cricket Club.

After about an hour of pacing the room and checking the cost of the cheapest possible fares on teletext, Marshy called back. The news was good. Benoni were willing to pay me a thousand rand a month to return until April. This wasn't huge money, and after paying digs etc, wouldn't leave a hell of a lot, but I didn't care. Then the news got better. Marshy announced that his Mam and Dad had just completed converting their garage as an annexe for him to live in, and he said that I could shack up with him there rent free, and I'd also have use of the family's beaten-up VW Combi Van – the closest I was ever to get to becoming a Beach Boy.

He then said something that pricked at my cricketing conscience. Since I'd played there last, Eastern Transvaal had been granted first-class cricket status and would be competing against the other South African first-class teams such as Border, Boland and Western Transvaal, in the Castle Bowl Completion. He said that if I played as well as I did a couple of years before, there was no doubt that I'd get called up and would spend the bulk of my time being flown round South Africa playing at the better grounds against the country's top players. I couldn't admit as much to Marshy, but I felt like telling him that after a couple of games, I doubted that I'd still be in Benoni's first team. He also announced that Mike Haysman, who had been a first-class cricketer in South Africa, and was now their equivalent of Richie Benaud as a TV commentator, had also told Marshy

A late 1980s' team photo with me standing near two of the biggest influences in my cricket career. On the far left of the middle row, Don Shepherd, my current BBC Radio Wales colleague, and sitting in front of me, Alan Jones.

'No, he's definitely not a jockey,' Hugh Morris assures Prince Charles and the late Princess Diana.

On our way to Colwyn Bay – Viv Richards wasn't as happy getting off!

As pro for Benoni, at a presentation for Denis Compton, with Terrence Marsh (second left) and Jim Pressdee (far right).

Ravi Shastri and me at Abergavenny with our respective player-of-the-month awards.

Robert Croft, resplendent with sandwich board, spreading the Glamorgan gospel in 1993. Size does matter, Crofty!

At Ebbw Vale. Future Glamorgan coach John Derrick always smiled when he was back in the valleys. You can take the boy out of Aberdare . . .

A team night out in Barbados. The legendary Michael Cann (left) playing hide the football with Simon Dennis (centre) and equally legendary Stephen Royston Barwick.

Viv Richards finishing on a high with Hugh Morris at Canterbury in 1993. Minutes earlier Viv had been in tears of joy.

Celebrations at Canterbury: as good as it gets.

Captain Marsh thought he'd got me – a huge moment for me that day.

It never got better than this. Viv Richards and I steer Glamorgan to victory to the sound of 'There's Only Two Tony Cotteys'.

Trophy No. 2, Taunton, 1997. Clockwise from captain Matt Maynard (with trophy), Darren Thomas, Alun Evans, Waqar Younis, Dean Cosker, myself, Adrian Dale and Adrian Shaw.

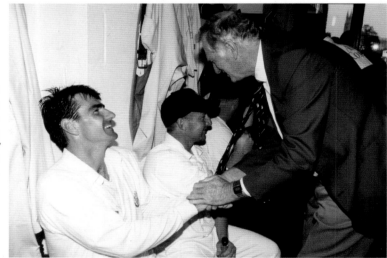

Cricketing journalists past and present – Mr Walker, late of the BBC, congratulates Mr James, future *Telegraph* correspondent, in the Taunton dressing room.

'Waqar is a Welshman' was the chant. And, at Taunton, Darren Thomas agrees!

Sweet success! The man in the Welsh Rugby shirt is the ever-supportive Fletch. The youngster far right is Tom Maynard.

An unbelievably proud moment at the Palace – even though it was the only time His Royal Highness smiled all day!

Glamorgan at the Palace with H.R.H. Prince Phillip.

Proudly receiving my Player of the Year trophy from the late Glamorgan scorer Byron Denning, a true friend.

Another wicket for Waqar. Always happy to oblige.

'You spawny Welsh…' Essex's Mark 'Ramble' Ilott was never lost for words.

Cottey vs the Rest of The World. Sunil Gavaskar and Gordon Greenidge look on admiringly!

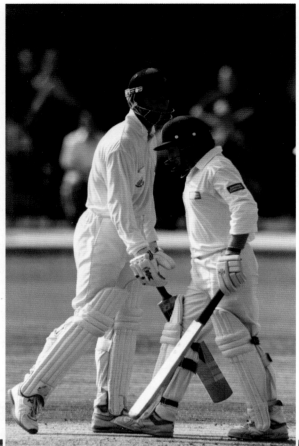

At the crease with Matt Maynard. Captain and vice-captain taking stock. Time to declare?

On my way to a hundred against Australia A at Neath in 1995. Adam Gilchrist has the gloves as Ricky Ponting ducks for cover.

Mark Waugh, Allan Border (above), Kapil Dev, Navjot Sidhu (below) – I bet they've got to pinch themselves that they shared a cricket field with me!

Leaving St Helen's after career best 203 against Leicester. Neil Kendrick follows me up the steps.

Walking in the shadows of greatness – Viv and me at Swansea.

Runs again at St Helen's, my favourite ground. This time, 191 against Somerset.

My first hundred at Cardiff – all the better for having Durham's Ian Botham and Dean Jones looking on.

A skilful steer off the intimidating Franklyn Stephenson. The despairing keeper? A certain Peter Moores.

Messrs Irani, Hussain, Gooch, Such and Waugh celebrate my passing at Pontypridd. I don't see the funny side.

A young Robert Damien Bale Croft, not a steel toecap in sight.

The four proud new county caps in 1992 with captain Alan Butcher. The seeds sown by this night would lead to my unhappy exit six years later.

Celebrating a Crofty wicket – an extremely regular occurrence during the 1990s.

The long and the short of it. Captains Tom Moody and I discuss the weather up there.

Somerset's Andrew Caddick and Dermot Reeve celebrate my demise.

'Duw, it's hard!'

A half century at Swansea for Mike Cann – my rival in the early days. There's no reason why he shouldn't have had a long career in the game

The legend, Baz. The eyes have it!

Watty – exactly as I remember him –
the perfect action.

that he would let him have an area of his indoor coaching school for us both to host some specialist coaching sessions for extra money. This was turning into the best telephone conversation I'd ever had.

So that was that, and I left for South Africa. I did ask Gail if she wanted to come, but wasn't surprised when she refused, and openly admit to feeling extremely guilty when we parted on that wet Thursday morning. I realised that I was putting an extreme strain on our relationship, and it was all borne out of my selfishness. To this day I'm not proud of what I did.

I spent the first couple of days in South Africa getting reacquainted with the area and the people that had been so welcoming to me two years earlier. I sensed though that there were tensions just under the surface, largely due the massive change that was beginning to take a grip on this wonderful country. The best way I can describe it is that when I first went to South Africa, people did what they did because they'd always done it. I'm not referring to any abuse of black people or anything like that, but the attitude people had toward the black people was born of generations of teaching and examples set by their forefathers. As a result, the first time I was there in 1989 the overwhelming feeling was one of a calm, matter-of-fact, even laid-back attitude to life. Now I sensed that people were aware that change was expected of them, and the pressures of immediate change were proving slightly more difficult to bear. People were more on edge – as if they felt they had to justify themselves to me. When I hooked up again with Don, he asked me if I remembered the Chicago Rib Shack incident in 1989 when he, Glamorgan colleague Michael Cann and I went out for a meal. I shuddered as I recalled it.

We'd finished our meal at the Rib Shack and were having the obligatory half a dozen Castle Lagers, when we heard a load of shouting and screaming from outside. We went outside to see what was happening – just as we would've done in Swansea or Cardiff – to see if we could help out more than anything. We then saw two black lads running out from a butcher's shop, which was odd, as it was 11pm at night – and all the lights in the shop were on. We heard the 'Stop them' shout go up, and aided by the Dutch courage of the lager, set off to catch them. In a situation like this you act very much on instinct. I guess if I'd thought about it, what I was expecting to happen in my lager-fuelled state was, along with Canny, to rugby tackle the pair of them, restrain them, and then hand them over to the police and they'd be in court the following morning to be charged with whatever they had done. We'd have both been heroes.

I was soon to discover we weren't in Swansea or Cardiff.

We'd only run about thirty yards when a van shot past us, mounted the kerb, and started ploughing over the front gardens of the houses in the street, in pursuit of these lads who were now literally running for their lives, and hurdling the small hedges that separated each house. In what seemed like seconds, and about 150 yards ahead of us, the van just ploughed into one of the lads, and appeared to break his legs. The driver – and owner of the shop – got out and started piling into the lad as he lay howling on the floor. Canny and I got there as fast as we could and tried to pull him off the lad and were screaming at him to stop. He then turned all his venom on us. He knew that we were from overseas and basically told us that we didn't know what the hell we were getting involved with. These two blokes had, *apparently*, held him up at gunpoint in his shop the previous week, but this time he had a gun with him when they arrived again tonight and they'd bolted from the shop when they'd realised.

This story illustrates how complex the situation was two years before in 1989 – it could be a real battleground – and I wondered what it must have been like living your life like that, not knowing if your next customer was going to shoot you. However, whatever the circumstances, I just couldn't see that taking the law into your own hands – especially as brutally as this guy had done – could ever be the right thing. I didn't then, and I don't now, express a view that could contain any solutions to the problem, all I know is that it was a very distressing and sobering experience, and luckily, the only one of its type I was to witness.

But it was two years later now, and things in South Africa were beginning to change. There was a sense of expectation and concern in and around the town about what the future held, but as usual, and as a fully paid-up member of the selfish sportsman's club, I was more concerned with my first game of cricket which was to take place on Saturday, than any of the political change that was occurring.

My first game was against Boksburg and this was the second game of Benoni's season. I was more nervous than usual when I padded up for my warm-up before the game. Marshy announced that the captain of Boksburg was Peter De Vaal, a left-arm spinner of some repute in South Africa, but more importantly the captain of the newly-formed Eastern Transvaal.

'Get runs today Cotts and he's bound to pick you,' said Marshy.

'Yeah, right,' I thought quietly, 'I'd be happy to get off the mark!'

I scored 150.

To this day, I have absolutely no idea where that innings came from. All I know was that, ultimately that innings went some way to saving my career. In the bar later, Peter De Vaal came over, bought me a drink, and asked me what my plans were for the summer and would I like to play for Eastern Transvaal.

Would I like to play for Eastern Transvaal?!

I suppose I should have played it cool and said 'Let me have a think about that, Pete – and I'll get back to you some time next week.' But I didn't. What I did was nearly spit my beer all over him so eager was my response.

'I'd love to' is what he heard between the gurgling.

He said that I'd be paid 350 rand – plus expenses – per game, we'd be flown around the provinces, and he was hoping it was going to be a really exciting time because there were plenty of people hoping we'd succeed as underdogs, but more importantly plenty others who were hoping we'd fall flat on our arses. I couldn't wait.

During this time I really cemented my friendship with Don Campbell. He was the marketing manager with Gillette in South Africa and I began to chat to him about his career and how he got to where he had and what opportunities he had in the company.

'Don't tell me you're after a job?'

I explained to him how I felt about my freefalling cricket career, and how much I enjoyed the South African way of life and maybe there was more to keep me here than I had ever really considered before. He told me that there were jobs with Gillette and that he'd be happy to put me up for one but that I'd have to go through the recruitment procedure with the other candidates and see how things panned out. He told me that there was no rush; I was there for five months, after all, and that I needed to have a real think about what I was potentially giving up.

I mulled it over for a few weeks and the more I thought about it, the more it made sense. The money that Don had mentioned was more than decent in South African terms. Thrown in was a company car, and added to that, Gillette were more than happy for me to continue with my cricket in South Africa with Benoni and East's, which, if it continued, would obviously supplement my income. My mind was made up. I was going to go for it and give up my final year with Glamorgan. I wasn't even going to go back home.

I had the interview with Gillette, had an absolute flier, and was offered the job. I hadn't discussed it with Gail up to this point – told you us sporties are inherently selfish – and rang her with the good news, and then asked her the most important question of all. Would she give every thing up and join me for a new life under African skies?

No.

Absolutely not.

Not under any circumstances.

We then did what most young couples do at this point: we had a stand-up row on the phone! With my blinkers firmly on, I couldn't see her point of view at all. I'd secured a great job, the cricket wasn't as high a standard as Glamorgan back home which meant I'd probably be able to eke out a living from it for much longer than my probable one final year back at Glamorgan, and we'd have a fantastic lifestyle in a wonderful country in the perfect climate. The beer was great here too . . . Pointing that one out was a tactical blunder, I must admit.

This lady, however, was not for turning. I was facing the ultimate ultimatum. Gail or my new life. The choice was mine and despite everything that made sense to me about my new South African life – I made the decision there and then. And it was an easy one to make in truth. I wasn't going to leave her.

This was February 1992, and I was 25 years old. When I look back at what I achieved in cricket from 1992 onwards on a personal basis, professionally in terms of trophies, along with the friendships I've made, none of it would have happened had I remained in South Africa. Maybe I'd have become a rand millionaire and head of Gillette's corporate training arm in Pretoria – highly unlikely I know – but when I was a kid, I don't recall having many dreams about heading up anyone's corporate arm. All I had dreamt about was sport. Living and playing in a world of sport.

As a direct result of Gail's refusal and ultimatum to me, I would live out, and, in many ways, surpass the wildest schoolyard dreams I'd had years before, and in reality, it's all down to her. If she'd said 'Yes', God, how my life would have been so different! There's only one thing I can say, thanks Gail. Thanks a lot.

Once the decision had been made, and at the time I was still pretty pissed off, I decided to buckle down and sort my head out. The cricket went really well for Eastern Transvaal. I averaged just under 40 for them finishing in the top fifteen batters in the competition, and in each of my final three innings for them, I scored a half century. We even managed to win the Bowl competition, which did my confidence the world of good. I resolved to get back to Glamorgan in as good nick as I could, and attempt to succeed in my final year, instead of shying away from it and bowing out with a whimper. My mindset became so far removed from how it had been the previous October when I arrived, and there was one final part in my recuperation, and it came in the form of a brief friendship with someone who would not just hit the highest cricket headlines in years to come, but at one point, world headlines – Hansie Cronje.

I met Hansie through Canny, who was playing in Orange Free State. Hansie was a really lovely, gentle guy, highly intelligent, very witty and you could tell he was destined for the highest level as a cricketer. Thanks to Canny, I was lucky enough to meet his family, notably his father Ewie and brother Fransie. For those of you that don't recognise Hansie's name, after you've read the next bit, I think you'll remember him.

Hansie was captain of Orange Free State by the time he was 21, which is where I ran across him, and by the age of 23, in 1993, captained South Africa. He became regarded in a career of 60-plus tests as one of the most astute captains in test history, and also became the face of modern South Africa by the way he embraced the rainbow nation idea on the world's sports fields, and promoted equality and fair play wherever he went.

But, in April 2000, he confessed to the largest match-fixing scandal in cricket history. He was subsequently banned from playing and coaching cricket for life. When it was all revealed, I just couldn't believe what I was hearing.

The day before my 36th birthday in June 2002, he was killed as the plane he was travelling in crashed into mountains as it circled the airfield in low cloud. He was only 32.

I know it's a cliché, but when the scandal broke, I remember thinking that he was the very last bloke that I've come across in cricket who would have been involved in stuff like that. There's a list with plenty on that I wouldn't be surprised about – but Hansie? Never. I look back on it now, with obvious sadness. At that time, when I was at a bit of a crossroads of my life in South Africa, he'd been very positive about what I should do – the gist of it being never, ever give it up, and some years later, when we shared a beer after a Sunday League match at Grace Road when he came to Leicestershire in 1995, I remembered back to then, but said nothing to him about the small, but quite significant part he had played in me not throwing my cricket away. To this day, I wish I now had. To think he's no longer with us is terrible, but I also view it from another, more positive angle realising that I only ever got to know him simply because I could hold a bat and hit a ball to a decent standard. It really astounds me the number of fantastic people I've met and friendships I've struck up, simply because my sporting ability has opened a few doors for me. This is one of the true benefits of playing sport.

Which brings me nicely onto Peter Conway's son.

I mentioned earlier that I was able to return a favour to my South African saviour Marshy by putting him in touch with former England fast bowler Jeff Jones, dad of current England fast bowler, Simon. Once Marshy had landed in Wales and got settled in thanks to Jeff, he got to know a great guy called Andrew Brown who ran the Carmarthen Bay Holiday Camp. Within weeks, this 21-

year-old semi-professional South African cricketer was spending his working week hiring out bikes to countless young ladies spending their holidays in this particularly beautiful part of West Wales. With his on-camp accommodation at close hand, I think Marshy had a summer most young fellas can only dream of.

After he'd been there a while, Marshy mentioned to Andrew Brown that I'd be happy to pop down and do the ocassional prize-giving at the camp for the odd couple of quid; after all, young cricketers in the early 1990s were always looking at ways to supplement their income. After a few of these prize nights, I also got to know Andrew very well. In turn, he then introduced me to his entertainments manager, professional comedian and singer, and all-round great bloke, Peter Conway. Now Pete and I got on like a house on fire right from the start. He loved his sport and always wanted me to give him the low down on what Viv Richards was like or what it was like to face really fast bowling and so on. He was a true sports nut. I, on the other hand, used to nag him about telling jokes, how he remembered them all and how he timed his delivery etc. To watch him on stage was an education in itself – he was an absolute natural.

In return for the hospitality that Andrew and Pete had showed me I was able to do what all good sportsman do, and leave them tickets at the gate whenever we played at Swansea. It was always a pleasure to see them after the games and chat about the day's events. I remember one day when Pete began telling me about his son Robert, who was a young lad with hopes of following his Dad into entertainment. This was around about the time of New Kids on the Block and I remember Pete telling me one weekend that his lad was having an audition that week for a group who hoped to be Britain's answer to the New Kids. Hope it works out for him, I remember thinking.

A few weeks later after I'd played for Ammanford in a South Wales League game at Gowerton, I arranged to meet Marshy at the camp, and Pete called over this sixteen-year-old lad to introduce to me. It was his son, Robert. I remember thinking what a bundle of energy he was – very similar to his dad – and after chatting to him about the cricket and some football times with the Swans, he was off and up dancing on the stage like a madman. I remember saying to Pete how good he was, and Pete proudly saying 'He's a professional – like you.' I laughed and said,

'Yeah, good luck to him – I hope there's more money on the stage than in cricket!'

I was to meet Robert on a couple more occasions over the years. When his professional career took off, he would often call down to stay with his dad at the camp, to get away from it all. Though Pete eventually moved away from

Carmarthen Bay, we've kept in touch over the years, long after he moved back to the Midlands. It's always great to hear from him.

One day in 1999, I had a phonecall from Pete saying that Robert was performing in Cardiff, and Pete wanted to return the favour of the tickets that I'd often left for him at St Helen's, and invited Gail and myself, along with Andrew Brown and his wife, up to the Cardiff International Arena for the concert.

At this point, you might be wondering why we were going to Wales's premier concert venue to see Pete's son? Well, in case you haven't worked it out, sixteen-year-old Robert did get that job with Britain's version of New Kids on The Block, he did achieve a career where he earned a couple of bob more than your average cricketer. Because by 1999, young Robert had become Robbie Williams, one of the biggest stars on the planet, but far more important than that, a helluva nice bloke.

I know it sounds trite, but I was more pleased to be going because he was my mate's son. Over the years, most of my best days in cricket have been watched by my Dad, and on many of those occasions, Dave has been stood next to him. One day Dave asked me if I had any idea how proud my dad was of me, and proceeded to tell me of his reaction when I completed a century for Glamorgan once, at St Helen's. Dave said Dad just stood there, looking out from his position under the floodlights to me as I stood in the middle of the pitch raising my bat to the crowd, with tears pouring down his face. When Dave said to him, 'Not a bad day Bern', he just looked at Dave, nodded – unable to speak – and turned back to watch me. The pride that story gives me is beyond explanation. Now at a worldwide level, I couldn't help but wonder how Pete felt as his son was achieving such monumental acclaim. It must've been wonderful.

I came off the phone and broke the news to Gail, who was absolutely thrilled to bits when I explained that we were going to get to meet him after the show too; I swear she swooned. Wives – you've got to love them!

We made our way up to Cardiff on the afternoon of the show and met Pete, Andrew and partners at our hotel. After a quick drink, Pete announced that Robbie had said it would be OK for us to call around to his hotel in the afternoon to meet him for an hour or so. For once in my life, I became a bit starstruck. I remembered my first day at The Vetch when all the top players walked in and past me, and that feeling of awe that I experienced – it was returning to me now. It was odd really. As I say, I'd met Robbie when he was still Robert, a really nice young kid, and as much as I wanted to meet him and tell him how chuffed and delighted I was for him at the way it had all worked out so spectacularly for him, I just really felt that we'd be intruding. Some cricketers I played with didn't want anyone coming near them or into the dressing room area before a game – I never worried about it myself – but understood why they didn't like it. I now had this overwhelming feeling of worrying if Robbie didn't really want to see us that afternoon, in case he was busy preparing and that our presence would be an unwelcome distraction. The last thing I wanted to do was to divert him from his preparations for his performance, so I walked over to Pete and asked if it would be OK if Gail and I waited until the show was out of the way before we went to see him. I think Pete understood straight away where I was coming from and said it was no problem at all.

We met in the foyer of the CIA in the evening, and Pete handed out the tickets. We were then treated to nearly two hours of just about the best concert you could wish to see in your life. I've seen a couple of decent bands in my time, the Rolling Stones in Tampa, Florida for one, but Robbie totally eclipsed everything I'd seen, before or since.

He was simply incredible. He's got this gift of just getting thousands of people in the audience in the absolute palm of his hand. Not only can he sing excellently live, his energy on stage is truly incredible, and so is his humour which he must've inherited from his dad (his hair's a lot better too – sorry Pete!) But the other great talent he's got is that he makes everyone feel as though they know him, just as Elvis Presley did in his films when we were all kids. His manner on stage is so down to earth and normal, the way he chats to people between songs, before launching into some incredibly powerful performance, is unreal. I totally understand how he's become such a massive draw at his live concerts. When the concert ended we cheered with the rest of the crowd, and then when he finally left the stage and the lights came on, Pete said for us to wait ten or fifteen minutes, until he had the nod to go backstage. Now I couldn't wait to see him, but still had all the usual worries that we all have: Will he recognise me? Will he know who the hell I am?!

I'll never forget when we walked into the dressing room, and Robbie was just sitting there at his table, eating a prawn salad. He smiled, got up and welcomed us all really warmly. We started talking about sport straight away – especially football.Robbie's a huge football fan, even though he does support Port Vale! We all had a few beers and after a while he asked me if I fancied a game of basketball. Another slightly surreal moment in my life – one of the world's most famous people, asking me, a bloke from Swansea, to have a game of basketball. Sounds good to me, I said. He said to wait until they pulled the first

152

few rows of the arena back, and after about twenty minutes, and another bottle of Bud, off we went.

Talk about a beating. He absolutely murdered me!

He'd obviously played before – that's my excuse anyway – and he didn't show me any mercy in our impromptu game of oneon one. By the time we'd finished it was past midnight and we went back to join the others in the dressing room. The night was about to get better.

Robbie announced that he didn't like going back to the hotel in the tour bus because of all the fans etc., but would we like to? The next thing I know, we're on the tour bus with God knows how many people screaming at us from outside. All the curtains were closed on the bus for people to think that Robbie was on board and as it pulled away I stuck my hand out between the curtains and waved. The screams were incredible – I couldn't believe it. My only ever moment of superstardom – impersonating Robbie Williams's hand.

Robbie joined us later at the hotel where he and his band were staying, the exclusive St David's Hotel on Cardiff Bay. He had the entire top floor as a penthouse suite affair. When we walked into the main room, there was just about the most exclusive buffet I'd ever seen and a table in the centre, on which, stacked high in a pyramid, were countless bottles of Budweiser – just about my perfect hotel room, I thought. Robbie came in and joined us, and when his band started to get a touch rowdy, he asked if they'd move along to the room next door, and sat with us for about two or three hours, signed some photos for my kids and just chatted. Robbie Williams has received all manner of stick in the press over the years, and I guess this is the price for living your life in the spotlight. But I've always been brought up to speak as you find, and I've got nothing but good things to say about him.

CHAPTER THIRTEEN

Daffodil Days

Some away trips you tend to remember more than others. Maybe it's because you got some runs or took a spectacular catch; maybe it's because of the venue – Lord's for example – or maybe it's because it was a nail-biter of a match in which you came out on top. One away trip I'll never forget was to Hove in 1994, and for a place where I was to spend such happy times years later, it's quite ironic how poorly lady luck was to treat me on this particular occasion.

The old saying goes, 'Good things come in threes'. Well, I can vouch – thanks to Hove 1994 – that so do bad things.

After breakfast at the Imperial Hotel on the morning of the game, I left to get my car from the small hotel car park, which was located underneath the ground floor. By now, thanks to my improved stature in the game, not to mention great sponsorships deals for the players from Paul Russell's contacts, I was driving around in my third cherry-red sponsored Volkswagen Corrado. Giving me one of those was like giving a machine gun to a monkey – and I certainly made the most of my boy-racer years whilst at the wheel. Imagine my horror therefore when I approached the car to see the tell-tale shattered glass on the floor by the driver's door, just below where a window used to be. I looked inside and saw that some delightful soul had relieved me of my in-car entertainment. Furious doesn't cover it. I went back to the hotel, explained to the lads – most sympathetic as you can imagine – and made the various telephone calls to insurance and car repair companies. By the time it was fixed, I was running quite late, but as it was absolutely pouring down, there was no danger of me missing the start of the game.

When I finally arrived at the ground, the lads were in the dressing room, suitably ensconced in various forms of entertainment: newspaper reading (don't believe any sportsman who tells you they never read what is written about them, especially when they've had a good day, it's the first thing they all do in the morning), the obligatory card school, and Crofty and Matt picking an ugly cricketers' XI – in scorecard order of course. I settled down, and after the mickey taking about my earlier misfortune had subsided, pulled out my latest Wilbur Smith, plonked myself in a corner and began to read.

By about 3pm, as it had rained on and off all day, I realised it was unlikely that there was to be any play. I went outside to stretch my legs just as there was a break in the weather, finding that the rain had almost stopped and had been replaced by a very light drizzle. As Peter Kay would say, it was that horrible wet rain. At the far corner of the ground, I could see one of the car parks, containing Glamorgan's kit van, a brand-new Mercedes, heaps better than the old rusty Sherpas of my Vetch days – but a van nonetheless. Unfortunately, about one in every four away trips, I'd have to park up my beloved Corrado in Cardiff, and jump in the front of the van, along with another budding Nigel Mansell, and trundle off to some remote part of Britain, arriving a couple of hours after everyone else. Everyone hated their turn driving the kit van. The van's purpose was that it contained all the kit for the team. Not only did it include equipment for training and warming up – stumps, balls, cones etc, but it also acted as transporter for the chosen luggage carrier of the professional cricketer – The Coffin. The Coffin was a large cumbersome box, about four feet long by a foot deep and wide, which resembled, well, a coffin. In this was kept everything you used during the season. Three or four bats, three or four sets of gloves, batting pads, box, thigh pad, inner thigh pad, jockstraps, boots (batting and fielding), sweaters (2), shirts (4), trousers (3) and various other bits and bobs that got you through the season. When coloured clothing came in for Sunday league matches – which was absolutely fantastic for spectators – it was an absolute pain in the arse for us, as we had to cram all the items mentioned above (only this time in navy blue) into our already bursting coffins. This was why we needed a kit van, and this was why every now and again I had to drive the bloody thing.

As the rain was by now obviously stopping, I went to fetch my coffin before the rush from the rest of the lads began, in the unlikely event that we were going to go on for the last hour or so. I walked back into the dressing room, saw the keys for the van on the table, grabbed them and went out to the car park. I hadn't bothered to tell anyone – there was no need. When I reached the van, the rain began falling heavily again so I opened one of the back doors, and jumped in quickly before getting a soaking . I don't know how it happened but the door then slammed shut behind me. Locked.

I was in pitch darkness, I couldn't even see my hand in front of my face. Memories of Darren Gale and the Swansea City dressing rooms came flooding back.

Unfortunately, I'm a fully paid-up member of the South West Wales

Claustrophobia society, and, as is our wont, I did what we do best when confronted with a situation such as this – I panicked. For security reasons, the van had been installed with a plywood wall which sat behind the driver and passenger seats, which in the event of a break in to the cab, would prevent the intruder from getting to the kit in the back. This, however, now revealed its second, far more sinister purpose, of not allowing even the merest chink of light into the back of the van, where I now found myself totally trapped. I instantly started sweating, so took off my tie and blazer. All I could feel around me were those bloody coffins – not a good image for a trapped claustrophobic to have in his mind in the pitch dark. I remained calm, for at least a good thirty seconds, then I went nuts. I was banging the sides of the van, the doors, anything I could reach to bang, and screamed as loud as I could. Nothing. Nothing except the sound of rain. What does rain mean at a cricket ground? It means everyone's in the dressing room playing bloody cards. I stopped banging for a minute – all I could hear was the rain hitting the roof of the van. I started banging and screaming again, then stopped, then started banging again, a procedure I faithfully followed for the next twenty minutes. I stopped again and tried to think. I quickly thought of the real consequences. There was a fair chance that the game would be washed out for the day. It was the start of a four-day match, and as such we'd be back tomorrow – whatever the weather. The Hove car park was a secure one within the perimeter of the ground, and therefore, there was no need to remove the van tonight, it could stay here until tomorrow. Whoever had driven the van that time – I think it was Steve James and Adrian Dale – would just get a lift back to the hotel, and leave the van here. All night. With me in it.

As unlikely as this was, I really freaked, I picked up a coffin and hurled it at the back doors, and as I did so, a miracle occurred: a light came on, only to reveal a strange ghostly presence standing in front of the doors. Only joking. No, what it revealed was the doors, and with it the lock. I sat down on a coffin and began my best safecracking attempts, and after about five minutes twisting and clicking, I finally managed to free the lock from the inside. I was out. After 25 minutes of purgatory, I was sweating like a safe-cracker too! This really was turning into my nightmare trip. But there was one final piece of misfortune awaiting me.

Overnight the rain had stopped and the ground started to dry out. Hove is a decent drying ground, and play started on time the next day. We won the toss and batted, with Hugh and Daley making up for lost time with a century each. By the time I was called upon with the score at 355 for 4, the second new ball was being taken and there were now only six overs left in the day. This meant the bowlers knew that for these last six overs with a brand new, hard, shiny ball, they could charge in, giving it the full kitchen sink, knowing that they'd soon be putting their feet up for a rest.

The trouble with batting in these circumstances is that from a batsman's perspective, you've got absolutely nothing to gain. No further members of your team want to bat that night. In fact, some almost plead with you as you're getting ready 'Nothing silly, Cotts, I don't want to get my pads out tonight' – which brings with it its own little pressures. From a purely selfish point of view, there's nothing in it for you either. At best you're going to scratch around for 10 or 15 runs, you have no thoughts of a 50 or a 100, which you do every other time you go into bat. In these circumstances you just want to get in, get a not out, get it over with and start again from scratch in the morning. Not many batters enjoy these little testing spells.

I'd faced about eight balls when Paul Jarvis came down the hill to me, with the kitchen sink billowing in his wake. He was a lot quicker than people gave him credit for was Jarv, and he also had a skiddy action, which meant that the ball was often onto you quicker than other bowlers, as he got less bounce. I remember getting into position as he pitched it short, and I moved onto the back foot for a regulation pull behind square for at least one, maybe even a boundary. But I missed it. It kept low, and I bloody missed it. It didn't miss me though.

Before I knew it I was doubled up on the floor in the worst agony I was ever to experience in my whole career. I've broken bones, dislocated joints, strained ligaments, but this was by far the worst. It felt that I was going in and out of consciousness for the briefest of moments, then I couldn't breathe, and all I was aware of was everyone around me laughing. And laughing a lot. Now where is the one spot that a sportsman can get hit, where everyone always see the funny side. Yes, that's right – the bollocks; and that's where Jarvis's quickest delivery had hit me, smack on. Every cricketer has been hit there, and I've spent many a happy time laughing at some other poor bugger who's taken a smack in the privates, but this one was the worst one I'd ever had in my career. The ball had kept low – the cricket ball I'm talking about now – and had smashed into the underneath of my protective box at about 85 mph. Hitting the *underneath* of the box had two effects:

1. Splitting it straight up the middle and jamming some flesh between the resulting crack.
2. Pushing my bollocks two feet up inside my chest cavity.

The pain was extraordinary. I lay on the floor, on my side, unable to move or make a sound. It was as if the life had been sucked out of me. In reflex, my legs had come up to my chest into the foetal position, and there I lay on my side until Dean Conway, our physio, reached me. He gave me water and tried to rub my stomach, but I couldn't move. My body just wouldn't release my legs. There I remained after five minutes of treatment, hardly able to get my breath, but more worryingly with my legs clamped vice-like up into my stomach.

Then the final indignity. They had no option: they had to carry me off! If I hadn't been in so much pain, I'd have been laughing as much as everyone else. My only saving grace as I was carried up the steps, like a little boy to see the doctor, was that there wasn't much of a crowd in. I was taken to the treatment room, plonked on the table, where Dean shovelled ice down the affected area, and after about ten more minutes of this, my body relaxed the death grip it had given my legs, and I finally, gingerly, straightened out. It was one of the few times I retired hurt in my career, and there was one point during it all when I wished I was just retired full stop. This most undignified of episodes brought to a conclusion a trip, a terrible trip, which, if I may pinch a line from The Beach Boys' anthem 'Sloop John B', most certainly was 'The worst trip I've ever been on'.

Despite this painful yet ultimately 'amusing' setback, I was pretty much part of the furniture of the team, and unbeknown to me at the time, was moving into the next phase of my career. For that I had one person to thank, and that was Matthew Maynard. Within a couple of seasons of my Hove disaster, Matt had made me his vice- captain and this was a role that I was honoured to carry out.

Matt and I go back a long way. It's funny when you look back at your career and realise how often people's paths crossed long before they lined up together in a crunch match at Lord's or somewhere similar, live on Sky TV. What the armchair fan doesn't often realise is that when someone like Dominic Cork is having a full go at Ronnie Irani or the like during a live game, and assume that they must hate each others guts, in reality they both probably played schools cricket against each other from fourteen years of age and may well have played for England age-group teams together for many years before becoming pros.

Back in the late 1970s, I played for West Glamorgan schools in the Under 13 Welsh Cup and we were drawn to play North Wales schools on a sunny afternoon in Port Talbot. We were all aware of their star player, a very aggressive batsman by the name of Matthew Maynard. We batted first and I made my way to the crease. It's at this point that the Maynard and Cottey version of events begin to differ. Matt has an *extremely* flawed version where he reckons he ran into the wicket to bowl the first over, saw me advance down the wicket, couldn't believe his eyes that one so small could be so cheeky, rolled his fingers across the seam, beat me through the air and bowled me – 'Get out!'

My version is slightly different and *far* more factual. Matt trundled in like the part-time pie-thrower that he is, lobbed one up, and my eyes now the size of saucers, advanced down to wicket poised to smack it back over his head for the six it deserved.

Then it pitched.

Unfortunately for me there was a stone embedded and slightly hidden in the pitch, the ball landed on it, turned square, and just caught the outside of off stump. I was livid – he was laughing. The seeds of a long friendship were sown.

Matt was to be the very heartbeat of Glamorgan in my time at the club, such was his zest for life, and many of the funny stories in Glamorgan's dressing room in this period centred around him.

Despite Matt possessing a really sharp wit in defence and attack in the often brutal dressing-room environment, there *was* the odd occasion which demonstrated that had cricket not been his chosen career, then he may not naturally have graduated to a higher seat of learning!

For many years, cricket's professional Sunday League had been sponsored by the John Player cigarette company, resulting in the imaginatively named John Player Sunday League. This became quite an iconic competition, televised for many years on BBC TV, long before cigarette-advertising laws prevented such companies sponsoring sports. To the everyday fan the league was well known and well liked, and provided a great vehicle to watch talented cricketers, including all the current test match players of the time (long before central contracts) display their talents. When I first got called up to play in this competition for Glamorgan against Gloucestershire in 1986, I was even more excited than when I made my first-class debut – the John Player League was something special. Pardon the pun.

It was however more special to some players than others, as I was soon to discover. Prior to every game, home or away, the local John Player rep would turn up at the dressing room, armed with a very smart blazer and a box of 200 fags. The idea behind this was that the packs would be liberally placed around the dressing room, for the general use of all the players. This was long before someone pointed out that smoking might not be that beneficial to the average sportsman. However, our dressing room, being particularly fit and aware of the dangers of nicotine, contained only two smokers, Steve Barwick and Matthew Maynard. As a result, every Sunday they'd be primed, almost jumping on the rep as he arrived, and quickly splitting the box between themselves, in an act that became a weekly ritual. Their haul would last Matt the week, and Baz about a day-and-a-half.

This process carried on until 1987 when John Player's period of sponsorship came to an end and the search began for their replacement. At the time Rothmans, Embassy, Benson and Hedges and so on were big players in sports advertising and we assumed that one of these would take up the mantle, certainly Baz and Matt hoped so. When the new sponsors were finally announced we were well into pre-season, and Matt was less than happy. Deadly serious he shouted to us, 'Have you seen who the new sponsors for the Sunday League are?' We smiled. We had. 'Refuge Assurance?' he said. 'Refuge Assurance?! What are they gonna give us now – bin bags?'

We all paused for a second then pissed ourselves laughing wondering if the financial wizards at Refuge Assurance had ever considered that their Blue Chip company would one day be confused with refuse sacks.

Matt was the first of our age group (which included Steve Watkin, Steve James, Adrian Dale and Mike Cann) to really breakthrough into Glamorgan's first eleven. We always knew he had the talent: he was one of the few players I'd take time out in order to sit and watch bat after I'd been out. And boy, did he announce his arrival in style! He not only scored a century on his debut against Glamorgan at St Helen's, but he reached three figures with three consecutive sixes off the vastly experienced Yorkshire bowler, Phil Carrick. What this gave the rest of us was the belief that we too had a chance of succeeding in the first team, and Matt was the trailblazer who gave us this faith. His record for Glamorgan turned out to be one of the finest in the club's history, and I feel it's a pity that a player of his undoubted ability didn't have more opportunities afforded to him by the England set up during his time, to take his undoubted talents onto the highest stage.

A person who I'm convinced would have helped Matt achieve the success in the test arena that his talents warranted, had he been around when Matt was a youngster, was Duncan Fletcher. When he arrived at the club in 1997, Matt was captain, and they hit it off from day one. A strong relationship which endures to this day.

One of the first things I remember about Fletch was his perceived indifference to taking the plaudits. To his credit he never took the spotlight away from the lads. His firm belief was that he'd prepare us to the best of his ability, but the moment we crossed that white line onto the pitch, it was totally up to us. His view therefore was we should reap the rewards – or cop the flak – accordingly.

When he was interviewed on television, however, he was very

uncomfortable, partly due to what I've just outlined, but also because he was a genuinely shy, quiet man. As a result, he tended to come across as quite grumpy and humourless. This followed him around as England coach and didn't help him when the critics eventually turned against him. When the England team were all gathered together in Lahore for a satellite link for Sports Personality of the Year in 2005, when they collected the team award for winning the Ashes that summer, Gary Lineker couldn't resist having a pop at him: 'Nice to see you looking so happy' or something in that vein. I don't think you'd ever accuse Fletch of being life and soul of the party, but generally he was fine. Unless of course you cut out the toes of his socks. Step forward, Robert Croft.

The lads were playing in Abergavenny, the lowest point of my season: Mike Powell had replaced me in the team, so I, the vice-captain, was carrying out twelfth-man duties. Once more the weather had got the better of us. As our idle minds began to wander, Crofty's mind switched onto a spot of tomfoolery and zeroed in on Fletch's socks. He went over, pulled them out of his shoes, got a scissors from Dean Conway's physio kitbag, and cut the toes out, then placed the now-open ended socks back into Fletch's shoes. I don't think I was alone in thinking that this was probably a prank too far from Rob, as there was nothing we had yet witnessed in Fletch that led us to believe he was into the odd practical joke. Anyway, we'd just have to wait and see.

They called the day's play off at about four o'clock as I remember, and with Crofty already changed, having second guessed the umpire, he decided to shoot off home straight away. The rest off us went into the dressing room, showered and began to change and pack up. By now Fletch had joined us, showered and began to dress. He was sat on the bench and reached down for his socks. He pulled one out of his shoe, put his foot inside, and pulled it vigorously up. His foot went straight through it, and the sock came up somewhere over his calf. We all corpsed, but said nothing – neither did Fletch. Then astonishingly, without checking, he pulled out the second sock, put his left foot in, and did exactly the same. There he was, stone-faced, sat on the bench, a middle-aged man in his pants, with two socks up around his legs and two bare feet flat on the floor. We couldn't contain ourselves. He could, luckily, because he was absolutely furious. He didn't say a thing, he just dressed in silence, got his gear together and left, without a word to anyone.

The next day we turned up as usual and got changed for our warm-ups. Fletch still hadn't said a word to anyone. He started the daily fielding drills which included him wearing a baseball glove, and hitting balls at fielders to swoop in, pick up the ball and return it at pace to his mitt. Mike Powell made a crass comment and was seized upon straight away by Fletch, who really bawled him out and told him to just get on with it and concentrate on the cricket. He then turned to Adrian Shaw our wicket keeper to hit some balls at him as he did everyday, but this day he was firing them like shells at a startled Shawsy who was trying to keep hold of them for dear life. Matt finally got hold of Crofty and told him that he should apologise. Crofty protested because he was annoyed that Fletch couldn't take a joke – maybe he had a point – but we just wanted to put it behind us, so Matt explained to Crofty that he had gone a bit far, and should apologise. Crofty reluctantly agreed. Now I'm not certain exactly what was said, but Crofty apologised, and being Crofty, also had a little dig at the same time, which resulted in Fletch only grudgingly accepting his apology. I don't think that their relationship really ever healed after that day

In hindsight I feel that Fletch might have taken the joke a bit better, and just sought Crofty out and at some point given him a bit of a bollocking and reminded him where the lines of authority were, and that would have been that. But what was done was done, and we just got on with it. I don't want anyone to think that we thought any less of Fletch for this, because we didn't. I don't think I've ever come across a more loyal coach in my career in terms of protecting the 'lads' – and especially me when my form started to suffer in our Championship year. An example of his loyalty to the team in general occurred not long after the socks' episode. We played Middlesex on the day that one of the live rugby union test matches was to be screened of the British Lions taking on South Africa. This was one of those occasions when some of us would have given up being a sportsman for the day, just to join the rest of the nation down the pub watching the rugby.

Though a cricketer, I've hardly ever watched a cricket test match, or one-day international, let alone a Wimbledon final, or even an FA Cup final, for the best part of twenty years. I'm not complaining at all; it's just another example of the little things you always take for granted as a sports-mad kid, yet when your dreams come true, and you become a sportsman, you never get to see those great occasions again until you retire. Weird that. Anyway, the dressing-room code at the time was that the TV was allowed on, but with no sound, so as not to distract the outgoing batter. As we were not in the field, the players not at the crease were trying to keep an eye on the TV watching the Lions game. Unfortunately, Middlesex were having a good day and our wickets began to drop alarmingly regularly, and we were busy compiling one of the lowest scores in Glamorgan's long history. I batted through most of it, having gone in with the score on 7 runs for 3 wickets. When Crofty came to join me at the crease, the score had zoomed along to 11 for 5, and as is his wont, he walked all the way out to bat, shaking his head and loudly bemoaning the lack of professionalism of his colleagues.

'They're more interested in the fucking rugby that saving this match,' he shouted to me as he was taking guard. 21-year-old rookie James Hewitt was the bowler, and as Crofty's first ball came in, this model professional played back to a short one, which didn't bounce, just pitched and ran all the way along the ground, bowling him first up. As he walked back past me red-faced and furious, I was biting my lip until it nearly bled to suppress my laughter. The damage had already been done though. We were stuffed – all out for 31 and Middlesex had beaten us by an innings. I'd top scored with 12. That said it all.

After the game, we were all sitting quietly in the dressing room when Fletch came in, and shut the door silently behind him. It was still only 3pm; a packed crowd were going home early, robbed of a day's entertainment, and we all thought he was going to slaughter us for not focussing fully on the job in hand. We sat there in silence for a couple of minutes waiting for the inevitable bollocking to begin.

He finally spoke.

'Lads, days like today can happen to anyone. You probably didn't help yourselves a hell of a lot, but forget about it now and put it behind you. Get changed and then follow me to the Beverley [pub], and we'll drown our sorrows. One thing though – remember this feeling – remember how bad it is, how much it hurts, and never, *ever* let it happen again. Now let's have a drink and some fun.' And he just walked out.

We were gobsmacked. Dressing room psychology? Yes. Did it work? Judge for yourself. We won our next game by an innings, went on a six-match winning run, never lost another game all season, and ended up winning the County Championship for only the third time in the club's history. I often think back to that quiet dressing room and Fletch's speech and I prefer to think of it as extremely good man-management, designed to bring us all together as a team and a group with him at the centre, at a time of deep crisis. Our whole season could've gone completely off the rails at that point, but, for the way Fletch dealt with it, every player felt a huge loyalty to him after that – I know I certainly did. In hindsight, I'm just glad I was given the opportunity to work with someone who I believe is one of the best cricket coaches in history. There's almost an inevitability in this country that if you hold a national position in sport – as a manager or coach – the press pack will get you in the end. I guess it was always going to happen to Duncan simply because he never appeared to go out of his way to cosy up to the media. If, in his first ever press conference, he had said that by the time he leaves, England will have beaten the Aussies in the Ashes and be ranked the second-best test nation in the world, most present would have said – 'Yeah, we'll settle for that'. But obviously they didn't – they wanted more. The problem for Fletch was one-day cricket. His final rites with England were played out at the 2007 World Cup in the West Indies and were beset by Flintoff's Fredalo incident, massive defeats by Australia and South Africa and only registering wins against Kenya, Canada, West Indies, Bangladesh and Ireland. By then the hounds were out to get him and he never stood a chance really. He cut an extremely forlorn figure at that time as this decent and proud man was essentially being judged on a form of the game at which England have always underachieved, with apparently his past successes in the test-match arena being conveniently forgotten. In the end though, as happens to all involved in sport, he was gone, and a new man appointed.

His name? Peter Moores and he was my professional and personal mentor for the six years I spent at Sussex, and his choice was absolutely correct and well deserved. On his appointment, I reflected on the fact that I was the only player in domestic cricket in England and Wales who'd played consistently under both men. One man's exit meant another man's opportunity. It was certainly one of life's bittersweet moments.

CHAPTER FOURTEEN

The Royle Family

On May 4, 1989, Glamorgan entertained Gloucestershire in a four-day championship match at Sophia Gardens. Nothing too noteworthy about that you might think, and normally you'd be right. However, this one was different. This fixture is about as close as Glamorgan get to a local derby, and as this one fell during Glamorgan's centenary year, the occasion demanded that the Patrons of both clubs be invited onto the pitch to meet the teams prior to play on the first morning of the game. And in 1989 the Patrons were a very famous husband-and-wife team. You may have heard of them.

Prince Charles and Princess Diana.

One of the pleasant spin-offs of earning a living in the public eye is that you get to meet all sorts of famous and well-to-do people whose paths you would never normally cross. Meeting Princess Di, however, tops the lot. On that lovely day in May there was plenty of mickey-taking in the dressing room beforehand – people daring each other to ask her for her number, or for an autograph – that sort of thing. Then Hugh came into the dressing room at about quarter to eleven, told us the official arrangements and instructed us to get our club blazers on and make our way out onto the pitch. There the Gloucestershire team came out similarly attired and lined up outside the pavilion. We were then joined by our special guests, and all the lads began craning their necks to get a good look at the stunning princess as they waited to be introduced to her. As she moved down the line toward me, greeting each of the lads as she came, it was as if I was looking at a cartoon. She'd stop in front of a player, shake hands, have a brief word with him and move on. As she did so each player would almost visibly swoon as she passed on. I almost expected their tongues to unfurl and drop down onto the turf. As she reached me though, I quickly realised what the fuss was about. She was absolutely, almost unbelievably, beautiful. She smiled, shook my hand, said hello and moved on. It was over in a second, but it's a moment I'll always remember – it was certainly my time to swoon. Then came Prince Charles. But he hardly registered with anyone after his wife had passed by! Then, each team in turn sat down for a team photo with the royal couple. It was a really nice interlude before the seriousness of the game began. Unfortunately, any hopes I had of impressing the princess with a cavalier century were dashed as I was caught by Bill Athey off David Graveney for a duck. Typical!

I had to wait a long four years to attempt to impress her again, and my chance came in 1993, when we were graced by her company again, this time at the picturesque ground of Abergavenny, and again, clad in our blazers, we lined up outside the small pavilion to meet her. This time I was standing next to Crofty and again patiently waited my turn to be introduced to this iconic woman – secretly hoping that she'd have more to say to me than just 'Hello' this time. She reached Crofty, shook his hand, and showing that she'd done some research asked him how his England career was progressing. Delighted by this, Crofty began chatting to her and immediately struck up a rapport. Then she turned to me, looked down – well she was quite tall! – held out her hand and said 'Hello, you must be the wicketkeeper.' I was too flustered to say anything witty in response, and out of the corner of my eye I could just see Crofty's shoulders starting to move in suppressed laughter.

'No, I'm just a batsman' was all I could offer in response.

'How nice' she replied then moved on. After she'd moved along a few more players, Crofty let a bit of his laughter out and turning to me said from the side of his mouth – 'Could have been worse – she might have thought you were our mascot!'

Bastard. We giggled away like a pair of naughty schoolboys. Still, I had the last laugh, I had the chance to impress her with my innings after my duck last time. I got off the mark with a cracking back-foot drive for four off the first ball. That must've impressed her, I thought. Unfortunately, it didn't last. Two balls later I was trudging back to the dressing room having not added to this imperious beginning, caught by Ball off Hancock and glanced up to see her having a nice cup of tea with the committee, totally oblivious of my endeavours.

Sadly, I wasn't to meet the princess again, but did meet her estranged husband though later that same year. Following our 1993 Sunday League Championship success against Kent, he kindly invited the team and staff, including wives, to his Highgrove estate in deepest Gloucestershire. Our chief organiser was Mike Fatkin who, for the previous five or six years had basically run the club, and always had a battle to keep this particular group of free spirits in line. This time though he needn't have worried about the players, it was my wife he should've kept his eye on!

Basically, Mike was panicking that we'd disgrace ourselves when being introduced to the future King, so he went to the front of the bus, grabbed the microphone and began his lecture on etiquette. His rules were quite simple. Firstly, wait to be introduced to the Prince by his representative. Secondly, on first introduction, we were to bow (or curtsey!) offer our hand and say 'Hello, your Royal Highness'. Thirdly, we then had to allow *him* to instigate conversation, and finally, if we met again during the evening, there was to be no handshake, just a plain 'Hello Sir'.

Simple as that.

The bus soon arrived at Highgrove and we trooped off, looking around at the estate, trying to take in all the sights, and peeking through the odd window, hoping to stumble across a bit of royal gossip. As we walked, Gail and Crofty's wife Marie edged ahead, and passed a window that was occupied by a security man who was staring at a bank of TV screens which contained security views from all over the estate. They both carried on walking, craning their necks to get a better look, perhaps into a royal bedroom or boudoir, when Gail became aware of someone standing on some steps to the left of her. She swung around, looked up to see the smiling face of the Prince, and remembering Mike's etiquette lecture, greeted him with a cheery 'Ooooh, hello.' I looked back to see Mike collapsing into a small heap of despair on the driveway!

My impressions of the Prince have always been good. He always seems to be interested in you or the occasion he's attending, he seems well informed (or well briefed) and really knows how to work a room! Later in the evening Matt, Crofty, myself and the wives were together chatting when the Prince joined us. He started chatting to Matt about his England experiences, asking how he enjoyed it etc, then talked to Crofty about his A Tour and then moved onto me and asked me how my season had gone. Somebody mentioned that we'd just had our first child Lowri, and he seemed really pleased for us and asked Gail how she was feeling, and enquired whether she was getting any sleep in the nights. He really knew how to put us at ease, and impressed us all even more.

Whenever I think of him, I also think instantly of Glamorgan colleague Alun Evans. Al and I now work together and I often give him stick about his 'chat' with the heir to the throne. This was also at Highgrove, but this time in 1997, after the County Championship win. Alun had already drawn attention to himself when he inspected a collection of swords placed on a table. Moving forward for a closer look, he knocked the table and sent the swords clattering to the floor. He was mortified. Then, later, when in conversation with the Prince, he mentioned that he hailed from Fishguard. His Royal Highness was interested in this as he apparently used to stay in Fishguard when he was younger, telling us that he always enjoyed the hunting and fishing he took part in with his father and brothers. But he couldn't remember the name of the place where he used to stay. So, Alun thought he'd help him.

'Must've been the Caravan Park, probably,' said Al in all seriousness. We all choked. The Prince, ever the gentleman, just smiled and said

'I don't think so. It was on an estate, just outside the town.'

I can't speak highly enough of Prince Charles. Everyone who attended that night had a story to tell about meeting him, and how interested he'd been in them. And as we left, he even made a point of coming across to Gail and me to tell us that he hoped we'd not have too many sleepless nights ahead of us. He was a classy guy.

My meeting with his old man wasn't quite as friendly, though.

When Glamorgan won the County Championship in 1997, it sparked weeks of celebrations, award dinners, interviews, and even an open-top bus trip around the streets of Cardiff. Heady days. For all the team's success, however, 1997 was pretty much a personal disaster for me: the worst season I'd had since cementing my place in the side five years earlier.

In my heart, I knew I hadn't really contributed in any acceptable way to the success, despite everyone saying that I was an integral part of the team and had played my part in other areas. OK, so I got 30-odd in a key partnership with Matt in a game we looked like losing, and had we done so the title would have been lost, but that was scant consolation to me, because I'd reached a point of my career when I wanted – no, expected – to perform at the peak of my powers in every game. Unfortunately, during the Championship season, the powers were at the crest of a slump. That season I'd averaged just 27.94 in the first-class game, with a top score of just 83, and that was against the Oxford students in a friendly. In the middle of this bad run, I felt my world was coming to an end, and it was made worse because it appeared that everyone in and around the Welsh media were saying how sad it was that I was having such a disaster in such an important year. I must admit I think I started to believe everyone and began to accept that I'd really had a nightmare, and as a result, started to doubt my worth to the side. Putting this book together, however, has allowed me to do some research, into not just my career, but also the careers of my teammates of the period, and I've come up with some stats that I wish someone had been able to point out to me at the time.

From the early to mid-1990s, Glamorgan basically had five regular batsmen: Hugh, Jamer, Daley, Matt and me. In 1994, Hugh averaged just 30.51. In 1993, Jamer averaged 28.24. In 1995 Daley averaged 29.61 and in 1996, 28.75. The year after our Championship win, 1998, even Matt averaged only 28.74. All these compare favourably (?!) with my championship year average of 27.94. At the time I don't remember any press coverage about any of these poor returns, or suggestions that any of these players should be dropped, as had happened to me. I guess it was just a case of me being unlucky enough of having my worst year at the time of the team's greatest success.

I tried to put it all behind me, and the boys were great, as was Duncan Fletcher.

Fletch also knew that I had other things on my mind in that Gail was suffering from some complications whilst carrying our second daughter, Seren. I was so worried about Gail that Fletch even relaxed the rules on mobile phones in the dressing room during the season for me, just in case I needed calling away urgently. I was extremely grateful for the compassionate way he handled the whole situation. Throughout it all, he never put any pressure on me and as I was part of the three-man team committee, along with Matt and Hugh, who basically discussed everything about team selection and make up, he always gave me the impression of valuing my contribution, and never made me feel anything but part of the team. I really appreciated it.

As I reflected on my lack of contribution at the end of the season, I finally decided to stop dwelling on it, took the rough with the smooth and accepted what was gone was gone. I tried to realise that the old adage was true about it being a team game where everyone makes a contribution to the whole, no matter how small that might be, and expelled the feelings of regret that my form hadn't been better.

Easier said than done.

As consolation there was to be an unexpected spin-off and I was to benefit from someone else's misfortune. Basically, the winners of the County Cricket Championship get presented with the trophy twice. Firstly, the trophy is taken to the ground where the most likely winners are playing, therefore, the ECB arrived in Taunton with the trophy, where following Matt and Hugh's magnificent hundreds, and not forgetting a brisk undefeated half century by my great mate Adrian Shaw, the result was never seriously in doubt. When the win was wrapped up, amidst typically jubilant and passionate Welsh scenes, Matt was presented with the trophy on the balcony. A truly fantastic, emotional, exciting and joyous experience. I can still see the scenes now.

On November 13 though, we were to be presented with the trophy officially.

At Buckingham Palace.

That certainly concentrated the mind. A couple of days after we'd come back from the celebrations at Taunton, I had a phonecall from Mike. 'I knew you were a good appointment as vice-captain,' he said. 'Don't let us down at the palace!' I had no idea what he was talking about. In the excitement of the previous few days, I had forgotten that Matt was flying off to spend the six winter months playing cricket in New Zealand. This now meant that I, as his vice-captain, would accept the trophy from the Duke of Edinburgh at the official presentation at Buckingham Palace.

Matt was probably disappointed and I genuinely felt sorry for him, and not a little bit embarrassed, bearing in mind my poor form that year. I always had a lot of time for Matt. We were very much kindred spirits, and even though our friendship would cool for a period over the circumstances of my leaving the club in 1999, at the time, that was all in the future. For years we were as thick as thieves and Matt was, and had been for some time, one of the most gifted and destructive batsman of his generation. Inexplicably, he failed at the highest level, but of all the domestic batsmen I played with or against in my career, in terms of pure ability and all-round game, Matthew Maynard – along with Graeme Hick – was the best. It's strange that neither player ever really succeeded at the highest level, but I suspect the only reason for that lies deep within each players own heart and mind. Sometimes, ability alone is not enough in sport, especially cricket, and for whatever reason, many batsmen have flourished at the highest level for England, without possessing anywhere near the pure talent that Matt and Graeme possess. Mark Ramprakash is another who seems to possess everything you need, but never really could transfer it to the highest stage. I guess the mystery behind this is one of the many reasons why people find sport, and cricket in particular, so compelling.

Anyway, Matt had been our talisman for some time, and enjoyed the happy knack of pulling it out of the bag for Glamorgan when we desperately needed it, and to those that know Matt well, you'll know that being centre of attention never fazed him in the slightest, so I guessed that missing out on being the focal point of the presentation might have been a bit of a blow to him.

Since 1890, when the first official championship was contested, Glamorgan had only won twice. I was to be only the third Glamorgan player in the previous 107 years to be in this position, following Wilf Wooller in 1948 and Tony Lewis in 1969. It started to dawn on me what an honour this was to be, and I couldn't help but feel extremely humble that I was to represent the team. Then I thought of some of the other guys in our team, more deserving of this privilege. Hugh Morris, Steve Watkin and Crofty had all played for England, Hugh was a former captain of the side, and was also retiring. Adrian Dale and Steve James had both played for England A. Waqar Younis was simply a legend and so on. Given my anxieties about my inadequate personal contribution to the winning of the championship, I started to have real doubts about whether I should pass the honour on to one of the others.

I chatted to friends and family who were themselves torn. They all understood how I felt, but were also desperate for me to pick up the trophy as they would all be so thrilled and proud. This is one of the twilight-zone areas of being a professional sportsman. To me, and probably every other person who plays sport for a living, it's the best job in the world. But after a period of time, whoever you are, and whatever sport you are employed in, you become pretty blasé about it, and largely you treat it as you would any other job. You get up in the morning and go to work. Same as everyone else. It's just that work can appear a bit more glamorous to those outside the game than more traditional jobs. My friends and family, however, always had a different take on this throughout my career. They, to a man, were sports fans, and every single one of them would have swapped places with me at the drop of a hat. My Dad, who had some ability as a batsman, would have given anything to play professionally, and Reeso, my former colleague at Swansea City and previously Arsenal had tasted it briefly, and if he had his time over again, I know he might have done things differently.

These were the people who were now urging me to accept this honour, as they could see from the outside that the likelihood of it happening to Glamorgan again, let alone me, was pretty remote. I was still unsure though. What swung it in the end was a bit of straight talking from Dave. He asked me if there was any point in having a vice-captain in sport in general and cricket in particular. I thought about it and said that there obviously was. He then pointed out that captains can get injured or lose form at any time during a season. The whole purpose of selecting a vice-captain according to Dave, is that you choose someone who has the respect, ability and stature to take over, with the least amount of disruption to the team, and that's why I'd been chosen. Then he started to ask me questions. What if Glamorgan had lost their first six games of the season and Matt had got injured, and I'd been put in charge for the rest of the season? Would I have thought of giving it away? Of course I wouldn't. He also asked if I had any idea how proud my mam and dad would be when it happened, and how disappointed they would be if I gave the honour away. That swung it, and I made my decision there and then to go ahead and do it. 'Final answer, Chris.'

The actual presentation is organised by the Lords Taverners. They arrange a top London Hotel, in our case The London Hilton, and also the ceremony at Buckingham Palace. As we approached the Palace and passed the usual sights that greet the London tourist, the atmosphere in the bus reminded me of a school trip. There were plenty of happy faces, general hilarity and an unexpected suggestion of awe on the faces of usually cynical, hardened cricketers! The only person not really joining in was me.

I had a knot in my stomach the size of a Windsor! My speech was worrying me, and the magnitude of the venue, responsibility and occasion was starting to get to me. Gail asked if I was OK. I replied that I would be in about an hour-and-a-half. I didn't say it with a smile.

We pulled through the gates of the Palace, and were driven under the arches into the courtyard where visitors are taken. We left the bus, lined up and waited to be shown into the building. A footman came out and showed us to an anteroom where the royal snacks and drinks were laid out. I'd have killed for a vodka and diet coke, but settled for the OJ. The knot in my stomach tightened again as I looked around at everyone surveying the splendour and opulence, when all I could do was look at my watch, praying that the moment would arrive quickly so that I could relax and enjoy the rest of my day.

My main problem was my speech. By then I'd done quite a few after-dinner speeches either on my own, or with Cofty, and attended countless sports forums for various clubs or businesses, and was very comfortable both with the task of standing up in front of people, and with the nature of my material, which I must admit was more Mike Reid than Peter Ustinov. But this was different. Totally different.

I'd been given an approximate time slot of two to three minutes, which doesn't sound a lot, but is plenty of time to hang yourself in front of the Queen's husband and a group of your peers. I wanted to find the right balance between having respect for the occasion, the surroundings and those present, but also injecting a respectful amount of humour. I thought about having a gentle dig at the Duke and his official title of Lords Taverners' honorary twelfth man, but bottled out of asking if he'd ever bowled the Queen a googly or a flipper.

Many thoughts were swirling round in my mind when a pair of doors opened. In walked the Duke, and we were ushered into the Buckingham Palace cinema room, where the presentation was to take place. The players and wives were shown in first, and I was told to hold back and walk in, just in front of the Duke, who would then make the presentation to me.

As I was introduced to him, I was struck by his general lack of feeling and interest. I thought I'd try to break the ice by mentioning my speech.

'I've been worrying about my speech all day,' I smiled.

He replied without turning to me,

'Don't worry about making a speech today, there'll be no time for that,' and off he walked. Now I didn't know whether to feel relieved or let down. For all my worries, I still wanted to do the decent thing and make my thank yous. We joined the others and lined up in place. I showed the Duke along the line of players, introducing them all to him, hoping there'd be a little banter, but the Duke just did the bare minimum of a gruff 'hello' and a quick handshake. When we got to the end, he was handed the trophy, said a few words which I've never remembered, unsmilingly thrust the trophy at me, said 'Thank you all for coming,' leaving me in no doubt that my oratory skills were not required at the Palace that day.

Despite all my anxieties, I couldn't help feeling a little flat. The boys saw the mixture of a crestfallen relief on my face and were suitably sympathetic: 'Great speech, Cotts,' and 'Who's your scriptwriter?' are among the lines I remember.

The afternoon at the Hilton was far more to our liking. Again the Lords Taverners had left nothing to chance. It was truly memorable. The knot in my stomach had gone completely, and after I made the loyal toast, my stand-in-captain duties were over and I happily slipped back to the ranks.

The presentation was far better than at the Palace. We all received our own personal mementoes of our championship success from the one and only Nicholas Parsons, President Elect of the Taverners. The personalised County Championship trophy, was the most treasured trophy I'd ever received in my career. It's in the style of a small ornate silver goblet, about six inches high, with an elaborate but tasteful design all carved around it. It came in a small leather box, and sat on a satin lining. On the back of it was carved 'Champions 1997' and on the front 'P.A. Cottey'. I'm hugely proud of it.

An amazing – and often surreal day – ended on a fitting note. About twenty-odd years after sitting down with Mam and Dad on a Sunday evening after tea to hear the announcer say 'From Norwich, it's the Quiz of the Week – Sale of the Century' and then watching Nicholas Parsons stride out to eventually present that week's winner with a kitchen or speedboat or something equally random, the same was now happening to me. This modern TV icon was striding toward me, smiling, and asking if I'd join him for a photo. Sadly, there wasn't a speedboat in sight.

CHAPTER FIFTEEN

Life in the Fast Lane

On the afternoon of April 24, 1997, a cricket ball left the hand of South African test-match bowler and all-round cricket legend, Allan Donald. He delivered it to our captain Hugh Morris, who at the time was 233 not out.

It's fair to say Hugh had his eye in.

In the split second it took to leave Donald's hand, the ball smashed into Hugh's face, knocking him off his feet, and making him momentarily unconscious. Blood immediately spewed from the wound onto the hard, pale batting strip. All the players watching on our balcony knew straight away that it was serious, and we all jumped up to try to get a closer look. Our physiotherapist Dean was already out of the door and running down the steps and out onto the pitch to help Hugh. I took a little more interest than most. I'd seen the pace that the ball was bowled at – it must've been over 90mph – and I'd seen, and heard, the sickening moment of impact. There was another, more selfish, reason why I took a keener interest.

I was in next.

Dean tended to Hugh out on the pitch for about ten minutes, then signalled to the dressing room that he wasn't fit to continue, and began to help him off the field. This was my cue to grab my gloves, bat, and most importantly my helmet, and set off to meet my executioner. My stomach was like a tumble drier. I remember my good friend Jamer look across at me with a forlorn look – 'All the best, Cotts,' he said. It's all right for you I thought, you've already scored 80-odd against him today, now it's my turn. Here goes.

You know that feeling when you arrive at the front of the queue of the biggest, fastest and meanest roller coaster at a theme park, and all around you, people are laughing and joking – as are you. But deep inside, you've got to stop yourself from holding your hands up and saying 'Sorry lads, I just don't fancy this at all – I'll meet you later at the burger stand.' Then the adrenaline of the moment kicks in and you get on the ride and have a whale of a time? Well, that's the best analogy I can give you of how it feels to walk out to meet someone of Donald's pace and calibre.

I've always been a bit of an adrenaline junkie. I've done a parachute jump, paraglided and done several bungee jumps, so even though I had the greatest respect for the pace that the fast bowlers I faced could generate, and even though I always walked to the crease with feelings of trepidation, once it all began, I must admit that it I thrived on it. Subconsciously, I'd treat the situation as my own private test match. As I was never to experience international cricket, I'd set myself up to treat the particular fast bowler I was facing – especially if they were test players themselves – as my own yardstick of how good I could be against them, and to maybe find out if I'd have been good enough to have played at the highest level.

In my career, I've batted regularly against most of the quickest bowlers ever to play the game – Donald, Shoaib Akthar, Courtney Walsh, Malcom Marshall, Patrick Patterson, Wasim Akram, Waqar Younis, Devon Malcolm, etc. And all these bowlers have one thing in common.

They've all hit me – hard.

Adrian Dale, who, to be fair, was a good player of pace, always said to me how much he loved facing quick bowling. It's not for me to say whether Daley really meant this or not, or whether it was a bit of bravado; all I know is that I didn't meet many fellow batters who loved it. It was just something you had to endure. When discussing the merits of such bowlers with many of my teammates and contemporaries over the years, most had nothing other than a very mournful tone in their voice when remembering the times they'd been hit and dismissed by these aggressive speed merchants.

Generally, as a batsman, you had two options. You either gutsed it out, took the smacks and the bruises as badges of honour, or alternatively you flinched, backed away, and showed your soft underbelly to the bowler.

If you ever – even for a split second – adopted the second approach, not only would the bowler seize on it in an instant during that innings, but also he'd never forget it for the next time he met you, and would rough you up accordingly. I know plenty of batsmen who, consciously or not, revealed this approach to playing pace bowling, and I also know plenty who were as brave as anything – John Hopkins at Glamorgan, for example. It's for others to judge me, of course. Indeed, it would be quite interesting to find out from some fast bowlers how I shaped up – that is if they remember who the hell I am in the first place! All I can say is that I never knowingly took a backward step and tried as hard as I could to get through the test. Sometimes I came out on top, and often didn't.

I mention John Hopkins with good reason at this point. 'Ponty' played for Glamorgan for eighteen years, and by the time I joined in 1986, he was coming to the end of his career. In fairness, he played for Glamorgan at a time when every season was almost always spent fighting off the wooden spoon at the bottom of the table. As I was to find myself at periods in my career, playing in a struggling team as a batsman brings its own unique pressures, especially when a fast bowler senses he's in for a quick kill.

The first time I witnessed Ponty's unique approach to dealing with fast bowling close up was during the first pre-season I had with Glamorgan as a pro back in 1986. This story illustrates quite well how an average supporter, however well meaning, has no real idea what effort a professional batsman has to go through, just to get up to the standard to take the field as a first-class player in the first place. When that player then trudges off after recording their third duck in five innings, and receives a bit of stick from the disapproving crowd, it's worth remembering the following story.

It was the first time that I'd batted at Neath's indoor cricket school as a member of Glamorgan's first-team squad. The club were struggling at the time – as they had for several seasons, but we had one real nugget, one genuine world-class player. Greg Thomas, our opening bowler. He had just broken into the England test team during the preceding winter's tour of the West Indies and was generally regarded as the quickest white bowler on the planet. At that time – and for a decade prior to this – the fastest bowlers in the world had all been West Indian: Courtney Walsh, Joel Garner, Andy Roberts, Colin Croft, Malcolm Marshall, Michael Holding, Patrick Patterson, Ezra Moseley, Sylvester Clarke and about ten others who only played when one of the above were injured. I shudder just looking at the names on that list.

In terms of pace, however, Greg was not out of place in that exalted list of quicks. Viv Richards and Desmond Haynes both said that Greg was as fast as anything they'd ever faced. I looked across at him from the spinners net at Neath in awe and thought 'I'll stay in here with Barry Lloyd and his off-spinners for a while!'.

There were three nets at Neath. The first two were occupied by the medium pace, spin and part-time bowlers, and the third was 'the fast net' which was Greg's territory, and one or two of our other seamers like Denis Hickey, Simon Base, Steve Barwick and Steve Watkin. I'd already had my turn this day, and was now bowling in the middle net when John Hopkins walked out of the first net where he'd been batting for ten minutes to get his eye in, and headed for the fast net. The surface of the fast net was quite a bit quicker than the other ones so you knew you were stepping up a gear as you took guard. Ponty motioned to Greg to open the curtain at the far end of the net, as well as the dressing-room door behind it. This added about six more yards to Greg's previously cramped run-up. As bowlers never had to worry about no-balling in the nets, all the seamers generally bowled off twenty, not 22 yards.

The length of a cricket pitch from stumps to stumps is 22 yards. The amount of time it takes a cricket ball bowled at any reasonable pace to leave the hand and reach the batsman is around a half a second. If a bowler bowls the ball from closer than 22 yards, then this obviously reduces that time still further. Now, Greg was plenty quick enough from 22 yards without bowling from twenty, but that's precisely what he and the others did in the net. I watched for the next 15 to 20 minutes in absolute awe, as John Hopkins dealt with everything Greg could throw at him. He hit a lot, he missed a lot, he was hit a lot – but he never flinched, never took a backward step.

Greg used this session as a decent warm up for himself too, and by the end of the session he would be steaming in at Ponty. My abiding memory of this, apart from Ponty's bravery, was the rebounding of the balls that passed him by. Because of the cramped conditions of the building, the wickets that Ponty was protecting were no more than a yard in front of the brick back wall. So when one of Greg's deliveries smashed into the back wall about six feet high, it would fly straight back at Greg in a pacey arc and land about ten feet back down the track. The sound this ball made as it thumped into the wall was sickening, the pace Greg generated was awesome, and as I mention, Ponty just soaked it all up.

At the end as we all showered and changed, I asked Ponty if he'd enjoyed that.

'Enjoyed it? Are you mad? No way. I do it because it sets me up for the season ahead. If I can cope with Greg in here, then I'm going to have no fears when I get outside during the season. I'll have dealt with all that in here. But enjoy it – no – it's just got to be done.'

Needless to say, from that day on, Ponty became, and remained, one of the batsmen I respected most in the game.

From this point on and over the next few years my career began to splutter into life. I was very much a fixture in the second XI, but on occasion, I broke into the first team – and when I did, it seemed always to be against Gloucestershire! They weren't really any better than Glamorgan in those days – apart from one key player: Courtney Walsh. Courtney is without exception the best fast bowler I ever played against in my life. Those early career figures of mine are testament to that: he got me out heaps of times, usually for less than ten runs. Unlike many fast bowlers who tried to shake you up with express-paced short deliveries which largely went over your head (especially in my case!),

Courtney never wasted a ball. Generally, if you missed a Courtney Walsh delivery, it hit you. His stock delivery was a very quick ball that pitched just outside off stump, but he had the ability to almost always make it jag back into your body. This obviously made you a candidate for leg before wicket or bowled, so you could never leave many deliveries from him. Once he worked out your strengths – in my case rocking back to pull or cut – he'd make sure he'd cramp you for room, which generally resulted in being hit around both thighs, midriff and chest. I always felt I earned my money facing Courtney.

I remember a sunny August day in 1993 when we played Gloucester at Abergavenny. We were batting in our second innings, hoping to set Gloucester a decent target to take a victory from them. Matt and Viv had both scored 90s in compiling our first-innings lead, but I'd missed out, having only scored 4, despite my best attempts to impress a certain princess. When the second innings came around, Viv was missing hurt, and as a result I was to bat at four in the order. By the time we'd reached 21, Courtney had sent both Steve James and Adrian Dale back to the pavilion for 1 and 10 respectively. As I walked to the wicket, I glanced down to the other end at Courtney who was just standing there, waiting, smiling. In all the times I ever played against him he never, ever slagged another batsman off, he was like the silent assassin. He always used to refer to me as 'youngster', probably because he didn't know who the hell I was, but at this moment, I didn't care – I just wanted to survive.

I tried to clear all the usual negativity from my head, took my guard and watched him run in hard. The first ball was a short one, and I managed to move back and pull it in front of square, for a one-bounce four. It felt really great and I remember thinking to myself – 'Christ, I'm in good nick here.' Courtney just stood there, hands on hips, looking at me. He raised his eyebrows, in a gesture I took to mean 'What have you just done?', turned round and walked back to his mark.

My adrenaline was absolutely pumping now. Not only was the battle on, but I'd just played a fantastic shot to get off the mark, and here he was, running in again. My heart must've been doing 170 beats a minute.

He bowled exactly the same ball, same action, same spot, same line, same everything. Except it was about 30% faster. I moved to get in the same position, to play the exact shot that had just got me four, but as I pulled back my arms to go through with the shot, the ball just hit me smack on the middle of my helmet, right where my forehead would have been, which was instead covered by the club crest, the famous Glamorgan daffodil. The ball smashed into the daffodil, nearly ripping the helmet off my head, flew high in the air, and landed about a yard inside the boundary rope for four.

I'd nearly headed a six.

For that split second when I'd totally lost sight of the ball and it smacked me on the head and I spun around wondering what the hell had happened, I must've looked like Norman Wisdom. As I struggled to straighten my helmet and to regain some dignity, I looked up at the big man in front of me. I almost wanted to apologise for my ineptitude! He smiled and said 'Oh, youngster', then laughed, and turned back toward his mark again.

We didn't score another run for three-and-a-half overs.

I had to face another three balls in that over, which I hardly laid a bat on, then Matt played a maiden out to Kevin Cooper, before Courtney bowled another full over at me. In total in that twenty-minute period, Courtney Walsh bowled twelve balls at me.

And he hit me ten times.

Talk about getting worked over.

As brutal as this was, the beauty of the torture was in the sense of achievement I enjoyed when I began to fight back. In football parlance it's called getting stuck in, challenging for headers and making lots of tackles – generally throwing yourself around. In cricket, as a batsman, you get in the same mindset, and create a battle between you and the bowler. The bowler nearly always wins – at the end of the day the most common score in cricket is 0 – but on certain days a bit of luck goes your way, and you see it through. I managed to hang around for the best part of three hours, and by the time I was out, caught off Cooper's bowling for 63, Courtney had long since finished his unplayable spell, and as I walked passed him, he called across, 'Youngster! Well played.' I was chuffed.

As I mention, Courtney never sledged – he didn't need to. But there were plenty who did. And in my career, the most verbose were Martin McCague, Shoabib Aktar, Andrew Caddick, Dominic Cork, Glenn McGrath and Phil DeFreitas.

I remember once at Colwyn Bay when I was batting with Canny in the early days and he'd been playing and missing for a couple of overs against DeFreitas. When 'Daffy' walked back to his mark and turned to run in to Canny, he just stopped dead, started whistling the tune for 'The Big Top' at the circus, and pretended to be juggling half a dozen cricket balls! He'd do anything to put you off.

What always made me laugh during my career however was the moral high ground that many of these bowlers took. Allan Donald was one of them. I can make this assertion now (I daren't have made it when I was playing for health-and-safety reasons!), but I don't feel that any fast bowler I ever played against was a hard man – bullies, yes, plenty of them, but hard, no. Hard men for me were the batters who never took a backward step against this onslaught, people like Mike Gatting, Robin Smith, John Hopkins and above all others, Viv Richards.

Viv in his 41st year was still batting without a helmet, an absolute and pure sign that he had no respect at all for the fast bowler desperate for his wicket. The number of times when I batted with Viv and a fast bowler would tear in and try and take his wicket, then, after two or three fruitless overs which involved being smacked back over their heads for six, the bowler would take his foot off the gas and just tamely bowl dot balls was remarkable. This was when the true bully in some fast bowlers would come out, because, when Viv was off strike and someone like me was facing, these bowlers would then go all out to crank the speed back up to soften us up. If I managed to squirt a single away to bring Viv back on strike, you'd visibly see the bowler change his impetus and just avoid being smashed away, until muggins was back on strike and then out came the kitchen sink again. Viv was always great here, though, because if I did take the bowler on and maybe hit a boundary, his huge voice would boom out for all to hear – especially the bowler – 'Biiiiig shot, Biiiiig Shot. That was a Big Shot for a little man.' I don't remember too many bowlers shouting back and telling him to shut up. Funny that!

What then was the rationale behind the quicks' moral high ground? Here was I standing motionless, 22 yards away from a fast bowler tearing in at express speed, knowing that one mistake or error of judgement that I would make in the 0.5 of a second I had to react, would either result in the loss of my wicket or serious injury or both. Yet the bowler, who would be snarling and staring back at his mark like a snorting bull always had six attempts to knock my block off. If I was to play and miss off the first ball, Andrew Caddick for example would just walk down the track at me, look at me like a piece of absolute dirt, and just say something like 'You're crap', leaving me in no doubt what he thought about me. Then the next ball would fly in, and if it was a bouncer that I chose to duck under, then the real taunts would begin: 'This fella doesn't fancy it' or 'If you don't like it out here, just piss off.' Then maybe the third ball would find me swaying out of the way too – 'This bloke really doesn't fancy it boys,' or 'Could do with a courage pill, fellas' and so on. Next ball, he bowls one right in my slot and I smack it square for four – this is greeted by a torrent of abuse that I can't begin to repeat, followed by the quickest ball of the lot which nearly takes my head off, and is accompanied again by more choice words questioning my courage.

Now then, fast bowlers, I've just stood my ground as you've hurled down leather missiles at the best part of 90 mph – never taken a backward step, and after each ball, watched you get angrier and angrier and the bowling get faster and faster and *you* question *my* courage? I always found it laughable. I know they will say they are trying to unsettle me – fair enough, some do – but the vast majority of them mean every single word they say. They really believe we have no courage because we duck and sway out of the way. As I mention, the very best bowlers, like Courtney for example, never said a word, they just got on with their job.

Significantly, when those really chopsy bowlers came into bat late in the innings, it was time for me and my fellow batters to laugh as we watched them backing away to square leg and wafting at a wide ball with an eye shut, just a few hours after abusing the shit out of me for my lack of moral fibre. One or two of these impostors would then strut around the bar afterwards like they were the baddest boys on the planet, yet the truth with most of them was they were just empty vessels, and you know what they say about those.

One exception however was Darren Gough. He'd deliver plenty of verbals but as soon as the day ended, he'd leave it all out on the pitch, come and find you in the dressing room after play, and if he'd given you a going over, grab you a beer and tell you if you'd played him well.

But back to Sophia Gardens in April 1997 with Allan Donald again on the warpath. It was with all these experiences somewhere deep in my mind, that I took my deep breath and replaced the injured Hugh Morris, as he was led from the field, in a daze, with a pink (previously white) towel over his cut head.

Matt, who was captain and had watched as Hugh was treated by Dean, came to greet me, looked at the scoreboard, and surveyed the situation.

'God, Cotts, he's bowling like lightnin'.'

'Thanks, pal,' I replied.

The score was now 515 for 3. I walked like the condemned man to take my guard. To Mr Donald and the chirping fielders, I tried to appear as nonchalant as possible, but inside my heart was pounding. As I looked down to place my bat for the umpire to give my guard, my concentration was broken by the amount of Hugh's blood that was all around the crease.

Then, Donald came careering into me. The first ball hit the shoulder of my bat almost as soon as it left his fingers. It remains the fastest delivery I believe I ever faced, and it just kicked up high into the air, bouncing just a foot or so inside the boundary for four – a la Courtney Walsh four years earlier at Abergavenny. I must be getting better at this game, I thought; at least it didn't hit me on the head.

I managed to survive the over with another streaky four thrown in and Matt came down for a chat.

'We really need 600 to declare, to bat them out of the game.'

We looked at each other and said nothing. We knew that was 80-odd runs away, which meant another hour of dealing with an increasingly aggressive Mr Donald. We both took a few runs off Gladstone Small in the next over, and with more luck than judgement we hung around and survived Donald's barrage for twenty minutes. By now I'd moved to 20 and Matt was on 16. Matt was facing, and took evasive action to a couple from Donald that nearly took his head off, then same as I'd done, fended a fiendishly quick one away over the slips for four, taking the score to 551 at the end of the over. Donald just stood there, hand on hips, looking at Matt with utter contempt.

Captain Matt, slightly knocked off his stride, came down the pitch, took one look at vice-captain Cottey, who was about to burst out laughing, looked at the new milestone on the scoreboard and enquired:

'What do you think Cotts?'

'Bloody right – five fifty's enough,' I said.

Matt laughed and turned to the umpires. 'That's it, Umps. We've declared.'

I don't want you thinking that us batsman are stupid as well as brave!

CHAPTER SIXTEEN

Fighting Fire with Fire

Fast bowling can be physically frightening. But equally intimidating is the mental and psychological pressure exerted on the batsman. It is given many names: sledging, chirping, mental disintegration, abuse. But call it what you want, it all has the same effect.

Sledging is not unique to cricket, of course; it goes on at the very highest level in all sports. As regards 1980s professional football, the sledging was extremely unsophisticated, to say the very least. If I was up against an old gnarled pro whose best sprinting days were behind him, and if I had the temerity to nutmeg him or make him look silly, I'd get away with it initially, but the next time the ball went dead he'd make a point of coming over to me, pretending to bend over and check his shin pads or something and then say, 'If you ever try that again you little prick – you won't be walking home tonight,' or words to that effect, but with many more colourful expletives thrown in for good measure. Another one that the established players loved trotting out to the young pros was 'Hey – how much money do you earn? Can you hear me, how much? Can you beat a grand a week? No? Well until you do just piss off out of my sight.' They would of course probably be earning five or even ten times more money than me. Another favourite was 'How many medals have you won?' or 'How many caps have you got?'

As you can see, the football sledger was often a very spiteful one, but not a particularly clever one. Cricket, however, was an altogether different business. Some of the lines were downright hysterical. Indeed, you often wanted to laugh at a good one yourself, even if it was aimed at you personally.

My all-time favourite sledge happened in a game that had nothing to do with me. In a game like cricket, domestically or internationally, good stories spread like wildfire. So when an overseas player returns to his county after a couple of months of international cricket, he'll come armed with an array of stories that took place during the series. Now, when it comes to curiosity about celebrities, your average cricketer is no different from your average fan.

Teammates will often ask an overseas player to spill the beans about the superstars: 'What's Shane Warne really like?' and 'Is Curtly Ambrose really as miserable as he looks?' etc. Now the story I have in mind has well and truly done the cricketing rounds, but I make no apologies for repeating it here.

It apparently occurred in a test match in Sydney between Australia and the touring Pakistanis in 1990. The Australia team of the time was captained by Allan Border and included such legends as Steve Waugh, Dean Jones, Mark Taylor and Ian Healy, but undoubtedly the heartbeat of the team was Merv Hughes. Big Merv had been bowling to the brilliant (and in-form) Javed Miandad, who had hit him for three successive fours and was now one short of another test fifty. As he smashed the third of those fours to the boundary, he apparently walked down the pitch, stopped just ahead of Hughes, and as he was tapping down the surface with his bat, looked up and said to Hughes – 'You're nothing but a big fat bus conductor,' and turned back round and went back to his crease.

Cue the steam to escape from big Merv's ears.

Merv retrieves the ball, walks back to his mark, turns, runs in, bowls a slightly quicker delivery – fuelled by the anger, no doubt – and watches as Javed plays another expansive drive. This time however, he fails to control the shot, and the ball flies to Dean Jones in the slips – out for 49.

As all the Aussies rush to congratulate Hughes, and, as the batsman walks disconsolately past him, Merv turns, and at the top of his broad Australian voice shouts at Javed:

'Tickets, please!' much to the hilarity of the rest of his team.

Now this is could well be an apocryphal story, and unless we can check it with Merv and Javed, we won't know if it's really true. Real or not, though, the point is that this type of thing goes on every day in any first-class cricket match. Sometimes it's funny, sometimes it's not, and sometimes it's just plain abusive.

I remember early in my career with Glamorgan when I became victim of the undermining sledge. This is when the comment is so dismissive that it hits you straight in the heart and almost takes your breath away, leaving you with no adequate comeback. My first experience of this was at the hands of the ever-so-well-spoken Mark Benson, onetime captain of Kent and now international umpire, and someone that we Welsh would describe simply as 'posh'.

I came into bat in our second innings at Canterbury in September 1992, and having dealt with the usual abuse about my lack of inches, had nurdled my way to 42 not out. As I nudged another one behind square and jogged through for the run at the end of the over, the tannoy announcer at the St Lawrence

Ground gave the news that 'With that run, Tony Cottey has passed 1,000 runs for the season.' Cue polite applause from the ground, and a slightly embarrassed raising of the bat from yours truly. As I did so, Benson, who'd gathered the ball up to give to his bowler for the next over, stopped dead in his tracks right in front of me, and said to me with the most quizzical of looks – *You've* got a 1,000 runs?' He shook his head disbelievingly, grunted and walked off.

Cheeky posh bastard.

I was livid, but had no retort. What could I say? If I'd given him a flustered 'Fuck off', he'd have just said something like 'How clever – you must be very proud?' or something equally disdainful. But he'd done his job. He'd cut me to the quick, made me really angry and got right inside my head – and that's what sledging's all about.

I remember years later when Sussex played Surrey at the Oval. This was when Surrey were winning everything and had developed a real confidence, based largely on an unbelievable level of arrogance and dismissiveness. Sometimes you wanted to punch them, but at times they were hugely amusing. On this occasion our young fast bowler Billy Taylor was going into bat, with us eight wickets down, and only Mark Robinson to go in after Billy. Now Billy had decided to fight fire with fire earlier in the game, and if there's something the experienced sledgers don't like it's a noisy little upstart having a go at them. As a result of this, we expected the Surrey boys to have something special planned for Billy. We weren't disappointed.

As Billy walked down the steps and onto the field all padded and helmeted up, he had to walk past the fielder at long-on. As he did so, the fielder walked straight up alongside Billy, and started peering strangely under his helmet visor with a puzzled look on his face. As Billy tried to ignore him, the next fielder Billy walked past did the same and so on until he got to the crease. At the crease the great Alec Stewart joined in and did the same. As we found out later, with much hilarity, they were all calling out 'Who the hell's this lads? Does anyone know who he is? Anyone ever seen him before? Nah – I don't know him. Does he play for Sussex? Surely not?' and so on.

Now Billy tried to laugh it off, but it had got under his skin. He was primed for the full abusive verbals, but this knocked him a bit off kilter. The funniest part however was still to come. Billy hung about for a couple of overs, and then nicked one to Stewart. As Billy turned round to walk off, we all turned to Robbo to wish him luck as he was next in. Then Stuart Osborne our physio shouted out – 'Hey lads, take a look at this'.

We all turned round to see Billy trudging off, and the whole Surrey team walking off with him. Billy glanced nervously round to see why they were doing it. The umpires appeared a bit confused to: there was still a man to come in. As they got closer, we could hear the Surrey lads all chattering. 'That must be it surely – there's no one left in there after him is there? There can't be anyone after him. He was so bad he must've been last man, surely? Who was he again? Anyone know? Anyone seen him before?'

With that they all pissed themselves laughing, and turned back, leaving a suitably chastised Billy Taylor to contemplate his future sledging approach. We sympathised with Billy when he recounted his ordeal with us, but I'd be lying if one or two of us didn't do so with a wry smile.

Further evidence of the often unique nature of the pursuit of mental one-upmanship occurred when I was batting against South Africa in 1994 At Ynys Angharad Park in Pontypridd. It was a lovely venue; the local council always pulled out all the stops when we played there, and as it was against the tourists who were fielding an almost full-strength test-match side, BBC Wales were televising all three days live. For players of my class, days like this were as close as we would get to playing test-match cricket. Whilst we always knew the tourists wouldn't play with the intensity of a test match, what they didn't like was losing, and if at any time during the match we were to get on top, then they would really crank it up and the sparks could start to fly. I loved it.

When we went into bat, led by Jamer and Daley, the rest of us took an interested look as to who was taking the field for the South Africans. They were still big news back then, as it was still only a few seasons since they'd been readmitted to the national stage, and nobody had seen any of these players in Wales before. We weren't disappointed. Hansie Cronje (capt.), Hudson, Kirsten, Wessels, Cullinan, Richardson, Symcox and Matthews, all test-match regulars, and last but not least, Jonty Rhodes, all took the field. Now Jonty was a bit of an idol to me. I certainly held him in high regard, but more than anything, I looked at his career from afar and often thought, if he can do it, so can I. We were a very similar stature. He was maybe an inch-and-a-half taller than me, but appeared to offer the same to his team as I did to mine. We both excelled in the field, indeed many judges commented he was in the team for his fielding, which had certainly been the case with me when I started out. But he'd now established himself in the middle order, coming up with important runs at crucial times of a match, which was very much how I was developing, albeit at a level below the test tier.

By the time I got the crease we were 72 for 3, joining David Hemp, the not-out batsman, who would go on to make 126. By the time I'd left the crease we were 309 for 5, and I'd contributed 84. Our partnership was great fun, and we started to get under their skin a touch. Hempy was an excellent runner – he was lightning quick, and always had the ability to turn a single into two, or two runs into three, and every time we managed this, we'd meet in the middle and have a little laugh together. This didn't go down well with the South Africans at all. At some point, I nudged the ball to the left of the right-handed Rhodes, and set off to pinch a single to his weaker hand. Quick as a flash he was onto it, gathering the ball cleanly, and switching it to his right hand in an instant. I knew straight away I was struggling. For me it was head down and arse up as I desperately ran my bat in as I rapidly approached the safety of the crease. As I got there, I felt the ball fly past me, and then heard the audible gasps and groans of the South Africans. He'd missed. I'd have been out. Comfortably.

Hempy came down the track, smiling. 'Well run, Cotts,' he shouted. I just grinned back and walked to meet him. With that, Rhodes walked closely by, and was not a happy bunny. To nobody in particular, but aimed at me I think, he shouted out 'C'mon lads we're not here to play this Mickey Mouse cricket, we're only here for the test matches.' I was gutted. If he'd had had a go at me personally, about my lack of ability, or just abused me in the ways we were used to, I wouldn't have given it another thought, but this slight did get to the marrow a bit. The reason being, I knew that to me this was a big game, a very big game, a real occasion. Like everyone, I had ambitions to play the game at the highest level, and if that wasn't to be then these games were as close as I was going to get. They were really important to me. Then to hear a guy I really admired basically dismissing the contest, and therefore me really – as Mickey Mouse – really hurt. I think at the back of my mind I knew that's what top test match players thought of playing the likes of Glamorgan, but to hear it so publicly, and said with such venom really hurt. But hey, that's life.

The South Africans also employed another, more sinister tactic. One fielder would shout something in Afrikaans at another, and they'd burst out laughing, usually to be joined by one or two of the others. Nothing wrong in that you might think; we couldn't understand what they were saying after all. But what was unnerving about it was that they'd end the sentence with 'little Cottey' or 'Hemp', and then burst out laughing. Quite quickly I realised I was being faced with a new type of sledging that I'd never come across before, and I must admit, I didn't like it at all. It was quite simple when you think of it, they were just planting thoughts in your mind – 'What are they laughing at', 'What have I done that's so funny' and so on. When I'd had to deal with direct sledging prior to that, it was fine. I was known in the game as someone who gave as good as he got, and was never really troubled by the sledgers. But this had been different, and had certainly handed them the mental edge.

At the end of the day, I had a chat with some of the lads, and told them what had happened, and how uncomfortable it had made me feel. I could see a plan starting to form in Robert Croft's furtive brain as I spoke. On the final day, Crofty scored 27, and whilst he was out there, he had the same treatment, and similar to me, it got to him a bit.

The following season, Australia were on tour here, and we played them at Neath. The team was badged Young Australia, but in reality it was their A team, and contained some class acts. If I run you through some of the names we took the field against, you'll realise they were quite a tasty outfit: Matthew Elliot, Martin Love, Justin Langer, Ricky Ponting, Stuart Law, Adam Gilchrist and Mike Kasprowicz. I think some of then had decent careers!

Anyway, we batted first and I copped a fearful amount of stick from their close fielders, namely, Ponting, Langer and Law. Law was unreal: he remains the first player I'd seen who sledged the bowler while he was batting! Fortunately for me, I got a hundred that day, and as far as I was concerned, they could call me what they wanted if it meant I'd get a hundred – especially against a team of that calibre. Crofty wasn't so lucky though. He got summarily abused, and then got caught behind by Gilchrist for a duck. He was not best pleased.

When we took the field, he unveiled the plan that had been maturing in his mind since the previous summer at Pontypridd . He asked if we remembered the South African sledging, and then suggested his own version, created in the Principality. He announced proudly that we'd sledge them in Welsh!

So we did. And they absolutely hated it.

The best one was Langer. We had some right fun with him. Crofty would trot past him at the end of the over say *'Dere cwningen Langer'* ('Come here Langer, my rabbit') and we'd fall about laughing. Langer didn't like it at all. Crofty kept on taunting his rabbit, and we kept laughing. Then our resident Englishman, our left-arm spinner Neil Kendrick, joined in. Every time he walked within earshot of Langer, he'd shout out the only Welsh phrase he knew – *'Hufen iâ, Langer, hufen iâ, Langer'* then burst out laughing – as would we. *'Hufen iâ'* is Welsh for ice cream! Whilst it was successful from the point of view of annoying Langer, and amusing us greatly, the main flaw in our plan appeared to be that the more annoyed Langer became, the further he hit the ball.

He scored 111. Back to the drawing board then.

But Crofty wasn't finished.

Some time later we played Sussex at Hove. Crofty thought it was about time he re-introduced his grand sledging plan again. This, however, was to be the last time it was displayed. He decided to pick on Jason Lewry, who was to become one of my best friends at Sussex. Jason was a hugely talented bowler, who, but for a catalogue of injuries, would surely have played for England. On the county scene, you won't find many players arguing against the statement that he's been one of the most talented and destructive left-armers of our generation. I remember Hugh Morris getting out against him after playing and missing five balls out of six for five overs against Jason some time earlier. Hugh said it was the best spell of bowling he'd faced in his career, and was glad to be put out of his misery in the end.

Trouble was though, Jason had *clustiau mawr*. Big ears.

Crofty jumped on this with relish. '*Clustiau mawr Lewry*' it began. And on he went. When he came into bowl and Crofty had defended, he'd shout out '*Bowlio cachu, Lewry*,' and laugh insanely. ('Shit bowling, Lewry,' I'm able to confirm.) After a spell of this, Sussex's lads were seething. But Crofty continued, making a comment in Welsh almost after every ball he faced. Jason walked back to his mark, and this time turned and ran in with a bit more purpose. He fired in the perfect ball to Crofty, it swung, it pitched, moved off the seam and beat Crofty all ends up – bowled – stumps flew everywhere.

Jason ran down the track like a madman, celebrating his wicket ecstatically, and from mid-on, courtesy of the normally mild mannered and eloquent Mark Robinson came the retort 'That's out in any fucking language'. He pointed Crofty the way to the dressing room, which is exactly where Robert proceeded to go. It was now the Sussex lads' turn to have a laugh at our sledging translation plan. I don't remember Crofty using his Celtic master plan after that.

Shane Warne, as you probably know, never died wondering on the field and has dished out as much abuse as anyone who's ever played the game. I'm very proud to say that I'm one of his victims, and also proud to say that I gave as good as I got.

It was when Glamorgan were playing the touring Australians at Neath and they pretty much had a test side out. Captained by Allan Border they included David Boon, Mark Waugh, Michael Slater, Damien Martyn, Ian Healy and Merv Hughes. But there was only one person the crowd came to see, and that was Shane Warne.

Now I can't claim that I know Shane Warne; all I can comment on is his demeanour on and off the field over the three days of the game and I can best describe him as brash, (surprise, surprise) cocky and bordering on the arrogant. At the time his hair was bleached the blondest of his whole career, and his habit of wearing bright lip salve, gave the impression of a tart on a Saturday night out. Like every cricket buff at the time, I was fascinated with Warne, and professionally tried to work out how best I could play him. The main delivery I had a worry over was his slider. This was almost impossible to pick and, if you didn't, you'd either get bowled or stone-walled LBW. He bowled this ball by almost squeezing it out of the front of his hand as his arm came over, almost as if it had backspin on it. To the batsman's eye, it appears as though it's going to be a short ball – almost a long hop – that's going to sit up and beg to be hit. On seeing this, the batsman would therefore rock back onto the back foot and the only decision then was to hit it for four or six through the off or on side. Trouble was, Warne was a genius, and it was perfectly disguised. Instead of it pitching short, as your brain was telling you it surely must, it would actually keep coming at you almost like a low inswinger, and the result was the ball – at pace – would smash either into your pads or the stumps. I'd seen him bowl it to a few of the lads – Matt for one rocked back to cut it, and the ball missed his off stump by centimetres. So I developed a plan. I decided I was basically going to get forward to every ball he bowled me and only use the sweep shot to score runs. My plan was quite successful really – I got 68 in the first innings and 38 in second but by the end of my second innings, Shane was more than pissed off with my approach and started to give me the verbals, which centred on my diminutive stature. He bowled one particular ball to me when I was on about 30, and as I swept, I caught it too high on the bat, and it just looped over the head of Michael Slater whom Warne had placed just backward of square for the catch. Relieved that I'd escaped, I just jogged through for a single. As I grounded my bat I sensed Shane was just standing still and staring at me. Finally, as he started to move away he shouted to me

'Oi – is that the only fucking shot you've got you little fucking pygmy'?

I let him take a stride further, and as he'd turned I just shouted,

'Thanks for the advice, Sharon.'

I judged from the laughter of Merv Hughes at mid-on, and the startled look on Shane's face, that he might not have heard that one before. I'm pretty certain that Warne wouldn't remember that incident – in fact he probably doesn't remember me at all! But now, all these years later, as we realise what a truly great bowler he has been – maybe the best that has ever lived – I feel strangely proud that I was one of his victims, bowled by him in that first innings for 68. My second innings was ended by a slightly less illustrious bowler, who only took 106 wickets in the whole of a twenty-year career – Allan Border! Told you that I probably wouldn't have made it at the very highest level!

190

CHAPTER SEVENTEEN

Partners in Crime

As I've mentioned elsewhere, I've been really lucky with the players I've shared my career with. Simply because I had some ability to hit a ball with a cricket bat, I've been blessed with some great friendships, at both Glamorgan and Sussex, and been really privileged to have been in a position to enjoy these friendships. But for ten years or so in my time at Glamorgan, I was pretty much inseparable from Robert Croft.

Crofty and I were roommates for nearly all my time at Glamorgan and, as such, were often the centre of much of the hilarity that went on in the dressing room. Crofty is the type of guy that has attracted much comment throughout his career – not all of it flattering – and sometimes, I hope he agrees, that has been of his own doing. Nevertheless we became kindred spirits, and really close friends, and I was honoured to be his best man when he married Marie. What is more, I saw first hand Crofty's good times – and there were many – and also the times when he occasionally had a bad day.

I remember the late Tom Cartwright telling me of Crofty's first coaching session with him at the Neath indoor nets. Crofty, who was about eleven at the time, bowled, and as you'd expect, Tom could see straight away that he had some talent. He was a little on the plump side – no change there – but those who were there could all see straight away that here was a lad with big potential. Toward the end of the session, Tom asked him if he wanted a bat for ten minutes at the end, so off he went pad up. When he walked back into the net Tom couldn't believe his eyes. Crofty had all the gear: Gray Nicholls' pads, gloves and bat, along with an impressive new helmet. But there was something wrong – it was his feet. As Tom looked closer, he could see that instead of lightweight batting shoes or trainers, he had brown industrial boots on, complete with steel toecaps. Tom couldn't believe it. Robert Croft was well and truly in the building.

Early on in our careers at Glamorgan, I guess the external observer would believe that you couldn't get two more contradictory characters than Rob and me. I was straight out of the school of hard knocks at Swansea City and brought to my cricket a fitness work ethic drummed into me by Tosh and Phil Boersma. Rob, it appeared, was more of a technical animal. Along with Steve James, for example, I'd always be off, road running between innings or after being dismissed. In those days the only time you'd see Crofty running on the road was when he was trying to make it to McDonalds before it closed. Despite this image, I should burst the first public misconception about Crofty. No, he was never the most dedicated trainer in regard to road running for example, but with regard his cricket skills, I never, ever played with anyone in my twenty years who practised harder. The hours that he put in during net sessions, bowling over after over was exceptional. It didn't happen just during scheduled training session's either. If, after a long day in the field, Crofty had bowled a couple of spells where he'd taken none for plenty, he'd come straight to me at the end of play and ask if I'd go back out with the baseball mitt and let him bowl at me. Obviously some times that was the last thing I'd want to do, but as he was often very insistent, it was hard to refuse. He'd then plonk a cone down at the batting crease, return to his mark and bowl ball after ball to me until he was satisfied he'd noticed some improvement, and thankfully, call it a day. If he continued to struggle during the next day's play, out we'd be again the following evening. He was like the golfer staying out on the practice range perfecting his swing. This area was where our cricketing beliefs fundamentally differed. I believed fitness was paramount, vital for me to base the rest of my game on. Crofty was different. He believed technical excellence was far more important, and as such, his fitness didn't interest him as much. Which of us was right? You decide. He played for England. I didn't.

However it was socially that we really bonded, and off the field, larking around in the bar and at team meals and days out, we were like peas in a pod. We always tried to find the humour in every situation, and I'm sure we pissed some people off along the way with our antics. We both had the same approach to a bad day, for example. Whether I'd got out first ball or Crofty had got none for a hundred, neither of us thought the best approach was to head for the hotel room, stay in, and watch *Coronation Street*. After we'd got rid of our disappointments in the sanctity of the changing room, we'd generally draw a line under it and head out for a few beers. Some other members of Glamorgan treated these disappointments the same as we did, Matt, for example; whilst others preferred a more studious approach. But it worked for us, and kept us from cracking up. The unwritten Glamorgan motto of the time was 'work hard, play hard' and to be honest, I feel this approach really contributed to the club's success both during my time, and in the years following my departure.

On the field Crofty was unbelievable at times too. I remember when we played Worcestershire in a one-day match at Sophia Gardens. It was around the time when Premiership footballers would dream up extravagant celebrations to bring out for the crowd when a goal was scored. Things like this were far too genteel for cricket. Not if your name was Robert Croft they weren't. He was fielding down at long-on in front of a big crowd, and as usual, between balls, Crofty had been enjoying some banter with both the home and away fans. Next thing, Steve Rhodes smashed the ball way up into the air, straight at Crofty, and it was obvious it was going straight down his throat. The ball was up there for ages – the worst ones – and when it finally came down, Crofty took a great pressure catch. What he did next stopped us all in our tracks. He just spun straight round to the spectators, threw down the ball and began machine gunning the crowd, spraying them with round after round of imaginary bullets and making that 'doof, doof, doof, doof, doof' sound you made as kid when you played war in the back garden. We couldn't believe our eyes. This was classic Crofty – if he planned it, he hadn't mentioned it to me or anyone else, and we just stood there pissing our selves laughing until he turned round to face us like Rambo. All he needed was Stallone's red bandana.

He's recently achieved an unbelievable personal milestone on the field too. In 2007 he succeeded in taking 1,000 first-class wickets, which in this day and age of covered wickets and perfect batting conditions – the best in the history of the game – is an astonishing achievement. When you factor in the 11,000 odd runs he's scored in the middle order, not to mention the important runs opening the batting in one-day games, I think people often underestimate the impact he's made on the domestic game, and also he's one of the few Glamorgan players in history to have consistent success over a decent period with England. And as I mention earlier, I firmly believe these results are testament to his commitment to practising his art.

There is however one period that I know Robert regrets to this day, and if he could turn the clock back, I'm sure he'd deal with it differently. It was when he was first left out by England, and returned to Glamorgan to be one of the foot soldiers again. I've never played at the highest level, but I know what it's like to be dropped from the first team to the seconds, after years of being an established pro. You go through a whole gamut of emotions: why has this travesty has happened; will I ever get back; is it gone for ever; will I ever play in front of a crowd again etc. But I'd imagine that being dropped by England must be ten times worse. The overarching feeling however is self pity, and that was something that Robert displayed, and to be frank, the boys in the team didn't react well to it. I felt that I was between a rock and a hard place as I was so close to him. I didn't think his behaviour was too crash hot – and told him too – but because the lads knew he and I were so close, it often fell to me to try and bring him back into line. 'Go and have a word with him – he'll listen to you,' was a frequent comment to me at the time. It took him a while to come round, but when he did, he became the life and soul of the party again.

One of the reasons he was picked for England is that Rob relished the big occasions, and if you look at his record in the Glamorgan quarter finals, semi finals etc, you'll find, that along with Matt and Hugh, he often performed at his peak. I viewed these games as a personal Everest and, as a result, my record isn't great – I probably made too big a deal out of the importance of the occasion and what it meant to fans, family and friends and so on, resulting in heaping un-needed pressure on my shoulders. Crofty however was born to it – he loved the big occasion. The bigger the crowd, the bigger the stakes, the better he liked it, and more importantly, the better he played. Maybe that's the key difference between a test player and a county player like me, the unshakeable belief in yourself and your ability, and the absolute relish with which you viewed the big occasions.

There have always been questions asked about Rob dealing with the short-pitched ball at the highest level which began with his dealings with a certain Mr McGrath from Australia in the 1997 Ashes series. Now I mention elsewhere in this book about my theories of facing fast bowling, and the intimidation that goes with it. Everyone accepts that it's an extremely tough area of the game, but, as a front-line batsman, you should possess the skills or reflexes to deal with it. On the international stage, Rob wasn't a front-line batsman, but as he wasn't a tail ender either, McGrath and co, quite legitimately were able to throw the kitchen sink at him – which they did with glee, McGrath getting him out four times. Unfortunately, the Aussies decided that Rob wasn't dealing with the barrage too well, and made this known extremely publicly. The result? Every time he came into bat they absolutely pasted him with short-pitched balls, and every man and his dog with access to a TV mike, a radio mike or a newspaper column dismissed Rob as someone who couldn't deal with the demands of fast bowling at the highest level. The whispers obviously focussed on a lack of bravery and heart, and to be honest I think that's very harsh. I'd be lying if I said that Rob didn't have issues with fast bowling at that time, but I genuinely think that the problem lay with his technique rather than anything else. The reason that I know this, is that I saw what Rob's critics didn't get the chance to see when this became a real issue in his career. Rob, quietly, without shouting it from the rooftops to his detractors, went to work in the nets against the bowling machine for hour after hour. Again, like his attitude to the practising of his spin bowling, he'd crank the bowling machine up to 85mph, and set it to bowl short lengths into his body and just gutsed it out, time after time to try to bring his technique up to a level to deal with the fast stuff dealt out on the international stage.

I hope he eventually swayed the doubters; whether he did or not is up to them, but all I know is the hard work he put in culminated in that fantastic rearguard action for England against South Africa in 1998, where for three-and-a-half hours he stayed his ground against the fastest, most hostile bowler on the planet – Allan Donald – to secure England a priceless draw, when the then peerless Donald took 6 for 88. You don't manage to do that at the highest level against one of the fastest bowlers who has ever played the game without possessing heart and bravery in some measure. And there were no steel toe cap boots in sight!

Unusually for sportsmen who are no longer teammates, Crofty and I remained close even after I moved to Sussex. This was partly because we only live about four miles away from each other, but also because we still appeared as after-dinner speakers as a bit of a double act. Our approach is quite an amusing one and often begins with Rob telling people how short I am and me telling people how fat he is! One of our earliest speaking engagements together was when we spoke at a benefit dinner for the club in Halliwell Hall at Trinity College in Carmarthen. There were plenty of tables filled by the great and the good of Carmarthen, and a table of the boys from Glamorgan. The fact that it was a mixed do with plenty of ladies in the audience added to the pressure slightly as I knew I'd have to watch my p's and q's a touch more than I was used to. Crofty was a bit late arriving which left me mixing with the dignitaries on my own, which I'm never too comfortable doing, until finally young Robert made his entrance. When he did, I knew we were in trouble. Much to the delight of the boys, Rob had obviously called in to a Carmarthenshire pub for a couple of nerve settlers beforehand and was now feeling no pain. He was quickly introduced to the VIPs as we were being shown to our seats on the top table. Rob and I were split by the Lady Mayoress, and on his right, was the Deacon of the college. We settled down to our starters and as I moved to my third mouthful of watercress soup, I nearly choked. Robert, having surveyed the splendour of the religious surroundings of the great hall, motioned to the Deacon, pointed to one of the effigies of Christ on the cross and said, a la Chubby Brown, 'I see you caught the bugger who stole all your silver'. I nearly choked. Crofty burst out laughing and the Deacon, looking quite startled, went back to his soup.

Worse was to come. Rob and I were introduced and, as is his wont, Crofty gets the microphone first, stands up, tells a few tales – hurls an insult at me – then hands the microphone over and sits down. I stand up, respond, tell my stories, and hand the mike back, and this is how it continues for an hour or so, and generally it's pretty effective. This time however Rob decided to open with a truly filthy joke, and one that was doing the rounds at the time. As soon as he began, I knew what was coming and sat there open mouthed not quite believing that he was going to tell this joke in mixed company. I glanced at the rest of the squad sat on the players table, who equally open mouthed, waited to see how far he'd go.

Over the next five minutes Crofty proceeded to tell, in ever more lurid detail, a fictional story relating to his recent England A team tour to Zimbabwe. It is a safari story that has done the rounds over the years, and featured many famous names in its many and various forms. In Crofty's version, it was his rival off-spinner, Peter Such, who became the butt of the joke; a joke which also features a violently amorous elephant. (Those who have heard it before will know the one I mean. The rest of you will, I hope, be suitably curious – but, I have it on good advice [Don Shepherd's, mostly], that re-telling the story here would not be in good taste!)

Anyway, as he ventured further and further into his tale, I watched the enthralled faces of the audience. They were hanging on Crofty's every word. And he revelled in the atmosphere he was creating.

As the punchline approached, I winced and awaited its delivery.

And sure enough it came. Crofty hit them with the most near-the-knuckle punchline that this (or any other) mixed audience would ever be likely to hear, and duly paused for their response.

It was received in total silence.

The hush in the great hall was only broken by the strangled guffaws of the Glamorgan lads and Crofty, laughing like a jackal.

I was ashen faced. He then handed the mike to me, and sat down.

'How do I follow that' was the best I could come up with, before launching into a tale about the hard work involved in getting psyched up to face fast bowling. Thanks, Rob.

To be fair, however, Crofty and I have continued to tour the country in tandem, telling our (usually) humorous and half-witted stories, confident in one another's ability to keep an audience entertained at formal, and more informal, functions.

I have to say that the biggest compliment I can pay Rob is that the happiest times in my whole career were those I spent in his company both on and off the field at Glamorgan when we were roommates, in what transpired to be a golden period in Glamorgan's history, and I'm as certain as I can be that the sustained success Glamorgan achieved during that magical period would not have happened without such a talented all-rounder in Glamorgan's side.

CHAPTER EIGHTEEN

Movin' Out

Monday, September 14, 1992, was one of the proudest nights of my life. At Swansea's famous Dragon Hotel, during Glamorgan's end-of-season player-of-the-year dinner, in front of players, club officials, supporters, friends and most important of all Mam, Dad and Gail, I was capped by Glamorgan.

Being capped is about the highest honour your county can bestow upon you, and is only really surpassed by being made captain of the club. It not only confirms your value and worth to your county, it also gives you added credibility in the cricket world at large. There are obvious financial benefits too; you get a pay rise which is always welcome (mine went up from £8,000 to £14,500 p.a.), you got a club car, and your bonuses for wins and cup or championship success also grew. As I've mentioned earlier, you also get to wear the proud Glamorgan daffodil on your cap and jumper. It's a fantastic honour to be given.

That night when I was called, along with Steve James and Adrian Dale, I thought all my Christmases had come at once. When you start out in cricket, you obviously set your self some goals – some achievable, some probably not. You dream of playing in a Lord's final, winning a league or even playing for England – some make it, some don't. But what you really nail your hat on though is getting capped. After you've secured your first couple of contracts, and realise that you've got a chance to make a career in the game, you really only set your eyes on one goal – getting capped. When it happened to me that evening, as I was presented with my cap by captain Alan Butcher, it was as proud and emotional a feeling as I'd hoped it would be. Little did I know then that it was going to also be the very reason why I would leave the club I loved so much just six short years later.

The facts around my leaving Glamorgan have remained a bit blurred to say the least as far as the public is concerned. This wasn't helped at the time by the club 'suggesting' to me that it would be a good idea to release an amicable joint press statement which would give the usual bland reasons for my leaving: 'new challenge', 'time to move on' – the usual soundbites. I've never spoken publicly of the real reason until now, and have no desire to re-open old wounds, it's simply that when I chose to write this book, I had no option but to write it with accuracy and honesty, and therefore it would be wrong of me to avoid any of the issues that occurred in 1998 when I had to leave the club that I loved, over what basically came down to a point of principle.

I have no problems with any of the central characters who will be outlined in the saga. At the time, certain friendships became strained, and after reading this, they may become strained again – but I make no apologies for this, as what happened, happened, as these people well know. While I can swear on the lives of my nearest and dearest that I hold no bitterness or ill will towards the club or the people concerned, a small part of me will always remain crushed that the powers-that-be at the time allowed my love affair with a club that was my whole life to be ended in such a disappointing and unsatisfactory way. I remain convinced that had it been any one of Glamorgan's other first choice first-teamers at the time – Hugh, Matt, Crofty, Watty, and Jamer, a way would have been found to keep them. Unfortunately that wasn't to be the case with me.

Looking back, the first thing that strikes me about the whole sorry saga was that the whole situation – my failure to agree a contract with Glamorgan, my leaving, and my discussions of a move with first Derbyshire and finally Sussex – was done without the aid of an agent or advisor. This was late 1998, and whilst agents had well and truly arrived in soccer, athletics, tennis and almost every other sport you care to mention, in cricket they were still regarded with an extreme feeling of suspicion. There were one or two cricketers at the time who boasted of having an agent, and by and large, these players were regarded as being total prima donnas. How wrong we all were. If I could give any young cricketer – or any professional athlete come to that – one piece of advice, it would be to get a good, trustful agent or solicitor to act on your behalf. The reason for this is not just to get yourself the best deal, longer contract or a bigger car or whatever else may be important to you, but far more importantly it's to take the emotion out of the equation. The circumstances of my leaving Glamorgan were not pleasant – for anyone. Now, nearly ten years on I can see both sides, but at the time I couldn't, and in a situation like that, hurt, pride and emotion begin to cloud your judgements. What you need is a financial expert to sit down with you and discuss the bald facts, someone to say 'I know how let down you feel, I understand how hurt you are – but from a financial point of view, my advice . . .'

When you are the person right in the middle of this wrangling and trying to sort out the best deal and also trying to protect your own pride and self worth, you unwittingly move away from what could be a sensible compromise. I chose to leave the club I loved, leave the best friends I had lived and worked with for the best part of fifteen years, purely over a point of principle. As a result, I also made a really bad financial decision. I'm convinced now that had I received some level headed, forthright advice from a professional person detached from the situation, I would never have left the club. The people I did turn to for advice, my family and closest friends, were similarly affected by the emotion of the situation, and on my behalf, were as hurt and upset by my treatment by the club as I was. As a result, the underlying feeling all of them had was one of 'Bollocks to them, Cotts – you're best off leaving'. At the time, this is precisely what I wanted to hear, so this more than vindicated my feelings about leaving. Whilst I'll always be grateful for their help and support throughout my career – the only type of person who could really have helped me at the time would have been a total stranger with no sentimental attachment to me or the club.

But what brought me to this point? Well, it was two separate events really: first was getting capped in 1992 and second was my bad batting year in 1997, Glamorgan's championship season.

Early season 1992 saw the club recognise Crofty's achievement of being called up to England's A team tour of the West Indies, aged just 21, by awarding him his county cap. The cap system factors in achievement, not just loyalty and consistency, and even though Crofty was four years younger than me and had leapfrogged the likes of Jamer, Daley and myself, we had had no qualms whatsoever about this richly-deserved recognition. Later that year, Jamer, Daley and I would all be capped on the same night, which meant that there were more capped players on Glamorgan's books then than at any time during my stint at the club, and this also meant that there were more players than ever before pinning their hopes on getting a benefit season at some later point in their career.

Every player always knew where they stood in the order of things in terms of a possible benefit. If players were fortunate enough to get a benefit season, then the order was always dictated by who was capped first. We all knew that Crofty was ahead of us three, fine, but what we didn't know was the order that Jamer, Daley and me were capped, as essentially it was done at exactly the same time, on that night in Swansea. This was to prove a vital issue.

The other problem was my 'bad year' in 1997 when we won the championship.

One thing I hope you've learnt from this book so far is that I haven't 'bigged myself up' in relation to my career. I've never been comfortable with that side of things; I've always been more than happy to be one of the unsung members of the team. I've often found it amusing watching other players almost fighting for the limelight but I've never thought any less of them for it, the exact opposite in fact; good on them all for seizing most of the opportunities that have come their ways. I'm starting to realise that there's a long old life after cricket, and I'd urge any young player reading this book to make as much of the opportunities they have in cricket, and also make the most of any financial spin-offs that are available to them – believe me, you'll need them after you've finished playing!

But I hope you'll bear with me now as I attempt to give some statistical justification to my career with Glamorgan to try to smash a bit of a myth about me that I was only an 'old-fashioned hard-working, bits-and-pieces cricketer', as I was often called.

From the five seasons since I was capped by Glamorgan in 1992 to 1996, prior to my annus horriblis of 1997, I scored 6,496 first-class runs for Glamorgan. In that five-season period my batting average was 47.41. During that same period Glamorgan had five regular front-line batsmen, including me, who more or less played every game, and all of whom (apart from yours truly) either played for England or England A: Hugh Morris, Steve James, Adrian Dale, and Matt Maynard. In the same five-season period, their averages for Glamorgan were as follows:

Hugh: 45.18   Jamer: 39.26   Daley: 33.72   Matt: 45.80

In the same five seasons there were several other very well known batsmen playing for England on the highest stage: Mike Atherton, Alec Stewart, Nasser Hussain and Allan Wells – whom I include as I more or less replaced him at Sussex. Their county averages for the same five seasons were respectively 42.25, 45.14, 45.26 and 44.75.

Please don't think that I'm claiming that I was a better player than any of the players listed above, because I'm not; all I'm trying to illustrate is that for five years – which is a pretty sizeable chunk of a player's career – I had a higher batting average than them all. I felt therefore that when contract talks next came around, my record over this period would be taken into account, and would count for something at that time. Maybe it was my fault.Maybe the county weren't aware of these facts, perhaps I should have taken them in with me at contract time – I don't know. However, I had the feeling in 1998 as the talks about my contract began, that my poor year of 1997, was becoming one of the major factors in the negotiations from the club's point of view.

The contract I was about to be presented with was to be the eighth one I had been offered in my career and the previous seven all had one thing in common – I'd never argued about a single thing: length of contract, amount of salary, bonuses, nothing. I'd always accepted them all and signed straight away. I was about to do exactly the same with this one. I just had one question, one that would turn my professional, and more importantly, personal life, upside down.

'What is the order of the benefit for Jamer, Daley and me, when we were all capped in 1992?'

I took the deafening silence as the first hint of a problem.

The issue in my mind was quite simple. I wanted to know if the contract I would sign would keep me at the club long enough for the <u>possibility</u> of being awarded a benefit. Of all the full-time professional sports in this country, cricket is one of the most poorly paid. It's improved a hell of a lot in recent years, but still lags behind most sports which enjoy a similar level of prestige. I'm not moaning about that, just stating a fact. The contract I was being offered was £35,000 per year for two years. This was effectively for two periods of six months because in those days – as with many cricket clubs now – you were only employed by the clubs from April to September, and if you chose to, you'd have to get another job in the winter. Some worked in the Glamorgan's commercial department in the winter months, all the younger players would find some way to get abroad to Australia, New Zealand or South Africa, as I'd done years before. People of my age – then in my early thirties – would stay at home and do some coaching and try to get the money spread throughout the year. I often worked for Dad in the winter, back amongst the axle grease again. The summer lifestyle of a cricketer was fantastic, it was less so come wintertime. One thing however was always on the horizon of the cricketer who managed to carve out a career in the game.

A Benefit Year.

A benefit year or testimonial was basically a reward given to a cricketer who satisfied two criteria – firstly they had to be capped, and secondly, it was usual that they had spent ten years in consecutive service with the same club, since being capped. At Glamorgan, this second rule wasn't rigidly adhered to as, during my time, several players had received benefits before their ten-year period was completed. The award of the benefit was seen by the players as very much a conveyor-belt process that every player became aware of, the more established they became at the club. When I joined Glamorgan, people like Hugh Morris, John Hopkins, Geoff Holmes, and Steve Barwick were all well established. As I became more of a fixture in the dressing room myself, I would notice that the talk amongst them would often return to when they would be receiving their benefit. These lads would be planning ahead to make certain that their next contract would encompass their tenth capped season with the club. If this date fell in the first year of, say, a new three-year contract, it more or less guaranteed that they'd receive their benefit year at some point during the three years of the contract. The problems came when they signed a two-year contract, which would only take them up to their ninth capped season. If they were shown the door by the club at that stage, they would never be entitled to a benefit.

In today's money, a benefit – which is untaxed – would probably get you between £100,000 and £150,000, which pretty much sets you up for life after your retirement. It's not enough to never work again, but it would certainly clear the mortgage and give you a few decent options up to 'proper' old age.

Hugh, John, Geoff, Baz, Matt, Colin Metson and Rodney Ontong all received benefit seasons whilst I was at the club. For a player, there's an unwritten code that ensures that he supports the beneficiary at every turn. This means playing in about three or four benefit games at local cricket clubs as a Glamorgan XI on your day off – usually a Tuesday – and attending several dinners in support of the player concerned, and in my case often speaking for 40-odd minutes at the dinners to the great and the good of the local business community in the area. Golf days were also popular and were fitted in on other days off, when you acted as the 'celebrity' partner with three other business types who paid for this privilege. (Why anyone would want to pay to play golf with me and my duck hook for four hours is anyone's guess?!)

At the end of the year all the money raised from these events, along with buckets passed around during several Glamorgan games, would be presented to the player as a reward for their continued commitment to the club. The time given to a player's benefit year by the other players in the squad was never questioned, usually for two reasons; firstly, the beneficiary deserved it and we were more than happy to do it, and secondly we all hoped and prayed the players would do the same for us one day, if we were fortunate enough to be in the same position.

By the time contract talks came around in late 1998, I was now in the position that had been occupied by Hugh, John, Geoff, Baz and Rodney when I'd first joined the club. I was on the fringe of the benefit scenario, and had celebrated thirteen years on the playing staff of Glamorgan – seven of which were as a capped player. Hugh, Matt, Metto and Watty had received their benefits, and I knew I would have to wait my turn. Fair enough, no problem with that at all. The next in line was to be Crofty as he was capped earlier (in 1992) than Jamer, Daley and me – order unknown.

I'd been at the club longer than both Jamer and Daley, but that was irrelevant as the guide to the order of a benefit was always who was capped first. What was needed – certainly in my mind – was publication of the order in which we were capped on that night back in 1992. Apparently – nobody at the club knew. I couldn't believe that something that would have such a massive financial bearing to all three of us, had not been recorded somewhere. That's what I was eventually told, and therefore, that's what I had to accept.

It's at this point that I'd like to put straight the first of several rumours that have followed me around since this time.

At no point during contract negotiations did I ever insist or demand that the club offer me a benefit. My view was then, and always has been, that a benefit is awarded – not demanded or requested. As a cricketer, all you could do is hope you were at the club long enough to be in a position to accept a benefit if one was offered.

When the club could not tell me the order of the cap awards, they asked why I wanted to know. I stated that it would affect the length of contract I would like to negotiate with the club. I reiterated that I would have absolutely no problem whatsoever with whatever order of the 'capping' that they decided on. If I was to be last of the three – fine; I'd be disappointed yes, but at least I'd have known where I stood. If I was to be first – fine too – but this was why I had to hold out for a three-year contract as that would take me to 2001, which was the earliest I would become entitled to a benefit. This meant that I'd then be in a position to accept a benefit if offered. That's all I wanted.

The club however were insistent. They were saying that there was no order. I'd just have to wait to find out and they would only offer a two-year contract, nothing longer. I went to see Mike Fatkin the club's chief executive. He had autonomy over money; the club's cricket committee had autonomy over the length of contract. Mike was extremely sympathetic and outlined straight away that he would do everything he could to keep me at the club. He instantly offered me more money. The offer on the table from the club's cricket committee was two years at £35,000. Mike said that as I was vice-captain of the club, it was perfectly in order to offer me a premium in addition to this £35,000, so he offered me an extra £2,000, and a two-year contract now increased to £37,000. I really appreciated this extra offer and thanked him, but I explained to Mike that the money was not the issue here at all, and reiterated that for me, the issue here was about one thing only – the length of contract.

The next myth to explode? *I never, ever asked for more money, nor when refused, walked out.* In fact, it was just the opposite. I actually asked for less money (Told you I should have had an agent!). I wanted to demonstrate how important the issue of the three-year contract was to me, so I said to Mike that I would like to be offered a three-year contract, and in return for this would be willing to come down from the £37,000 a year now on the table to £31,000 a year. Now hindsight shows us that I played for six more seasons in first-class cricket after 1998. The way cricket works is no different to an incremental system at any company: the longer you continue to serve the company, the more established you become, the more your monetary contract is increased as time goes by. We can safely assume, therefore, that had I stayed with Glamorgan for six more years and signed that two-year contract for £37,000, in two years' time, my next contract may have been for, say £40,000 or maybe even more. What I was proposing to Mike was effectively a minimum saving to the club of at least £6,000 per year for three years – £18,000. I don't think Mike had ever dealt with a player asking for less before! He still urged me to accept the two-year deal for £37,000, and take the risk that in that two years I'd be offered another contract. I said I just couldn't take that risk – what if I got injured and my career was ended – and asked that my proposal be officially put before the club.

Looking back now, I realise that one problem above all prevented me taking the risk of signing the two-year deal. Even though I'd bounced back from my bad year in 1997 by getting a thousand runs, I still felt that there was a growing perception about me that my career was on the wane. I'll never know if this is true or not, but that's the feeling I was given. I'd never been a player to attract the headlines, even in my best period between 1992 and 1996, and I'd grown used to that and it never really bothered me. What did bother me increasingly though was the regularity with which my bad year was always brought up: 'Cottey still battling to rediscover his touch', 'Cottey not as fluent as he's been in the past', 'Cottey needs to impose himself at the crease as he used to before 1997' were all examples of comments printed in the media around this time, and I felt that the people in power at the club were reacting to these, and as a result, feared offering me the longer deal. If that was their opinion, fine, but I'd have liked to have been given the opportunity to debate the matter, and point out just how good my career stats were up to 1997, and how I viewed that year as just a blip. As it was, my mind became filled with these sub plots – imaginary or not – and I began to adopt a bit of a bunker mentality of basically 'It's three years or nothing'.

All I really wanted was someone in power at the club, whether that was Matt as captain, Mike Fatkin, or, more importantly, members of the Cricket Committee to say 'Cotts, you're an integral part of the team and club here, we see you playing a key on-field part in the future of the club, we hope to have you on board for many years to come, so please sign the two-year contract and stay and help us all move Glamorgan forward'. I'm certain that's all it would have taken, and I'd probably have climbed down from my point of principle and changed my mind and signed. As Steve James correctly points out in his 2004 autobiography *Third Man to Fatty's Leg*, I had a bit of a reputation for changing my mind, but on this issue, when everyone apparently hoped I would do a u-turn, I didn't. The key reason for this is that it was becoming increasingly obvious that the club didn't see my first-class career carrying on after this two-year deal, and this view would be proved beyond doubt, just three or four weeks later.

As all this uncertainty continued, there was still cricket to be played. Our next game was against Derbyshire, and at the end of play on one of the evenings, I found myself talking to their wicket keeper and vice-captain, Karl Krikken, someone I'd become friendly with on the circuit over the years. I chatted to him about my situation, and told him that if the worst came to the worst I'd leave, and look for the security of a longer term contract elsewhere. He seemed very keen that if that was the case, he was certain that Derbyshire would be interested. I pushed my luck a bit and asked if a five-year contract was a possibility. He said he couldn't see why not, but as Dominic Cork, Derby's captain was not playing in the match, he couldn't take it any further, but suggested we all meet to talk it over. The following weekend Karl was getting married, coincidentally to a Welsh girl at Barry near Cardiff. Corky would be at the wedding and it was arranged that I'd pop along in the morning of the wedding to meet him. Corky was really keen and talked about a five-year deal in the region of £38,000 per year. I was so relieved that someone of Cork's stature in the game actually thought that my best years may be ahead of me, and was willing to invest significantly to confirm that fact.

I went away from the meeting feeling more positive about myself than I had for several weeks. Another fact that should be pointed out here, and can be proved by Cork's involvement, and subsequently Chris Adams' involvement when I eventually joined Sussex, was that a cricket captain always got the player he wanted. The only rider to that was unless there was a budgetary issue that ruled it out from the start. I realised that I'd have to speak to Matt officially to find out where he stood on the whole issue, and to see if he backed me. Now that I was armed with an offer of a five-year contract, I felt a little more confident to fight my corner for a three-year deal with Matt.

The discussion took place in the Beverley Hotel near Sophia Gardens in Cardiff after a game. There were four of us talking, Matt, Crofty, Dean – our physio and general voice of reason and common sense – and me. The conversation came around to the contract deadlock and I mentioned how I felt that 'I hadn't been treated very well'. I think the boys felt it was just a storm in a teacup and would soon be resolved and the feeling from them all was 'Don't be stupid – you'll never leave.' Dean tried to assure me that I would eventually get a third year, and not have any silly thoughts about leaving. I then turned to Matt who hadn't really committed himself either way and asked him a simple question.

'Matt, bearing in mind I'm your vice-captain, do you see me as part of Glamorgan's first team in three years time?'

I was desperate for him to say 'Yes, of course, don't be stupid.' Had he said that, I'd have forgotten all about Derby's offer there and then and would have signed the two-year deal the following day.

'Nobody can see that far ahead. We can all get injured and lose form – it's hard to say.'

My heart missed a beat. I was gutted.

'OK,' I said. 'Do you see me as part of Glamorgan's squad in three years' time?'

'Yes,' he replied.

That was better than nothing I thought.

'OK, then,' I continued, 'All I'm asking you is will you do all that you can to get me the three-year contract I discussed with Mike'.

'Yes I will,' replied Matt.

It had been a very awkward few minutes, but I honestly didn't think I was asking for the earth here. All I was trying do was protect mine and my family's future by ensuring I would be at the club when my possible 'turn' for a benefit came around. I don't feel I was asking for anything excessive, nor do I feel I was putting the gun to anyone's head. Bearing in mind I'd been offered a much longer contract at better terms by Derbyshire, I honestly hoped that with Matt now on board, I might just get the deal I craved.

A few days later the cricket committee convened, and one of the items on the agenda was my request for a three-year deal. This was where I hoped Matt would come into his own, and whilst he didn't have a vote, the captain's view on occasions like this was generally the clincher.

I lost the vote with only two members of the committee voting my way.

When the news was broken to me I could have cried. I was going to have to leave.

In late 2007, I was talking to Alan Jones about the circumstances of my leaving and brought up the fact that I'd been told some time ago that Matt never attended that meeting that was so critical to my future at Glamorgan, despite him telling me he would do all he could to secure me the three-year deal. Not only did Alan confirm that Matt didn't attend, he also had worse news. Alan had been on the coaching staff at the time, and, though he had no vote, he had been at the fateful meeting where his opinion was sought. Alan told me Matt, First XI coach John Derrick and he had met to discuss the issues of contracts prior to the meeting, and my particular situation was discussed. He confirmed that Matt indicated that I was only worth the two-year contract on the table. John and Alan apparently took a differing view and pointed out to Matt that it was their opinion that every effort should be made to keep me and that I should be offered the three years that I was requesting. During the actual cricket committee meeting that took place later that day (attended by amongst others Gerard Elias, Huw Davies, Peter Walker, Wyn Walters, Brian Shackelton and former Warwickshire player and broadcaster Jack Bannister) John and Alan were asked their opinion as coaches. They both confirmed that they believed I was certainly not asking too much for a three-year deal and it was their opinion that I should be offered such a deal and not backed into a corner that may see me leave the club. Apparently, Jack Bannister said that if that was the opinion of the coaching staff, then that was good enough for him and he voted for me, as did Shack. All other votes went against me.

Former Glamorgan legend and later, respected journalist Peter Walker voted against me. He tracked me down, told me how he voted, and gave his reasons why. As disappointed as I was, and as much as I disagreed with his reason, I have nothing but the utmost respect for the way he dealt with me.

I retreated to the confines of friends and family and went through the options. Now that I knew I had to leave, the upshot of our deliberations was to approach some other counties to let them know I was available, armed with the knowledge that Derbyshire had already made a concrete offer. This whole process left me cold. I hated the thought of phoning and contacting people out of the blue – I felt I was just prostituting myself. To show you how naive I was about the whole situation, I based my criteria on playing for someone where I wouldn't mind living. I'm from Swansea and have always had an affinity with the sea and the wonderful sweeping Swansea Bay, so a seaside club became my first choice. The first county that came into my head was Sussex. I can't believe that looking back I didn't first consider a county with a proven track record of success – say Warwickshire, or a county renowned for high wages and big bonuses – say Surrey or Lancashire. No, I went for one with a beach! In truth, what would have precluded me contacting any of the big-name counties was that deep down, my self-esteem had taken a real battering at Glamorgan, and part of me thought that I had no right to consider a 'big' county. I was just going to be grateful to secure a contract with any one of the seventeen counties out there. Sussex, however, ticked all the boxes. We've established they had a beach, I'd always played well at Hove and always liked the ground, I'd also never had any bad experiences from any of their players, and knew one or two – Pete Moores included – and got on quite well with them. That all seemed good enough reason to give captain Chris Adams a ring. I managed to get his mobile number from somebody, and sat down one evening, took a deep breath and took the plunge. He answered straight away 'Hello, mate' came the friendly reply when I told him who it was. I began to awkwardly explain why I was ringing, and after a moment he stopped me and I heard him say to someone 'Excuse me a sec, I've got to take this call'

Years later Chris and I were chatting about that phonecall, and I was squirming with embarrassment remembering how I felt ringing him up out of the blue that way and hawking my services. 'You didn't go to the PCA awards dinner that year did you?' asked Chris.

'No – how did you know that' I asked.

'Because that's where I was when I took your call.'

I told Chris I remember he was speaking to someone and heard him ask to be excused to take the call.

'Yeah, I know,' he said. 'It was Matt Maynard I was speaking to when I answered,' he laughed. Talk about unhappy coincidences!

Anyway, after Chris had ducked away from Matt, he confirmed that he, as captain, and therefore Sussex, were definitely interested, and didn't think that five years for the contract would be a problem. He said that he'd have to speak to coach Pete Moores and chief executive Dave Gilbert, the former Australian Test player, but he promised to get back to me soon.

I was quite relieved Chris had been so positive, and thrilled that he took the five-year contract issue in his stride. I took great confidence from the fact that the only two counties I'd spoken to had not seen any problem with a five-year deal, when my own county had taken an official vote to only offer me two years. This only strengthened my resolve to leave – misguided or not.

Pete Moores rang me back a day or two later, was hugely positive about the situation, and said that the club were extremely interested in speaking to me, and hoped he could offer me something that I would find attractive. I thanked him very much and agreed, at his suggestion, to meet with him and Dave Gilbert at Newbury Services two days later. I put the phone down and my head began to spin. This was such a different approach compared to the one that Glamorgan had decided to use. I felt that with Glamorgan they made me feel that I should be grateful that they were offering me a contract at all. Sussex however were approaching it from a totally different angle; it appeared that they were actually bidding for my services and were pulling out all the stops to get me.

The day of my clandestine visit to Newbury Services came, and my good friend Anthony Rees came with me for moral support. Reeso had played professionally for Arsenal as a youngster in the same youth team as Tony Adams, Martin Keown, David Rocastle, Niall Quinn and many others. He'd also played briefly with me at Swansea City fifteen years earlier, so at least had some idea of the workings of professional sport. But with the greatest respect to Reeso, a sports agent he wasn't, and when I left him in the car and went in to meet Pete and Dave, I was very much alone, and had no real idea what I was about to discuss.

We got the niceties over with and I briefly outlined my situation with Glamorgan. After this was explained, we then got down to brass tacks.

They both said they wanted me, and were delighted that I'd considered Sussex. 'Considered'? If only they knew the truth!

When I reflect on this meeting I blush at the absolute naivety that I displayed, and am eternally grateful that Pete and Dave are such honourable men as they could have absolutely fleeced me. Dave asked how much money I wanted. Believe it or not, until that moment I genuinely hadn't given it a thought. I quickly remembered my offer from Derbyshire – £38,000 and Glamorgan's improved offer – £37,000. I thought to myself 'in for a penny, in for a pound' and said 'I was thinking of £40,000 to £45,000.

Dave just nodded and said 'Do you have an exact figure?' He probably couldn't believe his ears when, hard bargainer that I am, replied

'We can split the difference if you like – call it £42,500.'

He said that would be fine.

Another myth to explode here – this time for Sussex fans. In my six years at the club, there was a rumour doing the rounds that I was the second highest paid player at the club after Chris Adams. I can categorically deny that fact here; there were plenty of players who earned more than me and that was fine. It just stuck in my throat a bit having to put up with that innuendo for six years, but now they'll all know – I certainly didn't cost a fortune, good wage that it was.

We then went to discuss other titbits – accommodation, for example. I asked if they'd put me up for the first season. They agreed. I had use of a lovely flat near Brighton's Preston Park for my first year. Why on earth I didn't ask for accommodation for the full five years, God only knows? I think I felt it was a bit rude, a bit too forward. This proved to be an expensive mistake. For the final five years of my six spent at Hove, I had to pay £350 per month in rent – which already started to eat into my 'big new deal'. Then I asked about a car. No problem, I was told, you'll have one for six months every season. Thanks very much, I said. I forgot to point out that at Glamorgan my car deal was for a full twelve months each year. At the end of my first season with Sussex when I handed back my club car, I had to lease one off a sponsor for the winter – something I continued to do for the next six years, which cost a decent amount of money. I hope you can all begin to see that I didn't leave Glamorgan for the money, and how naïve I really was.

Dave and Pete then tied up the discussions. Pete said that he agreed to everything, but that the contract would be for four years not five. This was the only time I really held my ground. I explained that it had to be five years or nothing. By leaving Glamorgan, I would be throwing away my chance of a benefit for ever – and the only thing that would come close to getting me the security for my family that I was desperate for was a five-year deal. I told them there was no way that I'd budge on that, and the deal was dead in the water otherwise. Dave Gilbert paused, looked at me, then nodded 'OK, five years and we've got a deal.'

I agreed. Dave then said that the professional thing to do now would be to sign a contract here and now. I refused, because I wanted to tell Glamorgan first, but if we shook hands on it, that was good enough for me. Dave said that was fine, so we shook hands, and I joined Sussex, in Newbury Services, ending an association with Glamorgan, the club I loved, which dated back sixteen years to 1983.

I was extremely relieved to know that I would be a professional cricketer for the next five years at least, but more so that my family were financially secure for the same length of time. My daughters Lowri and Seren were aged five and one at the time, and as we'd decided to educate them in Welsh-speaking schools, I also realised that I would be effectively leaving them for six months of the year for the next five years as Gail would stay home in the summer in Swansea, and I would pop back as often as I could. On average that would turn out to be about 25 days over six months. I'm sure you can understand therefore that the feelings I was experiencing as I left the meeting and drove away from the services with Reeso were mixed to say the least.

As we pulled away from the services and headed back to Wales, I couldn't help but smile at the song that came on the radio by one of my all-time favourites, Billy Joel. It was 'Movin' Out (Anthony's Song)' That said it all really.

The next day, Gail, the girls and I flew out for a holiday. Before I left, I rang the lads in the Glamorgan dressing room individually to make sure they got to hear the news from me directly. It was the hardest list of phone calls I ever had to make. I'll never repeat to people what the individual lads said, but I was touched that they were genuinely shocked, and after the last call was made I just sat there almost in a void thinking, 'What the hell have I done?'

When I came back from my holiday, my answer phone had nearly gone into meltdown with the messages it displayed. Lots of different people had called but the ones that stood out were Huw Davies, chairman of Glamorgan's cricket committee and Gerard Elias, the chairman of the club. There was also a letter from Mr Elias suggesting I contact him urgently on my return – which I've still kept to this day.

I rang Hugh first. It was a very strained conversation because I don't think Hugh ever rated me that highly (that's a personal view and I may be wrong of course) and by now I also knew that he was one of the committee who'd voted against me at that meeting. Unlike Peter Walker, he'd not said a single word to me about it since.

I'll never forget what he said to me. 'Cotts – what can we do to make you stay?'

I'm not overly proud of my response, but it indicates to you how much I felt let down by this man –

'Nothing you couldn't have done six weeks ago,' I replied tersely. The conversation ended soon after that.

I then tracked down Mr Elias. He came out with what I took to be the final nail in the coffin. He said that he understood my dilemma over the situation with the benefit and explained that the club never guaranteed a benefit to anyone. I replied and told him I'd never asked to be guaranteed a benefit, I simply wanted to know that if Steve, Adrian and I were ever to awarded a benefit, what would the order be. He replied that he couldn't answer that. I was experiencing déjà vu here. He then made what I assume to be the club's final offer. He said that if I signed the two-year contract that was still on the table, he would guarantee that Glamorgan would retain me for a third year as captain of the second team at a reduced salary if I couldn't make the first team.

I nearly dropped the phone.

Here I was, having shaken hands on a five-year deal at £42,500 with Sussex, with another offer from the only other county I'd spoken to, Derbyshire, of five years at £38,000 and my own county were writing my obituary as a first-class player. I realised at that moment I was making the right moral decision – maybe financially it wouldn't turn out to be the smartest move, but I don't think I could have gone back to the club after those comments. I said as much to Mr Elias, who started to say that I'd got it wrong, and he'd didn't mean it to come across as it sounded. In fairness to him, he probably didn't, and in hindsight he was probably making me a genuine offer to keep me at the club, but I was past caring by now and just felt totally let down, so I just informed him that I'd shaken hands on a deal with Sussex, and I wouldn't be going back on my word.

I think there was bad feeling on both sides by now, and as a result, the press release I mentioned earlier was drafted to show it was a mutual decision, and that we both wished each other all the best etc. etc. I'd never say that I left Glamorgan a broken man, that would be ridiculous, but broken hearted? I think that would be a fair description.

CHAPTER NINETEEN

The New Recruit

After I'd made the painful decision to leave Glamorgan and arrived back from my October holiday with the family, I contacted Sussex to find out the exact course of events that would lead to my official 'transfer' to the south coast. I'd never been in a situation like this before – obviously – and hadn't really known anyone else who had either, so I didn't really know the form. I spoke to Dave Gilbert who informed me that I didn't have to report with the rest of the players until the April 1 of the following year, but that he wanted me to come up to Brighton in November where he intended to set up a press conference to announce and complete my signing.

When the time came, Gail and I travelled to Brighton, and again, my naivety about the whole situation hit me between the eyes. It took us over four hours – door to door – from our home on the outskirts of Swansea to the plush Grand Hotel in Brighton where the club had booked us in. I remember thinking that I never thought it was that far or took that long when I travelled to Brighton before, but then realised that we'd often travelled there from other venues after a previous game had been completed elsewhere in England, and had therefore never really considered the length of the distance from Swansea before. I was going to be a long way from home indeed, and my plans to 'nip home' on my odd day off looked scuppered already.

We arrived at the Grand and were met by Mooresy, Dave Gilbert and club chairman Don Trangmar, and after the usual introductions and a spot of lunch, I was let loose to be received by the awaiting press pack. In fairness, it was hardly a pack: I was hardly David Beckham! I do remember Bruce Talbot of the Argus being there and being very welcoming to me. Anyway, I signed on the dotted line, discussed a few bits and bobs about where I would be staying and where I'd be getting my car from, was taken to the ground and showed around. The Sussex club and representatives couldn't have been better – they were first class and treated Gail and me superbly well. However, as we took a stroll along Hove seafront that evening, I had a feeling in the pit of my stomach that I'd made the biggest mistake of my life, but as usual, I kept those thoughts to myself and said nothing to Gail.

The following springtime rapidly approached when I had to make the next trip up to Brighton, and begin my new career as a Martlet. Over the winter I'd tried to be a big boy and just get my head around the fact that life moves on and that the Glamorgan part of my life was over and a new chapter awaited me, but in truth, it was not as easy as that. The loyal cricket fan probably assumes that when players up sticks and leave one club for another, they do it brimming with confidence and ready to take on the world. Well outwardly that might appear true, but inwardly, I suffered from all the worries, doubts and fears that anyone who has ever left any job they were comfortable in and begun a new career in new surroundings elsewhere similarly feels.

Even though my contract didn't begin until April 1 – which meant that I was technically unemployed until then – I decided I wanted to get up to Brighton as soon as possible, so along with my Dad, I packed the car to the brim, and set off for my new sporting life on March 18. Once settled into my new flat, I made my way to the ground to get acquainted with my new surroundings and I hooked up straight away with Peter Moores, Mark Robinson and Keith Greenfield who were to become my closest friends in my six years at Hove, and they proceeded to show me round and made me feel at home. In the couple of weeks that followed I worked on my fitness every day at the club and met players as they all drifted in, often coming from all four corners of the globe after wintering away. I was not the only new boy thankfully – from Middlesex came the promising all-rounder Umer Rashid; from Northampton came the studious Richard Montgomerie; from Holland the male model that was Baz Zuiderent and from deepest Tasmania, the wonderful Michael Di Venuto, who was to have such a massive impact on the team both on and off the field. It was great to meet these fellow new boys, and I began to stop feeling so alone and isolated.

April 1 was photo-call day. The day the squad met up for the first time. The day when all the shirts and cricket bats are laid out at the ground for everyone to sign in preparation for the season's charity requests. It was also on this day that I was introduced to our opening batsman Toby Pierce, and very sheepishly said a quiet hello to him.

The reason for my reticence was that my last meeting with Toby – and I prayed that he didn't remember it – had happened just in the previous season when Glamorgan played Sussex, and took place in the heat of battle. As I've

215

mentioned, Glamorgan had built their spirit largely on a 'them and us' situation, very much using our Welshness and creating an underdog or siege mentality, especially when we played the upper-class English, which teams like Sussex – to us – represented. Toby Pierce had become the centre of our attacks when we played Sussex, and this was not only due to the educated English lilt to his voice, but the overall demeanour he displayed whilst he batted against us. Toby absolutely loved the cut and thrust of the on-field sledging regime, and actually added fuel to the flames when he came out to bat with the absolute disdain with which he appeared to treat us. On this occasion 'Juice' (we nicknamed him this because he walked around as if he had a carrot stuck up his arse) strutted to the crease to take guard against Steve Watkin. Watty seemed to remember that Toby played shots off his legs quite uppishly, backward of square, early on in his innings, and as such set a very unorthodox field to try to capitalise on this. Therefore, after Toby had taken guard, he looked behind him surveying the field to see Crofty placed at a slightly deeper than normal backward square leg, and about ten yards behind him, Wayne Law was positioned almost as a leg-side fly gully. These were not normal fielding positions, and Toby took no time in letting us know. As he turned round, head high in the air, he looked in disbelief at our field, then looked down at Crofty and with the mixture of a haughty laugh and disdaining scowl, gave out a large 'tut' as if to say 'what rubbish have you prepared for me – please!'

Crofty was on him in an instant – 'Don't you fucking tut me,' and we all joined in:

'Who do you think you are, you upper-class knob?' 'Why don't you just piss off back to Eton, you tosser?' and other such gems. As I now stood shaking hands with Toby Pierce as he welcomed me to Sussex, I remembered that I had been one of the more vociferous that day with the insults. Anyway, in came Steve Watkin and he bowled to his Celtic bodyline field, and Toby flicked the wide, hip-high, leg-side delivery straight to Wayne Law, the deeper of our two men, who snaffled the catch comfortably. Toby was given the loudest and most colourful of send-offs, and again, I was one of the most vocal.

Imagine my embarrassment when Toby finished welcoming me to the club by saying

'Hope you have a great time here, they're a great bunch of lads and are all looking forward to playing with you'.

I just smiled and sheepishly thanked him, and wondered again if he remembered our abuse. I was to discover that Toby Pierce was a great guy, and I thoroughly enjoyed playing on his side for a change. Actually, Toby was one of the reasons I started to feel at home so quickly. He possessed a dry wit and really made me laugh. Throughout my career I usually ended up the centre of the fun and frolics in the dressing room – nowhere more than at Glamorgan – but in the early days at Sussex I felt that I was back down to the bottom rung of the ladder again as I had to build friendships from scratch, so it took a while before I really began to feel at home. Before long – to my relief – I realised that Mooresy was trying to build a sense of unity and togetherness within the dressing room that was extremely similar to the atmosphere at Glamorgan. He believed it was vital that harmony was achieved throughout the team both on the playing field and in the dressing room, and equally away from the game when we were socialising. If you managed that then you were halfway to having a united and successful team. Due to Pete's vision, my new workplace became an easy environment to thrive in.

Above all though, I wanted to prove my worth on the field, and I had a decent start with 46 against Lancashire at Old Trafford on my debut. This was also memorable because it was just two days after Wales had beaten England 32 – 31 at Wembley, thanks to Scott Gibbs's wonderful last-minute try – which remains one of my favourite sporting moments. As the lone Welshman in a dressing room dominated by England's finest, I sat down in the corner of the room and quietly tippexed in large white letters 'Wales 32 – England 31' on the outside of my coffin lid. When it came time to bat, I turned the coffin round, lifted up the lid, and walked out proudly leaving the score on full view for all my colleagues to digest. When I returned an hour-and-a-half later, the lid of my coffin was nearly hanging off because it had been kicked so much. I laughed. At least I was fitting in. I got five fifties in that first season and disappointingly only one hundred, which came against Gloucestershire in the match that Di Venuto ('Divver') also scored a hundred, whilst Umer scored the winning runs that saw us score Sussex's largest ever second-innings total to win a match. More of that later. I also remember it for a sledging incident with an unknown Australian called Ian Harvey.

Nobody had ever heard of Ian Harvey back in 1999. It was only his third game for Gloucester and it didn't take him long to start to roll out the abuse to me while I was batting, and as I'd once survived sledging from the greatest Australian bowler who'd ever lived, I was certainly not going to take any stick from this upstart. I ignored him and his insults for a while, but he just kept on and on and on. At the time Gloucestershire were largely cricket's under achievers, little was I to know that they were about to embark on a period when they would dominate one-day cricket totally – with Harvey of all people – right at the forefront. On this day though, he appeared to me as just another rent-an-Aussie, so after yet another of his chirps, I just turned to him and said

'Listen, mate, let's just get one thing straight here. You're only over here for a season and a holiday, then you'll be going straight back to the bush to live out the rest of your life, so gives us all a break and shut up, get on with it, cos we'll never ever hear of you again.'

I really should learn how to judge a player before opening my big mouth.

Over the next few years, Harvey became one of the best players to play the one-day game in this country. He won numerous medals with Gloucester, played 73 one-day internationals for Australia, won the Lawrence Trophy in 2001 for the fastest hundred, was man of the match in the winning Cheltenham and Gloucester final at Lord's and became one of Wisden's five cricketers of the year in 2004. If I'd had even a slight inkling of this on that cold afternoon at Hove, I might just have kept my thoughts to myself!

At least Harvey can claim that he witnessed the only hundred I was to score that season – and a very ugly one at that. We set a Sussex record that afternoon by achieving what was the seventh highest winning run chase in the history of first-class cricket, with me contributing 126. However, despite our victory, I was nearly embarrassed as I'd played so poorly on my way to the magic three figures. Mooresy sensed this, and came over for a chat. He asked why I was looking so down and I told him that my bad run of form had got me down, and the lack of quality in my knock hadn't done anything to lift me.

Mooresy considered for a moment and then said 'Listen – use this as a stepping stone to kick on from here. The only other option is to stay down about the quality of the knock, and that will only drag you down further. The choice is yours.'

I desperately tried to adopt the latter approach, but I still spent the rest of the season scratching around, and my end-of-season average of 27 told its own story. Strangely, however, my one-day form was the opposite. My season's average of 48 was the best I was to achieve in my time at Sussex and culminated in us winning a trophy. Our top three batters that season were fantastic – Divver, Monty and Grizz – and my job became one of making sure I was there at the end of an innings to attempt to either post a decent score or see the team home. One game that sticks out is our game at Taunton against our title rivals Somerset, a couple of games before the end of the season. Grizz scored a magnificent 115 not out, and my contribution of 62 not out with him in a stand of 159 set them a target of 260 to win. It developed into a fantastic game, which saw Somerset wanting four to win off the final over, in more or less darkness.

Step forward James Kirtley who proceeded to bowl a fantastic over where he removed their danger man Marcus Trescothick for 47, then a run out, then another wicket, Jason Kerr's. This was a massive win for us, which gave us the belief that we could take the title from here, and following massive nine-wicket wins over Surrey and Notts, we arrived in Derbyshire knowing victory would give us the title.

Then it rained – and rained – and rained.

There was no way that we were going to get any play at all. I'd been in the game long enough to know the signs, and we were desperate that Somerset would somehow slip up in their game handing the title to us. The weather was so bad that my mother and father who had set out from Wales early in the morning, turned back after driving through the worst of the weather after hearing the poor forecast for the afternoon.

Now I don't know whether Sky TV had any influence as they were televising it live, but at about 4pm, when it stopped raining, all hell broke loose on the outfield and everyone went to work. Even though areas of the ground were still soaking, we were informed that a ten-over-a-side match would take place at 5.15.

Derby batted first and the ever dependable Phil DeFreitas top scored with 34 in their score of 93. We got off to an OK start, but lost a couple of wickets and when I got to the crease we had four-and-a-half overs left and still needed 49 to win. I made a pre-determined decision that I was going to try to walk across my stumps, and help the ball over the leg-side field. Fortunately my plan worked, and I managed to hit two sixes off Matt Cassar on my way to 28. I was chuffed to bits to be standing there at the end with Keith Greenfield, who'd come out of retirement after Lewey was left out due the need for an extra batsman. Grubby had borrowed kit from everyone, and it was an absolute pleasure to see such a stalwart of the county scoring the winning runs. Grizz was very kind to me in the after-match interviews calling me 'a winner' and pointing out that was the reason why he'd brought me to the county was that I could do it when it mattered. I was also awarded the man of the match award for the only time in my professional career, and must admit that the short cameo I played that afternoon pretty much rescued my season, and had helped deliver what we all wanted at Sussex – a trophy. Little was I to know then that, in time, winning and losing a game of cricket would become quite unimportant in the grand scheme of things.

CHAPTER TWENTY

Umer

On April 1, 2002, in Grenada, West Indies, whilst Sussex were on a pre-season tour, Umer Rashid died. He was 26 years old.

He was my roommate on that trip, and on that fateful morning we'd woken as normal, had a quick chat about nothing in particular, and went down for breakfast. He'd arranged a trip with his brother to a local beauty spot waterfalls. Initially I'd said I'd accompany him before changing my mind. After breakfast we went back to our room, and when he left, he was in a rush and left a half-eaten muffin on his bedside table in our room.

I never saw him again.

I first met Umer in 1999 when I joined Sussex. We signed on the same day. He was from a Pakistani background, and was joining Sussex from Middlesex. He was a talented left-arm spinner and more than capable middle-order batsman. I have so many good memories of him that I don't know where to begin. He was one of the most engaging characters I've ever come across. People who've played professional sport often get a bit precious about their careers, and I've known some who've almost lost grip on reality because they've lived a life so feted as a sportsman that they begin to believe that they are more worthy and more special than people who have lived their lives in other, less glamorous, environments. Umer was about as far away from these people as it was possible to be. I know it's an almost worn-out cliché, but I never heard Umer say a bad word about anyone. Nor anyone about him. Whichever career Umer had followed, he would have been extremely popular. He was a really special man.

Were it not for sport, we never would have met. Our backgrounds were so obviously different that I doubt that that the paths of the Islamic Londoner and Welsh country boy would ever have crossed in any other profession. But from day one we got on like a house on fire. Now I must point out here that I'm not claiming to be Umer's best mate. In sport, as in life in general, people are thrown together, and have to make the best of it. Umer and I did, and we became mates. But what was so special about Umer was that he built the sort of relationship I had with him with everyone else in the squad too. He was never part of a clique, which often exists within the world of sport where people ally themselves with one or two others because it may benefit them in the long run. He never took sides with people in arguments or disputes, and he never annoyed people with the kind of selfish, petty behaviour that is an all-too-frequent occurrence in the world of sport. Umer was above all that. I'll never know if it was a conscious decision he made in life to get on with people, or whether it came naturally to him – second nature – but whatever it was, I don't think I ever played with a more popular, unassuming sportsman in my whole career.

To this day, some of the stories that the boys recount about Umer make you laugh until the tears come. There was an occasion when we were training at Hove, when the chief executive was expecting the club's insurance assessor at the ground to see if he'd renew the cover on the old main wooden stand for another season. We'd been doing some drills on the field and most of us had come back to the dressing room. Umer decided he wanted to slope off for a sly cigarette, and went upstairs to the players' area in the stand and stood on the balcony and lit up. After a few minutes he heard voices, and tossed the remnants of the ciggie into a wastepaper bin that was out on the balcony. As he did so, and left to go back to the dressing room, the chief exec and the insurance assessor came onto the balcony. Umer smiled and said hello, and walked past them. After a few strides, he looked back, and to his horror, behind the Chief Exec – who was now proudly showing the insurance assessor the panorama of the old ground – the wastepaper basket, which held the discarded ciggie, burst into flames. Umer didn't know whether to laugh or cry – the stand that the assessor had come to insure was about to go up in flames. What a sight it must've been seeing an insurance assessor stamping out a fire – it was too far fetched even for *Fawlty Towers!* I'm not sure what the financial implications of Umer's unintentional bonfire were, but I doubt if the club's excess was reduced.

Umer used to lodge with our groundsman, Laurence, who often had a go at him about not closing the door of their house. Laurence kept budgies in a cage in the kitchen and didn't want them getting out, or more importantly, something getting in and killing them. Anyway, one day an exasperated Laurence caught up with Umer in the dressing room and berated him once again. Umer was mortified – 'Oh Laurence, I'm really sorry mate – nothing's been taken from the house has it?'

'No,' Laurence replied , 'But a cat got in and has eaten my fucking budgies.'

We all collapsed – the birds that Laurence kept there were his pride and joy. It was a measure of Umer's character that Laurence saw the funny side too, and wasn't angry for long.

On another occasion, we had an away game at Northants and Umer came to my digs, left his car, and we drove to the game in my new sponsored Volkswagen. I'd had the car for just three days. I drove up to the game, and Umes drove back. When we got home he dropped me off and jumped into his car and went home. About two minutes after I got in there was some banging on my door. I answered and it was my next-door neighbour who pointed out with glee that my new car had rolled 40-odd yards down the road and ploughed into a parked BMW. Umes had forgotten to put the handbrake on! When I told him the next day, he was instantly apologetic again, and once more, you just couldn't be angry with him.

Though I'm not a big hoarder of memorabilia – I've given a lot away over the years –one thing I do have in my hallway is a montage of photographs of the Sussex versus Gloucestershire match at Hove in the Championship in 1999 – the Ian Harvey match. This was my fourth appearance for Sussex, and apart from 40-odd on my debut, I hadn't really scored any runs for the team, and was starting to feel the pressure a bit. Added to this, the match before had been a return to Cardiff to play against Glamorgan, a game I desperately wanted to well in for obvious reasons. Not only did we get easily beaten by six wickets with my own contribution a poor 6 and 9, but when I walked off the field after my first innings dismissal, I took a wrong turn and headed up the steps to the Glamorgan dressing room, not Sussex's. I took heaps of stick for that. I failed again in the first innings of the Gloucester game, and when I came to the wicket in the second innings to join Michael Di Venuto, we were 72 for three, chasing an improbable 455 for victory. If we got it, we would have had to have recorded Sussex's highest ever run chase in their long history to do so.

I remember John Hopkins telling me years before in the Glamorgan dressing room that there was no such thing as an ugly century. Well Ponty, you should have seen this one! How I scored a hundred remains a mystery to me today – it was horrible – but three hours after coming to the crease, Divver and I had put on 256 for the fourth wicket, until I fell for 126. Divver kept going, until he too went, for 162. By now Umer had come to the crease in what was only his second game for Sussex. The light was going, the overs were running out and we were eight wickets down. It looked like we were going to come up just short. Umer however had other ideas. He played beautifully. He farmed the strike to protect James Kirtley and took his score onto 40. He stylishly drove Gloucester's strike bowler Mike Smith for four through cover point, and ran off the field like a mad man – he'd won the game for us. We all went absolutely apeshit in the dressing room. This was one of the few times in all our careers that we won a match totally against the odds – it really doesn't happen often – and the only real reason we'd won was that when it came down to the wire, the most crucial time, when the wickets were falling, when time was slipping away and when Gloucester believed they were coming back to win it, we found a man with the calmness, poise and ability to take us over the line. That day, that man was Umer.

A few days later the press came down and took photos of Divver and me in front of the scoreboard which had been set up to show our record partnership, and also one of Umer on his own, showing his 44 not out and the record-breaking winning total. As usual, he's beaming in the photo. A couple of weeks later, we were presented with a framed montage of these photos, which had been signed by every member of the team. I'm lucky enough to have won five major medals in my career, but that signed souvenir remains still one of my most treasured possessions.

When the pre-season trip to Grenada was announced, naturally, we were all thrilled to bits. One of the massive spin-offs of professional sport is the travelling, and we all hoped this was going to be a fantastic trip, the usual mix between hard work and hard play. Umes and I were roommates on the trip and also sat next to each other on the plane on the flight out. Once the flight was over and we'd fought over the best bed in the room, we went to check the territory out. The tour had been organised by two former cricketers – Nigel Felton formerly of Northants, and the larger-than-life England legend, Allan Lamb.

After a few days' training, netting and playing against local sides, we were told tomorrow was a free day, to recharge our batteries, relax or just go off and do some sightseeing. Umer's brother Burhan had saved money to come out to Grenada at the same time as us, and came along with his girlfriend. We didn't know him as well as Umer obviously, but he seemed a nice guy. Umer told me the three of them were going to go up to a popular tourist waterfall called Concord Falls that they'd heard of and were taking the video camera to do some filming. He asked me if I'd like to come and I said yes. On the morning of the trip I changed my mind – the main reason being that I was nursing the mother of all hangovers after a memorable team night out the previous evening, and I later told Umes I'd give it a miss.

(It's worth pointing out here that as a squad we were still reeling from the news from Australia just ten days earlier about the tragic death of Surrey's Ben Hollioake in a car crash in Perth. He was just 24. We all knew Ben, and cricket is quite a small community really, and when something like that happens you all feel like you've lost one of your brotherhood.)

223

About three hours after the three had set off on their expedition, Richard Montgomerie took a distressed phone call from Burhan's girlfriend. As the news of the accident at the waterfall was being relayed to us by Monty, we still all had hope that Umer and Burhan had just drifted downstream and would be found safely. Then about half an hour later, Pete Moores took a call from Allan Lamb saying that they'd both drowned, and were gone.

I simply do not have the words to attempt to describe the reaction of us all at that moment.

Apparently, an eyewitness had seen them playing about in the plunge pool of this waterfall. It was very deep, but only very small in circumference, just a few strokes and you were back to the side of the bank. Unfortunately, neither Umer nor Burhan were accomplished swimmers. We were told that it appeared that Umer had jumped into the pool along with Burhan's girlfriend, both treading water, waiting for Burhan to join them. It seems that when Burhan did jump in, he must have taken a big mouthful of water, and struggled to resurface. Umer, knowing straight away that something was wrong, shouted to the girlfriend to get help, and dived under to rescue his brother. Nobody saw either of them alive again.

To tell the truth, I don't know how I felt. I suppose 'numb' best describes it. I didn't cry, I just went up to my room. Our room. I unlocked the door and walked in. The first thing I saw was that half-eaten muffin – I can never get it out of my mind to this day – and then all the 'if only's' started to come. If only he'd stopped to finish it. If only I'd gone with him. If only he'd stayed with us. If only we hadn't had a day off. If only. If only.

I was tasked with sorting and packing Umer's clothes, kit and belongings. A more solemn duty I have since to perform, and never wish to again. I had to go through his mobile phone to see if there were important numbers held within that club officials might need to have to contact relatives and friends. I did it all on auto pilot. I didn't feel I had the emotional tools to deal with this responsibility, but I also felt a great sense of duty to Umer to do it.

The tour was abandoned straight away – Northants were out there with us in a friendly tournament. Nothing mattered now anyway. We hired a bus, and the whole team and staff decided it was right and proper for us to visit the scene at the waterfalls and pay our respects. Or exorcise some demons. I didn't really know what to do when I got there. I noticed a shop selling some postcards, and I bought one with a pretty view of the falls. I sat down on my own, looked into the water where his body had been dragged from less than 24 hours earlier, and wrote a message on the back of the card to Umer. I don't know why I did it – it just seemed right. I keep this card with all my cricket stuff to this day.

Underneath my message I wrote the words to Umer's song – 'The Gallow Tree'. We all had a song we had to perform on club trips or nights out, and we all became associated with it. Umer's is almost unbelievably poignant now as I look back. After a short while we all trooped back onto the bus. It was totally silent. After about five minutes I thought of his song again. Something deep within me wanted to start to sing it, hoping the rest of the lads would join in. Somewhere else deep inside prevented me from doing it, in case it was perceived to be in poor taste. To this day I regret not singing it – I know the lads would have joined in, and I think it would have been a fitting tribute. I was just too scared that it might be taken the wrong way. I miss Umer very much – I just hope he is 'safe'. All I know really is that this world is a far poorer one without him in it.

These are the words to Umer's song:

> Slack your rope Hangman,
> Slack it for a while,
> I think I see my mother coming,
> Running many a mile,
> Father, do you hear me call?
> Can you hear my plea?
> For I still see you hanging,
> From the Gallow tree.

CHAPTER TWENTY ONE

Brothers in Arms

Team spirit, morale, belonging, commitment – call it what you will – is the single most important factor in achieving long-term success in team sport. Of course, ability is important, but when you are talking about professional team sport, on the whole, everyone in the team can play. And, obviously, there's always a Viv Richards, Waqar Younis and Mushtaq Ahmed who supplement the team by performing at a consistent level that the rest of us can only dream of, but if they too don't buy into the team ethic, a la Michael Bevan then quite quickly it will all start to stall.

When I first joined Glamorgan, we were largely in the doldrums. As much as I loved the players and characters who were there at the time, on many occasions you felt that we were often adopting a negative attitude before the first ball was even bowled. There were periods later on with Glamorgan in the 1990s and also with Sussex in our championship year, where, before we even stepped out of the dressing room, we were certain we were going to win. Absolutely certain – and we often did. To get to that level of belief is not a short journey, and involves many other factors: the technical brilliance of coaches like Duncan Fletcher and Pete Moores; the natural brilliance of players like Matt Maynard, Steve Watkin, Murray Goodwin, Jason Lewry. But what the Glamorgan sides of the 1990s and the Sussex team built by Peter Moores had in abundance was team spirit. They were without doubt the best periods of my sporting life.

Glamorgan based their team spirit on total unity and a common focus – Wales. We turned representing Glamorgan into, in our minds at least, playing for Wales. In our Sunday League-winning year of 1993, Roland Lefebvre was Dutch, Colin Metson English and Viv Richards West Indian, every other member of the team was either Welsh born or had represented Welsh Schools. We revelled in everything Welsh and used that as our base to create a them-and-us attitude between 'us' and the seventeen 'English' counties. We tried to turn the matches into internationals, and tried to ride on the intensity and passion that playing for your country gives you.

226

What underpinned that even further, however, was our friendships. Pretty much everyone in the team got on. As with all walks of life, some got on better than others; Crofty and I were pretty much inseparable for example, but I don't recall any of the real falling outs that I'd witnessed in my early years at Glamorgan, or certainly in my time at Swansea City. Many friendships were fostered at our team meal every Saturday evening. This night became our weekly ritual, our reward for the week's hard work, when we would let our hair down a little and have some fun. We had to be careful not to overdo it too much because at 12pm the next day we'd be starting a 50-over Sunday League match, but we'd certainly have a couple of drinks, and basically relax.

I'd had a chat with a couple of the lads about bringing in a daft shirt award that had to be worn by the victim for the duration of the night. This would be based on the events of the previous week, culminating with nominations and a vote on Saturday morning. I'd found a horribly loud Hawaiian-style shirt, and got a shocking kipper tie, which in no way matched the shirt, painted a ship's anchor on it, with a capital 'W' above it. I'll leave it to you to work out what that signified. Once the nominations were in, and the offending player was voted the award winner prior to the day's play, they knew that tonight at some nice restaurant or other in Tunbridge Wells, for example, they would be dining with their esteemed colleagues, but dressed like a pillock. The only rule we had was that the nomination could not be performance-related – such as dropping a catch at a crucial moment, for example. This was simply to be your penance for doing something stupid.

Hugh Morris, our captain, for example was an early winner. The day after a Sunday League victory in our blue-coloured clothing, Hugh marched out to bat in the four-day game, resplendent in his pristine whites, but wearing bright blue batting pads. He beat a hasty retreat to the dressing room when it was pointed out to him – but it was too late – we'd seen it. He was suitably rewarded with being 'Wanchor of the Week'.

Other winners were Darren Thomas for the now legendary story concerning his booking of that week's team meal. We took it in turn to arrange the restaurant, often relying on previous knowledge if we'd eaten there before, or if not, you'd do your best to find out from the opposition where was a decent place to eat. Darren settled on a restaurant not far from the ground where we were playing in Liverpool. He announced it specialised in French Food and was called the 'Massiez Vous'. He'd written the address down, and gave it to the driver of the taxi who said he knew the address but had never heard of the restaurant. When we arrived – all became clear. It wasn't a French restaurant at all, it was your bog-standard Beefeater situated on the banks of the River Mersey, from where you had you uninterrupted 'Mersey View' as told to him by the receptionist. That story still gets told on the after-dinner circuit.

The restaurant theme was continued by Adrian Shaw when a few of us were strolling around Hove looking for a restaurant to go to after we'd first had a couple of pints to quench the day's collective thirst. We passed a nice Italian restaurant that looked promising called 'Sole Mio' after the famous song. Shawsie stopped, had a glance at the menu as we walked on ahead, then shouted after us,

'Lads – this Sole M Ten looks pretty decent.'

Coach John Derrick won for this culinary classic when being served with his pizza. The helpful waitress enquired whether he'd like his pizza cut into four or six slices – 'Better make it four,' said big John, 'I'll never eat six.'

The first joint-winners were Darren Thomas (again) and young spinner Stuart Phelps. They were overheard in the shower:

'What's that on your arm, Dar?' asked a concerned Stuart,

'Oh that's just my birthmark,' he replied.

'How long have you had that then?' pursued Stuart,

'I dunno – since I was born I think.'

The shirt became a core point of our week, and as with everything it evolved. Crofty changed it first when he introduced a lime-green, skin-tight, capped sleeve T-shirt, complete with zip from neck to navel that was a gift from a very loving relative. When one of the lads would wear it they resembled a green condom full of walnuts – not a pretty sight.

The final version of the shirt whilst I was at the club was the punishment of having to wear your own Sunday League shirt, complete with your name emblazoned on the shoulders. It was the height of bad form for any cricketer to be seen wearing this anywhere away from the ground, and I'll never forget how gutted our England batsman Steve James was to wear it at a restaurant at one away trip. He was so self-conscious that people might actually believe that he would wear his jersey for an evening out on purpose that it really started to worry him. At one point in the night I went into the toilet where I found him washing his hands and explaining to one of the locals that he was only wearing the top because he'd been chosen to wear it this week by the lads as part of a team-building exercise.

'Bollocks,' I said as I walked past. 'He always wears it out on a Saturday night so people will know who he is.' He was suitably crestfallen!

The Sussex equivalent was based on the same ethic of bringing us together, but was altogether more advanced, and that was down to one man. Mark Robinson.

Whereas the common focus for our unity at Glamorgan was Wales, at Sussex it was far more the club, and the traditions it stood for, and, more than anything, our anthem 'Good Old Sussex By The Sea'. As much as I looked forward to my new life at Sussex, I didn't really believe I'd ever experience at Sussex the close-knit feeling I'd been central to at Glamorgan. Part of me felt that I'd never really fit in with these people from the heart of England's South, and as anyone who knows me well can testify, Lord Ted Dexter I am not! However, in reality, at the end of my six years at Sussex I felt just as much of a wrench driving through the club gates at Hove for the last time as I did when I drove away from Sophia Gardens. As I suggest above, that was largely due to the people skills of Mark Robinson. Now I'm not certain how much of what we did on our team nights was created by Robbo or carried on by him from previous senior players. All I do know is the amount of thought and preparation Robbo put in to made our team nights some of the best I ever experienced, and also the most important in terms of team-building and bonding.

Robbo was always the chairman. He devised countless games – most of them involving drinking or 'down downs' as we called them, but he did it in such a way that no one was singled out and the fines and forfeits were always spread evenly around. Some of his pranks, and the attention to detail, were legendary. There was a period when James Kirtley appeared to be setting his stall out to become vice-captain to Chris Adams. I was asked to do it in my first season there, but in truth was glad to hand it back to Michael Bevan when he returned the following year. After Bevan left, it was up for grabs. It was around this time that we started to notice that James hardly appeared to leave Grizz's side. As a result of this at our next away trip, Robbo decided to marry them. He booked a conference room at the hotel we were staying at, arranged for the hotel to set up the seating as if they were pews, created a makeshift altar and dressed as a Vicar. James was made to dress as a bride, with Grizz as the lucky groom. The rest of us – all wearing flowers – were sat in the pews of the 'church', watching Robbo perform the full wedding service and then, as tradition dictates, we greeted the new Bride and Groom. I'm not sure who caught the posy at the end – probably Mushie!

He'd also set up games of 'Who Wants to be a Millionaire', 'Mr & Mrs', 'Family Fortunes' – you name it, Robbo staged it. One thing was common though on our night out – the five Sussex oaths. Prior to each meal, Robbo would select five players to stand, and proclaim one of the oaths each. If any slips or mistakes were made – it was down, down time.

Oath One: 'The Queen' (Raising the toast with your glass in your wrong hand).

Oath Two: 'Wives and sweethearts – may they never meet'. This was subsequently replaced by 'Absent Friends' following the tragic death of Umer.

Oath Three: 'To the Jolly nice chaps of Middlesex' (or whoever our next opponents were due to be) – but this had to be delivered whilst remaining seated.

Oath Four: 'Good Old Sussex By The Sea' – which would cue the rest of us to loudly join in with this rousing team song, whatever the venue – no matter how refined or well attended!

Oath Five: 'United we believe – together we achieve' (invented by Jason Lewry and our unofficial motto which hung on a banner in every dressing room we played in).

Once the oaths were completed and we began our meal, Robbo would throw out instructions as he saw fit, eg 'No one is allowed to touch their face for five minutes,' at which point you'd develop the most irritating of itches on your cheek; 'hands up if you need to go to the toilet' and so on. Throughout it all Robbo would appoint a chief clerk whose job it was to let Robbo know of any unseen misdemeanours that required punishment. I know in the cold light of day you might feel this is all a bit childish, but I can only speak from experience that the effect these sort of evenings have on a group of people drawn together by a common bond – team sport – is startling.

Robbo also had the idea of spreading the gospel slightly further. He thought it was only fair that our sponsors and committee members who do so much welcome, yet largely unseen work on the players' behalf should be rewarded by joining in. So it was agreed that once a year, during pre-season, we would invite these good people into the sanctity of the team, and treat them all as though they were players of Sussex, and let them join in with all the games, the oaths, the meals and the general fun and good times. I'm sure they always enjoyed it, and we enjoyed having them.

As befitted his role as coach, Pete Moores brought in more organised and official team-bonding sessions. We'd all take a dip in the sea in April for one – not a pleasant experience! All the players would gather on the beach at Hove and would strip to our shorts. We then had to walk – slowly – straight out to sea, until the water came up to our necks. Running was not allowed and if you made any sound you were fined. It had become well known down at Hove, so there was often a gathering of spectators to witness the torture. Once the water came to the level of your neck, you turned and walked back to the shore. It was absolutely freezing. It's probably the only time in my sporting life that my lack of height was a bonus! Spare a thought for Robin Martin-Jenkins though, at six feet six inches he was nearly out in the shipping lanes before he could turn back!

Another unique exercise was painting the ground at Hove. It was deemed a bonding week, and we were all issued with paint, brushes, overalls, sandpaper the whole lot, and basically re-painted the ground. The stands, the scoreboards the fascias – everything. Pete also involved the office staff and it gave everyone a sense of unity and belonging and certainly brought everyone together. Another occasion was when all the players were given a budget of £500, the use of a chef as a consultant, and invited all the ladies and office staff who worked at the club to the Jim Parks bar, where all the players prepared and cooked a meal for them. Those that didn't cook acted as waiters and again, a fantastic night was had by all. Now I'm sure that some of you won't agree that events such as this would count a hell of a lot towards the winning of the county championship, but I'd argue that when the chips were down – as they often are in professional sport – a kind word or a glance from someone you've got to know via these sort of evenings goes a long way, and the feeling that you'll go the extra mile to make these people proud of you is very strong indeed. I'll leave it for you to judge.

By the time my third year at the club began, after Michael Bevan had negotiated a release from the final year of his contract, a definite dent in the togetherness of the team had developed. In my opinion it's no coincidence that the team ethic was at its worst when Bevan was at the club. He had such total and utter belief in his own ability and strengths (which in fairness were vast) that he had little time for those who didn't match up. During team meetings he was never ever wrong, his was the only opinion that carried any weight, and he'd happily shout down any youngster who wished to disagree or offer an alternative view. It was the only time in my period at the club that Pete Moores struggled a wee bit. I think he wasn't certain how best to deal with someone of such outstanding ability, but who gave so little to the team ethic – the one thing above all that Pete believed in. In my opinion Bevan was given too much latitude, and was allowed to get away with behaviour that wouldn't have been tolerated from the rest of us. I don't know the circumstances of Bevan's exit from the club, whether he ended his contract, whether the club did or whether Pete didn't want him back. What was certain though was that he was history, and Pete now had his work cut out to try to re-build some of the spirit and trust that had been lost during the previous year. After a few weeks it was clear that certain people still felt that they had nothing to contribute in team meetings, for example – as if people were either afraid of stepping on people's toes, or because of petty disagreements

Pete decided to take a big risk in my opinion – but it came off.

He called us all into the dressing room, and we were greeted with boards upon which were pinned eighteen envelopes. Each envelope had the name of a player on it. We were asked to sit down and were handed eighteen blank pieces of paper that were split with a line down the middle which had 'Likes' as a heading on the left and 'Dislikes' as a heading on the right. Our instructions were simple. Pick a player – in any order (and you had to do it for each teammate) – and complete each column with relevant comments about your chosen player. We were encouraged to be as honest as possible without being insulting, and when we had finished we had to place the pieces of paper in the relevant player's envelope. We also had to sign our name on the paper.

At the end of the exercise we were then given our own envelopes and went away to read the positive and negative comments of our peers. Quite powerful stuff. The final instruction was that if we had any issues whatsoever with what somebody had written, we were to go to the dressing room, alone, and thrash it out between us. Everything that was said was to remain in the dressing room – Pete didn't even want to know – and once sorted, it was to be forgotten and left behind. At the time I thought that this was a very brave thing to do as one thing that some pampered sportsmen don't like to hear sometimes is the truth. And this process was giving them the truth straight between the eyes – with both barrels. I was in and out of the dressing room like a yo-yo that day – on both sides of the fence – and, as per the instructions, what was said remains where it was said. However, it speaks volumes of that squad that I don't remember one incident of bad feeling, and I'm as certain as I can be that wouldn't have been the case if Bevan had still been at the club.

With hindsight though, I think Pete knew exactly what he was doing. Firstly, he knew he wasn't dealing with any pampered sportsmen, and secondly, even though we may not have realised it at the time, Pete trusted us absolutely. He could never have taken that risk otherwise. He knew we would deal with it professionally, and also knew that we wouldn't take anything personally. And he knew the end result would re-invigorate us and bring us back together. He was 100% correct. I was starting to realise that I was working for a very gifted man here, and by the end of my association with him in 2004 after six years, I would've walked over broken glass for him – and there were ten other players in the dressing room who felt exactly the same.

The thing that marked out my time at Sussex as so rewarding was the fact that the dressing room contained a very similar mix of characters to the one in Glamorgan. Some of the finer points – or not! – of a selection of these teammates follows here, and in classic cricket style, appear largely in scorecard order.

DIVVER – MICHAEL DI VENUTO.

Divver was as talented an opening bat as I ever played with. We shared a season together, my first, and we bonded straight away. He was a one-year overseas replacement for Michael Bevan, and the highest compliment I can pay him is that in the runs column, the team didn't miss Bevan at all. Divver's nature and demeanour was also a massive positive on the side – he was a brilliant team man, far more so than Bevan. He was good enough to play for Australia in one-day tests, with a top score of 89, and he was welcomed by all, playing huge part in the bonding of the club. We got quite close as we roomed and travelled together. He was a typical Aussie – played hard, and loved a night out. He, Umer, Monty, Baz and I all signed for Sussex on the same day, and as such I think we all shared a similar bond. I mentioned that we travelled to away games together, and a certain trip springs to mind. It was when we played a minor county – Cumberland – in a C&G match at Kendall in the Lake District. We both had identical VW Passats at the time as sponsored cars, but as Divver had only ever passed his test on automatic cars, his was an auto and mine was a manual. From time to time he nagged me about having a go on my manual version, but after my experience with Umer and the handbrake – I was a bit reluctant to say the least. Anyway, this day at Kendall he nagged me all day about driving it back to the hotel as it was only five minutes away, and by the end of play I'd had enough so agreed. We got changed in to our club tracksuits, had a quick drink in the clubhouse then went out to the car park. Divver got in, started up, and very gingerly drove toward the exit. Now this exit was one of those that began about ten feet lower than road level, then sloped up to the road via a small rise. By the time we approached the bottom of this little rise, Divver had lost control of his accelerator foot, and we were violently kangarooing our way out of the ground. The more the car lurched, the more I started to laugh, and competitive Aussie that he is, the more Divver started to get angry. He eventually stalled just at the bottom of the little rise. By now, not only had a small crowd gathered to witness the kangarooing, but a steady queue of supporters were waiting in cars behind us to get out of the ground too. Divver tried to compose himself, started the car, lurched forward and stalled. I burst out laughing once again. Divver, screamed, swore and tried again. Exactly the same result – lurch, laughter, swearing and abuse. This must've happened about four or five times, and each time we succeeded only in lurching a further yard up the slope, the queue behind us growing. By now Divver was begging me to take over – through my tears of laughter, I, of course, refused – so he gave it another go – with exactly the same result. With that, he just got out of the car, screamed, walked around the front of it, took off his club baseball cap, threw it down onto the bonnet, and reached in and started dragging me out of the car. I finally obliged and drove us back. Divver's remained in English cricket to this day – I wonder if he's still driving an automatic.

MONTY – RICHARD MONTGOMERIE.

Divver's opening batting partner that year was Monty, who has become a true mainstay of Sussex over the years, and must be one of the best signings the club has ever made in the modern game. Now we Welsh sometimes have a bit of a chip on our shoulder about the upper classes. We can't abide posh. Richard Montgomerie is quite simple the poshest friend I have. He was educated at Rugby School and Oxford University and those who assume that this sort of background doesn't cater for the toughest of people in professional sport are quite wrong. You see, beneath the horn-rimmed glasses, perfect manners and faultless diction, there lies one of the toughest and most determined batsmen to grace the game in my time – and with no little talent, as his 29 first class hundreds testify. Like me, you've probably heard the stories of how much Geoffrey Boycott lived for batting, I assume they must be true, but, the great Yorkshire opener apart, I can't believe anyone has lived for batting more than Monty. I'd bet my mortgage that he sleeps with his bat – his commitment to his trade is absolute. I'll never forget his comment to me after he'd scored his first century for Sussex. After I congratulated him, he just looked back at me and said in his dulcet tones, 'Put a bat in my hand and I'm in heaven.' A great bloke, and one you'd always want on your side.

TIM AMBROSE

In almost every way imaginable, Tim was at the absolute other end of the spectrum to Monty. I had the dubious honour of living with Tim when he joined the club after leaving his home in Newcastle (that's New South Wales – not the North East) to play club cricket at Eastbourne, before swiftly being picked up by Sussex. He was eighteen years old, raw to say the least, but a great lad, full of fun, and a pleasure to be around. He quickly earned the nickname 'The Freak' due to his uncanny ability to pick up a sport that he'd never tried before, to the highest standard in no time at all. He excelled at rugby, soccer, golf – anything we tried really. When he joined the happy home of Cottey and Robinson, Robbo and I quickly became surrogate fathers to him. Most men are hardly naturals when it comes to household duties, but Tim was just about the worst I'd ever come across. He didn't really get the process of washing and cleaning plates and dishes and one particular story still makes me smile. Robbo and I were playing away at Old Trafford on the following day, and after breakfast we were preparing our gear for our trip north that afternoon. We heard a bit of a crash in the kitchen and popped our heads in to see Tim surveying a smashed egg and pile of sugar he'd somehow managed to drop on the floor in a neat pile. Just as we were leaving a few hours later, there the mess remained, and Robbo and I both told him to get it cleaned as it had been there all morning. Tim wasn't in the first XI at the time and stayed behind after we left. When we arrived back home – five days later – there was a towel in the middle of the floor. Robbo picked it up, and underneath was the egg and pile of sugar! As Catherine Tate would say – 'Dirty bastard!'

Tim was also party to one of the lowest moments of my life. It was in our second year together and the shopping needed doing. Tim and I popped off to Sainsbury's – and bearing in mind this was in Brighton, and both of us are hardly six footers, I was often concerned as to whether people might have thought we were an item! Anyway, we did our circuit of the shop, then queued at the checkout. When we finally got served, Tim began to empty the trolley onto the conveyor belt and I grabbed some bags to begin filling them, when the pretty young assistant turned to Tim and asked the worst question I've ever heard in my life: 'Do you think your father wants a hand packing the bags?' I've never seen someone laugh so much as Tim in response, whilst I – for once – had nothing to say. As you can imagine, I've never been allowed to forget that one!

Tim left Sussex at the end of 2005 for Warwickshire in search of regular first-class cricket. It was always likely to happen as Sussex were blessed with two of the best young wicketkeeper-batsmen in the country – Tim and Matt Prior. Untilk very recently, Matt had snuck ahead of him in the England rankings, but after an excellent season in Birmingham, Tim has now got the test match gloves.

MUZZA – MURRAY GOODWIN.

If Tim Ambrose sticks at his game and flourishes as I believe he will, he could do no worse than copy the style of Muzza. Muzza was quiet simply the biggest character I've ever met in sport – both on and off the field – and there have been a few. He never ceased to be great company and that was whether it was out on the pitch when the opposition were 375 for 3 and we'd been chasing leather all day in the hot sun, or best of all, when were in the bar at the end of another fulfilling day's sport. He had the natural timing and mannerisms of a comedian and he always had us in stitches. Like me, he wasn't shy of a lager! Despite the fun, which was never too far away, he was extremely serious about his cricket, and on the field could be as intense as anyone. From the day he joined the club I looked at his batting game in awe. Everything I tried to base my game around – cutting, pulling, sweeping etc – he did too, only to a much, much higher standard. Every player carries a mental picture in their mind about how they play at their best, and hope that it comes to fruition a few times in their career. The picture I had in my mind was of Murray – but he had the ability to do it far more often that I was ever able to – it was almost like the norm, and I yearned to be as good, and as good *as often* as he was. We became really close at Sussex, and he remains a great mate to this day, but close though we were, he wasn't always the best person to ask for advice.

Pete Moores was a big believer in batsmen who had just got out, passing on information to those yet to bat, about the pitch, conditions bowlers etc. We were playing Lancashire at Old Trafford once, and Muzz had just got out, and like most of us, absolutely hated it. I gave him about twenty minutes to get his head right, and as I was batting at five that day, wandered over and asked 'What's it doing out there Muzz?' He just looked up from his despair and began.

'Well, to start with it's swinging . . . both ways. The pitch is very up and down. (Uneven). Chapple's darting it round both ways off the seam. It's even bloody turning for Keedy.'

He just looked at me forlornly, and put his head back down. I said thanks, moved away and thought that even Bradman would struggle to score runs out there!

TUCKER – ROBIN SIMON CHRISTOPHER MARTIN-JENKINS

Tucker's got more names than we had put together in the village I grew up in on the Gower! Radley School educated and in the Montgomerie class for poshness. Our backgrounds again were poles apart, but I really enjoyed his company. He's a very funny man with a very sharp, dry wit. As an all-rounder he's sublimely talented and can count himself very unlucky not to represent England in some format of the game. Tucker was very much Robbo's right hand man when it came to organising the entertainment for team nights out and was Robbo's chief snitch! I enjoyed batting with him, and we figured in a number of partnerships, which as you can imagine were a sports photographer's dream as there was over a foot difference in height. His party piece at our team meal was that he told the same joke for five years – and still got a laugh out of us.

DOXY – MARK DAVIS

Another of my roommates at Sussex – why did I have so many? I first came across Doxy when I played for Glamorgan against Northern Transvaal in 1995.

He was a mate of my South African host Terrence Marsh, so I knew him quite well before he joined Sussex. The ultimate accolade I can pay him is that he's my best Ginger friend – private joke I'm afraid! He's got a fine middle name – Gronow – named after his Welsh grandfather – no wonder we got on so well.

MUSHIE – MUSHTAQ AHMED.

Without doubt, the finest spin bowler I ever had the privilege to play cricket with was Mushtaq Ahmed. He joined Sussex in 2003, and despite the massive differences in our backgrounds, our culture and our stature within the game of cricket – he became one of the best friends I had throughout my whole career.

The friendship was based largely on humour, in our respective searches for the funnier side of life, and taking the form of general mickey taking. This wasn't confined to taking the mickey out of other players, but often saw both of us trying to take the rise out of each other. One such memorable occasion came to a head at Canterbury, prior to a Championship match against Kent.

Now for all my many failings, one thing that I won't be criticised for is my fitness levels. From the very start – back during my football days – I worked out that if I could become the fittest amongst my peer group, then at least that would be one string to my bow that might give me the edge over people if ever tight selection decisions involved me. Now, Mushie is about the same height as me – he may beat me by an inch or two – but as for our respective statures, well, as I've told him many times, Mushie is a fat little bugger! There's one thing I have to hold my hand up to however: over 50 yards, Mushie is faster than me. We once had a race which he won, and you've no idea how much it hurts me to admit that in print, but there it is. Mushtaq Ahmed is faster than me!

This became a recurring theme over the matches leading up to the Kent game, and Mushie just kept winding me up, going on and on about how he was not just faster than me – but fitter too! In the end I bit and said in front of the rest of the lads, 'Right, I'll race you over any distance over a 100 metres and I'll beat you – you just name the distance.'

Mushie just laughed and said it didn't matter what distance, there was no way I could beat him, as he was much, much fitter. He was really starting to wind me up now, and this was sensed by the boys who leapt on it. They decided that the next morning, during our warm up, they'd mark out a 400-metre track on the Canterbury outfield, where Mushie and I would take part in a properly organised race. In the bar that night, it was decided that the race would be over four laps – just under a mile. I was raring to go, and couldn't wait, but still Mushie laughed and said

'Cotts, my friend, there is no point, there is no way you can win, I am just too fit for you.'

I must admit, the confidence he displayed was a little disconcerting, and I became a little worried that maybe underneath the skin of this rotund little Pakistani was in fact the body of a middle-distance runner. After all, for all I knew he might have once been the Under-16 mile champion of Karachi. I was starting to get a little concerned.

Next day at the ground, the lads meticulously laid out the cones in a lap on the outfield. I nervously warmed up and stretched, indulging in the usual banter with Mushie, who again exuded this almost serene level of confidence. The lads all lined up for the start of the race alongside the start-finish line, and by now had opened a book on the race, which only marginally had me as favourite. Marginally! I couldn't believe it. I'd never, ever seen Mushie run over a hundred yards, and I'd run half a dozen marathons! What was going on?

The next thing I heard was Robbo saying 'Marks, Set – Go!' and off we went.

Well Mushie went off like the proverbial cannonball, he absolutely sprinted away from the line as he had done in our 50-metre race. I smiled inwardly and thought he'll never keep this up, but increased my pace a little just to keep slightly in touch with him. He reached and passed 50 metres at the same speed, and before I knew it he was passed 100 metres and was still going full out. I started to panic, and really lifted my pace. 200 metres came and went, and still he was going – this is ridiculous I thought, we'll both die if we keep this pace up for a mile. I was panicking so much now that I started to sprint as hard as I could, and as we passed 300 metres I started to gain on him, but still he kept going. As we got to within 50 metres of the end of our first lap of four, I just about pulled level with him, and he was busting every sinew in his body to keep ahead, I was getting a bit freaked out now, because if he was capable of keeping this pace up, I knew he'd beat me – and I'd never, *ever* live it down.

I decided that if only I could get ahead of him as we passed the start-finish line at the end of that first 400 metres lap, psychologically, that might just be enough, and I'd be able to enforce my pace on him, and outlast him for the next four laps. As we got to within ten yards of the line, I just about managed to edge him and, as we reached the line, I'd managed to get about two or three strides ahead. I kept going through the line onto lap two and then heard the laughter and the sound of only one set of feet running – mine.

I looked round and there was Mushie, in a state of absolute collapse and the boys pissing themselves laughing all around him. I jogged back sensing I was the butt of something – but still not too sure what. When he got his breath back, Mushie announced that all the lads were in on it, and what he intended to do was run as fast as he could – to his absolute limit – and get to 400 hundred metres before me, and then just stop dead, proclaiming himself the winner. He was then going to argue that as far as he understood, the race was only ever going to have been over 400 metres and as he'd won – he'd have succeeded in beating me 'over any distance over 100 metres' and was therefore the fitter out of the two of us.

I took the stick as it was intended, and just laughed at this spin-bowling genius, who was just about the biggest rascal you could meet, and reflected on what would've happened had I not passed him on the line.

Earlier in my career I had the misfortune of batting against Mushie on numerous occasions, either against Pakistan, Surrey or Somerset, and surprise, surprise, I never came out on top. Then after he joined Sussex I batted against him in the nets nearly every day for the best part of two years, not to mention fielding at first slip to him during championship cricket over the same period. I used to tell people that one thing remained constant between the early days as his opponent, and during the two years we had as teammates – 'I couldn't pick him then, and I couldn't pick him now'.

Years after the Wanchor-of-the-week award at Glamorgan, I was finally snared at Sussex, and boy did I receive my comeuppance, in spectacular fashion. I'd always been the instigator of the piss-takes at Sussex and without my knowledge, the boys got together to see if I could take the stick as well as dish it out.

Their plan was that I had to wear a specially designed bib for our warm-up routine at our next match at Edgbaston. I thought something was up when we took the field for our touch-rugby warm-up game, and as I joined a group of the lads, someone said – 'No, Cotts – you're bibs today.' As the red bibs were handed out, mine was kept until last, and then revealed in all its glory. We were in the middle of one of the *I'm a Celebrity Get Me Out Of Here* series, when Wayne Sleep was one of the contestants. At the time I had my hair cropped shorter than usual, and according to some misguided fools, there was some passing resemblance between me and this five-foot-four, curly-haired, big-nosed ballet dancer. I had no idea what they were talking about! The lads, thoughtful as ever, decided to present me with a bib adorned back and front in bright yellow with 'Save Wayne – Call 0897 2255801', in front of the members stand, where you were guaranteed a good couple of hundred early bird spectators, taking in the warm-ups of the players. The laughter spread round quite quickly as they realised what it was all about, and I bowed, ran off, and got on with the warm-ups. We started as usual with some gentle touch rugby. There was only one real rule – no diving taptackles – it was too dangerous. We started the game slowly, and, as usual, after a couple of minutes the competitive juices started flowing. It was at this point that Matt Prior tried to ghost past me on my outside, making a burst for the try-line, just under the members stand. Before I knew it, I made a desperate diving lunge to my left in order to touch him. As I flew in the air past Matt as he was touching down for a try, the first part of my body that came into contact with the earth was the little finger on my right hand. It dislocated outward immediately, at right angles at the middle knuckle, and the pain was excruciating. My momentum continued to spin me round however, and combined with the dew on the early morning Edgbaston turf, I slid a few feet before coming to a stop. I jumped up, screamed in pain, and bent over putting my hands between my legs in some vain attempt of hoping for some comfort from the agony. My screams had alerted the players, who began to realise there was something seriously wrong, and also the members on the balcony directly above me. But they were treated to a very different view of events from the players'.

Unbeknown to me at the time, I was standing there hopping on the spot in pain, bent over at right angles, but with my shorts down around my ankles, having been pulled down there as a result of my slide. As this was match day, all I had on beneath my shorts was my jockstrap, meaning that the Cottey arse was fully exposed, bent over, and above it remained the request to 'Save Wayne – Call 0897 2255801'. It was when the laughing started that I realised something else was wrong and looked down in horror to see that I was inadvertently mooning the great and the good of the Warwickshire members. I instinctively shot down a hand to pull up my shorts and rescue my dignity, but I inadvertently used my injured hand – cue more agony, continued indecency and increased laughter from above – and now the players. It took me about four grabs to get my shorts to a respectable level, and ran, leaving the field for the safety of the physio, with a large part of one buttock still hanging out of my shorts. The funny thing was that after Oz the Physio put it back in (the finger that is – not the buttock), gave me a pain killing injection and strapped it all back up, I scored 137 in the first innings, and 64 in the second.

Not bad for a one-handed ballet dancer. The lads said I should break my fingers more often!

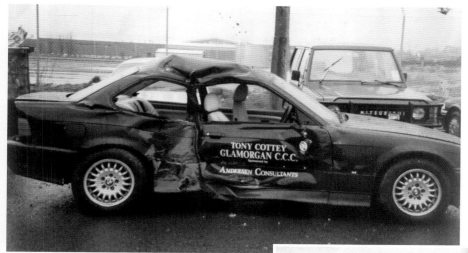

No one told me professional
cricket could be so dangerous!

Tiny Tonka Trucker Tony
passes his HGV test. Dad
thought I'd take over the
family business – never
gonna happen!

Gratefully receiving my
first sponsored car from
Mike Varley. Steve
Watkin, Matthew
Maynard and Paul
Russell look on.

Sussex fancy dress night: 'Scouser' Jamie Carpenter with 'the oldest swinger in town'.

Proud coach with the first trophy of his reign. Peter Moores celebrates the CGU Championship at Derby.

Keith Greenfield, me, Mooresy, Mark Robinson, Jason Lewry (and Toby Pierce in the mirror!) celebrate in the dressing room at Derby.

A different father and son . . . celebrating
my hundred at Arundel in the middle with
Tim Ambrose.

Celebrating at Hove – breathe in, son!

Housemates. Good mates.
Mark Robinson and me at Hove.

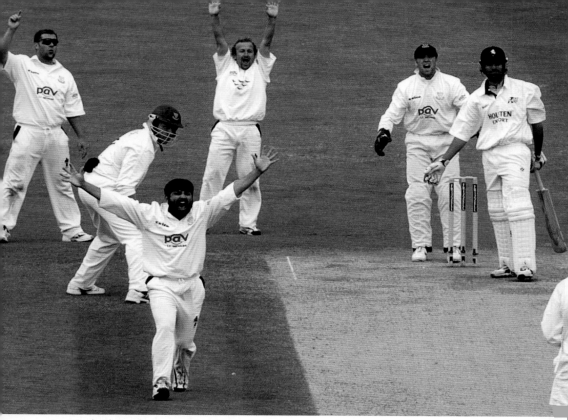

Ian Ward, Chris Adams, myself, and Matt Prior support a genius at work – Mushtaq Ahmed.

County champions elect – Sussex, 2003.

Champions at Hove 2003 – liquid celebrations.

2003 – Buckingham Palace revisited.

At Trent Bridge, contemplating the last fifty of my purple patch in Sussex's Championship year.

In my last season, batting in a Sunday League game against Yorkshire at Arundel.

Walking the Pembrokeshire Coastal Path for Tenovus Charity with Mike Gatting in 2002. Meeting us on the way are Mam (Ruth) and Dad (Bernard), and my daughters, Lowri and Seren.

Always loved my running, but London 2005 was by far the toughest.

A proper job at last! Working for ex-Glamorgan cricketer Mike Llewellyn at *Absolute Cricket* in Swansea.

The Cottey family:
Seren, Lowri, myself
and Gail.

Me and My Girls,

CHAPTER TWENTY TWO

The Search for the Holy Grail

Sussex County Cricket club was the very earliest of all the first-class counties to be formed, back in 1839. By 2003, the small matter of 164 seasons later, they remained one of only five counties, along with Gloucestershire, Northamptonshire, Somerset and new boys Durham, never to have won the elusive County Championship. That would all change in 2003, a season that seemed to encapsulate all the trials and tribulations that I'd experienced in my previous twenty-odd seasons, all wrapped up in five-and-a-half short months.

I began the season as I'd often spent large swathes of my career – under pressure for my place. Since I'd moved to Sussex in 1999, apart from helping secure the Sunday League Division Two Championship in that first year, I had largely underperformed. I think that had I been a home-grown player, or a player picked up on the cricket equivalent of a free transfer, there wouldn't have been a problem – my record was hardly dire – it was just that because I'd arrived in a bit of a blaze of publicity, I was expected to deliver every time I took to the field, and when that obviously turned out to not be the case, I quickly lost the support of the Hove crowd.

Michael Yardy is a very good friend of mine – I'd even helped to teach him to drive in my club car – and he'd regularly been scoring runs in the second XI. In 2003, there now a clamour for him to be given a run in the first team at my expense. The pair of us had lots of similarities: he too loved his football (West Ham), he worked extremely hard at his game, and was very gritty and determined. Now we were being perceived as rivals for a batting slot.

Much of this rivalry had emanated from the pages that the club ran on its official website which encouraged fans to air their opinions – or, in my case, grievances – in a web-board forum. I was taking an absolute pasting on this website. I'd been alerted to it by one of the other lads, and then by Dave who had taken it upon himself to defend me. I remember him being really annoyed about it at the time as the content was so abusive – and personal –·toward me. Unfortunately, I wasn't giving him too much ammunition for my defence. My last century for the club had been at the end of the previous July against Warwickshire, when I'd got 137. In the remaining nine innings of that season I only scored 161 runs with a top score of 41 at an average of 17.8. Hardly sparkling form, I'd have to admit.

In the final match of that 2002 season, also against Warwickshire, I was determined to end on a high, and was desperate for a big score. I made 5. When I went out to bat in my second innings, I heard a supporter shout out 'Piss off back to Wales, you waste of money.' I don't remember many fans contradicting him.

Two minutes later Wales was exactly where I felt like going.

I was run out without scoring. What a way to end the season.

I walked back into the pavilion in total silence. Not a single clap. I think I'd have felt better if I'd been booed. I felt professionally as low as I'd been in my whole career.

Back home in Wales, I spent the winter setting up a business that I hoped might look after me in my retirement, which I'd now decided, extremely reluctantly, would be the end of the coming 2003 season, which tied in with the end of the original five-year contract that I'd signed with the club back in 1999. My frame of mind was such that I very much felt the writing was on the wall, and therefore resolved to enjoy my final season as much as I possibly could, and was desperate to get in the team for the first game and even more desperate to start off well with a big innings.

I was picked for the first game of 2003 against Middlesex at my favourite ground, Lord's, a ground where I'd never scored a century. This would be my last ever chance.

I was out for a duck.

A situation then crystallised in my mind as I sat, watched and waited for the rest of our first innings to unfold over the next day-and-a-half. I began to realise that my grand plan of retirement might well be taken out of my hands. If I failed again and was dropped, then there was a chance that someone would come in and take my place, whether that was Yards or anyone else. If that person scored some runs, they would keep their place, and I'd be left on the sidelines, seeing out the final months of my career in the Seconds. This was something I couldn't begin to even contemplate.

My turn came around for the second innings, and I fared slightly better, scoring 38 in just over two hours. It was good to spend some time out in the middle but I was gutted to get out, and felt that I'd missed a great opportunity to get the big score that would have cemented my place in the side. Worse than that, we also went on to lose the match.

We won the next game at home against Kent, but my scores of 19 and 2 did little to curry favour with the Hove faithful, and the reaction to my performance was mixed to say the least. Next we were off to Birmingham to play Warwickshire, where I top scored in the second innings with 55 out of a pitiful 106, which saw us defeated by a massive 234 runs.

Despite this small personal victory, we'd hardly had a great start to the season which in itself brought its own pressures. Pete Moores and Grizz had really targeted 2003 as one to bring home a trophy of some description as they both felt that we had the best twelve or thirteen players in the six years that they'd both been at the helm. Also with the acquisition of the magical Mushtaq Ahmed, they felt that we now had the extra cutting edge needed to consistently win matches, by bowling teams out.

Yet here we were, three matches in, and we'd already lost two. Nothing was said to me by Mooresy or Grizz about my form, but the grumblings I heard and sensed from the crowd at Hove, and the vitriol that was being spewed about me on the website was starting to rouse the main demon of a sportsman – lack of confidence. All I could do was carry on trying to get that big score, and then hope I could relax and settle in to a run of form that would help the team move forward.

Our next game was Notts at home, but at Horsham not Hove, where we had a bit of a run fest, and enjoyed a resounding ten-wicket win. Even though I contributed by getting my highest score of the season to date (58), that was comfortably overshadowed by Richard Montgomerie, Matt Prior and Kevin Innes who all scored excellent hundreds. (Kevin incidentally became the first twelfth man in cricket history to make a century as he was replaced by James Kirtley for the rest of the match who had been released from England duty after Kev's innings.)

I have to admit to a feeling of envy at the majestic way the three of them had batted and the reception they all received from the home crowd, and hoped a bit of their good form might just rub off on me.

Unfortunately for me and my fragile confidence, things were about to take a massive turn for the worst.

After the one-day game against Notts on Sunday the 25th, our next Championship game was the following Friday at the Oval against the all-conquering Surrey side who absolutely revelled in taking the game to a new height of arrogance. I believe it came to be known as The Surrey Strut, and they certainly took to the field with a swagger and air of superiority I'd never come across in my previous twenty years in the game. These were the types of games that you played professional sport for. There is no doubt that Surrey were an exceptional side. Most of their team were household names and internationals – Ward, Ramprakash, Thorpe, Brown, Hollioake, Bicknell, Saqlain and Salisbury – and, by God, did they let you know it when they were out on the field. It was the one game of the year that you wanted to have your best day, and send them off the field at the end of the four days with their tails between their legs.

The way we operated as a team was so different to Surrey's approach. Our biggest star was Mushtaq Ahmed, and a more level headed, modest and humble man I've never met in my life – in or outside of sport. There were several players like me – journeymen pros as we are so often described – Richard Montgomerie, Kevin Innes, Mark Davies, Jason Lewry, Tucker and Mark Robinson, and we backed up those whose undoubted ability had been proved (or would later be proved) on the highest stage – Chris Adams, Murray Goodwin and James Kirtley. Throw in our talented youngsters, Matt Prior, Mike Yardy and Tim Ambrose, and here was a group of players who were a team with a capital 'T'.

Pete Moores never ever rated players on a one-to-ten basis, or showed any favouritism towards the perceived high achievers in our team. His firm belief was that everyone had something to offer, at any part of the match – on or off the field. His absolute priority at all times was that we acted as a team. He taught us that not only was it vital, but also very rewarding, to enjoy other players' success, and he promoted totally the ethic of team harmony, support and unity. 'Together we believe – United we achieve' was pinned up in our dressing rooms from day one that season, and if anything could sum up the reason for our success that season, it wouldn't simply be Mushtaq's wickets, Murray's brilliance or anyone else's timely contributions; it was the utter commitment to this statement of everyone who took the field for Sussex had. It was without doubt the most harmonious dressing room I was ever to inhabit in my whole career.

It was with this as a background that we prepared to engage with the Surrey Strutters, and as a team, we couldn't wait. But before that we had the Sunday League game against Notts, and again I desperately wanted to post a decent score for a whole host of reasons.

But then, I injured my back.

As we warmed up that Sunday morning, I was running around like a spring lamb, hugely looking forward to the contest, despite my indifferent form of late. I was taking part in the normal fielding drills when I felt my back go. It just locked up totally, and went into spasm. It was so bad I had to be carried off and taken to the dressing room, where Oz, our brilliant physio, set about trying to release it. I knew straight away I was in a bad way, and realised that there was no way I could play that afternoon.

My next thought was that I knew I had to play against Surrey to attempt to keep my place in the team for the long haul, and I now only had four days to get myself fit for selection. It was as simple as that. In my mind it almost became a life-and-death thing. My last two innings had been decent, and I knew how important it was for me to carry that forward. Surrey were such a good team that a decent score made against them – especially at somewhere like the Oval – carried more weight in the press and media than say a hundred against Somerset at Taunton. And don't ever underestimate the influence the press and media have in professional sport, especially in relation to selection issues. My big fear remained that if I couldn't play against Surrey and someone else came in and made a big or important score – probably Yards – that would be it for me. Career over, a summer in the second team, and twenty years of honest endeavour ending in a whimper. I wanted to avoid that scenario at all costs.

I went through big pain with Oz during that week leading up to the Oval, with him trying to manipulate my back to some sort of loose state as the spasm had completely locked it up. He worked on it for hours over the four days and it was absolute agony. I was wolfing down as much liquid anti-inflammatory as the Doc would allow me, and just prayed that my situation would improve by Friday morning at The Oval.

The morning of the Surrey game, I woke up, and gingerly got out of bed. I knew I was up against it. The back had loosened up a little, but I was in that zone where I felt that any particularly sharp movement might set it off again. I'd had the problem a couple of times before in my career, and I knew that just another 24 hours would see a marked improvement in my condition. I also knew that I didn't have 24 hours – I had about two-and-a-half.

I managed to guts my way through the pain at breakfast and the short trip to the ground from the hotel and got changed quite carefully. Oz came in and asked how I was. I took him to one side and asked if he'd give me the needle – cortisone.

He refused.

It's not illegal or anything; all cortisone does is get you through the day. It's injected directly into the affected area – which is unbelievably painful – and is basically a very heavy anaesthetic. The reason it's become frowned upon in recent years is that it does nothing to tackle the problem – it just takes the pain away. As a result, it's felt that in many cases it just exacerbates the problem and can turn it into much more of a long-term issue.

But I was desperate; I really did believe that if I missed this match, it could signal the end of my career. I was really that concerned. I should point out here that I'm fully aware that many of you reading this book will see my behaviour as totally selfish, and, to be honest, you won't get much of a defence from me. The only thing I feel I should point out in my defence is the conditioning – or even brainwashing – you experience whilst living the life of a professional sportsman. Right back at the start of my days with Swansea City where you were ostracised by the management if you were injured, through to my Glamorgan days when I played (as did many others) through finger fractures and ligament strains, you always tried to play, whatever the situation. As a player, you get used to these moments and begin to live in a world where the main ethic is 'no pain, no gain' and you get lauded by your peers – even winning their respect – for playing through the pain barrier.

Not all players do this – that's fine too – and I've got nothing against them. I've played with players who would refuse to take the field in football or cricket unless they were absolutely 100% fit. The reality of the situation is though that players in professional sport are seldom totally 100% fit, and those who refuse to give a little and at least approach the pain barrier don't tend to last too long in their profession. That's not my rule, it's just the way it is. The grey area in all this, of course, is when do you start becoming a liability? In my case, if I'm brutally honest, I couldn't guarantee the club that I would last the four days against Surrey. If my last four innings had been four hundreds, I'm pretty sure I would have declared myself unfit quite early on, but as I mention, the desperation of the situation – in my mind anyway – meant that I wasn't making a balanced decision anymore, I was just thinking about me. And looking back now, four years later, I really can't apologise for that, as I know, given the same circumstances, I would do exactly the same thing again.

So, I didn't get the injection I begged for – but I declared myself fit anyway. That however, wasn't the end of the problem for me. Sussex would still have the final say. I now had to take a fitness test under the watchful eyes of Oz, Mooresy and Grizz.

It was tough and it hurt like hell. But I was mobile, and I knew it would improve over the next 24 hours. If only the forecast had been bloody rain! I got through everything they asked of me, but I'd say at about 70% performance. After I was done they asked my how I felt.

'Fine. I'm OK to play. I'm fit'

The responses – or more accurately the lack of them – told their own story. Oz the physio was first to speak.

'Cotts – sorry mate – you're not fit. I'm going to have to pull you.'

The rest of them nodded. I was gutted. I started to protest but realised I was

246

wasting my energy. It was over. I was desperately hoping that this wasn't going to prove the case for my career as well.

As I walked back to the dressing room, I saw Mooresy talking to Yards, he was getting the good news – he was in. I just carried on to the dressing room. Mooresy came in a few minutes later.

'I know you're disappointed, but why don't you have a few days off, go home to Gail and the kids, take it easy and see us back in Hove in five days.'

As he left, I again got quite reflective. All the usual negativity came back and surged through me, and as I walked out of the Oval to the car park, I made a point of turning round and looking at the magnificent stadium, and really felt as though this was the end of my career. I thought to myself that I'd need a miracle to come back from this.

Three hours later I was back in west Wales, feeling thoroughly fed up, and as stiff as a board. Gail was in work and the kids in school, so I just slumped onto the couch and did what most frustrated cricketers do at times like this: put BBC 1 on, turned the sound down, and tortured myself by 'watching' the teletext cricket scores for our match at The Oval. As the screen updated through the day, I saw Graham Thorpe score a majestic 156, helping the cocky Surrey boys to an impressive 488 all out.

The following day I sat and 'watched' Sussex's reply. After just two overs Monty was dismissed and the name M.H. Yardy flashed up on the screen. I took a mournful gulp, and settled down to watch. It would have been my name on the screen at this point and I tried to imagine the scene facing Yards. Martin Bicknell steaming in, surrounded by two or three slips and close fielders, all chirping, piling the pressure on between balls. God, how I wished I'd been there. A couple of overs later the scoreboard updated and 'c Thorpe b Ormond 0' appeared alongside Yards's name. I took absolutely no pleasure from this – none at all – but I would be lying to you if I didn't feel a sense of relief.

I honestly never wished ill on a teammate throughout my career. If I'm honest, there were some occasions when I was less sad than normal when someone was dismissed and this might be for a variety of reasons: if someone particularly brash or obnoxious (and there have been a few of those) was out, just to bring them down a peg or two, and various other, generally childish, reasons that get lost in the mist of time, but this was certainly not the case with Yards.

I watched Ceefax on and off for the rest of the day and saw the lads manage to progress to 307, thanks to fifties from Murray, Tim and Tucker. Even though we were a hundred or so behind, we were still in the game. If we could just get some quick wickets, we might set up a bit of a run chase on the final day. It was vital that we took something out of this match, to knock a bit of the strut out of Surrey, as they'd be dangerous opponents and title contenders for the rest of the season.

It was not to be; Ian Ward scored 135, and Surrey declared at 233 for three, which meant that we'd have to score 406 in a day and three overs to win. Those sort of scores were and remain generally unheard of in the final innings of the match to win a game, in all likelihood it was now going to be just a case of survival.

On the final day, I again put the Ceefax on at 11am, and it was a good hour or so before the first wicket fell, Murray for 26. Enter Yards again. I was about to experience a very strange day of mixed emotions.

Yards began one of the great rearguard actions and batted all day as wickets fell all around him. He scored 69 from 241 balls in an innings lasting five hours and seventeen minutes. When I realised the type of innings he was building, my heart sank a wee bit. It was obvious he was playing a very brave and defensive innings, and apart from Tucker's 88, the hopes of saving the match sat largely with Mike. As the day progressed my emotions continued to seesaw – I didn't want us to lose, but I wanted my place back, and the better Yards did, the less likely it was going to be for me to get my place back, yet without Yards staying in, the clearer it became that we would lose. That had to be avoided at *all* costs, even more than my selfish situation.

About twenty minutes before the close of play, Yards was out. I was gutted – genuinely. He'd put up a fantastic effort, and he was last man out after batting for the bulk of the day, and nearly seeing us home. I pictured the dressing room and could see the desolation. Murray and Monty would be consoling Yards, but telling him what a fantastic job he'd done. Mooresy and Grizz would be trying to keep everyone upbeat and telling them to 'put this match behind us, but take out all the positives,' and Mushie would be saying it was Allah's will and that we would have better days soon 'Inshallah'.

The next day, I began the trip back to Hove. They wanted me back to see how I was progressing, and I set out on the five-hour trip. Most of the way I wondered what this all meant for me – selfish I know, but there it is – and wondered if I'd done enough in previous matches to get back in instead of Yards. I'd made the fatal mistake (again!) of looking at the club's web board. I hadn't even played and I was getting slaughtered! 'Hopefully Yardy's innings will see the end of Cottey'; 'If Cottey had played it would've be all over by lunchtime'; and my particular favourite, 'Yardy showed something that Cottey's never had –

bottle.' When you earn your living in the public eye you have to learn to accept the stick, and that's fine. But sometimes you just wish that on occasion these people realised that even us sports types do have feelings, and we also have family and friends who get even more hurt by the abuse than we do. But that's life I guess.

When I reached Hove I had a read of the Argus and it was saying pretty much the same thing, but in slightly more reasonable language, that Yards deserved a chance now and maybe it was time that I was left out to find some form in the Seconds, and came back fitter and stronger later in the season when injuries and loss of form to others take their toll. They had a very strong point to be honest; it's just that I knew in my heart I'd never make it back into the team if I was left out now.

The next day the first team were on the move again to Tunbridge Wells where we were to play Kent. My back was fine now, it had been by the second day of the Surrey game, but the management were still keeping me in cotton wool, and had arranged another fitness test for me, which thankfully I passed with flying colours. Then came the team news. It was basically between Yards and me.

They went with me. It was tough on Yards, but I was so relieved; I had to get a big score.

We lost a wicket with just one run on the board, and, batting at three, I went to the crease. I remember facing Sheriyar. With his second ball I was out. LBW.

For nought.

That was it. All over. I was inconsolable.

My mind was full of so many emotions as I trudged back to the pavilion, not just the ones specifically about me that I've referred to above, but added in for good measure, letting the team down, letting Mooresy down, (who knowing him would have voted strongly for me to be included in the first place), but strangely, I even felt that I'd let Yards down too.

I could see him hanging round, probably feeling the same as I did a few days before, not glad I'd failed, but relieved, but also probably wondering what the hell he had to do to get a run in the side. I knew exactly how he felt because I had those feelings when I was continually left out by Glamorgan during the early part of my career for players who I just felt were over the hill and were getting in my way of forging a career for myself. The reason I felt that I'd let Yards down is that it probably would've been easier for him to take if I scored 128 because that would have proved I was worth my place, but my duck just emphasised that I wasn't – certainly in many people's eyes anyway.

To say I was gutted is again an understatement. I was just glad that it hadn't happened again at Hove. By now my mind was a mixture of regret, sorrow, despair and, most worryingly, fear. The thought of my second innings scared me, the thought of letting the lads down again scared me, and the thought of having a peak at that bloody web board absolutely terrified me!

I actually never looked at it again, but months later, Dave told me what it was saying the evening of that second-ball duck in Tunbridge Wells. It didn't make pretty reading apparently.

I now had a day-and-a-half to reflect on things as we posted a first innings score of 311, with Grizz and Tucker chipping in with fifties, and most of the other lads contributing. I was the only player not to get double figures. That fact didn't exactly help my mood. I spent the next day or so in the field marvelling at the genius that is Mushtaq Ahmed. Even though I was going through the mill a bit, Mushie certainly took my mind off it for a while with his magical bowling, taking five wickets and ripping the heart out of the Kent middle order.

Now, at this point, I can also let you into a little dressing-room secret. One thing that is provided for the players of most counties these days are the scorecards of the last five or six games of your opponents, along with any other salient facts about certain players. This might be that he hasn't batted for a certain number of innings, or that he's back from injury, or that he's in a particularly bad run of form and his place is under threat, or that he frequently gets out caught behind early on, that sort of thing. The idea behind this is that when this player strides to the crease, apparently full of confidence, a little subtle welcoming committee awaits, sharing carefully selected personal comments such as 'God, he looks like a bloke who's only passed 30 once this season,' or 'Here he is, another attempt at getting his first hundred – he doesn't look like he's up for it today either,' and so on. It's purposely designed to try to get into the head or under the skin of the batsman. As I've alluded to, the vast majority of batters who make it to the professional ranks can play – there's no question about that – they simply wouldn't have made it this far otherwise. But, what the vast majority of first-class batsmen necessarily haven't got is a sound temperament. Many players can be coaxed into playing a rash shot or taking a risky single, simply because of some barbed comment made by a close fielder. When it happens to you, it's not pleasant, but when you take part in it yourself, it can be quite enjoyable. It's one of cricket's necessary evils.

That day when I walked to the crease for my second innings, with Monty losing his wicket with only one on the board and just three balls gone, under the most pressure I think I'd ever encountered since that day I walked out in

Glamorgan's Sunday League 'final' ten years earlier, I quickly realised that Kent had indeed done their homework, and one Andrew Symonds in particular.

Symonds was your typical Aussie cricketer – apart from one small fact. Years earlier as a young batsman for Gloucestershire he'd apparently made himself available for England as he'd been overlooked by Australia, and also by making this declaration, Gloucester could pick another overseas player. However, when push came to shove and England came calling, Australia conveniently came calling at the same time, and off he popped back to the outback. He was blessed with extraordinary ability, but had still not really established himself in the Aussie test team. One other Aussie feature he possessed in abundance was the skill that the Aussies called mental disintegration. Sledging.

As I walked to the crease, he started.

'Look out boys – dead man walking here. Duck in first innings, he needs the runs, boys, but he doesn't look like he's gonna get them.'

Cheers Symmo.

I took guard trying to ignore them, but my worries and insecurities were preventing me focus and I can hear almost every word even now.

'He hasn't got a hundred this year yet boys. Yardy should be playing here, not this old fella.'

I faced my first ball from Sheryiar who had me LBW in the first innings and I played and missed.

'Oooooo – he's shot, boys, he's gone, he won't last long. There's a career on the line here boys; if he doesn't get runs, it's retirement time. Keep at him'

And on it went.

I scratched around for a while, and then found a bit of form. Murray, as usual, was brilliant.

'C'mon mate, we're all with you. Let's just take it easy and get the score board ticking. No risks, you can do it – no trouble'

I'll always be grateful to him for that morning – he probably can't remember a thing about it, but he really helped me through that session. We stayed together for a little under three hours until I was out for 52. We'd put on 111 (Nelson for you cricket fans), and I felt heaps better when I walked off past Andrew Symonds. 'Well played, mate' he smiled. You've gotta love the Aussies!

All the lads seemed pleased for me back in the dressing room, none more so than Mooresy. 'Well played Cotts, you showed bags of character out there. Well done, I'm delighted for you'.

My depression was subsiding and my anxiety was receding. I'd finally contributed during a tricky spell of the match. The fact that we went on to win the match was a huge bonus, and I drove away from Tunbridge a far happier bunny than when I'd first arrived.

Following the Kent game, when I felt I was getting back into the groove after that three-hour knock, not to mention the choice abuse from Andrew Symonds, I was really looking forward to spending some more time in the middle, to build on the small foundation I had built. As it was, I wasn't to hold a bat in anger for another 23 days.

The reason for this was the introduction of a form of cricket that was to take the country by storm: twenty20. It caught the imagination of the Hove faithful, and cricket fans in general, succeeding spectacularly in encouraging younger fans and families in abundance to come and view this shorter version of the game. I've never been a dyed-in-the-wool traditionalist, yet despite having an extremely healthy respect for the history of the game, I've always believed innovation and new ideas are vital in keeping cricket an attractive and entertaining sport to allow it to compete with the many other options available these days to both the active and armchair fans. With this in mind I was really looking forward to this new experience, and because fielding had played such a big part in my career – and despite my advancing years – I was really looking forward to throwing myself around in the field for twenty overs.

We were chosen to be the first county featured on Sky TV in a live twenty20 match. The excitement was buzzing around the ground on the day, especially as the new rules and gimmicks were unveiled to us all. Bowlers had only 90 seconds to bowl each ball, lots of new fielding positions and restrictions were announced, a team dugout from which to enter the arena was placed on the boundary's edge instead of the long walk we usually undertook from the dressing room, and, most fascinating of all, some of us were going to be wired for sound to be interviewed on the go between balls by people like David Lloyd and Ian Botham. I couldn't wait – this was right up my street.

Unfortunately it was not to be.

Just before we all got changed for the warm-ups and the preamble to the game, I saw Mooresy coming over to me. It didn't look like good news.

'Cotts, I'm leaving you out today, I want to make sure that your back continues to improve, and I don't want to risk it in these games.'

I tried to hide my disappointment. I told him I felt fine, and was certain that it would be no problem and no risk, but he stood firm, and that was the end of that. It's a strange feeling when you're left out of a side on the morning of the game at the best of times, but this was slightly different as it was to be the first game of something different and new in cricket's colourful history. Pete had a point of course. There was no guarantee that my back would last the game, but my view was that there was no guarantee that it wouldn't either. But the decision was made and that was that. What you then do is try to blend into the background as much as possible, keep out of people's way and not be a hindrance.

As you now know, I've tried to live my career in cricket as the life and soul of the dressing room. I'm a massive believer in the 'team' and feel that the something extra I bring to the game, apart from any ability I have as a batter and fielder, is almost one of a type of morale officer. I'd seldom let myself get too down in public – even when inside I might be falling to bits – and I'd always tried to help others and cheer them up or reassure them when things were bad for them. I've had people do the very same for me, and I know how grateful I've been to many different people on these occasions. I feel really lucky to have won a bit of silverware in my career, but the proudest achievement I feel I have is the fact that for three of the six years I spent at Sussex, I was awarded the Team Man of the Year trophy. This was voted annually by the lads and management team, and even though I'd love to be sitting here having been voted Sussex's most gifted player of all time, I think in the grand scheme of things I'm happy if I am remembered by my peers as a handy bloke to have around the dressing room.

With all this in mind, I just kept my head down and took a spectator's view of the game, and hoped I'd be able to play in the second game the following day. But that day followed the same pattern as the first, as did the next day and the next. Every day Mooresy would tell me the same thing; he was protecting my back and the boys that had been playing had done well and that he didn't want to change the team. Therefore, I spent the bulk of June on the sidelines like a spare part. For a bloke that loves being at the heart of the dressing room, it's really tough to become a bit of a wallflower. Usually in my career if I'd been out of the first team, it was either because of injury, in which case I might not even be at the ground, or because of lack of form, resulting in being dropped to the second team. At least when dropped you're back in the dressing-room environment and enjoying the trials and tribulations of a match situation, but that period when I just spent the whole month basically as a supporter, I found a very strange and unsettling experience. I suppose it would have been easier to deal with if I was sitting there having scored 600 runs already in the season, knowing that I was a certainty to get straight back in the side when Championship cricket resumed on June 27 against Warwickshire.

But as we know, that wasn't the case, and it wasn't long before the good old-fashioned conspiracy theories flooded into my mind and began to take over. I began to convince myself that it wasn't because of my suspect back that Mooresy kept overlooking me, it was because he was trying all the other batters out in twenty20 to see which one would take my place against Warwickshire. I don't want you to get the impression that I'm a total basket case who thinks the worst every time something goes against me because I'm not – honestly! But self-doubt is the scourge of all sportsmen. Thankfully, I need not have worried.

On June 26 with twenty20 cricket finished, Mooresy told me I'd be playing against Warwickshire at Hove the next day. I can't tell you how relieved I was. I think he could see that I was really worried about my future involvement at first-team level, and the things he said to me that day not only reassured me, but also helped me realise that there were still people – people I respected – who still rated me at the club. It was a weight off my shoulders. There was only one problem left: I had to score some runs.

Up to that innings, my highest score for Sussex had been 154. And of the six hundreds I'd scored for Sussex up to that point, only one had been completed at Hove.

On that beautiful summer's day, I felt this was going to be my final opportunity to show the Hove faithful a glimpse of what I always believed I was capable of.

I scored 188.

As I walked off, I received a standing ovation from the whole ground. I remember taking off my helmet and raising my bat, and if I'm totally honest, I absolutely revelled in the moment, which was unlike me really. Amidst this joy I'd be lying if I didn't briefly wonder how many of those now cheering, clapping and shouting my name had openly abused me at Hove over the last couple of years, or had whacked the knives into my back in cyberspace on the website. But hey, what the hell? If they were clapping now, who cared?

When I got back to the dressing room, the reception I got was absolutely fantastic. I don't think any team I've ever played for celebrated so much with me for an innings of mine. I was genuinely touched, thrilled, proud and relieved in equal measure. The innings was one of the best and most fluent I was to play in my whole career. And I'd done it at Hove!

I went into bat with the score on just 3 after Murray was out for a duck, and joined Monty at the crease. As was usual at Hove up to this point, the announcement of my name as I walked to the crease was greeted with a muted response from the faithful to say the least. Irony of ironies, who do you think was standing at the other end waiting for me? None other than Pakistan's finest and former Glamorgan teammate, Waqar Younis. To my eternal gratitude, Wicky steamed in and bowled me a leg-side half volley which I clipped for four. I'm not sure if he was taking it easy on me, but I was grateful nonetheless.

By the time I walked off, the score had been advanced to 342, and most pleasing of all was that I'd hit a total of 31 boundaries in my innings, and only Murray – when he scored his mammoth 334 not out in the final innings of the season – would score more boundaries in a single innings that season. I can tell you that there's nothing like boundaries, and plenty of them, to win over the fans. The icing on the cake was that we absolutely stuffed Warwickshire by an innings and 59 runs, and, what's more, for the first time in a very long time, an innings of mine had been the crucial one in the match. Nothing can describe how good it felt.

I remember Mushie coming and sitting with me after we'd won, as I was having one of several celebratory beers that evening. Now if you think about Manuel in *Fawlty Towers*, and make him Pakistani instead of Spanish, you'll have some idea of Mushie's conversational skills. (Only joking, Mushie!) Anyway, he sat with me, and as a devout Muslim, joined me with a glass of water.

'I'm so pleased for you Cotts – it was Allah's will and you really deserved it.'

I thanked him and smiled, and, not being religious myself, felt like asking if he could find out if Allah could stretch to a hundred next innings too.

He then went on to explain how impressed he'd been with me this season even though I'd struggled for runs, because I'd kept positive through it all. If only he knew the truth, I thought! He finished by saying that he knew this day would come because everyone had said what a good player I was and that they were all so much behind me. I really appreciated his words.

I'll never know if Mushie did in fact have a word with the big man in the sky, but I was about to enter the best run of form I would ever experience in my whole career.

If I add in my scores from the Warwickshire game on 9th May, I managed to put together the following run of scores in the County Championship:

41, 55, 58, 0, 52, 188, 107, 98, 147, 58 and 53.

It was almost ridiculous; I can't believe now that I didn't fill in a lottery ticket during this period. I'd scored 857 runs in 11 innings, at an average of 77.91. At the end of the season someone told me that I had narrowly missed out on breaking a Sussex record which had stood since 1901 when no less a person than C.B. Fry scored eight consecutive championship fifties. I got seven, in a run of nine fifties in ten innings. I can't tell you how proud I am of getting close to such a revered figure. In hindsight I'm quite glad I didn't break the record; it's more than enough just to have got close to someone of his stature and mystique, whose association with Sussex carries so much weight.

Following the 188, everything fell into place mentally, and I was enjoying every second of my cricket, batting, fielding and all the shenanigans in the dressing room. The club was building serious momentum toward challenging for the Holy Grail – the County Championship – and I was having a very real impact on the positive results we were achieving. All through my career I've tried to work out how I was feeling at times when I was playing really well, and attempt to replicate that feeling at times when things aren't going so well. In the end, I now know absolutely 100%, that the key to success is purely and utterly a state of mind, based on high confidence. When it's with you, you feel as though you can take them all on – Warne, Donald, Walsh – you simply don't care, but when your confidence is gone, even a part-time trundler terrifies you. It really is bizarre.

Obviously there are times when technique is an issue, and your confidence can't really help you if you're doing something fundamentally wrong, but that's when the two best coaches I've ever worked with – Duncan Fletcher and Peter Moores – really come into their own. They were always willing to work with you, hour after hour, attempting to iron out some flaw, or introduce a small process which will have the effect of improving the situation as a whole. The two of them really border on the genius. Pete was always strong on 'controlling the controllables'. By this he meant never dwelling on situations or issues that you had absolutely no influence over. A good example of this is umpire's decisions. I've had so many bad ones in my career, it's laughable. But, by the very same token, I've had appeals for LBW against me that were so vociferous and strong that I nearly walked, yet then looked up to see the umpire turning the appeal down. Pete's point is that these will almost certainly even themselves out over a season or career – just deal with it and get on with it. When you're in the middle of a bad trot and you get caught at third slip off the boot, as I once was against Lancashire, that's very much easier said than done, but that's Pete's whole point – if you *can* achieve that, you really are halfway there.

The other issue connected with all this is relaxing and not getting crushed by the pressure. The main thing I remember about my 'purple patch' in 2003 was how relaxed I was and how much I enjoyed everything, and how I literally took each delivery at a time. I became almost nonchalant. It's almost as though I was taken over by another being. I remember early in my career playing against Colin Wells at Derby. In three consecutive innings (two championship and one Sunday League) he posted scores of 100, 90 and 100. I remember spending lots of time through these innings just watching him, not just his batting, but his whole demeanour. He absolutely exuded confidence, even arrogance. When he smashed another ball to the boundary, I felt like clapping I was so impressed, but there was not a glimpse of pride or pleasure on his face; his look was instead one of almost indifference. I remember our eyes met after one such shot, and the look he gave me was almost like 'I do this every day son – just get used to it.' I drove away from Derby that weekend hugely impressed by his whole approach and wondering if I shouldn't just give it all up – I'd never be able to bat in that relaxed and arrogant manner. Months later, at the end of the season, I stumbled across his figures for the season. He finished the season averaging around 24, and that weekend was far and away his best trot of the summer. The point of all this is that for one of the few occasions in my career, I felt exactly how Wells had looked to me all those years before. I had nothing in my mind that concerned me, and I played with the carefree abandon of a man who was pretty much sure that his career was drawing to a close and felt I had nothing to prove to anyone any more, regardless of what people may or may not have thought of me. How I wish I could've just switched that frame of mind on like a light during my career.

I then had another conversation with Mushie after my 98 in my second innings at Arundel against Essex where I narrowly missed getting a hundred in each innings – a feat I never managed to achieve in my whole career. The basis of the conversation was that Mushie suggested that I put off my plans for retirement at the end of the season. I hadn't really given it much thought since I got my 188 at Hove – I'm convinced that the very fact that I hadn't been thinking about it had a big impact on the run of form I enjoyed. I just put it all out of my mind and enjoyed myself.

'Have the club approached you about a new contract?' Mushie began.

I told him that they hadn't and that I'd not really been thinking about it. I explained that in my own mind I was preparing for retirement, but that I'd not made a conscious decision about it, nor had I mentioned it to Mooresy, Grizz or anyone else at the club.

'I've never retired before so I don't really know what I'm supposed to do,' I said.

'Listen, don't retire. I urge you not to. You are batting really well now and I just think it would be a terrible shame if you were to walk away from it all now. I'm certain that this team is going to achieve great things in the next few years, and I think you should definitely be a part of that – you've earned that right, and you are now showing everyone what you can do out in the middle. Retirement is a very final thing, and I will be putting that day off for as long as I can. You must do the same.'

I was really taken aback.

'Go and speak to Mr Peter Moores and ask him about next season and what the club are going to offer you. You need to put the decision with them.'

We chatted on about other things, but I guess Mushie had successfully planted the seed in my mind. What he'd also done – for the very best of reasons – is give me something to worry about again.

A day or so later I went to see Mooresy and brought the topic up in a roundabout way. He asked me what I was exactly saying and I blurted out

'Am I going to get a contract for next year?'

The delay and lack of clarity in Mooresy's response was its own answer.

He mentioned that it hadn't been considered yet and that he'd speak to Grizz and the board and would get back to me. As he walked away, I felt a little let down. Whether I'm right or wrong about this I don't know, but the feeling Mooresy gave me was that this was a problem he didn't want to deal with. I felt as if it was almost like I was outstaying my welcome suggesting this, and the twelve-year-old boy in me wanted to say 'It's not my fault sir, Mushie told me to ask you!'

I was left feeling almost as though I wish I'd never asked, because as much as I liked Mooresy, he was my boss after all, and now I didn't know whether I'd overstepped the mark by bringing this issue up, or whether I was right to do so.

The net effect? I began to clutter my mind with rubbish again after such a productive period of run scoring that had been totally underpinned by my clarity of thought. But it was done now, I thought, and as the runs still kept coming, the thought of securing a new contract became more important to me than I previously considered. I must stress here that at no time did I ever feel that a new contract was my express right – far from it; it was, and always should be, the decision of the club in the end, but in my career to date, any player who'd had a big year in the final year of his contract was always offered another. I truly hoped that this would be the case with me, but I also realised that I was 37 at the time.

Over the next few weeks a few of the lads got on my case in support of getting a new deal, which was extremely good for my confidence, but conversely the lack of response from Pete wasn't. This 'will they, won't they' feeling increased, and from going from a situation of turning up for games with my mind totally uncluttered, I was now being greeted with cheery 'Good mornings' followed by 'Heard any news yet? No? That's odd, I'd give you a contract straight away if it was me – they must be mad.' It was all incredibly well meaning by the boys, but began to prove unsettling. I've had to deal with good and bad news in equal measure in my career, and to be honest you just try to get on with it, but the worst situations are those born of uncertainty.

It came to a head when we played Notts at Trent Bridge and I'd just completed another 50, making it my ninth half-century in ten consecutive innings. Paul Franks came into bowl, dropped it slightly short, and I rocked back and cut him uppishly, but powerfully, just behind square. It looked like it might go for six, until it just dipped and arrowed straight into the hands of Andrew Harris at deep third man. It was a rank bad ball that I'd hit really well, and in the month prior would have probably sailed for six, this time though, it got me out.

As I walked past the ever so pleasant Mr Franks, who gave me a right send-off even though he'd bowled like a drain (these bowlers!), it was as if a veil was being drawn over me. And I just knew at that very point that my run was over. I just knew. Unfortunately, I was right.

A year after my career finished, I remember talking about this incident with my mentor Alan Jones, who as a Glamorgan opening batsman scored over 50 centuries for the club, almost twenty more than I managed.

'You'd just had your quota, Cotts,' he said.

He then went onto explain why it's important – especially for batters – to enjoy their days of success, because even for really successful players, those days are few and far between. Al defined a day of success as one where you scored a fifty or a hundred.

He pointed out that in the modern game there are seventeen first-class, four-day games a batsman can play in. That means a maximum of 68 days' play. For more or less half off those, you are in the field watching the opposition batters. That leaves 34 days. Of these some are always lost to rain or bad light etc – very conservatively four days. That leaves 30 days. A typical county batter will score three or four hundreds and maybe five or six fifties in a season out of their 30-odd batting attempts. That means twenty further days with no success – meaning ten or so days during the whole season where a batsman will experience success. That's not a hell of a lot. His view was simply that I'd had all mine together.

He explained that if you look at any decent player's record over a career, yes they will have had good runs of form, and one or two seasons will be better than others, but whoever they are, there aren't many batters who will experience more than ten to fifteen days of success in a season. It's just people's perception of that success, or sometimes lack of it, that changes. He pointed to my career average of 36.69.

'That's why the batting average is the benchmark in judging how good a player was. In your case it says that every time you went to the crease you were capable of scoring 37 runs. Now if you multiply that figure through your top six batters and all-rounder, and add in 30 or 40 runs for the tail, every time your team bats, they score 300 runs – that's 600 per match. There's not many teams in county cricket history who score 600 runs in a match and lose. It's all about perception. Whether you score those runs in ten or eleven straight innings, or every third match, is irrelevant really, it's just that the day you got out against Notts marked the end of your quota for a while.'

Alan was right about that. It really was the end of my quota, and I was only to pass fifty again once more that season.

CHAPTER TWENTY THREE

The Winners Enclosure

Things were now going well at Sussex. Up to the 'end-of-my-quota' game at Notts, we'd now played eight games, lost two and won the other six. The draw against Notts consolidated our position toward the top of the league.

I drifted through the next couple of games, still applying myself as hard and as desperately as I'd done prior to my purple patch, but the runs just wouldn't come. The bonus was that we were still winning, and despite my not contributing as well as I had, the fact that we were striding confidently toward the title was far more important. In the games that followed the end of my run of form, we drew against Surrey, then beat Lancashire, Essex and Middlesex and surged to the top of the table. My contribution to these wins had been 1, 41, 18, 0, 23, 15 and 7. Hardly a run of scores to threaten any other records held by C.B. Fry.

To be frank though, I wasn't that concerned. Personally, I wanted to score as many runs as I could every time I stepped to the crease, but now, as other batters like Grizz, who'd had a poor summer up to this point of the season, came to the fore, I was more than happy to play second fiddle if it meant the team continuing to win. If a cricket genie had come to me and asked if I'd like to swap, say, that innings of 18 listed above, and turn it in to 125 not out – with the price being a Sussex draw instead of a victory – I would have turned him down flat. Prior to my purple patch though, I'd have bitten his hand off. Such are the vagaries of sport! Now, the team was everything, and every single player was putting personal dreams to one side in pursuit of the prize that we could see tantalisingly up ahead on the horizon.

The balance between collective loyalty and individual ambition – between selflessness and selfishness – is a delicate one in all team sports. I think that cricket, however, has its own unique take on this seeming conflict of interests. Cricket can best be summed up as a team sport played by individuals. By that I mean that at the start of each season I guarantee you that every single player in a county cricket team will have their own personal and individual targets. Now some of these will be public, and some will be private. The bottom line generally however is that if these targets are reached – no matter how selfish they appear – the team will generally benefit.

Let me give you some examples.

Take players with ambitions of playing for England. I had them when I'd cemented my place in Glamorgan's side in the early 1990s, but when I looked in the mirror, I knew that in reality, it would take a bit of a leap of faith for the selectors to give me a chance. Apparently, for the seasons between 1993 and 1996, after Graeme Hick and Mark Ramprakash, I had the highest batting average for an England qualified player over those four seasons. At no point however did I ever think in that period that I *should* be picked, nor have I felt hard done by the fact that I wasn't selected. It just wasn't meant to be. Now at that same time, the press, especially in Wales, were really clamouring for Matt to be recalled to the squad, and that was fine. I hardly got a mention, and that was fine too. I believe Matt to be just about the most talented player I've ever played with in my career. The key difference between Matt and me, though, was expectation. He expected to be picked, and got really annoyed when he wasn't. It was hugely important to him, and when he was being overlooked it really got to him. It was a very similar story with Chris Adams at Sussex, again another very fine player with high expectations. Now I never discussed it with either of these players but I think I got to know them well enough to suggest that at the start of each season the following list of mental targets would not be a million miles from what they actually would have set themselves:

> Get off to a good start with a hundred as soon as possible.
>
> Attempt to go for a 1,000 runs by the end of May or early June, as that gives you pole position in the press for an early England call-up.
>
> If taking part in a televised game, ensure a confident, positive and hopefully big innings.
>
> If picked, do as well as possible for England.
>
> Help Glamorgan/Sussex up the league as far as possible.

As you can see, the first four of these targets are personal – extremely so – and you've got to get down to number six before the county team gets a look in. Now, in no way am I criticising either player – far from it. I'm just illustrating that in cricket, the first thoughts are often for a player's personal goals and circumstances, with the success of the team following automatically if these personal goals are achieved.

Other players would have similar, though probably less grand targets. Mine might have been:

Get a hundred in the first month of a season.

Make sure I get to a 1,000 runs sometime in August to take the pressure off for the final couple of games.

In any televised games, make sure I get off the mark early and keep the scoreboard ticking over.

By June, have scored enough runs to make sure I stay in the county side for the rest of the season.

If in the side for the full season, and 1,000 runs passed, have a look at my career record for runs in season and see if I can beat it.

Help Glamorgan/Sussex up the league as far as possible.

I can't over-emphasise the feeling of self-preservation a professional cricketer experiences; it's simply the level of perceived achievement that changes. It's also the same with bowlers and wicket-keepers. Bowlers don't want to be entering June having only taken 15 wickets. If they do, the press will begin to ask questions about their form and probably suggest that they be 'rested'. They want to bowl on seaming or spinning wickets taking 8 or 9 wickets in a match, and the odd five-for, while similarly, wicket-keepers want to take as many catches and stumpings as possible to improve their career record.

There's no other game like cricket for statistics, and if you ever meet a cricketer who leads you to believe that they don't know how many runs they've scored or what their average is or how many wickets they've taken, just watch their nose grow. I've spent enough times watching players pop off to see the scorer – me included – to 'see how I'm doing' to know how self-focussed we all are who play this wonderful game.

However, by the time we reached September in 2003, and entered the final two games – so close to team glory – all personal goals were now shelved. I'd still not heard whether I was getting a contract, but frankly, my insecurities on that had passed now; it would either happen or it wouldn't. I really felt that we were now on the edge of something great for the club, and all my energies were being focussed on that – as were the energies of every other player. We arrived at Old Trafford to play Lancashire knowing that a resounding victory would mean that in all probability we would win the title.

They smashed us by an innings and 14 runs.

There's very little to say about the game really. We were outplayed, they were better than us over the four days, end of story. One thing that did come out of it was a bit of unlikely team bonding. When the four-day match ended, we all trooped back to the dressing room feeling not only sorry for ourselves, but also wondering what damage we had done in relation to our championship hopes. We felt as a team that we'd come too far now to blow this, and we had to take the positives out of the performances and move on. This was the gist of Mooresy's talk after the game.

Pete, us usual, was excellent. He really lifted us and told us that when you've given your all and lost, there's no disgrace, the problem arises only when you've not given your best, and been defeated by an inferior team. He highlighted the good performances, such as Murray's hundred, Jason's bowling – taking three of the six wickets to fall – and even mentioned my welcome return to form, scoring 97 in the match. He then said 'Don't feel sorry for yourselves, don't sit in tonight and fret, enjoy yourselves and stay upbeat.'

Unfortunately for Pete, we took him a bit too literally.

That night we met back at the hotel – the usual suspects, Murray, Grizz, Matt, Tim, physio Oz, a couple of others and me, and went out for something to eat and a couple of drinks. One thing led to another and we followed Pete's orders to the letter, and ended up enjoying ourselves. We were hardly out of it in a rock-and-roll state, but we'd probably had about seven or eight bottles of Budweiser by the time we crept in at about 11.00. There was only one problem with this – we still had a one-day game to play the next day.

The following morning, one or two of the boys looked a little worse for wear, and Pete didn't need to be Betty Ford to realise what had happened. He waited until we started to warm up, and until the first predictable sloppy mistake was made, and then he gave us full barrels. He raged at us that we were unprofessional, foolish, immature and every thing else that fitted. We looked suitably glum as he climbed into us, and took it all as it was a fair cop really. Drinking and socialising plays a big part in cricket, even in today's fitness and nutrition-focussed world. However, when you play a sport that sees you spend four consecutive nights away from home on at least nine occasions during the year, you simply can't expect us to quietly go up to our bedrooms at 8.30 and watch *Eastenders*. It simply doesn't happen. There's far too much energy flying around, and most nights are lubricated by a couple or three lagers. I'm not talking excess here – that would be ridiculous too – but there has to be a balance. The night before this one-day match with Lancashire, I'd have to admit we got the balance slightly wrong.

As Pete was delivering the dressing down, Jason Lewry made a noise, and Pete tore a strip off him. Lewey looked a mess. His hair was all over the shop, he hadn't shaved, his eyes looked black and he hardly looked the picture of sporting excellence.

Pete wrecked him.

As he did so, the rest of us struggled to keep straight faces while witnessing Jason's bemusement in the face of this attack. There was one major fact Pete was unaware of as he was slaughtering Jason.

He was one of the few that stayed in for an early night – he'd not even had as much as a shandy.

To Jason's eternal credit he never said a word, and took it all. That's team bonding for you.

Oh, I forgot – the result of the game?

We returned the favour of the Championship match and smashed them by nine wickets, and I scored one of the best 1 not outs of my career.

When we arrived at Hove on September 17, 2003, we all truly felt that this was a day of destiny. The equation was simple. If we got six bonus points out of this match with Leicestershire – win, lose or draw – Sussex would become county champions for the first time in their long history. As a team we all knew what this meant to the club, fans, past players, and everyone in the area really. Since I'd been at the club I'd read through the club's yearbooks and listened to fans talk about the names that had graced the Hove ground: Jon Snow, Imran Khan, Garth le Roux, Ted Dexter, C.B. Fry, Tony Greig, David Sheppard, Colin Wells, Michael Bevan, Gehan Mendis, Javed Miandad, Maurice Tate, the Langridges, Ranjitsinji, Jim Parks – the list could go on for pages. And now we, the class of 2003, stood on the verge of delivering something to the club, that no one in the clubs history had been able to achieve. The County Championship. It made us all feel very humble.

But we had to do it yet.

We got together before the game and Mooresy had great balance to his speech: he covered everything from personal achievement to professional pride, and from making history to not taking anything for granted. We all knew exactly what we had to do.

Leicestershire won the toss, and my old adversary Phil DeFreitas, who had made his first-class debut less than a year before mine in 1986, chose to bat first. They made a decent, if slow start, and had taken the score onto 111 for 1, as we approached the final over before lunch. Our magician, Mushtaq Ahmed bowled to the Australian Brad Hodge, who was now well-set on 36, and looking extremely comfortable. Mushie bowled a decent length ball to him, outside off stump. For the first time all year, I picked his googly from my vantage point at first slip – and I was hoping Hodge hadn't.

He hadn't.

It turned back sharply, passing his forward defensive and smashed into off stump. It was magnificent delivery, and as Mushy wheeled away in total delight, arms raised, all present were fully aware of the significance. He'd just taken his hundredth first class-wicket of the summer. It was a truly remarkable achievement, by a truly remarkable man, and I don't think I've ever been so pleased by a milestone achieved by a teammate as I was at that moment – and I think all the lads felt the same too.

Lunch was taken straight away, and it tasted a lot better than we thought it would when Leicester had been grinding away for most of the morning. The rest of the afternoon was pretty much a Sussex bowling masterclass as we took the next eight Leicester wickets for just 68 runs with Mushy claiming four and Tucker three. When Mushy bowled Dave Masters for two, we left the field with our maximum three bonus points, knowing that if we could score 300, the three bonus points that score would bring, would secure us the title.

Still, it was far from over. The old mists had rolled in from Hove in the late afternoon, and the ball had already started to do a bit for our bowlers, and the pitch was not as benign as we hoped. The first four batters padded up as usual. Muzz and Monty were already in the zone, and I couldn't help but think that 300 was still a long way away as I watched them depart, and sat down in my own little world, knowing I'd be in next, but not knowing if that would be when we were 24 for 1 or 240 for 1.

It was 24 for 1.

Monty was caught behind by Nixon off DeFreitas, and I'd seen enough already by the way that Daffy was swinging the ball to realise that the next half hour of my life was not going to be without its stressful moments. There were about 32 overs left in the day, and that famous old sporting adage came straight to the front of my mind, and was certainly true in the circumstances – 'We couldn't win the Championship tonight, but we could sure as hell lose it!'

I joined Muzz, who had a quick chat – 'It's nipping around a bit but just play each ball as it comes and let's get a partnership going, mate.' I loved batting with Muzz and I simply hoped I'd be around with him long enough today. We stayed for about two-and-a-quarter hours that night until the close of play. I ended the day on 47, Muzz on 71 – both not out, which was a bonus. The way DeFreitas had bowled, it was nothing short of a miracle too. He bowled beautifully. He's always been one of the most intelligent bowlers in the game, and he was one that when he got older and his natural pace left him, he made up for it easily with guile and clever changes of pace, and he never forgot how to swing a ball. In that period, God, did he swing it. In terms of discipline and watchfulness, that innings was probably the best I batted all season. As Murray and I walked off together that night, to a rapturous round of applause from a still packed Hove, we both knew we'd done what we were paid to do. We'd batted through a very difficult session of cricket, without losing a wicket, and moved the score to 137 – almost halfway to our target of 300. I felt great, and couldn't wait for the next day, to find out what the sporting gods had in store for us.

The next morning, the team felt slightly more relaxed than the previous day. We definitely had one hand on the trophy now. Mooresy and Grizz had their say, and once again hit the mark perfectly. The comment I'll always remember though is when we were all huddled on the field after we'd finished our warm up. Grizz was giving us the final rallying call, and asked if anyone wanted to say anything. Muzz was the one to immediately pipe up:

'Lads, I just want to tell you that I want to be the one to score the winning runs today.'

I nearly burst out laughing when I saw Grizz's face. I think he thought he was always destined for that reward and he responded by saying that so did he. I wanted to chirp in with 'Fuck me boys, I'm not even out yet – I wouldn't mind doing it either!' I thought it was a really funny moment, but I kept quiet. In fairness to Muzz, he went on to elaborate and say that he hoped we all wanted to do it, as it showed not only a positive attitude, but also how proud he would be to achieve that moment for this great club.

A shudder went through me when he said it as I went straight back to Canterbury ten years earlier almost to the day, and I remembered how fantastic I felt when it happened to me. Maybe lightning would strike twice – perhaps it was to be me again.

Sadly, there was no lightning around Hove that day.

We'd added 14 to our overnight score, and I'd moved onto a fifty which was received with such warmth and joy by the Hove faithful, that I felt quite emotional, and as I looked around at the sea of fans applauding me, I allowed myself to wonder if I'd finally won them over – I'll never know of course – but I truly hoped I had, even if for just that season.

Six runs later and it was all over, caught Nixon, bowled DeFreitas, and off I walked, hugely disappointed as I'd have loved to have been there when the championship was won, but very relieved nonetheless to have contributed in quite a decent way. Grizz walked out, and I could just tell he was going to see it through with Murray – I just knew.

What followed was just as about fantastic as it gets. Muzz and Grizz played absolutely beautifully, the ball stopped swinging (I would say that wouldn't I!), the lads took advantage of every loose ball, and just batted Leicester into submission. After lunch that afternoon, at around quarter to two, and with the score on 298, Murray pulled a short-pitched ball from DeFreitas majestically for four. We'd done it! As good as his word, Muzz had hit the winning runs, and the whole place absolutely erupted. We'd been on 298 for a while, and as a result all the rest of us were primed for a bolt down onto the pitch from the players' balcony. We weren't certain that we'd be allowed on to the pitch as obviously we were still in the middle of a game, but the umpires, and more importantly Phil DeFreitas magnanimously agreed to a ten-minute suspension of play for us all to enjoy our moment, together, as the team that we'd always been.

In my twenty years in the game, I'd never known of such a situation, and will be eternally grateful to Trevor Jesty, Merv Kitchen and Daffy for allowing it. We had a big group hug, plenty of backslapping and a truly memorable lap of honour around the ground, to a tumultuous ovation from the fans at Hove. I'd never seen the ground as full in all my time there, and as I took in every cheer and every image on display, I felt a magnificent sense of achievement, more so than anything that I'd ever done in the game prior to this. I can clearly see the images and scenes in my mind right now.

There's no prouder Welshman than me, and if I'm being truly honest, I never thought that I'd ever top the experiences I'd had with Glamorgan down at Sussex. But since arriving at the South Coast in 1999, I'd struggled, really badly at times, and as I walked around with my teammates, Murray, Mark Davis, Grizz, Tucker, Matt, James Kirtley, Lewey, Monty, Tim Ambrose, Robbo, Mushie and Mooresy in particular, who'd been right behind me through thick and thin, I realised that I was part of the best 'team' that I had or ever would, play with in all my life. It was quite a moment of recognition, and one I'm certain I'll never forget.

CHAPTER TWENTY FOUR

They Think It's All Over . . .

My ultimate exit after 22 years as a professional sportsman was fittingly bittersweet. It certainly mirrored the ups and downs I had experienced in my career, and also the many sad but ultimately amusing moments. Pretty much as my sporting life has panned out really.

The situation was quite simple. At the start of my penultimate season with Sussex, I was in the final year of a five-year contract, which I'd signed at the start of 1999. It was 2003, and after four seasons of underachieving, which in fairness included the one ruined by injury in which I only played two games, I was under a bit of pressure for my place. I was 36 years old, feeling far from home, and was considering my future.

After the bitter feelings I'd experienced when I was deemed not good enough at Swansea City, and the despair I felt when Glamorgan effectively put a retirement date on my head by offering me that two-year contract and a letter confirming a third year as captain of the second team, I was determined that I'd end my career on my terms. It was with this in mind I embarked on what was to become the most joyous, fulfilling season of my life. By the middle of the 2003 championship-winning season, I felt in as good form as I'd been for ten years, and then it all clicked. As the previous chapter outlines, June and July witnessed a run of form the like of which I had never experienced before or since. I had twelve innings littered with either half centuries or big hundreds. I scored more runs than any other batsman in Britain, and was voted 'Man of the Month' in *The Cricketer* magazine. My run of form, alongside the genius of Mushtaq Ahmed and important contributions from most of the other players in the team had catapulted us to top of the league, and as such, meant we went on to win the County Championship for the first time in the club's history.

As the dust began to settle around this fantastic victory, I was finally offered a one-year deal. I thought about it very carefully, and discussed it with my closest friends and family, but ultimately I knew what I was going to do quite early on. I signed.

Part of me felt I shouldn't sign it, and that I should retire, as I'd planned to do, at the end of 2003, which would have been the perfect way to go out – right at the top – winning the most prestigious trophy available, and being right at the centre of that victory. I remember how flat I'd felt in 1997 when Glamorgan won as I'd not contributed as I'd hoped, but this time I felt an integral part of it and as such relished it. However, I also felt that there was no reason why Sussex couldn't win it again in 2004, nor was there any real reason why I couldn't perform again as well as I had in the championship year.

After signing my one-year deal, I did make a promise to myself though. 2004 would be my final season. Definitely. I would retire, whatever happened, even if we won the league again – end of story. It was funny really, because once I'd made the decision, I was strangely relieved. I decided to relax, play to the best of my ability, take each innings as it came (sorry – a cliché, but absolutely true), but above all enjoy it. And I did, every minute of it.

I had a bit of a purple patch again mid-season – nothing as good as the championship year's run of form – but one which proved I was still worth my place in the side. It was around this time that Chris Adams came to see me.

'Have you thought about what you'd do if you were offered another year?' This hadn't come out of the blue; a few of the lads had said much the same and the whispers were that I was going to be offered another deal. I should have replied – 'It's a lovely thought Grizz, but this is my last year – I'm going to retire.' But no, what came out of my mouth instead was:

'Not really. Is it likely?'

'Yes,' he replied. He went on to explain that they wanted to bring in another overseas player, but also wanted to keep Murray. If they decided to keep Murray, that freed up money to be able to keep me. I said I'd definitely think about it and get back to him.

I was now faced with a simple choice. Did I want to extend my life as a cricketer, or did I want to end it? I'd enjoyed the season so much – on and off the field – I began to realise how much I'd miss it when it was over. I now enjoyed every aspect of the game. I loved the fitness, I loved the batting, I loved the fielding, I loved being part of a great group of players. There was nothing I could think of that was negative, even the Hove crowd seemed to support me fully. I was as fit as I'd been for years, and after discussing the positive monetary impact another year would have on the Cottey household back in Wales with Gail, my mind was made up. I went from being committed to retiring to being committed to playing on at one fell swoop. What was it Steve James had said about me changing my mind? I told Chris I would sign.

He was really pleased and said that was great news.

I then put it all to the back of my mind, and just carried on with the season. Then, as often happened, my form tailed off as the season progressed. I've no idea why this happened – it was a bit of a constant throughout my career – I have no real explanation for it. About three weeks before the end of the season, a fella by the name of Maros Kolpak got involved. Heard of him? He's a Slovakian handball player who went to the European Court to be allowed to play in the German league without being classed as a foreigner. Not to do so, he argued, would result in restraint of trade. He won. I was dead in the water.

All the contract talk went quiet, and although it was never mentioned to me by anyone from the club in an official capacity, what this now meant was that Murray could be treated as a 'Kolpak' player in 2005 – effectively meaning he was no longer an overseas player – leaving the club free to bring in another overseas player from the massive pool that exists abroad. This effectively meant that the club could now do without my services.

Once I'd sat down and considered this, I understood perfectly. I would've loved to have had that extra year – my final, final year – but fully understood Sussex's position. Murray was a much better batsman than me – truly world class – and I'd have picked him above me if there was only one space up for grabs. There was no bitterness either – certainly not towards Murray. Nor was there any bitterness towards Chris Adams or the club either. If I'd had my time over again, I'd have preferred that Chris had never raised the matter, because up to then I was more than content to announce my retirement toward the end of the season and bow out quietly. But Mr Kolpak probably hadn't entered his head, so what was done was done, and it must be said, I'd thrown my hat into the ring quite eagerly.

Two days before the final day of the season at Hove, it was contract day at the club. This is when everyone at the club has a slot, and is called in to be told their fate by the club, represented in 2004 by Keith Greenfield, Robbo, Mooresy and the Chief Executive.

When it was my turn, I was called in. I walked in, sat down and waited for Mooresy to begin. In that split second I went straight back to how I felt as a kid with my dreams back at Swansea City, and hoped with all my heart that Mooresy was going to offer me another year.

'Cotts, we're going to have to let you go . . .'

I listened to the rest that he said, and I can remember most of it, and I was taken aback by the kindness and thanks he gave me for my efforts for the club. I was genuinely touched. I let him finish and asked if I could say a few words.

I began by publicly thanking Robbo, my former housemate, for his personal and professional help in my time at the club, and wished him all the best for his new role in his coaching capacity. As Pete was leaving for his new job as Cricket Academy Director, I then began to thank him, but after a few sentences, I began to fill up big style. I struggled to get my words out because of the utmost respect I have for Peter Moores and also it was dawning on me that this was the end. Rather than make an absolute arse of myself, I think I said 'Sorry, I've got to go' and just got up and left.

I walked out and blanked everyone who was waiting in the corridor outside. I quickly found the exit and walked away from the building, and for some reason walked over to the top side of the ground and sat down out of the way, behind the sightscreens. Then the tears came. It was amazing; history repeating itself twenty years after the bitter tears spilt when leaving the Swans.

This time though the tears weren't bitter. They were tears of regret more than anything. Regret that I hadn't retired as planned on my terms, as it meant that I'd completed an unwanted triple crown of rejection at three key points of my career – being released by the Swans, Glamorgan and now Sussex. Regret that my career itself had drawn to a close; it had ended and there was no going back on that. But the biggest regret of all was that I felt I had almost lost my immortality. So many people over the years had asked me what it's like to be a sportsman, and so many times I've just come back with a glib soundbite – 'fantastic', 'really great', 'I've been very lucky'. But do you know what it honestly feels like to be a sportsman? To be paid to play your chosen sport at the highest level? What's the best way I can describe it?

It feels like you're immortal.

It feels like you live in a privileged, parallel world, where people want to speak to you, buy you a beer, ask for an autograph, sometimes hang on your every word – and why? Just because you can hold a cricket bat the right way round and you've been blessed with the reflexes to avoid Shoaib Akthar hitting you on the head when he's bowling a cricket ball at you at nearly 100mph. Your every whim is catered for, cars are arranged for you, hotels are booked, doctors and dentists are arranged for you, and you are paid well too.

You feel immortal.

I instantly remembered Viv Richards's tears in that ecstatic dressing room at Kent eleven years before, sobbing in Hugh Morris's arms. I'm almost certain that he was crying over the loss of his own 'immortality' at the end of his long and fabulous career, and I understood exactly how he felt.

As I sat there on the outskirts of the ground, feeling a little sorry for myself and contemplating my newly acquired mortality, I pulled myself together, stood up and put my hand in my pocket for my car keys to drive away. Not there. Nor my phone. I checked again. Where the hell were they? I remembered. My colour drained again.

I'd left them on the table in front of Mooresy and Robbo. Typical. I even cocked up my own exit. With tail firmly between legs, I tapped on the door, went in pointed to my keys and phone on the table, apologised and picked them up. Mooresy looked as upset as I'd been. I just smiled and left.

It was all over.

CHAPTER TWENTY FIVE

Reflections

Following the success and joy of 2003, I entered 2004 feeling able to reflect on my nineteen years in the game for the first real time. I tried to understand what made a cricketer and what tools were needed to succeed. I know you might be thinking 'Well it's a bit bloody late to be doing that at the end of your career,' but that's the point really, when your career is trundling along nicely over the years, you don't ever give it another thought, you just keep yourself fit, keep yourself available, and when the opportunity arises, try to get some runs. You really delude yourself that this wonderful career may never end.

On reflection though I realised that there are three distinct stages a cricketer goes through in his career. I recognised this, not only by honestly assessing my career and how I pursued certain goals at certain times, but also from spotting these same traits in my cricketing teammates at various times.

The first stage, naturally, encompasses your entrance into the game. Largely, this is the most selfish stage of your career. I've seen cricketers at this stage being so ruthless and self-centred, it's unbelievable. However, their behaviour is totally understandable. This is the stage of your career that you are at your most vulnerable. It's the time when all your dreams can be ripped from you due to the vagaries of form, fitness or quite simply bad luck. I've seen so many players, comfortably as talented as me – some more so – being lost at this early stage. At Glamorgan, Mike Cann, Ian Smith, Andrew Jones, Alistair Dalton and Alun Evans for one reason or another were lost to Glamorgan in their early stages and never had the chance to develop a career in the game. As a senior pro at Sussex, Toby Pierce, Will House, Baz Zuiderent and one of my best friends Jamie Carpenter, all similarly were shown the door.

Early in this book I explained that I identified Mike Cann as my direct rival for a place in the Glamorgan team and as a result reasoned that if I outperformed him in all areas, then I'd probably be offered a contract before him. This had absolutely nothing to do with Canny personally – I absolutely loved the bloke – but the fact was that in my mind I felt that he and he alone stood between me and a career in the game. This marks out the first stage of a cricketer. Unless you're a prodigy like Kevin Pietersen or David Gower, you've got to graft and give everything – and I mean everything – just to get your chance. I'm not saying that Gower and Pietersen didn't graft, it's just that they were so exceptional as youngsters that they were always going to get a run in the team at the earliest opportunity. For the rest of us mortals starting out, our target for success as a player at the time is not the success of our team, or the wellbeing and development of our fellow players, and often not even the state of the game you find ourselves in. No, our target is quite simply personal success. It was the only time in my career, when I'd actually swap the team result – obviously a win – for personal glory. In those days, if I scored a hundred and we lost, I really didn't worry too much – I'd succeeded in putting my name up in lights and got myself on the map. Mission accomplished. It's a harsh fact of life that a batter who contributes lovely match winning cameo's of 30 or 40 in winning sides will not get the column inches of a player scoring century after a century in a team that loses every game. In this situation, at contract time, the player with the centuries will always get the contract before the player with the cameos. It doesn't take long as a young player to realise this, and as a result, your target becomes personal achievement – not necessarily team achievement. Every living cricketer will recognise this – even if they don't admit it!

During my personal stage one, I was like a sponge. On the batting front, I watched and listened to everyone at Glamorgan I could learn from – veterans like John Hopkins and Alan Jones, and overseas players like Ravi Shastri. On the fitness front, I got myself as fit as I possibly could and forced myself to become the best fielder at the club because it was vital to *my* development – again – not necessarily Glamorgan's development.

During this phase you also develop an attitude to competition which is extremely vigorous to say the least. You begin to convince yourself it's vital to prove to everyone at the club that you are a winner. In the touch-rugby warm-ups, for example, you have to win, you have to score the most tries, you have to make the most tackles, and sometimes this competition spills over into the odd unpleasant confrontation. I remember Crofty and Mike Powell falling out quite badly with each other over a game of touch rugby an hour or so before a one-day game, and having to be pulled apart from each other as they grappled on the ground.

The final thing I can say about stage one is that there is no long-term vision at all from the player concerned – it's all focussed on the here and now and getting your foot in the door and getting in the team. You may be dreaming of a long career or England recognition, but the reality is 'get me in the team' and this is at all costs and at the expense of anyone. I went through this at Glamorgan between, say, 1986 and 1989 and when I was finishing at Sussex nearly 20 years later, I saw youngsters doing the same down there. The lucky ones will make it to stage two.

Stage two is the political stage of your career. You've been a first-team regular for four or five years, you're about 25 or 26 and you think 'it's about time I took control of some things here.' You pretty much know now that you have a career in the game, and all being equal, you're looking forward to the next six to eight seasons. In stage one you're looking forward to the next six to eight months. You now feel it's vital to give your voice some volume and get your opinions heard – you've got your feet under the table, a few of the old pros have gone, there's a couple of new youngsters coming in – so it's time to create a bit of a persona for yourself. Again, most cricketers will recognise this, but some cricketers will make more of a meal of this than others. To use a cricketing term, some players become unplayable. They become arrogant, opinionated and generally believe that they know all the answers and have nothing left to learn. I'd like to think that I wasn't that bad, but looking back, I did make a concerted effort to get my views across and make my voice heard. On the cricketing merry-go-round, some players had reputations above others – Dominic Cork, Andrew Caddick, Dermot Reeve, Nasser Hussain, but to be honest I never played week in, week out, with any of these, so can only vouch for their arrogant and brash behaviour out on the pitch. I know at Glamorgan and Sussex, by and large, the egos in those dressing rooms were very much under control. There was the odd exception, an Australian one-day batting legend by the name of Bevan at Sussex, for example. But generally the players in both these environments recognised that people should be allowed to have their say, but there were plenty of strong characters to pull someone in to line if they were beginning to lose their grip on reality. This stage lasts for less than stage one, maybe a season or two, and then hopefully, you'll be lucky enough to move into stage three.

This final stage of your career is when you actually begin to do things for the right reasons. You realise that you're at – or just over – the peak of your career, and that there's a far bigger picture going on than just 'Can I get another hundred today to boost the old averages?' I decided that I wanted to give support to as many of the younger players as I could. Some of this support would go to those who probably didn't need much help from me as their talent was so obvious that it would carry them through anyway – Matt Prior, for example. Some support would be given to those players who were just like me twenty years earlier – very raw, with limited ability, and only an average chance of forging a career in the game. Because I knew it was so hard to build my own career from the very beginning, I just tried to help these players as much as I could, whether it was by mentioning something about their technique, or just a kind word of encouragement. I just remember someone like Chris Cowdrey being so kind and helpful to me at Glamorgan when I was making my way in the game, and him having such a positive impact on me, that I just hoped I might have the same effect on a youngster who might be wracked by self-doubt.

In 2001 I played only one championship game before going down with an injury which began as a sore elbow needing rest, and ended with a consultant telling me that the tendon had been really badly torn. During this time, I was so downcast that I, for the first time, began to fear for my career. The club were great – never put me under any pressure – but I felt awful as I could do everything – run, field and throw – except pick up a bat. I was really worried that people thought I was feigning – and I'm sure a couple did. I was given an unofficial option by the club. I could hang around Hove keeping fit and staying round the first team on home match days, or I could join the Seconds as a bit of help to Keith Greenfield. I didn't have to think twice. I joined Grubby at the seconds and mucked in helping him as much as I could.

In stage one I probably would have hidden the injury as much as I could, and if that didn't work, would've stewed around, hoping for rain in all games, and at the very least hoping that none of my rivals had any spectacular success. In stage two I would definitely have stayed with the first-team squad – absolutely no doubt about it. I would've tried to still win the touch-rugby matches – albeit one-handed; I'd have made certain that I won all the fitness tests and fielding drills, and would make sure that I participated fully in any team meetings and discussions. I would not want to risk losing my presence or importance in the dressing room. But now, in stage three, the reality was different. I genuinely wanted to make the best of it and be of as much use as I could to Grubby. I don't mention this for you all to think I'm the perfect pro – because there are many who would do, and have done the same – I mention it because it shows how you finally develop to realise that the hand that feeds – the game – is bigger than us all, but that it takes us the best part of a career to realise that. Unfortunately, there are plenty that don't ever realise that and get marooned in stage two, and finally leave the game very bitter and very twisted about being replaced by one youngster or another coming through.

The bizarre thing is that I knew toward the end of my career that by helping and encouraging say Matt, Tim, or Yards, there was every chance that I was helping to create my eventual replacement in the side – but that was fine – I'd now learned that was the bigger picture, and that everything you do, really, should be for the benefit of the team and the club. In stage one, that's absolutely the last thing you consider – it really is a case of everything coming full circle.

Looking back, my personal stage three began at Glamorgan when I was vice-captain, especially when struggling for form during Glamorgan's championship year under Duncan Fletcher. I was absolutely determined to do well that year, I knew we had by far the best side in all my time at the club in terms of talent, experience and youth – and I went out and had my worst season for six years! Halfway through the season I went to see Duncan and – despite being absolutely desperate to keep my place – explained to him that as vice-captain I didn't think myself above being dropped, if it would help him and the team. To Duncan's credit he dismissed this and spent hours working with me to try to coach me into some type of form. I did at the time, and still do, hold him in the highest regard for the effort he put in trying to help me. I also realised that it was far more important that I worked on my game – even if I were excluded from the team – as it was the best way forward for the team. I had absolutely no thoughts on who might come in and replace me, or how well they might do or how long they'd keep me out of the side, I just wanted to do the best for the team, which was getting me back to form – in or out of the side. Later at Sussex in my first season – again as vice-captain – I had exactly the same conversation with Pete Moores, who gave exactly the same response as Fletch. He worked overtime with me to try to get me right, and publicly stood by me. It's never been a surprise to me that Mooresy and Fletch have reached the heights of international coaches.

The final example of this stage three was when I signed my final contract with Sussex. I knew that I'd only been signed because there was still a doubt that Ian Ward was going to join from Surrey, and if he didn't and I was released, Sussex would be a batter short. When Wardy did eventually sign, we instantly became a batter too heavy. I went to see Mooresy to see if I was going to start the season in the team. His response was not good. He outlined that he obviously hadn't signed Wardy not to play him. Murray Goodwin would play as he was overseas, as would Chris Adams as he was captain. That was three of the six batting spots gone. Matt Prior and Tim Ambrose were the long-term future of the club so would also play. That left Monty and me for the final spot. I'd comfortably finished higher in the averages than Monty in the previous year, 46 against his 33. It all came down to who would bat at three. I had batted there all season, and Monty seldom did. However, I knew that another option was that Murray could drop down and bat three – he was world class there anyway –

leaving Monty to open with Wardy. This was the option Mooresy took. I heard him out. He felt that Monty had done really well over previous years, well enough that he could be forgiven for his previous season's average form, and that he had a longer-term future with the club due to his age compared with me. I told Mooresy that I was bitterly disappointed with his decision, and felt that I really thought that I had the ability to perform extremely well in the coming season. However, I also said that I totally respected his decision, but asked that I be temporarily released from the first-team squad, and be allowed to play – and captain – the second team. I didn't want to waste what was obviously becoming my last season hanging round the first team. I wanted to play, score as many runs as I could in the seconds, and force Mooresy to pick me if any of the batters lost form or got injured. I asked him for one favour and that was not to forget about me. He agreed. I then remembered the experience of several Glamorgan players whose careers fizzled out in the seconds when I was starting out, and also recalled how their bitterness to the coach, the club and the game in general sullied my memories of them, and I was determined that no future Sussex player would have that opinion of me. So, I went into the seconds, did the best I could when batting, gave 100% in the field and wanted to leave the youngsters with the message that at whatever your level of the game, and at whatever your stage of career, always adopt a positive attitude, and if you do, hopefully you, and more importantly the team, won't go far wrong. I wish I'd known all that during stage one – it would have made life a lot easier!

Before I move on, I mention the bitterness that some old pros carry around with them at the end of their careers, and this is largely related to the fact that they've found it hard to deal with the fact that their careers have ended and their time in the spotlight has come to an end. I remember being with a very unpopular former Glamorgan player when I was just eighteen years old and a young kid, prompted by his father, came up to ask for his autograph. The player just turned to the kid and basically told him to piss off as he was talking. The kid retreated almost in tears and I couldn't believe what I'd just seen. I resolved from that day that if anyone ever wanted my autograph or a quick chat, I would always try to find time to oblige.

I think there's a saying along the lines of 'The greater the man, the bigger the star' and this is no truer than in the case of Welsh rugby legend Phil Bennett. As I've made my way in sport, I've been hugely fortunate to get to know Phil really well and consider him a good friend. When I was spending one of my trips in South Africa, I was also doing a bit of one-to-one coaching for a few extra rand, and spent a day with Michiel Van Olst and his dad Dennis. After the session we got talking and it turned out the guy's great love was rugby union, and his all-time favourite player was Phil Bennett, largely due to his performances on the British Lions' legendary tour to South Africa in 1974. I mentioned that I knew Phil and the guy went into orbit and begged me to try to get Phil's autograph when I went home. When I got back I rang Phil and told him, and asked if I bought a replica Welsh jersey and brought it round, would Phil sign it for me to send to Dennis. Phil said he'd be delighted to. When I got to Phil's, he signed the shirt then showed me a little box he'd put together; in it was a signed team photo of the British Lions, a couple of his club ties and a signed programme of one of the matches Phil played on that tour in 1974, and asked if I'd send that to Dennis along with the shirt. I'm sure Phil's not alone in doing something as kind as that, and it just illustrates what I've learned throughout my time in sport, which is that by and large most sportspeople will go the extra yard for the true fan. Some like Phil do it as a matter of course and have done it all their lives, and some only really buy into that approach deep into stage three of their career. Sadly, the odd one or two don't buy into it at all.

To be a batsman in professional cricket – you must posses one talent above all others. It goes without saying that you must have a ability, technique, bravery and bottle, but on top of all that, you must possess the inner strength to bounce back from a bad run of form. It's the loneliest time of your career when you're in a bad trot and even more so if the team and the rest of your mates are doing well – as I found myself in our championship year of 1997. You enter a phase of the most acute self-doubt that, if you're not careful, could prove terminal to your career. You really begin to struggle to see where your next run is going to come from and the worse your form gets, the more your confidence seeps away until it's rock bottom. You soon enter the 'fake it till you make it' stage. This is when outwardly – even though you're falling apart inside – you display the cocky arrogance and indifference to everything that you think you exude when you are doing well. You try to send signals to the opposition that your bad run is just water off a duck's back, and you do this by chewing gum confidently when walking out to bat, or maybe introducing a bit of a strut to your walk, or if that fails, adopt a leisurely laid-back stroll. In reality, of course, it fools no one! Least of all yourself.

The hardest place to pull this off is in your own dressing room. I was always known as a big piss-taker, and when you're in the depths of despair about your personal form, you feel you must still act exactly as people expect you to, even though all you really want to do is curl up and hide away. It's really, really hard to keep up the façade. You then focus on trying to turn the slump around –

which often brings its own pressures. I always tried to take it back to basics – trying to remember what I did when things were going well. One thing was my preparation – I tried really hard. This meant warming up and training to maximum exertion levels, batting for as long as possible in the nets and working for as long and hard as the coach would allow. This hard work almost became my comfort blanket – I'd really start to believe that I must get runs soon: 'Look at the work I'm putting in'. And then I'd go in and get another duck, and it was back to square one. You start agreeing with everyone's well meaning clichés: 'You don't become a bad player overnight', and then you get out again and think 'Bugger me – was I ever a good player at all?' It's really hard to explain to non-batters how desperate you quickly become. The trouble is that yes, cricket's only a game, and there are far more important things in life, but this game was also my livelihood. It's what put food on the table and clothed my kids. At your lowest you just see this fantastic livelihood being taken away from you, and realise you may soon have to start heading your life in a totally different direction – which again just piles on the pressure.

And what's the worse thing? All this is acted out in front of a paying audience who may be basically calling for you to be dropped – only sometimes not as politely as that. Pretty soon you alter the way you play. When I was playing well, I'd generally get off the mark straight away with a nudge for one without even thinking about it. When I was struggling I'd do everything I could for that first run, but try so hard that all I'd end up doing is blocking it for 25 minutes because I was so scared of getting out. When eventually you'd fail again playing this way, you'd resolve that in your next innings you'd play with gay abandon. The next innings would come round and you'd smack your first two balls for four, think 'Wow, this is the way to do it,' then smack the third one straight into the hands of backward point, playing at a ball you'd never normally go after, and there you were again, back down to the bottom. It was at this point you felt you had nowhere to go.

As this book underlines repeatedly, I've known many, many times where I had nowhere to go.

You ultimately sit down, think about it and revert to a game plan that served you well in the past. Sometimes the most bizarre thing snaps you out of it, possibly a dropped catch, a close run-out decision or a poor umpire's decision. I remember once in my second innings against Notts at Swansea in 1993, after a shocking run of form in which I'd only passed 50 once in my previous twelve innings, I absolutely smacked the cover off one delivery from Chris Cairns which flew straight to the keeper Bruce French and they all went up. I was on 0 at the time and was nearly sick as it thumped into his gloves, as I'd also got a duck in the first innings. I always walked when I played – but this time I didn't – and lo and behold umpire Don Oslear gave me not out. I got the shit abused out of me by the bowler, slips and close fielders, and they really cranked it up when I edged the next one for four. I can't really explain it other than to say that a huge weight just lifted from my shoulders as I thought, 'That's it, bad run over. I'm going to get runs today' and I did – 100 not out! The most bizarre thing of all is that after this 'comeback' innings you often return to play at a better standard than before your bad trot and before you know it, absolutely everything in the garden is spectacularly rosy again, and all the off-the-field worries are immediately banished.

In time I learned to rationalise this by adopting a phrase I came to believe in 100% which was 'I'm only as good as my next innings, and definitely not as good as my last.' This basically covered both angles of getting too down on myself or getting too carried away. I started to realise that if I'd scored 2 in my last innings, I mustn't dwell on it as it would drag me down. Just start the next innings with a clean slate and try to get a big score. Similarly if my last innings was 142, I'd wipe it from my mind as I didn't want to get complacent. No, it was back to the clean slate and try to get as big a score as I could. It was hard to keep to this approach, and it took me years to work it out, but it's the approach I used in my big year at Sussex when things went well.

Mooresy's take on it was 'playing with no traffic in your mind'. That meant leaving all the irrelevant stuff back in the dressing room. Maybe you'd argued with the wife, or perhaps the dog had died, or maybe you thought the conditions were against you or maybe you were worried about a bad run of form, Pete's view was if you could get all that traffic out of your mind and just control what you could – i.e. your ability as a batsman, then the rest should take care of itself. He believed that the best players switched on when the bowler came in and that they raised the bat behind them to face him with a totally clear mind. I managed to achieve this on several occasions in my career and I am absolutely certain if I'd been able to do it more often my career average would be at least ten runs more than it is now. Sadly, the truth is, for large parts of my career, my mind was like the M25.

We were also warned of the dangers of getting into 'the endless loop of failure'. We were told that if you were playing poorly and acted as if you were, then there was more chance of that poor run continuing. When you then carry on playing badly and continue to fail, the loop gets harder to break out of. Baz Zuiderent who was our talented Dutch batsman suffered from this a bit. When he was struggling, he was in the depths of despair, and you felt he had nowhere to go, and nothing you could say would lift him. However, when his form returned and he got some runs, he would be out of his tree with confidence. I remember once that he'd been in a bad trot, but then burst out of the run by managing to get back-to-back hundreds. The next day when I went down for nets in the morning, Baz was basically coaching people and getting his voice heard – even though he was the youngest in the side. Just days before you could hardly get a word out of him.

Chris Adams's greatest strength was that you couldn't tell, just by talking to him or watching him, whether he was in the form of his life or the biggest slump of his career – and for that I have huge respect. I think Chris and I came from the same era and background, recognising that if you worked hard and stuck at it, then the runs would come eventually. In pre-season for example, no one had the bat in their hands longer than Grizz, and no one worked harder in training than him. Baz on the other hand worked very hard too but never really came to terms with dealing with a bad run of form.

I'm conscious that I keep referring to Pete Moores and his influence as I reflect back on the culmination of my career and it is only now, four years into my new life as an ex-cricketer, that I can truly judge him as a coach. I have now moved on from my active sporting days and taken the plunge into establishing a career for myself for the rest of my life. The best compliment I can pay Mooresy is that many of the lessons I learned from him in my six years at Hove, I keep with me today. He is a big believer in positivity, his mantra was always 'You only get out what you put in' and he believed absolutely that a happy positive attitude in life – let alone in cricket – will bring its own rewards and success. I believe in this totally, and I try to live my life that way. I now work for former Glamorgan batsman Mike Llewellyn at his snooker and cricket supplies company Absolute Snooker and Cricket, and many of the lessons of being positive and openly displaying a happy, upbeat demeanour I carry with me each day. Pete was a big believer that you have people in a dressing room – or in life for that matter – that absolutely suck the positive energy out of you. We've all met them or worked with them: they are the ones who grumble about the weather, their bad back, the state of the economy, global warming, *Eastenders* storylines – you name it, they moan about it. In cricket terms, these are the players who curse their luck at every dismissal, blame the conditions/umpires/opposition for their poor run of form, and who cannot bring themselves to say well done to others in their team who achieve success on a day that they have failed. Pete believes that players like this are as bad as poison in the dressing room and I agree with him totally. He preached to us constantly about being happy, about smiling, being interested in others, helping teammates, being approachable to fans and supporters and above all enjoying other players' successes. This results in a dressing room of energy givers. Try it yourself – it makes a huge difference. Put some upbeat music on the CD player on the way to work and arrive with a smile not an 'Oh god, here we go again' lament to your workmates. When someone takes the time to smile at you and ask how you are, respond by saying 'Really good thanks – what about you?' instead of 'Well, now that you ask, I haven't been feeling too clever and my job is getting me down. It's quite hard to embark on this if you are quite a negative person, but try it and you'll see how better you feel and you'll also notice how much more positively your presence will be received by your work mates. I'm sure this must be the approach that now underpins the England dressing room, one of fun, positivity and good humour – yet, importantly, all within professional limits. I predict that Mooresy will succeed as England coach and will usher in a new era of success on the international stage, based on good habits and optimism instead of anything related to an introspective approach.

I now leave this book, hopefully as I eventually left my professional career, on a positive note with absolutely no regrets. I feel blessed and privileged to have lived the life that I have lived in sport and seen the things I've seen. All the good, the bad and the ugly times now join together in my mind as a rich tapestry of vivid colour. If you look close enough there'll be the odd blemish, closer still will be the rare images of perfection, but overall, I believe it to be one of interest and relevance as we now move forward into the next golden era of sport, and more importantly, someone else's turn.

Thanks for reading, and good luck.

Nicknames

Sport in general and cricket in particular is littered with nicknames. Some are straightforward – mine is Cotts – others less so, Hugh Morris is Banners, so named after a perceived resemblance to George Peppard's 1970's TV detective Banacek . . . Don't ask me!

Anyway, throughout the book I've spoken about people in the same way as I would speak about them if I was telling you these stories face to face. John Hopkins, Glamorgan's opening batsman when I joined the club for example will always be Ponty to me and I don't remember the last time I called him John. Where possible throughout the book I've tried to introduce them first, but am certain that I've not managed this in all cases. So to help remedy that, I've included here a list of people referred to in the book in nickname order, giving you their real name and also a brief background about each one so that there is a little flesh added to their character. Hopefully this will give you a better picture of them in case you are not familiar with all of them prior to reading this book.

Al or **Senior** – Alan Jones. Without doubt the single most important figure in my cricket career. Was a hero of mine as a kid, and nothing has really changed since then. A true Glamorgan legend, he stuck up for me on more than the odd occasion during my career, and was one of the lone voices who said that Glamorgan should have offered me the three year contract that would have kept me at the club. Have never really thanked him for everything he has done for me, so will do it here – thank you, Al.

Banners – Hugh Morris. One of the best batsmen in Glamorgan's history, and one of the top three people in my career in terms of those who helped me get the most out of my limited ability and forge a career in the game. Now a big wig at Lord's, and thankfully recovered from very serious illness. Top bloke.

Baz – Stephen Barwick. Best one-day bowler in my time at Glamorgan, integral to the success the club achieved in the early and mid-1990s, all the more pleasing for him as he'd been at the club in the very dark days. A really great fella, who has sadly had to deal with personal tragedy in recent years.

Benny (1) – Phil Bennett. Welsh rugby legend and one of the nicest guys you'll ever meet. Has a fantastic knowledge of sport in general and rugby in particular and have enjoyed his company as a fellow speaker at many after dinner functions. Delighted to know him.

Benny (2) – Andrew Bennett. Apprentice professional at Swans when I was there and very talented striker. Like a lot of us at the time, never made it as a pro, but played in Welsh League for many years.

Boey – Phil Boesrma. John Toshack's right-hand man at Swansea City after signing him as a player from Liverpool, and the absolute scourge of the apprentices and young pros. Possessed a volcanic temper and you made sure you never, ever crossed him. Hated him with a passion at the time, but now realise that without his hard lessons I'd never have had a twenty-odd year sporting career. Would like to thank him if I ever saw him again.

Brayers – Dave Brayley. My most trusted friend and driving force behind this book. Some people queried me asking Dave to write this book, but I've never had a moments doubt. Has an encyclopaedic knowledge of sport and probably remembered more about my career than I did! Has read nearly every sports biography over the past twenty years, which is why I knew he'd be perfect to write mine. Once held a batting record for Swansea Cricket Club Youth XI – till I broke it! Still a bit fat.

Butch – Alan Butcher. Former England player, and captain of Glamorgan when I started to make an impact in the first team. Oozed class as a batsman and his record at Glamorgan was second to none, and his partnership with Hugh Morris started to give the solidity to Glamorgan's batting that had often been lacking, even though they didn't always see eye to eye. Another person who probably doesn't realise the impact he had on my career. A top professional.

Canny – Michael Cann. My teammate at Glamorgan during the early years and rival for a batting spot. Hugely intelligent guy bordering on the genius and one of the funniest I ever met. Our rivalry was to boil over once or twice but I hold him in the highest regard and remember him fondly. Extremely unlucky not to have made a career in the game, and looking back I have to say that if I made a career out of it, there was no reason why he shouldn't have.

Colin 1 – Colin Appleton. Swans manager who really gave me my first-team chance – then was sacked the next day! Stories about him are legendary and was a very eccentric man, with a very eccentric assistant manager, Colin 2.

Colin 2 – Colin Meldrum. See Colin 1 above.

Crofty – Robert Croft. Has his own chapter in this book, so I'm not saying much about him here!

Curt – Alan Curtis. Welsh International and one of the greatest players to have played for the Swans. Possibly the nicest footballer you will ever meet, and did things in training that I could only dream of. I hold him in the highest regard as a footballer and a person.

Daffy – Phil DeFreitas. A constant opponent throughout my career, tough adversary but good off the field. Great gesture when we won the title in 2003 by letting us all do a lap of honour mid-game.

Daley or Arthur – Adrian Dale. Our careers ran in parallel until I left Glamorgan in 1998. More than useful player both batting and bowling, but was often found in the shadows when it came to the headlines. Well respected by the rest of the players and as inseparable from Jamer as I was from Crofty. Now lives in New Zealand.

Deano – Dean Saunders, Welsh international footballer and hugely successful, much travelled striker. Our careers began within a year of each other back in the early 1980s at Swansea City, and we were both released on the same day by the same manager – John Bond. Now assistant manager to Tosh with Wales. A real character.

Divver – Michael Di Venuto. Quite simply the best pro I ever worked with. Great bloke to have on the field and even better in the team room. Replaced Michael Bevan at Sussex, and was himself then replaced by Bevan the following year. May not have bettered Bevan as a player, but certainly did as a man. Now at Durham.

Duffer – David (Dai) Hough. Fellow apprentice at Swansea City. We clashed on the odd occasion but I always had massive respect for him as a player and a man. The only one of our intake that had any sort of career with the Swans, staying with the club for ten years. Met up with him again recently – delighted to call him a friend. Now a senior ranking officer in the South Wales Police.

Fletch – Duncan Fletcher. Was an absolute breath of fresh air at Glamorgan and has so many qualities, it's hard to list them all here. Was a fantastic support to me during my crap championship year and took loads of unfair stick when his time as England coach ended. History will be far kinder to him than the press headlines he endured at the time – quite rightly so.

Gatt – Mike Gatting. Long-time county opponent and former England captain. Often badgered him for advice during the middle part of my career and always willing to spend some time with me in the bar – I'll always be grateful to him for that. Joined me on a charity walk along the Pembrokeshire Coastal Path in 2003 – only lasted three days – that's the trouble with old age, I guess!

Grizz – Chris 'Grizzly' Adams. My captain throughout my time at Sussex. A complex character but a great leader and one of Sussex's best ever captains. Very loyal to me when my form was inconsistent, and I will always be grateful to him for giving me the chance at Sussex when I was at my lowest ebb. Just glad I was able to repay his faith in 2003.

Grubby – Keith Greenfield. One of my best mates at Sussex. He is the perfect example of a team player and someone who everyone at the club had, and has, a massive respect for. One of my career highlights was being at the crease with him when he hit the winning runs in the 1999 Sunday League Championship win at Derby. Now Head of the Academy at Sussex.

Hempy – David Hemp. Gifted left hander who had the undoubted ability to play for England. Left Glamorgan for Warwickshire but returned to Glamorgan in 2002 where he's since matured into a senior member, and latterly captain, of the team – a far cry from his wild days when he wanted to hit Gordon Parsons of Leicestershire over the head with his bat.

Jamer – Stephen James. Long time friend and batting partner, also know as 'Sid' for obvious reasons. Our careers followed a very similar path in terms of establishing ourselves in the Glamorgan first team, but when he did, he never looked back. Huge respect for the way he turned himself into a top-line batsman. In common with several of the Glamorgan lads at the time, never given a run in the England team that his form deserved. Now a well-respected journalist.

JD – John Derrick. One of the most solid, honest and dependable guys I came across in my whole career. Deservedly appointed Glamorgan coach for several years, but sadly paid the price for a poor season in 2006. A man you could always rely on. Now heavily involved in coaching elite Welsh cricketers

Jimmy – Dzemal Hadziabdic. Yugoslav international and cult hero of the fans. Great fun guy who was often given swear words by some of the lads and told he could use them in interviews – much to our amusement. Along with fellow countryman, Ante Rajkovic, probably the most successful of the early foreign imports to the English game, a massive reason for Swansea's success under Tosh – both were perfect pros.

Josh – John Mahoney. Welsh international of great repute and one of the toughest, most uncompromising footballers I ever came across. Played the same way in training as he did in games, and as I was in direct competition with him in Reserves v First Team games, I still have the scars to prove it. No airs and graces, would do anything for anyone. Ignored pain and injury as if they simply didn't exist. In my eyes, a true legend. Tosh's first cousin.

Lakey – Huw Lake. Apprentice when I joined the club and as such always looked up to him. Very similar player to me but had far more success playing over 50 games for the Swans. A real character who always had the dressing room in stitches. Would have been a great character in *Dad's Army* as Lakey was the bloke you'd always go to if you wanted something – he had contacts everywhere.

Larg – Paul Gallagher. Quite simply one of the funniest people I have ever met in my life. Met him through Dave's brother-in-law Nige and some of the things he has done have left me speechless and crying with laughter. More out of the Matt Lucas school of looks than David Walliams. Once walked into a packed café for a business lunch, walked into the toilets, came back out dressed in red lycra one-piece long johns and shouted out in true *Little Britain* style, 'Bacardi and Coke please, Myfanwy,' then turned round, got changed and carried on with his business meeting. A staunch supporter of mine, for which I've always been grateful. Senior Manager in Nat West Bank. (Not for long after they've read this!)

Latch – Bob Latchford. Ace striker and best finisher I've ever seen. A real gentleman and pleasure to be around. Taught me lots about how to handle yourself in public and with fans in particular. Never refused an autograph. No longer involved in football and last I heard was living in Switzerland.

Lewie – Chris Lewis. My oldest friend from Three Crosses. Were as thick as thieves until we left Bishopston Comprehensive and went our separate ways. Lewie and I were neck and neck in all our sporting endeavours from about the age of eight onwards. He played for Wales Schoolboys the year I was dropped from Swansea Schoolboys for being too small. He probably doesn't realise how much our rivalry and his excellence spurred me on, and I owe him a lot for giving me such a high standard of competition from an early age. He's now a very successful businessman in Liverpool.

Lewey – Jason Lewry. Hugh Morris once said Jason bowled the best over to him that he ever faced. Massive ability who again should definitely have played for England in some format of the game. A man you could trust with your life and a real good mate to share a drink with. Very loyal to me during my time at Sussex.

Marshy – Terrence Marsh. My South African host in the early 1990's and all round lunatic. Loved a night out and some of our antics were legendary. Played first class cricket in South Africa, but gave it up in his late twenties to focus on business interests. Became a millionaire. Bastard.

Matt – Matthew Maynard, former England and Glamorgan player, and very close friend during my 14 years at Glamorgan. Just about the most talented player I saw in my career. Graduated to become assistant Coach to Duncan Fletcher with England before returning to Glamorgan as Director of Cricket.

Meto – Colin Metson. The most gifted wicket keeper I ever saw, but unfortunately, couldn't bat an eyelid. Can count himself unfortunate to have been around when wicketkeeper batsmen became the recipe of the day, and could therefore never compete with the likes of Alec Stewart at the highest level. Would have played for England in almost any other era of the game. A bit of a one off, and as such we never really hit it off.

Monty – Richard Montgomerie. Probably the most dependable batsman I ever played with. Epitomises the strength of character that many of the critics of the England side state that is non existent. Absolutely *loved* batting and has been the foundations around which Sussex have built their success in recent years. The best player of Spoof I ever saw. Retired at the end of Sussex's Championship season of 2007. Our First class career records are almost identical.

Mooresy – Peter Moores. One of the men to whom I owe so much. Stood by me when everyone else outside of the club were calling for my head in Sussex. Has influenced my thinking in life, not just cricket. I always told anyone that listened that he would eventually replace Fletch as England coach – which he did. The most positive person I've ever met, and definitely most loyal. Still influences me to this day.

Mushie – Mushtaq Ahmed. Genius. Played with him every day for two years and if he's the third best spinner after Murali and Warne, then those blokes must be superhuman. On his day unplayable – but cricket is only a small part of his life. Totally committed to his faith, and as such, is the most contented sportsman I've ever known. The most modest and self-effacing of all my teammates, and again, hugely loyal to me. How a borderline Welsh alcoholic and a Teetotal muslim became such good mates, I have no idea – I'm just so glad that we did. Would give you his last penny with a happy smile.

Muzza – Murray Goodwin. Along with Matt Maynard and Hugh Morris, the best batsman I ever played with. Very similar to me in terms of what we liked out of life, and was the epitome of work hard and play hard. Huge influence on my batting – just wish I could have been as good as him. A great mate. Can finally reveal publicly for the first time that Bruce Forsyth is his father. (For all lawyers reading this, that is a chin-related joke.)

Oz – Stuart Osborne. Every cricket side needs a good physio who is also a social worker, confidant and spiritual adviser. Dean Conway did it superbly at Glamorgan as did Oz at Sussex. Trust him with my life and a truly honest man, not frightened to give you the truth. Got to know the intimacies of my lower back extremely well, and should be on a bonus from the makers of Ibuprofen. Was awarded the Sussex Team man of the year award in 2001. That says it all.

Pasc – Colin Pascoe. One of the most talented young players at Swansea in the Toshack years. Was light years ahead at seventeen in terms of ability. Had a great career in the game playing for Wales and several top clubs. Now part of Roberto Martinez's backroom team at Swansea City.

Ponty – John Hopkins. Glamorgan batsman and long-time opening partner of Alan Jones. Played for Glamorgan during some lean times, but having spoken to many people about him during my career, had the respect of many in the game. Taught me a lot about preparing well for games, especially in relation to fast bowling. Was great to me when I was trying to break into the first team, and I have the utmost respect for him.

Razor – Ray Kennedy. Liverpool and England footballing legend. Our paths crossed at a bad personal time for him, but have nothing but good memories of him. Perceived by some as a big-time Charlie, but nothing could be further from the truth. The highlight of my time at the Swans was playing alongside him in midfield for the reserves for twenty-odd games before he left the club. I learnt more about football in those games than at any other time in my life. Sadly now very ill with Parkinson's disease. A real tragedy.

Reeso – Anthony Rees. One of the most gifted athletes I played football with. Still holds the Wales schools record for the 800 metres nearly 25 years later. He left our Swansea Schoolboy squad and was snapped up by Arsenal. Was so good, he was made a pro after only six months as an apprentice, beating the likes of Paul Merson and Tony Adams to a contract. Came under the wing of Charlie Nicholas as a pro, and then things went a bit pear-shaped for him – understandably really! Joined Swansea City during my final year and our friendship was cemented for life. Lives just down the road from me, and is one of my closest friends.

Robbo – Mark Robinson. My housemate for four years and my closest friend at Sussex. Another perfect pro whose belief revolved around doing his absolute best for every second of every game. I can think of no better person to be a role model for any upcoming cricketer, which is why he is now club coach at Sussex. A truly great friend.

Roly – Roland Lefebvre. One of the best one-day bowlers in the game in the early 1990s and very popular in the dressing room. A fantastic outfielder and took some catches in the deep that bordered on the miraculous. With Baz and Watty, created arguably the best limited-overs bowling attack in Glamorgan's history. Now involved with Dutch cricket in Rotterdam.

Shawsie – Adrian Shaw. Wicketkeeper batsman and one of the most underrated cricketers I ever played with. As he wasn't in Metson's class behind the stumps (not many were), he was probably under more pressure than any other batsman to perform once he replaced him in our Championship year of 1997. Massive character and one you would definitely want in the trenches alongside you. Now Glamorgan first-team coach, and despite the recent troubles of the club – which is more to do with lack of investment than anything else – will be a big success.

Tosh – John Toshack. My first, and best ever, boss. A hero to me even before he chose me to join the Swans where my impression of him only increased with every passing day. One of my saddest sporting days was when he finally left the club, but not surprisingly he went on to far bigger and better things. Unbelievable to think he was still only 33 when I joined the Swans. A man never, ever to mess with – possibly the strongest character I've come across in my life – in or out of sport.

Tucker – Robin Martin-Jenkins. Extremely talented player and all-rounder who should definitely have played for England. Very witty guy who is also a great conversationalist and someone to whom I'd always be happy to listen to and learn from. Will turn out to be one of Sussex's all-time greats.

Ums – Umer Rashid. Like Mushie, a truly great and lovely guy which must have something to do with their common backgrounds. Absent minded and as such, incredibly funny. In my opinion, would have gone on to play for England. His death has been one of the biggest tragedies in my life to date, and the only good thing to have come out of it is that he will be remembered at Sussex for eternity. Sorely missed by everyone who knew him.

Walshy – Ian Walsh. Wales and Swansea City striker. Very hard working striker who suffered real bad luck with injuries throughout his career. Played lots of times with him in the Reserves when he was returning from injury. Great attitude and really nice to the young pros. Now works as a soccer pundit for BBC Wales TV and radio.

Wardy – Ian Ward. Big signing from Surrey, whose arrival pushed me out of the first team in my final year. Nice guy, but never really worked out for him at Sussex, and his TV commitments took over to such an extent that he retired to pursue that area as a career. Now an anchor man of *Sky Sports Cricket* – and a very good one too.

Watty – Steve Watkin. Probably the most consistent bowler of his generation; why he didn't play more often for England totally mystifies me. Had the unbelievable knack of being brought back on to bowl mid-innings in tight one-day games for Glamorgan and nearly always taking a match-changing wicket. Bit of an absent-minded professor with a theory for everything, but loved being in his company in our time together at Glamorgan. Now a member of Glamorgan's coaching staff.

Whoolie – Michael Wholohan. Legendary Australian, bordering on the lunatic. Had so much fun with him in Penrith it was almost unfair. The centre of the *craic* in any dressing room and has had the uncanny knack of making friends with sports stars – one being Glenn McGrath. I still get the occasional drunken call at 3am from him telling me I owe him a beer.

Yards – Michael Yardy. I guess you could say he was my replacement at Sussex, and I'm absolutely delighted he's done so well. People tried to create a fictional problem between us but never the case – just ask him. Has a real chance to build a future with England in the coming years, and I truly hope he does.

APPENDIX B

Career Statistics – P. A. Cottey – 1986 - 2004

First Class

Team	Matches	Inns	NO	Runs	HS	Ave	100	50	Ct
Glamorgan	197	320	49	10,346	203	38.17	21	56	137
Eastern Transvaal	5	7	0	253	76	36.14	0	3	5
Sussex	74	119	2	3,948	188	33.74	10	14	40
TCCB XI	1	2	0	20	12	10.00	0	0	0
Overall	277	448	51	14,567	203	36.69	31	73	182

Limited Overs

Team	Matches	Inns	NO	Runs	HS	Ave	100	50	Ct
Glamorgan	195	171	31	3,607	96	25.76	0	21	67
Eastern Transvaal	3	3	0	68	66	22.66	0	1	1
Sussex	84	75	10	1,318	85	20.27	0	6	24
Overall	282	249	41	4,993	96	24.00	0	28	92

Overall Batting (Career)

Matches	Inns	NO	Runs	HS	100	50	Ct
559	697	92	19,560	203	31	101	274

Overall Bowling (Career)

Balls	Mdns	Runs	Wkts	BB	4wi	5wi
2493	47	1799	42	5-49	2	1

1,000 runs in season – 8 (1990, 1992-96, 1998, 2003)

Honours:
Tilcon Trophy Winners (55 Overs) 1992 Glamorgan v Sussex
Axa Equity and Law Sunday League 1993 – Champions, Glamorgan
Britannic Assurance County Championship 1997 – Champions, Glamorgan
CGU National Sunday League Div Two 1999 – Champions, Sussex
Cricinfo County Championship Div Two 2001 – Champions, Sussex
Frizzell County Championship Div One 2003 – Champions, Sussex

One of four centuries in single innings for Glamorgan (club record) v Gloucestershire – July 4-8 1996: S.P. James 118, H. Morris 108, M.P. Maynard 145 n.o., P.A. Cottey 101 n.o.

Scored 126 in Sussex's highest ever fourth innings total of 455-8 (club record) v Gloucestershire May 22 1999

Only Welshman to win the County Championship with two counties